RECONSTRUCTING POST-SADDAM IRAQ

Edited by
Sultan Barakat

Routledge
Taylor & Francis Group
LONDON AND NEW YORK

First published 2008 by Routledge
4 Park Square, Milton Park, Abingdon, Oxon OX14 4RN
605 Third Avenue, New York, NY 10017

Routledge is an imprint of the Taylor & Francis Group, an informa business

Typeset in Times by KnowledgeWorks Global Limited, Southampton, UK

British Library Cataloguing in Publication Data
A catalogue record for this book is available from the British Library

Library of Congress Cataloging in Publication Data
A catalog record for this book has been requested

ISBN13: 978-0-415-41371-8 (hbk)
ISBN13: 978-0-415-46424-6 (pbk)

RECONSTRUCTING POST-SADDAM IRAQ

Post 9/11 the USA developed a policy of 'war on terror' and as part of this the decision was made to democratize the Middle-East with a controversial policy of pre-emptive invasions in both Afghanistan and Iraq.

This volume seeks to analyze and investigate to what extent this policy was justified or effective. It looks at the evidence of democracy post-invasion and also considers the global, regional and internal politics leading up to the decision to invade. It attempts to answer the questions most troubling the international community since the invasion of Iraq, such as:

- Were the invasion of Iraq and Afghanistan an exploitation of military supremacy to secure a favourable balance of power for the USA?
- Is it possible to build a stable democracy after a pre-emptive invasion?
- What is the current outlook for a stable democracy in Iraq?

This book is insightful and vital reading for all those interested in international politics and the future in Iraq.

This book was previously published as a special issue of *Third World Quarterly*.

Sultan Barakat is a Professor of Politics at the University of York.

Contents

Notes on Contributors

Sultan Barakat is a Professor of Politics at the University of York. He is the founding Director of the Post-war Reconstruction and Development Unit (PRDU). He has published extensively on the social and economic rebuilding of war-torn societies, including most recently the edited volumes Reconstructing War-torn Societies: Afghanistan (*Third World Quarterly*, 23(5), 2002) and *After the Conflict: Reconstruction and Development in the Aftermath of War* (Tauris, 2005).

Alex Callinicos is a Professor of Politics at the University of York, where he has taught since 1981. He has written some 20 books on social and political theory and politics, including most recently *The New Mandarins of American Power* (Polity, 2003).

Tareq Y Ismael is a Professor of Political Science at the University of Calgary, Canada, President of the International Centre for Contemporary Middle East Studies at Eastern Mediterranean University, North Cyprus, and the Secretary General of the International Association of Middle Eastern Studies. He is the author and editor of over 20 books on the Middle East, Iraq and international studies. His most recent works include *Iraq: The Human Cost of History*, with William H Haddad (Pluto, 2004) and *The Iraqi Predicament: People in the Quagmire of Power Politics*, with Jacqueline Ismael (Pluto, 2004). **Jacqueline S Ismael** is a Professor of Social Work at the University of Calgary. She has also written articles and monographs on social change in the Middle East, including *Kuwait: Dependency and Class in a Rentier State* (University Press of Florida, 1993) and co-authored a number of works with Tareq Y Ismael, including The Communist Movement in Syria and Lebanon (University Press of Florida, 1998) and *The Iraqi Predicament: People in the Quagmire of Power Politics* (Pluto, 2004).

Michiel Leezenberg teaches in the Department of Philosophy and on the MA programme Islam in the Modern World in the Faculty of Humanities of the University of Amsterdam. Among his numerous publications are articles on the political economy of Iraqi Kurdistan (in K Mahdi (ed), *Iraq's Economic Predicament* (Ithaca Press, 2002)) and on political Islam among the Kurds (to appear in F Abduljabar & H Dawod (eds), *Tribes and the State: The Case of the Kurds* (Saqi Books, 2005)), as well as an award-winning history of Islamic philosophy (in Dutch; English translation to appear with Cambridge University Press).

Rolf Schwarz is Teaching Assistant in the Department of Political Science at the Graduate Institute of International Studies in Geneva. His academic interests include theories of the state, security studies and Middle Eastern Studies. Recent publications include *The paradox of sovereignty, regime type and human rights compliance*, *International Journal of Human Rights* (2004), and *Staat, Macht und Menschenrechte in Algerien* (2002). **Oliver Jütersonke** is Research Co-ordinator of the Programme for Strategic and International Security Studies (PSIS) at the Graduate Institute of International Studies in Geneva. His research interests include security studies, the history of ideas, in particular, the relation between law and politics. He is currently editing a PSIS Special Study entitled *Justifying the Use of Force: Ethical Considerations on Military Violence and Humanitarian Intervention* (forthcoming, 2005).

Eric Herring is Senior Lecturer in International Politics at the University of Bristol. He is currently writing a book with Glen Rangwala entitled *Iraq in Fragments: The Occupation and Its Legacy* (Hurst, forthcoming, 2006) with financial support from the Economic and Social Research Council. **Glen Rangwala** is a Lecturer in international politics at the University of Cambridge, and a Fellow of Trinity College. He is currently completing a book (with Eric Herring) entitled *Iraq in Fragments: The Occupation and its Legacy* (Hurst, forthcoming, 2006).

Philippe Le Billon is Assistant Professor at the University of British Columbia in the Department of Geography and the Liu Institute for Global Issues. His research interests include international development, conflict studies and resource governance. His recent publications are *Fuelling War: Natural Resources and Armed Conflicts* (2005) and (as editor) *The Geopolitics of Resource Wars* (2004).

Toby Dodge is a Lecturer in Politics at Queen Mary, University of London. He is also Senior Consulting Fellow for the Middle East at the International Institute for Strategic Studies, London. His recent publications include *Inventing Iraq: The Failure of Nation Building and a History Denied* (Columbia University Press, 2003); *Iraq at the Crossroads: State and Society in the Shadow of Regime Change*, (edited, Oxford University Press, 2003) and *Iraq's Future: The Aftermath of Regime Change* (IISS/Routledge, 2005).

Adeed Dawisha is Professor of Political Science at Miami University, OH, and Carnegie scholar for 200405. He is the author of some ten books, the most recent being *Arab Nationalism in the Twentieth Century: From Triumph to Despair* (Princeton University Press, 2003). He has lectured and written extensively on Iraq, including the co-authored 'How to build democracy in Iraq (*Foreign Affairs*, 2003) and Iraq: setbacks, advances, prospects (*Journal of Democracy*, 2004).

Nadje Al-Ali is a Lecturer in Social Anthropology at the Institute of Arabic and Islamic Studies, University of Exeter. Her research work focuses on the impact of war and sanctions on women and gender in Iraq; transnational communities and reconstruction, and secularism, Islamism and gender in the Middle East. She is co-editor of *New Approaches to Migration: Transnational Communities and the Transformation of Home* (Routledge, 2002).

Richard Brown is a chartered civil engineer with some 30 years experience. He is also an army reservist and has worked intermittently in post-war reconstruction since 1997, holding senior operational roles in Bosnia and Herzegovina, Kosovo and Iraq. He is a Visiting Lecturer at the PRDU, University of York and has contributed a chapter on reconstructing infrastructure to *Postconflict Development: Meeting New Challenges*, edited by Junne and Verkoren (Lynne Rienner, 2005). He is currently an Associate Director with international consulting engineers, Arup.

Kjell Bjork is a Visiting Research Fellow at the PRDU, University of York, researching the socioeconomic impact and developmental role of humanitarian mine action. He has recently returned from Iraq, where, as programme manager, he implemented a new Explosive Ordnance Disposal Operation for a German humanitarian NGO in Baghdad. **Richard Jones** is a Research Fellow at the PRDU, University of York. His research focuses on the economic impact of conflict and strategies for economic development and poverty reduction. He has undertaken funded research in a number of war-torn countries. He has recently contributed a chapter, 'Post-war poverty reduction', to S Barakat (ed), *After the Conflict: Reconstruction and Development in the Aftermath of War* (Tauris, 2005).

Frederick M Burkle, Jr is Senior Scholar, Scientist and Visiting Professor at the Center for International Emergency, Disaster & Refugee Studies, Johns Hopkins University Medical Institutions, Baltimore, and Professor, Department of Public Health Sciences and Epidemiology, and the AsiaPacific Center for Biosecurity, Disaster & Conflict Research, John A Burns School of Medicine, Honolulu, HI. He formerly served as Deputy Assistant Administrator, Bureau for Global Health, USAID, and in that capacity was a major health planner in the build-up to the war with Iraq. He later served as the Senior Medical Officer on the Office of Foreign Disaster Assistance's Disaster Assistance Response Team (DART) and was the first senior health diplomat to enter Baghdad and southern Iraq after the collapse of the health system. **Bradley A Woodruff** is Adjunct Associate Professor, Department of International Health, Rollins School of Public Health, Emory University, Atlanta, GA. He served as senior epidemiologist on the Iraq DART during the immediate relief phase of the war. **Eric K Noji** is a Visiting Professor at the Center for International Emergency, Disaster & Refugee Studies, Johns Hopkins University Medical Institutions, Baltimore. He served as the Deputy Senior Medical Officer on the Iraq DART during the immediate relief phase, MarchMay 2003.

John Warren is a Fellow at the PRDU, University of York. As an architect/planner with over 30 years' experience he worked extensively in Iraq during the 1980s, restoring buildings in devastated areas of the medieval city of Baghdad. He contributes to a range of academic journals on conservation and Islamic architecture. His work on Byzantine and Early Islamic architecture led to his election to the Society of Antiquaries. He is Chairman of the World Heritage Committee of ICOMOS UK and has been on its executive for over 20 years, carrying out a number of international evaluations for UNESCO.

Margaret Chard is a Research Fellow at the PRDU, University of York. Her research focuses on the impact of capacity building and institutional development in war-torn countries, having worked in this field in a number of countries since 1983, principally Mozambique during and after the civil war. Recent co-authored articles include: Theories, rhetoric and practice' and 'The composite approach: research design in the context of war and armed conflict' in the special issue 'Reconstructing War-torn Societies: Afghanistan' of *Third World Quarterly*, 23 (5), 2002.

Acknowledgements

This special issue on 'Reconstructing Post-Saddam Iraq' was conceived to mark the anniversary of handing over sovereignty to the Iraqi Interim Government. The intention was to produce a multidisciplinary volume of academic and professional substance, which could provide guidance and insight on the reconstruction of Iraq as it passes through the difficult transition from war to peace. I am grateful to all the contributors who, by their expertise and dedication, have made it possible to realise this ambition.

Shahid Qadir, Editor of *Third World Quarterly*, has not only encouraged the idea of this volume but has continued to give his advice and enthusiastic support throughout. It has been a pleasure for me to collaborate with him as a Guest Editor.

A number of anonymous peer referees were of great assistance in facilitating this publication. I would like to extend my thanks to them for their prompt response and constructive comments.

I owe a debt of gratitude to my colleagues at the Post-war Reconstruction and Development Unit: Roger Mac Ginty, Richard Jones and Mark Evans. I am particularly grateful to Margaret Chard. Without her assistance, this work could not have been completed.

I would also like to thank my wife Nisreen and son Noumay for remaining gracious, helpful and understanding.

Finally, special thanks are due to the Altajir Trust for their financial support, which has released some of my time to be able to undertake the necessary research and writing.

Sultan Barakat
York, UK

Reconstructing Post-Saddam Iraq: an introduction

SULTAN BARAKAT

> At this point they caught sight of thirty or forty windmills that were standing on the plain. And no sooner had Don Quixote laid eyes upon them than he turned to his squire and said "Fortune is guiding our affairs better than we ourselves could have wished. Do you see over yonder, friend Sancho, thirty or forty lawless giants with whom I mean to do battle? I shall deprive them of their lives and with their spoils we shall begin to enrich ourselves, for this is righteous warfare and it is a great service to God to remove so accursed a breed from the face of the earth."
>
> "Take care, sir," cried Sancho. "Those over there are not giants but windmills. Those things that seem to be their arms are sails which, when they are whirled around by the wind, turn the millstone."
>
> "It is plain to be seen," replied Don Quixote, "that you have had little experience in this matter of adventures. Those are giants and if you are afraid, turn aside and pray whilst I engage them in fierce and unequal combat."
>
> Don Quixote. Chapter VIII. Miguel de Cervantes.
>
> [Source in translation: Putnam,1972: 110–111]

Following the shock of the 9/11 attacks in New York, a deep sense of anxiety pervaded the whole nation of the USA, as one commentator graphically put it, 'causing us to feel like we have suddenly been told the floor of the room is actually built over a bottomless well'.[1] 'Paradoxically' it is this 'new sense of vulnerability' combined with the reality of US global dominance that 'have reinforced tendencies toward a muscular unilateralism in US foreign policy.'[2]

Having regained self-confidence by deposing the Taliban regime in Afghanistan, albeit with only reluctant support from the international community, the US administration under George W. Bush went on to develop a world vision in which the USA was to play the role of champion of the civilised world against the forces of evil, its actions justified by the zeal of its mission for freedom and democracy, rather than the consent of the international community.[3]

The danger of policy driven by such zeal and idealisation in a complex world is that it can be hijacked by those with questionable interests or become sidetracked by mission creep. Thus the US administration was driven by the agenda of its Defence Department to focus on Iraq, both to pursue its 'war on terror' and as the starting point for bringing its 'global democratic revolution' to the Middle East.[4] In so doing it allowed itself to be diverted from the two crucial issues for world security: the pursuit of the world-wide Al-Qaida network and the need to address the conflict between Palestine and Israel which had been Bush's main foreign policy concern up to the eve of 9/11. It is the many unresolved conflicts around the world (Palestine, Chechnya, Kashmir, and the former Yugoslavia and the treatment of Muslim minorities in Indonesia and the Philippines), which have led to the perception of Muslim persecution. From this perspective, the unfolding events since 9/11, the invasion of Afghanistan and the rhetoric of the 'War on Terror' requires another interpretation by many Muslims as a Western 'crusade' which has now provided Al-Qaida with a new generation of recruits.

To those fired by ideological certainties, small shifts in the complex political scene can be interpreted as signals that the desired democratic transformation is about to occur, and self-congratulatory speeches are prematurely made,[5] while the might and threat of the enemy needs to be exaggerated for them to be worthy of the great power wielded to crush them. Thus the hand-over of 'sovereignty' to an appointed Iraqi administration in June 2004 and the election held in January 2005 in which the candidates were unable to make themselves known to an electorate who could only vote in those parts of the country where military protection could be effective, are seized on as important milestones on the road to freedom and democracy. Similarly, the destruction of the city of Fallujah in pursuit of insurgents who were able to regroup elsewhere, is seen as a victory for freedom against international terrorists.[6]

The Middle East is a complex reality with many voices. Those who listen for vindication can easily hear voices of support. They can come from many vested interests that seem to coincide with the US agenda only to be later proved unreliable allies; in 1980 it was Saddam.[7] In 2005, demonstrators from factions of the Lebanese opposition demanding the withdrawal of Syrian troops seemed to herald the 'advance of democracy' only to be outnumbered by more than ten to one by counter demonstrations in support of Syria.[8] In this environment of contradictory messages, the USA too has failed to deliver a consistent message. The people of the Middle East, even those inclined towards the USA are confused by an administration that speaks in idealistic terms of freedom and democracy and the will of the international community. While it seemingly abandons the resolution of the conflict between Israel and Palestine to tilt at windmills in Iraq, it is apparently indifferent to the heavy cost in civilian lives or even the mounting toll of its own military deaths resulting from that adventure.[9] From its position of occupying military power in Iraq the USA demands the immediate end to Syrian occupation of Lebanon[10], yet has tolerated Israeli occupation of Arab lands for more than 50 years. The prevailing cynicism is then reinforced when 'deadlines' for action appear always to be set not in conformity with Middle East realities but with an eye to public opinion back home in the run up to elections and presidential inauguration speeches. The US message is inconsistent, appears ambivalent and is therefore not believed. Justifying the recent invasion of Afghanistan and Iraq as humanitarian and reconstruction missions has been the most deeply confusing message of all.

The objectors to the war in the USA were acutely aware of these contradictions and challenged 'the troubling precedent... of the world's only superpower' using 'preventive force' to overthrow other regimes' on the grounds of potential rather than actual threat. As such, objectors doubted the credibility of the humanitarian motive, given the far greater abuses and human suffering tolerated around the world in places such as Congo, Sudan and North Korea. They asserted that to be justified war must have 'serious prospects for success' and 'must not produce evils and disorders graver than the evil to be eliminated' neither of which could be assumed.[11] These were essentially the grounds on which the UN Security Council also refused to endorse the war with the UN Secretary General subsequently declaring it illegal.[12]

This volume was commissioned with the brief of examining the process of reconstruction in Iraq after the invasion. Yet it has been necessary to devote much of it to an analysis of the global, regional and internal politics leading up to the decision to invade, as well as its aftermath. This is because, uniquely, Iraq was deliberately deconstructed in order to be reconstructed to a new model. Post-conflict reconstruction in any context has never, of course, been a purely technical matter. How reconstruction is carried out has always been a crucial factor for rebuilding the institutional, economic and social life of a nation and in that sense is profoundly political. However, the invasion of Iraq and dismantling of the Iraqi state was justified on the grounds that its reconstruction will lead to a 'new', 'free' and 'democratic' Iraq. This has placed reconstruction at the heart of the political agenda of the occupying powers. Therefore reconstruction has to succeed to prove that the military strategy was correct. This is what challenges both the principles and practice, which have underpinned our understanding of post-war reconstruction until now.

In the opening paper, Barakat examines this dilemma in the light of the current consensus on the nature and needs of reconstruction in post-war contexts, of Iraq's unique history and strategic assets and of the very particular nature of the conflict that has led to the need for reconstruction but has also thwarted its implementation. He concludes by suggesting some approaches that could advance the process in a positive direction.

The 'Anglo-American invasion of Iraq' in its global political context, is then examined by Callinicos, arguing that the 9/11 attacks accelerated a policy shift from a coalition-building approach to one of exploiting military supremacy to secure a favourable global balance of power for the US. The change was driven by a heightened sense of insecurity but also by a perceived opportunity. However, the policy is being severely tested by the popular resistance in Iraq.

The two papers that follow use a reading of Iraq's recent past and present conditions as guideposts to understanding its possible future. Ismael and Ismael propose four possible scenarios that could emerge from the present interaction between history and contemporary political dynamics. Leezenberg examines the experiences of Iraqi Kurdistan in attempting reconstruction over the past last ten years as a semi-autonomous region, assessing to what extent the same destabilizing factors evident in Kurdistan are present in Iraq as a whole and suggesting how these might be overcome.

The challenge posed by the discrepancy between traditional international norms of sovereignty and actual practice in recent emergencies, culminating in the political impasse over Iraq, is tackled by Schwarz and Jütersonke. They suggest that the notion of sovereignty can still have relevance, and can therefore aid the evaluation of post-war reconstruction in Iraq, if it is analysed 'through the lens of divisible sovereignty'.

Moving beyond the 'sovereignty debate' and the apparent almost total dominance of the USA over the Iraqi state by means of the Coalition Provision Authority (CPA), Herring and Rangwala identify globalising forces outside US control that are shaping governance in Iraq from above and below: global capital and the transborder informal economy which is often closely associated with the insurgency.

Le Billon then examines the pattern of authoritarianism, corruption and violence that have marked the recent history of Iraq as a major oil producer. He questions whether the US administration's declared aim to break this cycle will in fact deliver a peace dividend from equitable sharing of the oil revenues or simply revert to a 'corruption-based patronage', which this time will accommodate to US interests.

The failure of the American intervention, to quickly establish a stable functioning administration is attributed by Toby Dodge to ideological perceptions and lack of understanding of the political and sociological legacy of Saddam's regime and of the size and nature of the task to be undertaken. The subsequent manifestations of violence and sectarianism are seen as a direct outcome of this failure.

All these negative trends are recognised by Dawisha who nevertheless sees prospects for real democracy emerging from the US occupation, arguing that the right policies could transform these challenges into opportunities. He too looks to Iraq's past experiences and finds cohesive factors that could be built on, also taking encouragement from the emergence of Iraqi civil society since the occupation.

Having looked at the political and economic forces shaping the context for reconstruction in Iraq the remaining papers examine the impact that this has had on personal and operational efforts for reconstruction. The manner in which immediate relief and restoration of basic services are delivered is seen not as a separate 'emergency' phase of activity but as the initial enabling stage of the reconstruction process in which it is therefore essential to involve national actors and international development agencies.

The negative impact that war, sanctions and occupation have had on Iraqi society are examined by Al-Ali, by showing how these are reflected in patterns of gender relations and compounded by women's decreasing ability to participate in society because of personal insecurity.

The following papers contributed by those engaged in operational aspects of reconstruction trace their frustrations and difficulties to the fundamental contradictions of the pre-emptive military operation combined with equally pre-emptive, and therefore ill-informed, planning of the reconstruction. They argue that this ignorance was compounded by placing the reconstruction and humanitarian operations under military command - sidelining expertise both within the US Administration (State Department) and in experienced international agencies, and preventing the adoption of developmental strategies.

From practical experience in infrastructure rebuilding programmes in Iraq, Brown examines the contrast between the expected scenario for which the USA had planned and the emerging reality after the occupation. He notes the effect of the insurgency and chronic insecurity in reinforcing a policy of short-term solutions rather than a developmental and therefore people-centred approach.

The implications of the policy of contracting the private sector to deliver aid in an unstable environment, leading to unprecedented and unregulated use of private security firms, the advent of the 'armed humanitarian' and consequent blurring of the boundaries between military intervention and humanitarian aid in the minds of the local population, are the subject of the next paper by Bjork and Jones.

Lessons learned from managing the execution of relief programmes in the aftermath of the war are examined by Burkle et al from their experience of working within the US administration and in the light of the decision to place both humanitarian and military operations under the single command of the Defence Department. They argue for clarification of the legal framework for a UN led response to the protection of civilian life and welfare outside the political arena.

The volume concludes with two papers that consider the question of value. John Warren's paper demonstrates, from a different disciplinary angle, the true value that Iraq has contributed to human civilisation, suggesting that in the present conflict its deep cultural values should be invoked to break the cycle of violence and contribute to reconstruction. He shows that Iraq is much more than a theatre of war, reducing the pretentious claims of present day invaders to their proper place in its five thousand year history. Finally, Barakat, Chard and Jones discuss how we may eventually evaluate the impact that the US led invasion and subsequent efforts for reconstruction have had on the development of the Iraqi nation. Recognising that such an assessment can only be made when sufficient time has elapsed for the ultimate effects to be evident to the Iraqis themselves, the paper sets out some possible approaches to recovering the lessons to be learned from their evaluation.

The contributions to this volume reflect the many ways of viewing the complex reality of post-Saddam Iraq and the huge challenge that rebuilding that nation represents. Iraq is revealed as a diverse society shaped by many cultural and ethnic strands in a long and complex history, within the Middle East Region and with wider global strategic significance. As in any nation, there is evidence of both a strong national identity and deep conflicts of interest that have to be negotiated. The motives and approaches of the international actors are seen to be equally diverse and often contradictory. Our hope is that this volume will contribute to an understanding of the danger of prescribing simplistic solutions to Iraq's problems and of looking for instant transformation. What we have learnt from many past experiences of recovery from repression, violent conflict and sudden regime change is that a better future has to be negotiated and built by the national stakeholders to their own vision. The role of outsiders is to understand and support their efforts.

Notes

1 B Thistlethwaite, (2003) 'Just War and a Post-Modern World' in *Would the Invasion of Iraq be a "Just War"?* Special Report 13–15 (Washington DC United States Institute for Peace USIP), p.15.
2 Powers, G (2003) 'An Ethical Analysis of War Against Iraq' in *Would the Invasion of Iraq be a "Just War"?* Special Report 3–8 (Washington DC, United States Institute for Peace USIP), pp 3–8.
3 'States like these and their terrorist allies, constitute an axis of evil, arming to threaten the world... Steadfast in our purpose, we now press on. We have known freedom's price. We have shown freedom's power. And in this conflict, my fellow Americans, we will see freedom's victory'. George W. Bush State of the Union Address 29th January 2002.
4 Remarks by President George W. Bush at the 20th Anniversary of the National Endowment for Democracy, United States Chamber of Commerce November 6 2003.
5 Peter Baker, Washington Post March 8th 2005 www.washigtonpost.com
6 www.worldpress.org 24.11.2004 and www.middle-east-online.com 29.11.20004
7 B. Rubin (1993) 'The United States and Iraq: From Appeasement to War.' in *Iraq's Road to War*. A. Baram and B. Rubin eds. 255–271 (New York, St Martins Press), p.256.
8 www.washingtonpost.com 08 and 09.03.2005.
9 According to the Iraq Health Ministry Figures, 3,274 people in Iraq were killed and 12,657 injured in conflict related violence in the six month period from 1 July 2004 to 1 January 2005. (www.newsvote.bbc.co.uk) (30 January 2005)
10 No mention was made of the fact that the Syrian Army came in as part of the Taif Accord which ended the Lebanese civil war, with US blessing.
11 Powers, 'An Ethical Analysis of War Against Iraq', pp 3–8.
12 'Iraq war illegal, says Annan.' Kofi Annan interviewed by the BBC 16.09.2004 (www.newsvote.bbc.-co.uk)

Post-Saddam Iraq: deconstructing a regime, reconstructing a nation

SULTAN BARAKAT

ABSTRACT *The reconstruction of Iraq, following its invasion and occupation by the USA and its allies in 2003, presents a challenge to the consensus view of post-war reconstruction that has emerged in the wake of the Cold War, in that in Iraq reconstruction is being seen as integral to a military strategy and external strategic interest. Iraq itself also presents a very different context in terms of its human and economic development, resources and recent history compared with other nations that have been the subject of reconstruction interventions. This paper draws on four key tenets of post-war reconstruction: understanding the context (historical, cultural, regional); developing a shared national vision of the future; developing collaborative governance; and inducing development as a framework for analysing the nature of the reconstruction attempted in Iraq. It traces the difficulties of effecting a peaceful transition to the failure to understand the implications of attempting to impose a pre-determined plan in the fragile conditions of Iraq, post-Saddam. Nevertheless, despite these many mistakes, the paper concludes by suggesting that a way forward can still be found.*

Over the past decade a diverse set of actors, such as the UN and its agencies, donor governments, international and national NGOs, national governments and global financial institutions, has increasingly focused attention on the management of post-war reconstruction and has committed specific resources to it.[1] This new focus suggests that reconstruction is not only part of a wider strategic agenda, beyond the familiar territory of humanitarianism, but, more importantly, that it is now recognised as a key element in achieving global stability, security and the eradication of poverty in the 21st century. However, when relating the reconstruction of Iraq to this current understanding of post-war reconstruction, it becomes evident that it does not conform to previous patterns of conflict and reconstruction.

Uniquely, reconstruction in Iraq was conceived by the invading US superpower and its allies as an integral part of the deliberate destruction and dismantling of an existing, and so far functioning, state with the declared aim that 'The establishment of a free Iraq at the heart of the Middle East will be a watershed in the global democratic revolution'.[2] It was on the basis of this grand idea that the US Department of Defense took control of reconstruction as well as destruction. Detailed plans were made on the simplistic assumption that a swift total military victory, with relatively little damage or civilian casualties, would provide a blank sheet for reconstruction in the liberal–democratic mould, as well as investment opportunities for corporate business and the grateful acceptance of the Iraqi people.[3]

Clearly, this was the primary motivation for the war and an ambition of some long standing, so that, when the immediate justification of 'pre-emptive self-defence' against a potential threat to world peace was challenged both by US and British military analysts and by a last-minute Memorandum from three European powers to the UN Security council in early 2003, they were ignored (Cortright *et al*, 2002: 21).[4] Thus, unlike recent interventions in Afghanistan and Kosovo, which had grudging international support, the military powers were operating outside the legal parameters of the UN charter and had cast themselves in the role of 'occupying powers' while claiming to be liberators.[5]

The Iraqi response also proved to have been misjudged: the invaders were not met with gratitude and euphoria but with a fair degree of scepticism (ICG, 2002b: 7), which rapidly turned to disillusion as the behaviour of the invaders seemed increasingly at odds with their high moral rhetoric.

As a result it is difficult even to classify the current situation in Iraq as 'post-conflict', since what has occurred is a military occupation followed by various forms of violent resistance, which are still ongoing despite the declaration by the Pentagon on 14 April 2003 that 'major combat engagements are over' (Kagan, 2003: 3). There has been no capitulation as at the end of World War II, no peace accord between warring parties as in Mozambique. What we are witnessing is more in the nature of a protracted conflict, not dissimilar to the Afghan resistance to Soviet occupation. As such it can continue indefinitely until there is a political settlement between all the parties and an end to military occupation. Perhaps only then will it be appropriate to talk about 'post-war' reconstruction. The current reality is that the reconstruction of Iraq is being attempted in the midst of an ongoing conflict and for the present the most we can say is that it is 'post-Saddam'.

Conceptualising post-conflict reconstruction

There is a notable imprecision when it comes to the terminology used to describe the process of rebuilding war-torn societies. Post-war reconstruction, recovery, rehabilitation, peace building, and nation building are often used interchangeably, and differentiating between these terms is very difficult. For example, World Bank definitions emphasise assisting economic recovery and normalisation (World Bank, 1998: 4–5), whereas the UN emphasises the importance of political reform (Boutros-Ghali, 1995: 11).

Often the direct use of the term 'reconstruction' is avoided, as some commentators have suggested that it implies the restoration of what existed in the pre-war society, when it is often the pre-war systems, or lack thereof, which contributed to the conflict in the first place (Kumar, 1997: 2). Others fear that the term reconstruction focuses attention on the restoration of physical infrastructure, thereby overlooking the less tangible issues of rebuilding governance, reconciliation and psychological readjustment. In this case the term 'peace building' is preferred. Yet others have suggested that post-war reconstruction is something more often initiated by the war-affected community, whereas 'peace-building' is biased towards external interventions that often adopt 'quick fix' and *ad hoc* approaches to war-torn societies. In short, there are as many different concepts as there are facets to this multidisciplinary process. Political theories of reconstruction tend to emphasise the importance of institutions for physical security and stability; economic theories, with their belief in the importance of financial security, take a more developmental approach (Haughton, 1998; Collier *et al*, 2003); religious or humanitarian theories of reconstruction focus more on people and their capacity to survive, reconcile and forgive.[6] Recognising that war, with its toll of human suffering, has revisited so many countries as a result of economic, social or political breakdown, one cannot but adopt an overarching definition that incorporates all of these theories.

As a starting point to this discussion, therefore, we have taken post-war reconstruction to mean a range of holistic activities in an integrated process designed not only to reactivate economic and social development but at the same time to create a peaceful environment by addressing the emerging deficits in security and political and institutional capacity that will prevent a relapse into violence.[7] In this sense, reconstruction can be distinguished for its corrective dimension in righting wrongs and addressing vulnerabilities that have their roots in the past and the present, while maintaining a focus on the future.

The practical implications of this definition lead to four overarching lessons for reconstruction. First, it is critical to have a clear understanding not only of the causes of the conflict, but also of the overall context in which reconstruction is attempted. Second, for reconstruction to take root it is necessary to create a shared vision of the reconstruction among all national stakeholders. Third, for reconstruction to be implemented effectively it is necessary to establish institutions and mechanisms for collaborative governance. Fourth, reconstruction should be seen as a process of inducing development. The following sections of this paper examine the current approach to reconstruction in Iraq in the light of these four conclusions.

Iraq in context

It is important to remind ourselves that Iraq is not a typical context for reconstruction. On the eve of the war it had little in common with the poor, underdeveloped, dysfunctional states that have been the subject of 'humanitarian' reconstruction interventions under the auspices of the UN. The main distinguishing factors include the fact that it was not a failed (or for that matter failing) state.[8] In contrast, it had been considered a functioning, modern state and it continues to be rich in liquid assets and human resources. Its economic incapacity was largely brought about through an international regime of sanctions and reparations. Finally, it has a heritage of mobilising for reconstruction.

Following the 1991 Gulf war the popular insurrections in the Shia cities and the Kurdish north were a visible manifestation of a deep 'longing of the Iraqi people for democracy'. As al-Jabbar (1992) describes, the potential support for this movement extended to Baghdad and the central region and to many in the armed forces. But the lack of organisation within the opposition, the disruption of communication as a result of the war and the failure of the international community to lend support allowed Saddam Hussein to regroup those forces, from across the whole Iraqi ethnic and social spectrum, which nevertheless remained loyal to him and ruthlessly to regain control.

Rather than a failed state or one breaking up as a result of prolonged civil or secessionist wars, Iraq continued to be a stable and so far functioning dictatorship no different from other totalitarian regimes around the world such as Burma or North Korea. The grip of the regime over the population in the central and southern regions was to remain total up to the moment of intervention by external forces.[9]

Iraq is again unique in that its economic and administrative decline and the growth of corrupt clientelism have been brought about not only by the dictatorship of the regime and years of war,[10] but also what has been described as the most rigorous sanctions regime ever imposed by the international community. To this was added the imposition of war reparations on a scale comparable to those imposed on Germany after the First World War (Niblock, 2001: 192). Although the international community mitigated the worst effects of their own impositions through the Oil for Food Programme, by still preventing economic recovery it consolidated the despotic regime,[11] 'making it no longer merely a dictatorship of force but also a "dictatorship of need"' (ICG, 2002a: 10–11). It is also argued that the punitive nature of the sanctions regime 'convinced the Iraqi public that there is an international conspiracy to weaken and divide Iraq' and led to 'popular acceptance' of some 'central tenets of the regime ideology' (Niblock, 2001:186–187).[12] As a result, not only the moral authority of the invaders but also that of the international community is seriously compromised in the eyes of the Iraqi public.[13]

In contrast to other nations that have recently emerged from war, where the lack of liquid assets, the neglect of human capital and poor institutional development have meant that there is a need for long-term dependence on international finance and technical assistance to support capacity building and development, Iraq is a rich developed country. It holds the second largest oil reserves in the world (UNDG/World Bank, 2003: 5).[14] By the 1980s oil exploitation had been developed and the revenues used to create a modern state with a largely educated population, public services and infrastructure. In fact at that time it stood out among its neighbours in the Middle East as a model of progress. This means that, apart from some short-term assistance to rehabilitate essential infrastructure, it can generate all the finance it requires for reconstruction because, following the war, it still has huge liquid assets with which to fund its own reconstruction.[15] Similarly, despite the recent decline in the quality of education provision and the need for professionals to update their skills, there is sufficient basic human capacity to develop and implement reconstruction strategies, not least because, uniquely, Iraq has had recent experience of, and therefore retains expertise in, reconstruction after war.

As the Iran–Iraq war drew to a close the Iraqi government had already initiated the reconstruction of Fao and Basrah, the two southern cities largely devastated by the war. In the December following the ceasefire in August 1988 a 'Supreme Committee' for reconstruction, headed by the president decided that Basrah was to be rebuilt first, by the following March, followed by Fao on a similar time scale. Only the government's own construction capacity was to be employed, deliberately cutting out foreign companies expecting a share in the enterprise. The reasons for this decision were both symbolic and practical. First of all it wanted to demonstrate 'Iraq's great power', celebrating the 'heroic stand' of the two cities against the Iranians and present 'Saddam Hussein, as a hero of war and defence as well as of peace and reconstruction' (Iraqi Ministry of Culture and Information, cited in Barakat, 1993: 20). From a practical point of view it would save millions of dollars in profits to foreign contractors.

Given these aims and the imposed time scale it is not surprising that the reconstruction was top down, concerned with visible and highly symbolic physical reconstruction rather than social and economic regeneration and involved no local consultation, let alone participation. For example, Fao was rebuilt to a plan in which each sector was named after an Arab state whose traditional architectural style was adopted for its reconstruction. This Pan-Arabic statement was to remain an empty gesture, since the Shat al-Arab water way was never reopened and without its economic heart the city was never reoccupied by its citizens (Barakat, 1992).

A second reconstruction was necessary soon after, following the invasion of Kuwait, retaliation by the USA and its allies in the extraordinary violence of 'Desert Storm',[16] and the short-lived revolts of the Shia in the southern cities, including Basrah, and of the Kurds in the north. This time Baghdad was heavily bombed, key military installations, civil infrastructure and industry were deliberately targeted and 'smart' bombs that inevitably missed those targets also hit residential areas. Twenty hospitals as well as civil defence centres and civilian shelters were also damaged by allied bombing.[17] The devastation of residential areas was even more marked in the cities involved in the uprisings, where looting and vandalism followed by the army's retaliation added to the war damage (Barakat, 1993: 34).

The response of the Iraqi government to the renewed task of reconstruction was as decisive as its restoration of political control. As in the Iran–Iraq war, measures for reconstruction were initiated during the war, mainly to secure emergency restoration of vital transport links and services. Immediately after the war the whole cabinet was engaged as the 'Reconstruction Government' overseeing the assessment by the ministries of levels of damage and remaining resources, on the basis of which a three month emergency phase was largely successful in restoring basic services (Barakat, 1993: 39; Clawson, 1993: 75). All this was played out in the context of UN sanctions, which obliged the Iraqis more than ever to rely on their internal resources and technical ingenuity (Barakat, 1993: 38–41).[18] Nevertheless, without some imported technology and materials these successes could not be built on nor in the long run maintained (Graham-Brown, 1999: 158).

A first-hand account of this earlier reconstruction is given by Gafar, who was directly involved at that time. He admirably demonstrates the technical and managerial skills and practical problem-solving approach of the Iraqis in this field and has some confident lessons to contribute. In particular he notes that: 'With sufficient motivation and good organization, Iraqi personnel can implement any reconstruction project with little or no on site help from foreign contractors' (Gafar, 2003: 37).

While Iraqi technical competence in reconstruction is beyond doubt, Saddam's vision of centrally directed reconstruction had some serious flaws. Thus a second less positive lesson can be learned from Iraq's approach to reconstruction in the cities of Basrah and Fao. By concentrating on restoring the physical environment, to express the symbolic message of national resilience and personal power that obsessed the dictator, without reference to the local inhabitants' need for homes and livelihoods, the reconstruction created monuments to national pride but did not in fact restore the fortunes of the two cities.

Both the positive and the negative lessons from these experiences are highly relevant to the present approach to reconstruction by the occupying powers and to understanding the Iraqi response. Many of the failings of the reconstruction efforts that are set out in a number of interim evaluations could have been avoided if this experience had been examined and built on (Dobbins *et al*, 2003; Pollack, 2004; Barton & Crocker, 2004).

With their own experience of reconstruction in mind as a constant yardstick, it is hardly surprising that the Iraqi public expresses frustration and disbelief at the slow progress being achieved by the present occupying powers in restoring basic services, despite the huge sums of money paid to foreign contractors (ICG, 2004: 2–3). Feeling as they do that they have been punished by the international community as well as by the dictator, though initially pleased to get rid of Saddam, they also believe they have the right to expect some minimum conditions from the occupying powers: a rapid restoration of services; maintenance of law and order; to be treated with respect (ICG, 2002b: 7–10). None of these expectations has been fulfilled.

Creating a shared vision

It is crucial to recognise that the creation of an effective reconstruction process involves the establishment of a *shared vision* beyond the complex technical and administrative process of responding to urgent needs. In the case of Iraq, a vision for a 'New Iraq' post-Saddam was developed within the US administration. It was founded on the concept of military victory leading to the removal of Saddam Hussein and his loyalists, creating a blank space in which to install a 'Western style democracy', favourable to US political and economic interests in the Middle East (Stansfield, 2003).

This vision was not the result of cohesive policy development but rather the outcome of a contest between the US State Department, the arm of US government that customarily manages post-war reconstruction, and the Pentagon, which was eventually awarded responsibility for reconstruction as well as for the prosecution of the war. Thus, reconstruction was planned in advance as an integral part of the military operation. Stage one was deconstruction by military means, stage two reconstruction by corporate US capital as a spoil of war and as an instant measure for privatisation.[19]

Huge contracts were awarded to major US companies to complete 'showcase infrastructure projects'. As Dobbins *et al* remarked 'that's what the Army Corps of Engineers does: it hires multinational corporations to build infrastructure'.[20] As Pei and Kaspar (2003: 6) point out, the danger of these 'sweetheart deals for American corporations' is that instead of injecting necessary capital into the local economy they are actually exploitative and present an image of 'the occupying foreign power…advancing its own interests', which quickly leads to rejection by the indigenous public.

The fact that the vision for the 'New Iraq' was not developed within Iraq or by Iraqis made it inherently unworkable, however it was conceived. A reconstruction vision must provide a 'national appreciation for recovery' that is essentially, an internal vision, not one that is externally imposed (Logan, 1996: 24–34).

The US scheme envisages replacing, not building on existing conditions in Iraq. There is no celebration of its direct descent from the oldest human civilisation or of its huge contribution to universal knowledge, art and culture.[21] Similarly, while denigrating the excesses of Saddam's rule there is no recognition of Iraq's achievements as a modern secular state. Reconstruction strategies have not sought to enlist Iraq's wealth of human capacity, nor to solve its short-term debt crisis in order to put its economic resources at the disposal of national development rather than international corporate profit. The contracting out of reconstruction, and the rapid privatisation of key industries that followed, marginalises Iraqi business, middle class professionals and the general public. A wider exclusion was to ignore regional and international stakeholders when developing a vision of Iraq's future. Since the invasion was focused on Iraq's past aggression against its neighbours and its supposed threat to world peace, positive economic and cultural ties within the region were ignored. Similarly, the positive roles Iraq has played in modern history as a founding and active member of the United Nations,[22] and later on of the Arab League,[23] were not acknowledged. On the contrary, Iraq's protracted and difficult attempts to negotiate with the international community through those organisations went unrewarded throughout the sanctions regime and its final compliance was to be swept aside in favour of an illegal invasion.[24]

A common impediment to developing a relevant vision of reconstruction is the failure to read the complexity of the socioeconomic and political conditions that need to be addressed, resulting in policies that are either too narrow, such as 'the UN's characteristic sectoral approach' (Barakat, 2003: 809) or too rigid. Thus in the case of Iraq it was not a lack of planning that led to the chaotic scenes that followed the invasion—after all, plans for reconstructing a 'new Iraq' had been in the making since October 2001. The problem was that much of the planning was based on serious misconceptions and was not open to modification in response to the reality encountered on the ground (Dodge, 2003: 163–165).

For a vision of reconstruction to engage people effectively all stakeholders need to feel ownership and commitment to achieving its goals and, as Diefendorf (1996: 8) reminds us, it must be 'reflective of the specific needs caused by the war and not of the perceived needs of those implementing the vision'.

In Iraq, however, rather than seeking space for dialogue with the resistance, the occupying powers have chosen visible confrontation. For example, in the second battle for Fallujah the US forces wanted to show that they could enforce security for the holding of elections, while the insurgents sought to prove that they could not. Meanwhile, what the ordinary citizens of Fallujah experienced cannot have seemed significantly different from previous horrors, such as the infamous chemical attack on Halabja back in 1988, in which whole communities were destroyed in a struggle for power between protagonists who showed no concern for human life or interest in people's needs.[25]

The development of a national vision is important not only for peace building but because it can provide a unified conceptual framework around which reconstruction partners can build relevant and integrated strategies in a collaborative coalition of international and national actors. The substitution of such a vision with campaigning zeal to bring about a predetermined change by military means has resulted in the fact that neither experienced entities within the US administration, nor its allies nor, since it was being sidelined, the UN, were consulted. International financial institutions were similarly not involved in any pre-war planning, since the US concept was that US private enterprise would lead economic reconstruction.

Restoring collaborative governance

Years of experiments in the reconstruction of war-torn communities in the wake of the Cold War have led us to conclude that, unlike short-term relief efforts, the success and the sustainability of long-term recovery is dependent on the existence of effective systems of governance. Therefore, whatever the challenges to creating the vision, the implementation of an effective reconstruction requires the existence, and as soon as possible, of a strong state structure that enjoys 'legitimacy' and has the 'capability' to deliver the post-conflict dividends equitably. Bypassing 'bureaucratic' and 'corrupt' state structures in favour of the 'lean' and 'transparent' non-governmental and private structures may deliver short-term results but has often led to longer-term dependency.

The US-led occupation, however, moved swiftly to implement its predetermined concept of removing all traces of the Baathist regime in order to have a clean slate on which to start building the new 'free and democratic' Iraq. Instead of identifying and strengthening capable and legitimate elements of the existing state, it moved to dismantle it by removing key institutional and human resources.

Possibly the most disastrous mistake of the US administration was dismantling the army by decree on 23 May 2002 after Paul Bremer took over as Administrator of the Coalition Provisional Authority (CPA).[26] Soldiers had their pay cancelled and were never asked to surrender weapons they had taken home with them when they abandoned the war; the officer core was humiliated by being debarred not only from holding rank in the army but from any public employment, on the grounds that it was by definition Baathist. This not only left the army with a deep sense of betrayal but created wider public resentment because of the close identification with the army as a symbol of national pride. It also removed at a stroke the one institution that could have ensured an orderly transition by excluding it from governance.[27]

The outcome was a rapid breakdown in law and order leading from 'widespread looting and violent crime' to armed resistance (Amnesty International 2004: 1–2). The US troops in particular, became 'obsessed with force protection and tracking down the insurgents who are attacking them', leaving the Iraqi public and their property largely unprotected (Pollack, 2004: 9–10) and heavily reliant on private (and therefore unaccountable and unvetted) security firms who were mainly protecting expatriate reconstruction personnel, equipment and key installations (ICG, 2003b: 21). This has led to the emergence of a gun culture, hitherto unknown in Iraq. Private security guards, many recruited from the ranks of the unemployed Iraqi military, as well as foreign mercenaries contracted from around the world, contest the streets with insurgents, also both national and foreign, as well as criminal gangs.

It is important to recognise that legitimacy cannot be based solely on re-establishing security and authority, but should be earned through advocating reconstruction policies that are inclusive and accountable. Rather than demilitarising Iraqi society and promoting civil governance, the disbanding of the army promoted the rule of the gun, thereby restricting not enhancing the participation of civilians in public life.[28]

The chaos of war often destroys or discredits traditional social structures and authorities, while new political structures may remain fragile, having yet to build their profile with the public—they too lack legitimacy and credibility and their reputation is frequently tarnished by perceived links to partisan interests. In Iraq, having dismantled the regular army and police without making arrangements for an international police force, the CPA began to rely on militia groups, as Saddam had done, and even to recruit intelligence and security agents who had previously served the regime, allowing themselves to be discredited by association (Dodge, 2003: 159–161). Thus the violence in Iraq is not solely an issue of security but also one of governance and credibility.

Building the capacity of government to deliver and account for reconstruction policies at the national and sub-national levels, while providing a conducive environment for recovery, is a difficult but very important aspect of successful reconstruction. Understandably a post-conflict situation brings with it high expectations from the people, in direct contrast to the low capacity of the state to deliver. If the state is not supported, the likelihood is disillusionment, with a corresponding diminution in the credibility and thus the legitimacy of the state, making the peace dividend hard to realise as far as the individual is concerned (Collier *et al*, 2003).

The second major error of judgement by the CPA was its 'debaathification' policy. Curiously, although this policy was clearly inspired by denazification in post-war Germany, the lesson that this policy had proved a blunt instrument when it came to ridding the state apparatus of regime supporters without loosing essential staff, seems not to have been taken on board. A blanket policy of purging the top four ranks of the civil service of Baath party members was excessive and denuded public institutions of experienced managerial personnel and frontline staff, either because of the actual purges or because many disillusioned civil servants remained at home (Dodge, 2003: 164; Pollack, 2004: 14).[29] Meanwhile, the figures at the very top, who were most involved with the regime, soon used their network of contacts and considerable resources to re-emerge in new guises, heading NGOs and private companies. Some were even re-engaged by the CPA. Thus the policy disabled rather than built the capacity of the state administration, without necessarily succeeding in removing the influence of key associates of the regime.

Another important dimension of collaborative governance is for the state to develop the ability to invite civil society groups and local communities to participate effectively in the identification and development of reconstruction programmes. This is critical not only to ensure the ownership and relevance of the programmes but, more importantly, to create spaces for political dialogue. This is particularly important in the case of emerging social groups which have become politically sensitised and aware, such as ex-combatants and their leaders, returning refugees, diaspora returnees etc, who tend to exercise a politicising impact on the local scene.

Those leading the US occupation, as we have seen, were mainly concerned to establish a new Iraqi government that would promote US interests in the region. The ICG (2002b) states that, as a consequence, they associated themselves with Iraqi exiles, such as Ahmed Chalabi and Ayad Allawi, who were deeply unpopular in the country, relying on their analysis and intelligence to formulate policy without questioning these men's credentials or how they fitted into the Iraqi domestic picture.[30] The exiles for their part sought to use the Americans for their own purposes.[31]

The problems of fragile relationships between people and institutions are related to and compounded by unclear or unstable divisions of power, transitory political institutions and poorly developed civil society and civic culture. In such environments, attempting prematurely to impose imported ideological imperatives may at best not take root and at worse be counter-productive, creating further dissent and fragmentation. For example, in the absence of a mature system of governance, elections rarely resolve such situations or lead to sustainable power-sharing arrangements.

Soon after the invasion of Iraq the CPA began to make arrangements for a civil administration with some semblance of Iraqi involvement. However, it sought not to develop a model for future governance with the Iraqis, but rather to enlist those who were prepared to implement the pre-planned US model. First attempts by Ray Garner to bring together Iraqis who would work with the CPA were 'more notable for those who chose not to attend' and for the fact that 'over half the attendees were recently returned exiles' (Dodge, 2003: 166). The Iraqi Governing Council (IGC) eventually appointed by the CPA under Bremer on the basis of ethnic quotas, reflected 'how the Council's creators, not the Iraqi people view Iraqi society and politics'. Strictly excluded from the Council were 'stridently anti-US Shiite religious leaders' and any former Baath party members (except of course those who returned from exile such as Ayad Allawi), in contradiction of the concept of collaborative governance discussed above (ICG 2003a: ii).

Meanwhile, a 'reconstruction from on high' approach, reminiscent of that adopted in the early 1990s by Saddam Hussein, was adopted in the public sector (Stansfield, 2003: 69). All ministries were under the control of US administrators, most of whom spoke no Arabic and therefore relied heavily on the unpopular 'Michigan bunch' of exiles as translators and interpreters of a reality on the ground of which neither had any current knowledge (Dodge, 2003: 165). As a result, instead of identifying and promoting Iraqi best practice to find solutions to reconstruction problems, attempts were made to reproduce US administrative norms (Pollack, 2004: 18). These strategies did nothing to arrest the deterioration in the security and employment situation.

After some months, attempts were made to put right some of the mistakes (recruiting and training an Iraqi police force and a new army for example (ICG, 2003b)) and on 15 November 2003 the CPA and the IGC announced an agreement for transfer of power to an appointed interim Iraqi government. The proposal was vehemently denounced by the leading Shia cleric Sistani and by the majority of Iraqis and had to be abandoned. The principle objection was not so much that it would be unelected (although a short time frame to a fully elected government was demanded) but that it would be selected by caucus along ethnic quota lines and accorded powers inconsistent with a caretaker government (Brahimi, 2004a.).

When the CPA at this point called in the UN to broker a solution, the U-turn in US policy appeared to be complete. However, the eventual composition of the Interim Government installed in June 2004 ignored Brahimi's advice, based on Iraqi public opinion, that a technocratic caretaker government, involving neither political aspirants nor sectarian interests, was needed in order to prepare for fully democratic elections (Brahimi, 2004b; 2004c). Despite a tactical retreat, the USA ignored the evidence that its vision of Iraq was not shared by the majority of Iraqis and, far from collaborative governance, pursued its original plan of installing a government sympathetic to US interests.[32] The transparency of this intention inevitably undermined any legitimacy that the formal transfer of sovereignty to an Iraqi administration with UN endorsement might have achieved. The armed challenge to the occupation escalated and was met with a show of US military strength.

It was in this context of intense military operations, counter-violence and mistrust, but equally of hopes that a turning point had been reached, that a moment of opportunity might, with the right kind of international support, afford the chance of a better future, that elections were held in January 2005. A substantial number of Iraqis were able and also willing to vote. Are we to interpret this as the achievement of the US vision of a democratic Iraq as the Bush administration suggests? The number of Iraqis who couldn't and didn't vote belies this. Nevertheless, it has created an opportunity for Iraqis to begin to take control of the reconstruction process and to negotiate their future.

Inducing development

It is critical to recognise that post-war reconstruction is fundamentally about getting development right. The need for approaching reconstruction as a development challenge can be demonstrated by assessing the recovery strategies of countries as diverse as West Germany, Mozambique and Cambodia. Key aspects of economic recovery have been identified as follows:

1. war inevitably de-regulates the economy, and often leaves behind a heritage of 'war-economy';
2. economic growth is critical for reconstruction and recovery to be sustainable;
3. there is a need for a balance between the macroeconomic policies designed to induce economic growth and microeconomic policies needed to develop human capital and allow people to feel the dividend of the post-conflict situation;
4. in order to get the balance right, appropriate timing and sequencing of intervention is a prerequisite for creating the right environment for investment and growth;
5. a word of caution is required concerning the 'false economy' that has the tendency to be created by the sudden arrival of emergency relief and its associated actors.

In the case of Iraq, as discussed, it is not only the impact of war that has had a detrimental effect on the economy. The legacy of sanctions and the oil-based corruption have also taken their toll. Since legitimate trade and public administration were severely restricted, Iraq under sanctions had become a breeding ground for nepotism, corruption and rampant accumulation by an elite group close to the regime's leaders, to the detriment of legitimate business. In this climate private contractors, sanctions busters and profiteers who were useful to the regime prospered and were hardly taxed, while merchants outside the circle of power were subject to appropriations and executions for profiteering (Niblock, 2000: 170–172; ICG, 2002a: 10). Thus before the US invasion of Iraq this was the country's only experience of operating in the private sector. The majority of people were not benefiting from this private sector, and became reliant on the state, rather than the family, which in traditional culture has always been the prime coping mechanism. This further distorted socioeconomic conditions.[33]

Economic growth is a crucial component for sustainable development. However, in the context of war-affected countries like Iraq there is the added cost of reconstruction investment. Therefore the simplistic notion that, in Iraq, oil revenues alone will pay for recovery fails to recognise that there is no supporting institutional and administrative infrastructure in place to ensure the trickle-down effect. While many commentators, such as Hill (1996: 85), consider economic growth to be critical to ease the transition from the immediate post-war recovery to longer-term development, this does not mean simply promoting national 'economic growth' by employing liberal market strategies, as the World Bank and other financial institutions have had the tendency to advocate in the past. Such an emphasis, particularly when it is purely ideologically motivated, as now in Iraq, can often lead to extra pressure on emerging societies. Privatisation and restructuring can result in large job losses and wider grievances at a time when reconstruction should be creating hope through delivering tangible benefits to individuals and their communities. As Kubrusi (2003) points out, the public may not have the means to purchase the enterprises or the enterprises themselves may not be attractive to the private sector when they are not functional. On the other hand, stimulating the economy through increasing the number of people employed has the added advantage of improving legitimacy and therefore security, as noted above.[34] However, the US strategy of inviting corporate US business to tender for the large reconstruction contracts, and its intended oil privatisation, is more likely to lead to asset stripping than to the investment in the economy which is so crucial for encouraging employment. In addition Iraq's $200 billion war reparations debt could seriously hinder any capital investment for economic and social development (Abdel-Fadil, 2003).

While traditional regional suppliers maintained strong links with Iraq following the 1991 Gulf war and continue to operate outside the formal economy, formal co-operation and the associated fiscal benefits have now ended because of the war and the US-controlled procurement policy (Kubrusi & Kadri, 2003: 48). This economic dislocation will continue as long as the USA remains obsessed with oil as the only form of economic salvation (Abdul Fadil, 2003). Kubrusi (2003: 30) argues that it is the agricultural sector, which has traditionally been an engine for growth, that should be seen as a priority and stimulated to complement oil revenue. This would not only restore the livelihoods of a substantial section of the population but also increase food security.

Contrary to the economic reconstruction needs discussed above, the US strategy neither addressed the immediate macro nor the micro economic priorities necessary to initiate development. At the macro level currency stabilisation, rehabilitation of the banking sector and national control of economic assets (oil) have yet to be addressed (Corm, 2003: 14; Abdel-Fadil, 2003). At the micro level the combined effect of debaathification, disbanding the army, privatisation of state enterprises, the dollarisation of the economy and the resulting insecurity has increased levels of unemployment across all classes of society.[35] It has also failed to stimulate alternative income generation from small businesses and agriculture (Abdel-Fadil, 2003). As a result Barton and Crocker (2004: vii) in their interim evaluation found that the continuing lack of economic opportunity and high levels of unemployment, combined with personal insecurity, are now the main concerns of the Iraqi public.

Timing and sequence are crucial to economic reconstruction and this should be coupled with the recognition that, in Iraq as in other war-torn contexts, protracted uncertainty and insecurity have existed for so long they have become normative. In such a context reconstruction cannot simply replace humanitarian assistance, or take societies back to what existed before the war started. Continual trade-offs between reconstruction and humanitarian assistance, while adapting to an ever-changing environment are necessary. Indeed, the dislocations that commonly occur during conflict are often so fundamental that a high adaptive capability is the first requirement in reconstruction interventions. This particularly highlights the importance of linking relief and development strategies within the rubric of post-war reconstruction. Jones (2005) goes further, stating that, without tangible improvements in livelihoods, people's receptive capacity for other recovery initiatives such as reconciliation is diminished. Hence the importance of re-establishing acceptable levels of public services such as health, education and power supply, as well as efforts to ensure stability by re-establishing the rule of law and creating a secure environment.

The rapid implementation of the pre-planned US recovery strategy pre-empted a more incremental approach based on an actual in-country needs assessment carried out by UNDG/World Bank in October 2003 that took a more balanced view of the priorities. On this basis the World Bank (2004:10) proposed an interim strategy to first 'build institutional capacity', second, 'generate employment/kick-start economic activity, restore essential infrastructure and services' and, third, 'lay the groundwork for Iraq's medium-term reconstruction and begin assisting in the transition from central planning to market economy'.

Reconstruction as a development challenge is about addressing the micro-level needs of communities (health, education, environment, employment and political participation) within a macro national strategy driven by the need to reinforce peace, as much as by the need to induce growth. In Iraq, while the World Bank analysis has taken this on board, the US concept of focusing reconstruction on achieving national economic growth through fast-paced privatisation and foreign corporate investment has prevented the development of a national economic strategy for reconstruction and has failed to address the microeconomic needs of the Iraqi public.

In summary, two different influences are apparent, which at times conflict and at other times come together. The first is the strong relationship between the concepts and practice of development and of post-war reconstruction. Reconstruction is thus viewed as a process of reactivation of development, which at the same time addresses the root causes of conflict to establish an environment of peaceful interaction and a shared vision of the future. The second is the strategic interest of rich nations, which do not necessarily coincide with the actual needs on the ground in war-torn countries. This point can be illustrated through a simple comparison of international aid pledged for a number of recent reconstruction challenges: Rwanda ($98 per capita); Afghanistan ($174 per capita); East Timor ($626 per capita); Bosnia and Herzegovina ($1200 per capita); Kosovo ($830 per capita); and Iraq ($1337 per capita) (Dobbins *et al*, 2003).

Applying these lessons to Iraq, we can see that the strategic interest of international actors has dominated the reconstruction effort to the exclusion of the developmental approach. While there is a vision for reconstruction, it is almost entirely external and, although there were elements of functional governance, these have been dismantled and their re-establishment has been limited by lack of stakeholder participation. The performance of the international institutions and agencies in previous post-war contexts such as Afghanistan was not without criticism and their co-ordination and information-sharing difficulties are still hampering operations in Iraq. Nevertheless, they have built up a body of expertise, experience and awareness of the need to proceed on the basis of local knowledge and consent, which could have averted some of the worst mistakes that have so far been made by the US occupation.

Moving forward

As has been argued, how reconstruction is carried out is more important than what is done. Reconstruction has to be planned for the contribution it makes to peace building and the restoration of a shared national life. Many mistakes have been made by all parties in the recent history of Iraq; these have worked against peace and reconstruction. If the process is to take a positive direction from here, transparency and coherence are first required from the international community, the occupying powers and the Iraqi leadership—there is a need for an honest admission of failures and a clear statement of intentions followed by consistent action, if trust in the process is to be established.

It is first of all important to acknowledge that in Iraq reconstruction is being attempted in the face of unresolved violent conflict and a continuing military occupation. The challenge that this is posing in Afghanistan in terms of diversion of reconstruction funds to the military and distortion of recovery strategies has already been documented (UNDP, 2005: 223–224). An even more difficult scenario has already emerged in Iraq.

Therefore the first priority for reconstruction and simply for improving the lives of ordinary citizens is security. However, this will not be achieved by higher and higher levels of military protection and the use of ever greater force. These will simply continue to absorb more and more resources without resolving the situation. Security will come through conflict resolution, which requires reconciliation of all parties in an accountable state-building process that results in responsible and sovereign institutions whose authority and legitimacy are recognised by all. That is, a state with the authority to regulate and strength to provide security for all to participate fully in society.

Starting this process without including all stakeholders will only exacerbate the conflict. Allowing the precedent of the recent elections to set a pattern of developing strategies for the willing in the 'stable' areas, while failing to resolve the conflict in the 'Sunni triangle', can only fuel the sense of exclusion and grievance on which the insurrection feeds. The whole country has to go forward together, redressing the inequities and injustices of the past, while avoiding creating new inequalities and exclusions.

There has to be a vision of where the state-building process is headed, the kind of society Iraq is going to be, but it cannot be the missionary vision of outsiders or of a small elite. There can be no pre-determined blueprint. It has to be a vision shared by all national stakeholders. It can be backed by international support but it has to emerge through dialogue between Iraqis in which all can participate. Democracy has to be negotiated and built, it cannot be imported.

Genuine and inclusive participation is the substance of democracy. Without it democratic forms can be subverted by the powerful, especially in the conditions that prevail in Iraq today, where participation is limited by personal insecurity and civil society organisation is still weak. Strengthening civil capacity to participate in the national dialogue can be promoted through participatory planning, community empowerment and international support for the new government's attempts to create space for dialogue.

Equity through balanced development and fair distribution of resources is another fundamental key to sustainable peace building, especially where unequal development and restricted access to opportunities have been a source of grievance leading to violent conflict. As we have seen, both Shia and Kurds have in the past resorted to violence provoked by their sense of exclusion and oppression. The equitable distribution of Iraq's oil revenues as the key strategic resource for reconstruction and development is therefore a key issue but, unless it remains under state control, it will be difficult to negotiate its management and sharing between the claims of the regions, key economic sectors and future generations.

The ability to participate in and benefit from economic reconstruction is also an equity, and therefore a security, issue. Rapid introduction of a classic liberal market economy while the majority of citizens are excluded from the formal economy by unemployment and poverty, and legitimate business devastated by years of decapitalisation, can be destabilising. Most will simply not have the capacity to take advantage of the market economy and the winners will inevitably be the war entrepreneurs and foreign (regional and global) enterprises. The rapid and illegal disposal of Iraqi state assets by the CPA has added this source of grievance and dissent to an already volatile situation (ESCWA, 2003).

Iraq's reconstruction requires a multifaceted programme but one that always has people and their perceptions in the forefront. This means starting to involve Iraqis from the community level upwards in decision making and facilitating, rather then trying to direct the work of Iraqi public servants and managerial and technical staff in restoring services and productive enterprises. Concentration should be placed on restoring livelihoods, wherever this is feasible, in state or private enterprise, family business and agriculture, not on doctrinaire privatisation (Corm, 2003; Abdel-Fadil, 2003).[36] All these approaches are designed to enable Iraqi capacity. As discussed above, Iraq does not suffer from the huge human and material resource deficits that afflict other war-torn countries: what Iraq has lacked at all levels of society is empowerment.

The international community, however, does also need to play an enabling role in Iraq's reconstruction as in other war-affected countries. It is essential that the UN resume a leading role as political facilitator but, as ESCWA (2003: 3) has pointed out: 'The United Nations would only be given a meaningful role in Iraq if the international community demonstrated that such a role was indispensable' and insisted on its 'independence vis-à-vis the occupying power'. However, the international community has so far not given its wholehearted backing to the UN, particularly for the role that it has tried to play in establishing a representative government in Iraq.

Financial enablement is also critical but Iraq does not need the customary long-term donor support, rather it is necessary to negotiate a solution to Iraq's debt and war reparations burden and restore sovereignty over its oil revenues. This would allow Iraq to negotiate its internal resource distribution to stimulate its internal economy, to compete in the global economy and to contribute to the regional economy as before.

Finally, the reconstruction of a nation is always dependent on the conditions and relationships with its surrounding region.[37] The reconstruction of Iraq therefore has to be tackled in the context of an agenda for peace in the Middle East, where the core problem is the unresolved conflict between Israel and Palestine. It is not the Bush vision of Iraq as a springboard for democratic revolution that will resolve the problems of the Middle East. It is an Israel/Palestine settlement that holds out the prospect of sustainable peace and development in Iraq.

Notes

1 Through entities such as the World Bank's Conflict Prevention and Reconstruction Unit, UNDP's Bureau for Crisis Prevention and Recovery (BCPR), or the Post Conflict Reconstruction Unit (PCRU) recently inaugurated by the British government.

2 President George W Bush, 'Remarks to the Anniversary of the National Endowment for Democracy', United States Chamber of Commerce, 3 November 2003.

3 This militaristic approach to advance planning for reconstruction is discussed in this issue by Burkle *et al.*

4 'Deliverable weapons of mass destruction in the hands of a terror network, or a murderous dictator, or the two working together, constitutes as grave a threat as can be imagined'. Dick Cheney, 'Remarks to the Veterans of the Korean War', 29 August 2002; and Memorandum of France, Germany and Russia, 24 February 2002, at www.nytimes.com/2003/02/05. See also Cortright & Lopez (2004).

5 The war 'was not in conformity with the UN charter. . .from the charter point of view it was illegal'. Kofi Annan, interviewed by the BBC, 16 September 2004.
6 Based on either 'Dunantist' or 'Wilsonian' approaches.
7 For the development of this concept see Barakat and Hoffman (1995).
8 For analysis of the definition of this concept see ICRC (1999).
9 It was only the military measures taken by the USA and Britain with UN backing on 'humanitarian' grounds that separated the Northern Kurdish region administratively from the rest of the country as a 'protected zone' but not as an independent state.
10 Iran–Iraq War, 1980–88; Invasion of Kuwait, 1990; Gulf war and Shia and Kurdish uprisings, 1991; Invasion by US-led coalition, 2003.
11 The UN Oil for Food Programme had the declared objective of 'improving the life of the average Iraqi citizen'. Its policy involved constant haggling with the Iraqi government to determine the amount of oil that Iraq could export and the price per barrel (based on a six monthly cycle). Under the UN sanctions Iraq was allowed to produce oil at around $\frac{3}{4}$ of the pre-1990 Gulf war level (over $12 billion per year). However, under the UN Oil for Food Programme 30% of the return was reserved for the compensation of those who had suffered losses or injuries during Iraq's invasion of Kuwait (US$3.6 billion); 13% of the return went to the three Northern Provinces (around $1.56 billion); 4% covered the operational costs of the UN ($480 million) and 49% were allocated to the part of Iraq under the control of the government ($6.36 billion). See http://www.un.org/Depts/oip/background/) and http://en.wikipedia.org/wiki/Oil-for-Food_Programme.
12 Oil for food did little more than halt the deterioration in nutritional status. UN surveys after 1996 still reported malnutrition in over 14% of infants and in children under five at over 20%. Babies underweight at birth had increased by nearly 20% since 1989. Only 1.2% of the total value of oil for food contracts approved up to 2000 were spent on education: the result was falling enrolment in schools, low teacher morale, intellectual isolation in universities and the doubling of adult illiteracy compared with 1989. Less than 5% of approved contracts were for inputs to agriculture. As a result, despite increasing the land under agriculture in an attempt to increase food self-sufficiency, without the necessary spare parts for plant and machinery and agricultural inputs '20–25% of the potential crop yield was being lost by the end of the 1990s' (Niblock, 2001: 142–154). The lasting effects of sanctions are reflected in the post-war needs assessments and surveys of social indicators: UNICEF, *Nutritional Status Survey of Under-Five Children in Baghdad*, Iraq, 29 April–3 May 2003; United Nations/World Bank, *Joint Needs Assessment*, October 2003. UNICEF, 2004. At a Glance: Iraq.
13 As the bombing of the UN headquarters in Baghdad, 19 August 2003 and of the International Committee of the Red Cross in October of the same year sadly confirmed. While the majority of Iraqis did not condone these acts, there was notably little public demonstration of outrage.
14 The US Department for the Environment (2005) states that according to the *Oil and Gas Journal*, Iraq contains 115 billion barrels of proven oil reserves, the third largest in the world (behind Saudi Arabia and Canada), concentrated overwhelmingly (80% or so) in southern Iraq. Estimates of Iraq's oil reserves and resources vary widely, however, given that only about 10% of the country has been explored. Some analysts (the Baker Institute, Center for Global Energy Studies, the Federation of American Scientists, etc) believe, for instance, that deep oil-bearing formations located mainly in the vast Western Desert region could yield large additional oil resources (possibly another 100 billion barrels or more), but have not been explored. Other analysts, such as the US Geological Survey, are not as optimistic, with median estimates for additional oil reserves closer to 45 billion barrels. In August 2004 Iraqi Oil Minister Ghadban stated that Iraq had 'unconfirmed or potential reserves' of 214 billion barrels. See http://www.eia.doe.gov/emeu/cabs/iraq.html. Country Analysis Briefs: Iraq.
15 At the ESCWA (2003: 20) workshop, Corm suggested that estimates of the financial needs of Iraq had been greatly inflated by the US authority in order to facilitate large company profits. This is substantiated by the quarterly report to Congress of the Special Inspector General for Iraq Reconstruction of 30 January 2005.
16 'The USA does seem to have treated the Kuwait crisis in a manner similar to the way the Nazis handled the Spanish Civil War. It became a laboratory for testing weapons (Pelletiere, 1992: 54).
17 The Amirya shelter hit by a US stealth bomber in the belief that it was a command and control bunker on 13 February 1991 with a total of 315 civilian deaths was the most notorious case of bombing error. The destruction of civil infrastructure and industry, however, was deliberate and left key public services such as the electricity supply and telecommunications barely functioning, roads and railways (especially bridges) 50% destroyed and the all-important oil industry at a virtual standstill (Barakat, 1993: 33).
18 In this round of reconstruction there was also some indication of administrative adaptation as regional planning and development decisions were decentralised by dismantling the Ministry of Local Government, although potentially wasteful competition between ministries was continued as an incentive measure.

19 These aspects of the reconstruction are examined by Ismael and Ismael, and by Brown in this issue. Herring and Rangwala also argue that his strategy in fact fed globalisation agendas, both corporate and criminal beyond and above the interests of corporate America.
20 J Glanz & E Eckholm, 'Reality intrudes on promises in rebuilding Iraq', at www.nytimes.com, 30 June 2004.
21 See John Warren in this volume.
22 The founding members of the UN in 1945 were: Argentina, Australia, Belgium, Bolivia, Brazil, Belarus, Canada, Chile, China, Colombia, Costa Rica, Cuba, Czechoslovakia, Denmark, Dominican Republic, Ecuador, Egypt, El Salvador, Ethiopia, France, Greece, Guatemala, Haiti, Honduras, India, Iran, Iraq, Lebanon, Liberia, Luxembourg, Mexico, Netherlands, New Zealand, Nicaragua, Norway, Panama, Paraguay, Peru, Philippines, Poland, Russia, Saudi Arabia, South Africa, Syrian Arab Republic, Turkey, Ukraine, UK, USA, Uruguay, Venezuela, and Yugoslavia.
23 The League of Arab States was formed in Cairo on 22 March 1945. The founding member states were Egypt, Syria, Lebanon, Iraq, Transjordan (now Jordan), Saudi Arabia and Yemen.
24 By 1998 the International Atomic Energy Agency (IAEA) was reporting that Iraq's nuclear capability had been eliminated and UNSCOM reported that, despite Iraqi obstruction 'the disarmament phase...is possibly near its end in the missile and chemical weapons area'. Nevertheless, and in full knowledge of the humanitarian crisis in the country, 'this partial compliance was not rewarded with the partial lifting of sanctions'. In fact the criteria for lifting sanctions were never defined (Herring, 2002: 42–43). UNMOVIC's (2003) final report to the Security Council before the war showed the disarmament process nearing its end. See also UN Security Council, 28 February 2003 [S/2003/232].
25 To this day, military analysts such as Stephen Pelletiere attribute the atrocity in Halabja to Iran, while others implicate Iraq with alleged US complicity or indifference. The arguments hinge on the exact nature of the chemicals used. See Hiltermann at www.iht.com; Nezan at http://mondediplo.com; and al-Obaidi at www.ajazeera.net. The International Committee of the Red Cross denounced the disregard for human life by both sides in Fallujah. www.icrc.org, 19 November 2004. See also BBC News, Voices from Falluja, 11 November 2004, at http://newsvote.bbc.co.uk.
26 President Ghazi al-Yawar in a BBC interview, 13 December 2004.
27 For the first time in Iraq's history there was no representative of the military in the cabinet (of the ICG) This policy was attributed by both returning exiled officers and those who remained in country to the US administration's exclusive reliance on the advice of the exile group associated with Chalabi, who had their own reasons for excluding the military. ICG, 2003a.
28 Al-Ali in this volume shows how the prevailing insecurity has particularly restricted the already limited participation of women.
29 Amnesty International (2003) contends on human rights grounds that 'mere past membership in the Ba'ath party should not in itself constitute grounds to deny a person the possibility to hold employment in the top three layers of management of government ministries'.
30 For example, Allawi's INA party is said to have been responsible for passing on a report that Saddam could launch weapons of mass destruction within 45 minutes. See http://english.aljazeera.net, 29 May 2004; and www.disinfopedia.org, quoting Charles Cockburn in the *Independent*, 29 May 2004.
31 When Chalabi's agenda diverged from that of his backers they had to withdraw support, substituting another exile, Allawi, rather than building relations across the political spectrum within the country (Stansfield, 2003: 70; Pollack, 2004: 18–19).
32 Pei and Kaspar (2003: 3–4) list seven other cases of attempts at nation building by the USA involving 'interim surrogate regimes' and note a 'record of complete failure'.
33 For further analysis see Graham Brown (1999) and the proceedings of the ESCWA Workshop (2003).
34 As the ICG (2004: 18) confirms, unemployment and violence (both political and criminal) go hand in hand. Unemployment is the main problem and the main source of resentment and creates a vicious circle: lack of security leads to lack of reconstruction, which leads to lack of jobs, which leads back to lack of security.
35 The flood of dollars into Iraq has a detrimental effect on the dollar:dinar exchange rate, which swung from 4000 dinars to 1500 dinars to the dollar because of the continuing closure of the Central Bank and the lack of dinar liquidity compared with the pre-war period. For most people this meant a 200% inflation rate (Haddad, 2003: 45).
36 The ESCWA workshop (2003: 4–5) concluded that 'reconstruction activities should be linked to the widest possible use of Iraqi industries and services...depackaging of large contracts should be considered to...maximise the local contribution'. Further 'execution or direct supervision should be entrusted to the relevant Government entities...technical ministries or public enterprises...the regulatory role of the State and policy-making institutions should be enhanced.'
37 A regional approach was advocated by the ESCWA (2003: 5) workshop: 'A regional integration plan should guide the reconstruction of the Iraqi economy, taking into account the interests of neighbouring countries'.

References

Abd al-Jabbar, F (1992) Why the uprisings failed, *Middle East Report*, 176, pp 2–14.

Abdel-Fadil, M (2003) Issues of economic reconstruction of Iraq, in: ESCWA, *Report on the Workshop on Iraq and the Region after the War, Beirut 9–11 July 2003*, pp 25–37 (New York: United Nations).

Amnesty International (2003) *Iraq Memorandum on Concerns related to Legislation introduced by the Coalition Provisional Authority* (London: Amnesty International).

Amnesty International (2004) *Iraq. One Year on the Human Rights Situation Remains Dire* (London: Amnesty International).

Barakat, SB (1992) The rebuilding of Fao City, Iraq: a case of central government post-war reconstruction, in: Y Aysan & I Davies (eds), *Disasters and the Small Dwelling: Perspectives for the UN IDNDR*, pp 194–206 (London: James and James).

Barakat, SB (1993) *Post-War Reconstruction in Iraq: The Case Study of Basrah and Fao*, Institute of Advanced Architectural Studies, Post-war Reconstruction and Development Unit, University of York.

Barakat, S. B. (2003) Setting the scene for Afghanistan's reconstruction, in: Barakat, *Rebuilding Afghanistan: Between Principles and Practice* (Basingstoke: Palgrave).

Barakat, S & Hoffman, B (1995) Post-conflict reconstruction: key concepts, principle components and capabilities in post-conflict reconstruction strategies, paper presented to the International Colloquium organised by the United Nations Industrial Development Organisation (UNIDO) and the UN Department for Development Support and Management Services (DDSMS), Stadtschlaining, 23–24 June.

Barton, F & Crocker, B (2004) *Progress or Peril? Measuring Iraq's Reconstruction. September 2004. The Post-Conflict Reconstruction Project* (Washington, DC: CSIS).

Boutros-Ghali, B (1995) *An Agenda for Peace* (New York: United Nations).

Brahimi, L (2004a) *The Political Transition in Iraq: Report of the Fact-Finding Mission*, Report annexed to S/2004/140 Letter from the UN Secretary General to the Security Council, 23 February 2004.

Brahimi, L (2004b) *Statement of the Special Advisor to the Secretary-General, Lakdhar Brahimi, to the Security Council on the Political Transition Process in Iraq*, UN briefing, 27 April 2004.

Brahimi, L (2004c) *Briefing of Special Advisor to UN Secretary-General, Lakdhar Brahimi, to the Security Council on the Political Transition Process in Iraq*, UN briefing, 6 July 2004.

Clawson, P (1993) Iraq's economy and international sanctions, in: A Baram & B Rubin (eds), *Iraq's Road to War* (New York: St Martins Press).

Collier, P, Elliot, V, Hegre, H, Hoeffler, A, Reynal-Querol, M & Sambanis, N (2003) *Breaking the Conflict Trap: Civil War and Development Policy* (Washington, DC/Oxford: World Bank/Oxford University Press).

Corm, G (2003) Identifying the main economic and reconstruction issues in Iraq, in: ESCWA, *Report on the Workshop on Iraq and the Region after the War, Beirut 9–11 July 2003*, pp 13–21 (New York: United Nations).

Cortright, D, Lopez, GA & Millar, A (2002) Winning the war: sensible security options for dealing with Iraq, *Policy Brief* (Indiana: Fourth Freedom Forum/Kroc Institute).

Cortright, D & Lopez, GA (2004) *Containing Iraq: Sanctions Worked*, available at www.nd.edu/~krocinst/.

Diefendorf (1996) West Germany after World War 2. Planning and the role of Preservation Thinking, in: S Barakat, J Calame & E Charlesworth (eds), *Urban Triumph or Urban Disaster: Dilemmas of Contemporary Post-war Reconstruction*, Post-war Reconstruction and Development Unit, University of York.

Dobbins, J, McGinn, JG, Crane, K, Jones, SG, Rolie, L, Rathmell, A, Swanger, R & Timilsina, A (2003) *America's Role in Nation-Building: From Germany to Iraq* (Santa Monica, CA: Rand Publications).

Dodge, T (2003) *Inventing Iraq: The Failure of Nation-Building and a History Denied* (New York: Columbia University Press).

Economic and Social Commission for Western Asia (ESCWA) (2003) *Conclusions and Recommendations. Workshop on Iraq and the Region after the War: Issues of Economic and Social Reconstruction, Beirut, 9–11 July 2003* (New York: United Nations).

Gafar, JD (2003) Rebuilding Iraq: samples of Iraqi reconstruction efforts during the period 1991–2002, in: ESCWA, *Report on the Workshop on Iraq and the Region after the War, Beirut 9–11 July 2003*, pp 33–37 (New York: United Nations).

Graham-Brown, S (1999) *Sanctioning Saddam: The Politics of Intervention in Iraq* (London: IB Tauris).

Haddad, A (2003) Social and humanitarian conditions in Iraq: challenges and priorities, in: ESCWA, *Report on the Workshop on Iraq and the Region after the War, Beirut 9–11 July 2003*, pp 41–47 (New York: United Nations).

Haughton, J (1998) *The Reconstruction of War-Torn Economies* (Harvard, MA: Harvard Institute for International Development).

Herring, E (2002) Between Iraq and a Hard Place: A Critique of the British Government's Case for UN Sanctions, *Review of International Studies*, 28, pp 39–56.

Hill, R (1996) Post War Reconstruction in the Post Cold War Era – Observations of a Practitioner, in: S Barakat, J Calame & E Charlesworth (eds), *Urban Triumph or Urban Disaster: Dilemmas of Contemporary Post-war Reconstruction*, Post-war Reconstruction and Development Unit, University of York.

ICG (2002a) *Iraq Backgrounder: What Lies Beneath, Middle East Report*, 6.

ICG (2002b) *Voices from the Iraqi Street, Iraq Briefing, 4 December 2002.*

ICG (2003a) *Governing Iraq, Middle East Report*, 17.

ICG (2003b) *Iraq: Building a New Security Structure, Middle East Report*, 20.

ICG (2004) *Reconstructing Iraq, Middle East Report*, 30.

ICRC (1999) *Failed States and International Law* (Geneva: ICRC).

Jones (2005) Post-war poverty reduction, in: S Barakat (ed), *After the Conflict: Reconstruction and Development in the Aftermath of War* (London: IB Tauris).

Kagan, F (2003) War and aftermath, *Policy Review*, X, pp 3–27.

Kubrusi, A (2003) Strategies for development under crisis conditions, in: ESCWA, *Report on the Workshop on Iraq and the Region after the War, Beirut 9–11 July 2003*, pp 22–25 (New York: United Nations).

Kubrusi, A & Kadri, A (2003) The economic consequences of the war on Iraq on the ESCWA region, in: ESCWA, *Report on the Workshop on Iraq and the Region after the War, Beirut 9–11 July 2003*, pp 48–51 (New York: United Nations).

Kumar, K (1997) The nature and focus of international assistance for rebuilding war-torn societies, in: Kumar (ed), *Rebuilding Societies after Civil War—Critical Roles for International Assistance* (London: Lynne Rienner).

Logan, W (1996) Hanoi After the Bombs: Post War Reconstruction of a Vietnamese City Under Reconstruction, in: S Barakat, J Calame & E Charlesworth (eds), *Urban Triumph or Urban Disaster: Dilemmas of Contemporary Post-war Reconstruction*, Post-war Reconstruction and Development Unit, University of York.

Niblock, T (2001) *'Pariah States' and Sanctions in the Middle East: Iraq, Libya, Sudan* (London: Lynne Rienner).

Pei, M & Kaspar, S (2003) *Lessons from the Past: The American Record on Nation Building* (Washington, DC: Carnegie Endowment for International Peace).

Pelletiere, SC (1992) *The Iran–Iraq War: Chaos in a Vacuum* (New York: Praeger).

Pollack, KM (2004) After Saddam: assessing the reconstruction of Iraq, *Analysis Paper 1* (Washington, DC: Saban Center for Middle East Policy, Brookings Institution).

Stansfield, RV (2003) Politics and governance in the new Iraq: reconstruction of the new versus resurrection of the old, *Whitehall Papers*, 59, pp 67–89.UNDG/World Bank (2003) *United Nations/World Bank Joint Iraq Needs Assessment* (New York/Washington: United Nations/World Bank).

UNDP (2005) *National Human Development Report: Security with a Face, Challenges and Responsibilities* (Washington: United Nations).

UNMOVIC (2003) *Twelfth quarterly report of the Executive Chairman of the United Nations Monitoring, Verification and Inspection Commission in accordance with paragraph 12 of Security Council resolution 1284 (1999)* (New York: United Nations).

World Bank (1998) *Conflict Prevention and Post-Conflict Reconstruction: Perspectives and Prospects* (Washington, DC: World Bank).

World Bank (2004) *Interim Strategy Note of the World Bank Group for Iraq* (Washington: World Bank Middle East Department).

Iraq: fulcrum of world politics

ALEX CALLINICOS

ABSTRACT *The Anglo-American invasion and occupation of Iraq must be understood in the context of the grand strategy consistently pursued by the US since at least the beginning of the 20th century. The Bush administration, breaking from Washington's reliance since the Second World War on coalition building, is seeking to use one of the main comparative advantages of the US—its military supremacy—to perpetuate a favourable global balance of forces. The seizure of Iraq seemed to favour this strategy, particularly since it would enhance US capacity to deny access to Middle Eastern oil to actual or potential rivals such as the European Union and China. But popular resistance to the occupation of Iraq is now testing this policy, perhaps to destruction.*

'Unhappy the land that needs a hero' says Brecht's Galileo.[1] Unhappier still the land that becomes the focus of major geopolitical forces, as the plight of Iraq today makes evident. To understand how the Anglo-American invasion and occupation of Iraq have come to dominate world politics it is, of course, necessary to address a much larger context. In this article I focus on a crucial part of that context, the grand strategy pursued by the US, primarily, though not exclusively under the administration of George W Bush.

The exhaustive debates in the US and Britain on the intelligence used to justify the invasion and conquest of Iraq in March–April 2003 have established beyond any doubt that the official pretext for the war—the continued possession by the Iraqi Ba'athist regime of weapons of mass destruction (WMD)—had no basis in fact. More importantly, it is clear that this publicly stated reason was not the real motive that guided either the Bush administration or its chief ally, the British government under Tony Blair. After the conquest of Iraq, Paul Wolfowitz, then the US Deputy Defense Secretary and the leading neoconservative ideologue in the administration, explained: 'for reasons that have a lot to do with the US government bureaucracy we settled on the one issue that everyone could agree on which was weapons of mass destruction as the core reason'.[2] An even clearer insight into the mindset that bound together Washington and Whitehall after 9/11 is provided by a leaked memorandum to Blair from his Foreign Policy Adviser, Sir David Manning, following a meeting with his American counterpart, National Security Adviser Condoleezza Rice, in March 2002:

> I said that you would not budge in your support for regime change but you had to manage a press, a Parliament and a public opinion that was very different than anything in the States. And you would not budge on your insistence that, if we pursued regime change, it must be very carefully done and produce the right result. Failure was not an option. Condi's enthusiasm for regime change was undimmed. But there were some signs, since we last spoke, of greater awareness of the practical difficulties and political risks.[3]

The British insistence that 'failure was not an option' reads rather hollow in the light of the increasingly bloody counterinsurgency war that has developed since the fall of Baghdad. But, retrospect aside, these and other official documents that were either leaked or published as a result of various investigations on both sides of the Atlantic make clear that regime change in Iraq was the prime objective and that Saddam Hussein's fabled WMD served to help 'manage' public opinion, particularly in Britain but also in the US itself, and in other countries that might be recruited to President Bush's 'coalition of the willing'.

Clearly ideology is an important ingredient in explaining why the overthrow of Saddam Hussein became such a priority for the Bush administration. The influence within it of the neoconservative wing of the Republican Party, which has developed since the early 1990s a quasi-Messianic programme of imposing 'democratic revolution' on the Middle East by armed force, is notorious and well documented.[4] A variant of the same outlook, based on a belief in the right of the 'international community' to override national sovereignty in order to punish evildoers, has come increasingly to motivate Blair's foreign policy.[5]

But simply to see the war in Iraq as the realisation of such world-views would be misleading. For one thing, even as right-wing an administration as the younger Bush's is not ideologically homogeneous: there have been many disagreements and tensions between the neocons led by Wolfowitz and more old fashioned conservative nationalists such as Vice President Dick Cheney and Defense Secretary Donald Rumsfeld. For another, pure ideology of course cannot explain why it was Saddam's Iraq that was selected for regime change rather than any of the many other obnoxious regimes under which so much of humankind still groans. This points to the fact that, if realists are mistaken in denying any role to ideological representations in motivating the action of states, they are right to emphasise the significance of economic and geopolitical interests.

American grand strategy

The fundamental truth is that Iraq has become the anvil on which a gigantic test of power has been undertaken. At stake in that test has been the future course taken by the US, widely seen, since the end of the Cold War, as a state exercising unprecedented global power. To understand what is at stake requires a closer consideration of US global strategy. Its essence was cogently summed up by George Kennan, the premier theorist of US foreign policy, midway through the 20th century:

> We can see that our security has been dependent throughout our history on the position of Britain; that Canada, in particular, has been a useful and indispensable hostage to good relations between our country and the British Empire; and that Britain's position, in turn, has depended on the maintenance of a balance of power on the European Continent. Thus it was essential to us, as it was to Britain, that no single Continental land power should come to dominate the entire Eurasian landmass. Our interest has lain rather in the maintenance of some sort of stable balance between the powers of the interior, in order that none of them should effect the subjugation of the others, conquer the seafaring fringe of the land mass, become a great sea power as well as a land power, shatter the position of England, and enter—as in the circumstances it would—on an overseas expansion hostile to ourselves and supported by the immense resources of the interior of Europe and Asia.[6]

In the 19th century British power—above all in the shape of the barrier the Royal Navy constituted to intervention by other European states in the Americas—provided the shelter behind which the US could expand across North America, come to dominate the western hemisphere, and develop the largest economy in the world. In the first half of the 20th century the very success of the US undermined Britain's ability to balance against the rising continental power of Germany. The Second World War marked the point at which the US stepped in decisively to assume Britain's role in preventing a hostile power or coalition of powers from coming to dominate Eurasia—an objective eloquently stated by Kennan at the beginning of the Cold War and reaffirmed by leading American strategic thinkers after its end.[7] John Lewis Gaddis argues that this shift, carried out with enormous skill by Franklin Roosevelt, represented a break with American tradition in foreign policy, defined above all by John Quincy Adams at the beginning of the 19th century in order to establish US hegemony in North America:

> the United States was able to move in a remarkably short space of time from a strategy that had limited itself to controlling the Western hemisphere to one aimed at winning a global war and managing the peace that would follow. Equally significant is the fact that Roosevelt pulled off this expanded hegemony by scrapping rather than embracing the two other key components of Adam's strategy, unilateralism and pre-emption.[8]

Under Roosevelt the US embraced rather than avoided the entangling alliances with other powers against which George Washington had warned and allowed Japan and Germany to take the initiative in drawing it into war. This strategy of securing US global hegemony through coalition building continued during the Cold War. The nexus of alliances centred on NATO gave the US a permanent military presence in Western Europe and East Asia and united the advanced capitalist world under American leadership. This bloc was, of course, also constituted economically through the international financial institutions (IFIs) created at Bretton Woods. Andrew Bacevich argues that since the beginning of the 20th century the USA has, under successive administrations, pursued a 'strategy of openness'. Its aim

> is to preserve and, where both feasible and conducive to US interests, to expand an American imperium. Central to this strategy is a commitment to global openness—removing barriers that inhibit the movement of goods, capital, ideas, and people. Its ultimate objective is the creation of an integrated international order based on the principles of democratic capitalism, with the United States as the ultimate guarantor of order and enforcer of norms.[9]

The ideal of a global order in which free markets and democratic institutions promoted peace and prosperity was eloquently articulated by Woodrow Wilson during the First World War, and by Cordell Hull, US Secretary of State for most of the Second World War.[10] The realisation of this ideal after 1945 was partially frustrated by the partition of the world into two superpower blocs during the Cold War, but the Bretton Woods institutions—the International Monetary Fund, the World Bank and the General Agreement on Tariffs and Trade—nevertheless served economically to integrate the advanced capitalist states. A transnational space—' the West'—was thus created in which economic and geopolitical competition were at least partially dissociated. In other words, the global struggle for markets and resources among firms did not, as it had tended to during the first half of the 20th century, fuel military and territorial rivalries between states.

The disintegration of the Soviet bloc and indeed of the USSR itself in 1989–91 offered the US the opportunity to make this space genuinely global. The Clinton administration seized the chance. On the one hand, the expansion of NATO and the European Union into Eastern and Central Europe was conceived by American strategists as a means of maintaining and extending US primacy in Eurasia.[11] On the other hand, the IFIs, strengthened by the creation in 1994 of the World Trade Organization, promoted a package of neoliberal economic policies—the so-called Washington Consensus—that, while generally favourable to the interests of transnational corporations of whatever national origins, tended to promote the Anglo-American free-market version of capitalism.[12]

Yet since the late 1990s this strategy of creating a US-led liberal capitalist global order has come to be increasingly contested. In part this is because, from the East Asian crisis of 1997–98 onwards, a growing number of voices have asserted, with increasing stridency, that neoliberal policies are economically dysfunctional and socially divisive; the result has been the emergence of the world-wide movement seeking another globalisation. At the same time the role of the US as a global hegemon constituting and maintaining a liberal capitalist world has been increasingly questioned. It is important to see that US primacy was already an issue under Clinton. By 1999 the veteran American security intellectual Samuel Huntington was warning that the US was widely perceived as 'the rogue superpower'.[13]

More than anything else this perception was promoted by the increased willingness of Washington unilaterally to take advantage of its military supremacy, most notably in the case of the 1999 war in Kosovo (mounted by NATO without the authorisation of the UN Security Council) and the bombing campaign against Iraq, maintained throughout the 1990s against the growing opposition of most other member states of the international coalition constructed to recapture Iraq in 1990–91 (with, of course, the signal exception of Britain). This unilateralist drift was partly a consequence of the sheer disparity between the military capabilities of the USA and those of all the other Great Powers either singly or combined. But the trend was also self-reinforcing: frustration with the conduct of 'war by committee' by NATO in 1999 led US Central Command to reject the offer of French troops for the war in Afghanistan after 11 September 2001. According to James Mann:

> French Ambassador to Washington François Bujon de L'Estang called this the Kosovo syndrome. During the 1990s American military leaders had been exasperated by the process of seeking consensus within NATO for military action in the Balkans...This particular strand of American unilateralism, then, did not originate with the Bush administration. It grew directly out of the military realities of the 1990s: the operational difficulties between the US and allied forces in the Balkans and the overall disparity in military power between America and Europe.[14]

Nevertheless, the global strategy adopted by the administration of the younger Bush in response to 9/11 marked a dramatic radicalisation of US unilateralism, particularly in the shape of the Bush Doctrine affirming Washington's right unilaterally to mount preventive wars to eliminate potential terrorist threats.[15] Gaddis argues that this represented in many respects a return to US grand strategy of the 19th century, when American leaders claimed the right to launch pre-emptive attacks as part of the process of continental expansion. But he concedes: 'It was one thing for a continental hegemon to threaten pre-emption within its own environs, as John Quincy Adams, Theodore Roosevelt, and Woodrow Wilson had all done. It was quite another thing for a global hegemon to threaten it wherever necessary, as George W Bush appeared to be doing.'[16]

The other side to this assertion of a right to wage preventive wars was the pronounced shift in the administration's attitude towards coalition building. Central to US global strategy since 1941, this policy wasn't actually abandoned—Washington constructed an *ad hoc* coalition to invade and occupy Iraq that included some major powers like Britain, Spain, Italy, Japan and South Korea. But the administration's response to France's and Germany's opposition to the war in Iraq—counterposing, as Rumsfeld famously did, 'Old' to 'New' Europe—seemed to represent a deeper shift in attitude towards the EU. European integration, promoted by the US since the 1940s, was now perceived as a threat to US hegemony, and the EU was accordingly to be controlled through a policy of divide-and-rule.

Why Iraq?

The Iraq war was, of course, the first test of this strategy. It is clear from a succession of books based on insider knowledge that, from the president downwards, Bush's team came very quickly after 9/11 to focus on attacking

Iraq, despite the absence of any serious evidence linking al-Qaeda to Saddam Hussein.[17] As numerous commentators have pointed out, seizing Iraq would have the obvious advantage of allowing the US to entrench its strategic dominance of Western Asia and its vast energy reserves. The 2001 war in Afghanistan introduced what looks set to be a permanent American military presence in Central Asia, another region rich in oil and natural gas. Wolfowitz has emphasised that occupying Iraq would permit the US to withdraw its troops from Saudi Arabia: an American presence in Iraq would be less provocative than one in the land where the greatest holy places of Islam are situated.[18]

It is important, however, not to interpret the role that oil played in motivating the conquest of Iraq too narrowly. Leading figures in the Bush administration have shown an even greater preoccupation with the potential threat to US hegemony by possible 'peer competitors'. This dates back to the administration of the current president's father, George HW Bush, in the early 1990s. In March 1992 a draft Pentagon *Defense Planning Guidance* document was leaked to the *New York Times*:

> Our first objective is to prevent the re-emergence of a new rival. This is a dominant consideration underlying the new regional defence strategy and requires that we endeavour to prevent any hostile power from dominating a region whose resources would, under consolidated control, be sufficient to generate global power ... we must maintain the mechanisms for deterring competitors from even aspiring to a larger regional or global role. [19]

Dick Cheney, now Vice-President under George W. Bush, was then Secretary of Defense. The document was drafted by Zalmay Khalilzad, now US Ambassador to Afghanistan, then an aide to Wolfowitz, Under Secretary of Defence for Policy under Bush *père*, and to Lewis Libby, his principal deputy – and now Cheney's Chief of Staff. [20] Though the document was repudiated by the administration, its outlook informed the global thinking of the neoconservatives whose influence in the Republican Party grew during the 1990s. The Project for the New American Century, launched in 1997 by William Kristol, editor of *The Weekly Standard*, provided the neoconservatives with their rallying point. Surprisingly enough given America's unparalleled military lead over all other states, their main preoccupation was US weakness. Thus Wolfowitz argued that rapid economic growth was making China a power with a potential comparable to that of Germany at the end of the 19th century for destabilizing the international system. [21] In the face of these potential threats, US military strength needed to be built up even further and asserted where necessary, in the first instance through securing regime change in Iraq.

The same thinking dominates *The National Security Strategy of the United States of America*, issued by the Bush administration in September 2002, which warns: 'Our forces will be strong enough to dissuade potential adversaries from pursuing a military build-up in the hopes of surpassing, or equalling, the power of the United States'.[22] This remarkable document was drafted by Condoleezza Rice's staff at the National Security Council. Rice emphasised that the attacks on New York and Washington offered the Bush administration the opportunity to do what it wanted to do anyway:

> an earthquake of the magnitude of 9/11 can shift the tectonic plates of international politics. The international system has been in flux since the collapse of Soviet power. Now it is possible—indeed, probable—that that transition is coming to and end.
>
> If that is right, if the collapse of the Soviet Union and 9/11 bookend a major shift in international politics, then this is a period not just of grave danger, but of enormous opportunity. Before the clay is dry again, America and our friends and allies must move to take advantage of these new opportunities. This is, then, a period akin to 1945 to 1947, when American leadership expanded the number of free and democratic states—Japan and Germany among the great powers—to create a balance of power that favoured freedom.[23]

For the Bush administration, then, 9/11 represented not simply a catastrophe, but the chance to remake the world on a scale comparable to the Truman administration's construction of a liberal capitalist bloc after the Second World War (an achievement that Dean Acheson, Truman's Secretary of State, with typical modesty, compared to the creation of the world[24]). From this perspective, the principal significance of the Middle East lay in the interrelation between oil and geopolitics. In May 2001 a team headed by Vice President Dick Cheney reported on US future energy needs. It estimated that by 2020 the US would be dependent on imports for two-thirds of its oil needs. This would tie America even more closely to unstable and potentially hostile regions—the Middle East, Latin America, Central Asia, Russia and West Africa. The Cheney report emphasised the importance of the US diversifying the sources of its energy supplies. But it also underlined the central role of the Middle East, home to about two-thirds of global oil reserves. Middle Eastern oil is even more important for other countries, notably the EU, Japan, China and India.[25]

Occupying Iraq would give the US control over the country with the second largest oil reserves in the world. It would also be in a stronger position to put pressure on Saudi Arabia, which has the largest reserves. Relations between the US and Saudi Arabia have been getting worse, especially since 9/11 (15 out of the 19 suicide hijackers were Saudi subjects). The conquest of Iraq would not only make the US less dependent on Saudi Arabia, but its military power in the Middle East—plus that in Israel, whose alignment with the US grew even closer under George W Bush than it had been under previous administrations—would give it a potential chokehold on the oil supply to the other leading powers in the world. As David Harvey puts it:

> Europe and Japan, as well as East and South-East Asia (now crucially including China) are heavily dependent on Gulf oil, and these are regional configurations of political–economic power that now pose a challenge to US global hegemony in the worlds of production and finance. What better way for the United States to ward off that competition and secure its own hegemonic position than to control the prices, conditions, and distribution of the key economic resource upon which those competitors rely? And what better way to

> do that than to use the one line of force where the US still remain all-powerful—military might? [26]

Conquering Iraq also had the function of demonstrating the scale of that might and the cost of defying it. 'Shock and awe'—the expression widely used to refer to the purely military effects of the rapid and dramatic use of the Pentagon's hi-tech weapons systems—also embraced the much broader political impact of the spectacle of American military supremacy during the short campaign of March–April 2003. Gaddis suggests that these consequences were intended primarily within the Middle East: 'If future terrorist acts were to carry with them the certainty of devastating reprisal, then that should generate resistance to those acts within the societies that spawned them—possibly even before they had been committed.' But he concedes that 'the resulting shock and awe extended beyond its Middle Eastern targets', helping to produce a dramatic change in international perceptions of American power: 'within little more than a year, the United States exchanged its long-established reputation as the principal *stabilizer* of the international system for one as its chief *destabilizer*.'[27]

Gaddis presents this shift in attitudes as an unintended consequence of the Bush administration's strategy. But it is not obvious that this is right. A number of commentators have argued that the US must now be seen as a 'revolutionary power'.[28] In his brilliant early study of the statecraft of Metternich and Castlereagh, Henry Kissinger offered a classic definition of a revolutionary power as

> a power which considers the international order or the manner of legitimizing it oppressive. . .The distinguishing feature of a revolutionary power is not that it feels threatened—such feeling is inherent in the nature of international relations based on sovereign states—*but that nothing can reassure it.* Only absolute security—the neutralization of the opponent—is considered a sufficient guarantee, and thus the desire of one power for absolute security means absolute insecurity for all the others.[29]

At one level it seems ridiculous to think of the US as 'oppressed' by an international system that it has reconstructed to fit its interests and in which it is the dominant power. But at the same time the idea that 'the desire of one power for absolute security means absolute insecurity for all the others' does resonate with the way in which the US has behaved since 11 September. The Bush team is motivated by a strange mixture of triumphalism and insecurity. Insecurity is present, of course, in the fear of further terrorist attacks: 9/11 reactivated historic memories of other surprise attacks—the British destruction of the Capitol and White House in 1814 and, of course, Pearl Harbor in December 1941.[30] Insecurity is also reflected in the perception of longer term threats to American hegemony—for example, the rise of new powers such as China that preoccupies Wolfowitz. Triumphalism is perhaps most evident in their faith in American military power and in the superiority of the US model of liberal capitalism, proclaimed by Bush as the 'single sustainable model of national success'.[31] This in turn is reflected in the administration's programme of 'democratic revolution' aimed at imposing this model by force on the Middle East.

This policy—what Bush calls 'our forward strategy of freedom for the Middle East'—is the most obvious respect in which the US is acting as a revolutionary power challenging the status quo in the international system. It is, moreover, presented as an explicit break with past US policy in the region, which has, of course, involved actively supporting highly repressive regimes such as those in Egypt and Saudi Arabia—what Bush describes as 'a bargain, to tolerate oppression for the sake of stability'.[32] Bush forcefully restated the policy in his second Inaugural Address in January 2005: 'The survival of liberty in our land increasingly depends on the success of liberty in other lands...So it is the policy of the United States to seek and support the growth of democratic institutions and movements in every nation and culture, with the ultimate goal of ending tyranny in our world.' [33] Underlying this policy shift is the Wilsonian belief that self-interest and principle dovetail in the promotion of democracy since, as Walter Russell Mead puts it, 'democracies make better and more reliable partners than tyrannies'.[34] Hence the formula, coined by Rice and taken up by Bush, of 'a balance of power that favours freedom'—or as Mann puts it, 'a slogan that represented another effort to combine the realism ("balance of power") that Rice had learned from mentors like [Brent] Scrowcroft [National Security Adviser under George HW Bush] and the ideals ("human freedom") of the neoconservatives'.[35]

Bush has elaborated on this idea in a number of occasions:

> In democratic and successful societies, men and women do not swear allegiance to malcontents and murderers; they turn their hearts and labor to building better lives. And democratic governments do not shelter terrorist camps or attack their peaceful neighbors; they honor the aspirations and dignity of their own people...by advancing freedom in the greater Middle East, we help end a cycle of dictatorship and radicalism that brings millions of people to misery and brings danger to our own people. The stakes in that region could not be higher. If the Middle East remains a place where freedom does not flourish, it will remain a place of stagnation and anger and violence for export. And as we saw in the ruins of two towers, no distance on the map will protect our lives and way of life. If the greater Middle East joins the democratic revolution that has reached much of the world, the lives of millions in that region will be bettered, and a trend of conflict and fear will be ended at its source. [36]

Here, of course, was the final respect in which Iraq came to be the focus of the Bush administration's global policy. Its seizure would not only provide the USA with a more secure base from which to dominate the Middle East. The incorporation of Iraq into 'the democratic revolution' would help to transform the region along liberal capitalist lines. Hence the demands by neoconservatives after the fall of Baghdad that the USA move against Iran or Syria next. Hence also their frequent affirmation that 'the road to Jerusalem runs through Baghdad'—in other words, that the progressive removal of Arab nationalist regimes hostile to Israel and their replacement by pro-

Western 'democrats' would make possible a Middle East settlement acceptable to the Republican right's Likud allies.[37]

The testing ground

History is ruled by unintended consequences—by outcomes unforeseen by and contradicting the aims of those whose actions produced them. Rarely has there been a more dramatic instance of this than the aftermath of the Anglo-American conquest of Iraq. By the first anniversary of the fall of Baghdad it had become clear that the occupiers were confronted with a classic counterinsurgency war spreading across the country. Neither the promise of eventual elections nor the hasty replacement of direct US rule with an 'interim government' headed by a man previously best known as an intelligence agent, first for Saddam's Mukhabarat and later for the CIA and the British Secret Intelligence Service (SIS), prevented the security situation from steadily deteriorating to the point that, following the unsuccessful American siege of Falluja in April 2004, the *Washington Post* could report:

> Army Maj Gen Charles H Swannack Jr, the commander of the 82nd Airborne Division, who spent much of the year in western Iraq, said he believes that at the tactical level at which fighting occurs, the US military is still winning. But when asked whether he believes the United States is losing, he said, 'I think strategically, we are'.[38]

At the beginning of the following year, after Falluja had finally fallen to American arms, the outgoing Secretary of State, Colin Powell, offered an equally bleak judgement:

> According to Chas Freedman, former US ambassador to Saudi Arabia and head of the independent Middle East Policy Council, Mr Bush recently asked Mr Powell for his view on the progress of the war. 'We're losing,' Mr Powell was quoted as saying. Mr Freeman said Mr Bush then asked the secretary of state to leave.[39]

Discussion of how the occupation came to such a pass has focused on a series of policy mistakes committed during its early days—for example, the hasty decision to disband the Iraqi army.[40] But the causes lie deeper than such errors of judgement, important though they were. Many have pointed to the flagrant contradiction between the high-tech military capabilities that allowed a relatively small Anglo-American force rapidly to seize control of Iraq and the Pentagon's lack of the training or manpower needed to sustain an occupation—a contradiction that, according to some commentators, is a symptom of the USA's inability to function as an imperial state that doesn't simply project power but is able to maintain long-term control over conquered territories.[41] None of this can be separated from what Gilbert Achcar calls the 'crackpot idealism' that encouraged the administration to believe its own propaganda, and the 'intelligence' supplied by Iraqi exiles close to the neoconservatives—figures such as Kanan Makiya, who told Bush in January 2003 that American troops invading Iraq would be 'greeted with sweets and flowers'.[42]

But underlying all these miscalculations and bungles is the simple fact that the overwhelming majority of the Iraqi people oppose the replacement of a brutal authoritarian regime with what evidently remained, after the 'transfer' of sovereignty in June 2004, alien rule. Although the Constituent Assembly elections in January 2005 were widely seen as a success for the occupation, they had been extracted from the Coalition Provisional Authority by mass protests called by the leading Shia cleric Ali al-Sistani. Moreover, the United Iraqi Alliance which, with Sistani's tacit support, won the lion's share of the seats was open in its desire to seek an end to the occupation. As the veteran US diplomat James Dobbins put it, 'Washington has lost the confidence and consent of the Iraqi people, and it is unlikely to win them back'.[43]

Western preoccupation with the religious allegiances of different political forces in Iraq may misdirect any attempt to understand the nature of the resistance to the occupation. No doubt the decline of the radical secular traditions that were so prominent during and after the 1958 Revolution—most importantly Communism, Nasserism and Ba'athism—has increased the political importance of Iraq's diverse religious faiths. No doubt also the removal of Saddam and the highly dysfunctional occupation have given the zealots of al-Qaeda an opportunity to mount operations inside Iraq that they never enjoyed under Ba'athist rule. But the driving force of an increasingly widespread if apparently highly fragmented resistance seems to be much more straightforward—the political rejection of occupation and rule by foreign powers. This cause could mobilise memories of past national struggles—the 1920 rising against incorporation into the British Empire, and the succession of revolts that punctuated the last 10 years of the Hashemite monarchy.[44]

There is an important moral here. A variety of factors—for example greater economic integration, the development of forms of global governance, the crisis of many postcolonial regimes—has encouraged the belief that nationalism itself is in decline as a political force, supplanted either by Western-style consumerism or by more regressive, often religious particularisms. This belief has in turn helped to legimitise the intervention of Western powers into societies whose internal collapse is deemed to reflect their incapacity to construct or maintain modern nation-states.[45] But the case of Iraq suggests that national identity remains a formidable basis for political mobilisation. This should give Washington pause before it contemplates bringing the blessings of its version of democracy to anywhere else in the Middle East. But it should also more widely discourage an attitude towards the peoples of even the most benighted societies of the South that treats them as the recipients of charity from the outside, or as the objects of social engineering by policy makers in Western capitals.

Meanwhile the US is left struggling to manage an increasingly unmanageable situation in Iraq. If the investigative journalist Seymour Hersh is right, Israel rapidly wrote off the prospect of Washington constructing a viable successor regime in Iraq and switched to 'Plan B', deploying forces in the

Kurdish areas of northern Iraq in the expectation that the rulers of an autonomous Kurdistan would provide a useful ally against Iran, even though this might undermine Israel's military alliance with Turkey. According to Hersh:

> Ehud Barak, the former Israeli Prime Minister, who supported the Bush Administration's invasion of Iraq, took it upon himself at this point [November 2003] to privately warn Vice-President Dick Cheney that America had lost in Iraq; according to an American close to Barak, he said that Israel 'had learned that there's no way to win an occupation'. The only issue, Barak told Cheney, 'was choosing the size of your humiliation.' Cheney did not respond to Barak's assessment.[46]

Here, too, older patterns are reasserting themselves, in this case the logic of guerrilla war, where victory or defeat depends less on the conventional military superiority of the occupiers than on the capacity of the insurgents to destroy the enemy's political will to fight. As in the case of the latter stages of the Vietnam War, the US military's politically determined reluctance to take casualties imposes a significant constraint on its capacity to fight insurgents who specialise in hit-and-run attacks and suicide bombings. The US faces a further limitation—in this case to a much greater extent than in previous wars such as Korea and Vietnam—in that the political costs of significant civilian casualties are very high. Among the terms of the agreement that ended the siege of Falluja in April 2004 was expulsion, at the Americans' insistence, of the al-Jazeera news team that had been working in the city and transmitting images of civilian suffering around the world. The revelations of systematic torture and sexual abuse of detainees held without trial by the occupation forces at Abu Ghraib and other prisons in Iraq—themselves outposts of the much larger carceral archipelago created by the Bush administration that stretches to Guantánamo Bay and to Bahram airbase in Afghanistan—have seriously, perhaps fatally undermined the moral authority of the occupation in the eyes of both Iraqis and the rest of the world: Blair has been especially strident in his claim to have waged a war for human rights.

Consequently even neoconservatives such as Robert Kagan acknowledge that the US faces a crisis of legitimacy.[47] This crisis can be interpreted in both broad and narrow terms. Specifically with respect to Iraq, the Bush administration is caught on the horns of an acute dilemma. To withdraw US troops from Iraq would, of course, drastically undermine Washington's plans to remodel the Middle East. Moreover, should an Islamist regime hostile to the US, and probably aligned with Iran, come to power in Iraq, the resulting shift in the regional balance of power in the region could have very dangerous consequences, perhaps, for example, encouraging Israel to launch pre-emptive strikes against Iran. At the same time, the Arab regimes most closely aligned to the USA, notably in Egypt and Saudi Arabia, would find their already shaky positions further weakened. And, more broadly, US authority on a wider scale would be reduced: having unsuccessfully talked loudly and used a big stick in Iraq, Washington would find other states less willing to toe the line on a variety of issues.

The alternative, refusing (as Blair puts it) to cut and run, and keeping US forces in Iraq seems equally unpalatable, given the scale of popular opposition and the growth of the insurgency. In the lead-up to the January 2005 elections, US strategy combined devastating assaults on guerrilla strongholds such as Samara and Falluja and a longer-term effort to built up viable Iraqi military and police forces capable, over time, of taking over the main burden of fighting the insurgents from American soldiers. Neoconservative commentators displayed an increasing willingness to play the Shia card—in other words, to hope that the Shia political establishment would take on the task of governing Iraq and fighting the insurgents, which are most strongly based in the Sunni areas around Baghdad.[48] But the success of the resistance in opening a new front by attacking Iraq's third city, Mosul, and overwhelming the police force there and in the smaller Tigris valleys to its south during the US assault on Falluja in November 2004 underlined the limited success of this strategy: 3200 out of 4000 police officers died or deserted as a result of the insurgent assault on Mosul on 10–11 November, forcing the US to redeploy troops back to the area.[49] In January 2005 the US Army announced plans to maintain its forces in Iraq at the prevailing level of 120 000 for the next two years, a number insufficient to contain an insurgency whose size was estimated that same month by the head of Iraqi intelligence at 200 000, but large enough to continue the serious attrition of American capabilities caused by the occupation of Iraq.[50] Military frustration could lead the US either to lash out itself against, or to encourage Israel to attack, the states—Iran and Syria—that it blamed for supporting the Iraqi resistance, dragging the region down into a further destructive spiral of warfare. It is not clear that a serious attempt to 'multilateralise' the war by giving the UN and NATO bigger roles represents a way out for Washington. France and Germany continue to oppose NATO involvement in Iraq. UN officials, despite their involvement in the formation of the Allawi government, seem to recognise that too close an association with the occupation would further undermine the UN's authority with the Iraqi people and make its personnel once again targets for attack (as, of course, they were on the occasion of the August 2003 bombing of UN headquarters in Baghdad).

This dilemma is, in its essentials, the same that the US faced in Vietnam. That in itself is remarkable given the dramatic changes in the global balance of power in the past generation—above all, the disappearance of the Soviet bloc, whose albeit inconsistent and cautious support for the North Vietnamese regime was one of the constraints on the Pentagon's ability to secure victory by conventional means. A war that was intended to demonstrate what the *National Security Strategy* calls the 'unprecedented—and unequalled—strength and influence' of the US has instead revealed the limits of American power.[51] It does not follow that the US does not command enormous resources, economic, military and cultural. In particular, the central role played by what Peter Gowan calls the Dollar–Wall Street Regime in the global political economy has allowed the Bush administration to finance the rapidly growing US trade and budget deficits by an inflow of capital, in particular from East Asia.[52] But the Iraq debacle has ignited a major debate with the US establishment over the appropriate political framework in which to exercise its resources. Zbigniew Brzezinski, for example, argues strongly for a return to the more multilateral strategy pursued by the Clinton administration and, more particularly, for a recognition that American interests are best pursued by treating the EU not as an enemy to be split, but as an indispensable junior partner in the exercise of hegemony.[53]

Brzezinski makes no bones about the fact that this strategy is a means of maintaining American primacy. But it is this that is precisely in question in the broader crisis of legitimacy currently being experienced by the US. The war in Iraq unleashed an unprecedented global protest movement. Between 3 January and 12 April 2003, 35.5 million people took part in 2978 demonstrations against war in Iraq. Fifty-seven percent of the total (20.3 million demonstrators) participated in protests in the expanded European Union of 25 states: the division between 'Old' and 'New' Europe was far more one that separated governments than it did peoples.[54] This extraordinary assertion of citizenship, like the European and World Social Forums that played a critical role in initiating and organising the protests, conjures up the image of a world beyond the Great Power competition that still frames the calculations of policy makers around the world. The continuing war in Iraq will no doubt carry on testing humankind's ability to create a more democratic way of shaping its future.

Notes

1 B Brecht, *Life of Galileo*, in *Collected Plays*, Vol 5, New York: Vintage, 1972, p 85.
2 'Deputy Secretary Wolfowitz Interview with Sam Tannenhaus, *Vanity Fair*', US Department of Defense News Transcript, 29 May 2003, at www.dod.mil.
3 'Iraq: the secret papers', *Daily Telegraph*, 18 September 2004.
4 J Mann, *Rise of the Vulcans*, New York: Viking, 2004, offers a detailed and, on the whole convincing, study of the leading figures in Bush's security team.
5 T Blair, 'Doctrine of the international community', speech at the Economic Club, Chicago, 24 April 1999, at www.number-10.gov.uk. See the detailed account in J Kampfner, *Blair's Wars*, London: Free Press, 2004.
6 GF Kennan, *American Diplomacy 1900–1950*, Chicago: University of Chicago Press, 1951, p 5.
7 For example, H Kissinger, *Diplomacy*, New York: Simon & Schuster, 1994, p 813; and Z Brzezinski, *The Grand Chessboard*, New York: Basic Books, 1997, *passim*.
8 JL Gaddis, *Surprise, Security, and the American Experience*, Cambridge, MA: Harvard University Press, 2004, p 48. This brilliant brief essay is the single best piece on the change in US grand strategy under the younger Bush. See also SF Bemis, *John Quincy Adams and the Foundations of American Foreign Policy*, New York: Alfred A Knopf, 1949; Robert Dallek, *Franklin D Roosevelt and American Foreign Policy, 1932–1945*, New York: Oxford University Press, 1995; and WR Mead, *Special Providence*, New York: Knopf, 2001.
9 AJ Bacevich, *American Empire*, Cambridge, MA: Harvard University Press, 2002, p 3.
10 See, for example, GJ Ikenberry, 'America's liberal grand strategy', in Ikenberry (ed), *American Foreign Policy*, New York: Longman, 2002, pp 274–296; and G Kolko, *The Politics of War*, New York: Vintage, 1970.
11 Brzezinski, *The Grand Chessboard*.
12 P Gowan, *The Global Gamble*, London: Verso, 1999.
13 SP Huntington, 'The lonely superpower', *Foreign Affairs*, 78 (2), 1999, online edition, at www.foreignpolicy2000.
14 Mann, *Rise of the Vulcans*, pp 304–305.

15 See especially *The National Security Strategy of the United States of America*, September 2002, at www.whitehouse.gov and the analyses of the Bush Doctrine in A Callinicos, *The New Mandarins of American Power*, Cambridge: Polity, 2003; and Gaddis, *Surprise, Security, and the American Experience*, ch 4. Some authors tend more than Gaddis to emphasise the continuities in US global strategy before and after 9/11. See, from very different perspectives, Bacevich, *American Empire*; R Kagan, *Paradise and Power*, London: Atlantic Books, 2003; and N Chomsky, *Hegemony or Survival*, London: Hamish Hamilton, 2003.
16 Gaddis, *Surprise, Security, and the American Experience*, p 100. On the 19th century, see *ibid*, ch 2.
17 See especially RA Clarke, *Against All Enemies*, New York: Free Press, 2004; and B Woodward, *Plan of Attack*, New York: Simon & Schuster, 2004.
18 'Deputy Secretary Wolfowitz Interview with Sam Tannenhaus, *Vanity Fair*'.
19 'Excerpts from 1992 Draft *Defense Planning Guidance*', at www.pbs.org.
20 See Mann, *Rise of the Vulcans*, pp 208–215 for an account of the draft and its origins that emphasises the continuities between the policies outlined there and those pursued by the Clinton administration.
21 P Wolfowitz, 'Bridging centuries: fin de siècle all over again', *The National Interest*, 47, 1997, online edition, at www.nationalinterest.com.
22 *National Security Strategy*, p 30. See Mann, *Rise of the Vulcans*, ch 20, on the background to this document.
23 'Remarks by National Security Adviser Condoleezza Rice on terrorism and foreign policy', 29 April 2002, at www.whitehouse.gov.
24 D Acheson, *Present at the Creation*, New York: WW Norton, 1969.
25 *Reliable, Affordable, and Environmentally Sound Energy For America's Future: Report of the National Energy Policy Group*, May 2001, at www.whitehouse.gov.
26 D Harvey, *The New Imperialism*, Oxford: Oxford University Press, 2003, p 25.
27 Gaddis, *Surprise, Security, and the American Experience*, pp 99, 100, 101, (italics in original).
28 For example, R Kagan, 'America's crisis of legitimacy', *Foreign Affairs*, 83 (2), 2004, pp 65–87; and WR Mead, *Power, Terror, Peace, and War*, New York: Knopf, 2004.
29 H Kissinger, *A World Restored*, London: Weidenfeld & Nicolson, 1957, p 2, (italics in original).
30 See Gaddis, *Surprise, Security, and the American Experience*, *passim*.
31 *National Security Strategy*, p iv.
32 'President Bush discusses Iraq policy at Whitehall Palace in London', 19 November 2003, at www.whitehouse.gov.
33 'President sworn-in to second term', 20 January 2005, at www.whitehouse.gov.
34 Mead, *Special Providence*, p 163.
35 Mann, *Rise of the Vulcans*, p 329. It is, however, important to understand that in practice neoconservatives tend to equate democracy not with popular sovereignty but rather with what Fareed Zakaria calls 'constitutional liberalism'—ie limited government that protects individual liberty and the rights to private property and free speech. Zakaria's warnings against 'illiberal democracy'—ie the consequences of unrestrained majority rule, though couched as a criticism of the neocons' project, in fact very much resonate with their concerns. See F Zakaria, *The Future of Freedom*, New York: WW Norton, 2004; and Callinicos, *The New Mandarins of American Power*, pp 23–34.
36 'President Bush discusses Iraq policy at Whitehall Palace'.
37 Callinicos, *The New Mandarins of American Power*, pp 80–92.
38 TE Ricks, 'Dissension grows in senior ranks on war strategy', *Washington Post*, 9 May 2004.
39 G Dinmore, 'Powell gives bleak assessment of Iraq security problems', *Financial Times*, 13 January 2005.
40 For an assessment that is all the more damning because it is written by a former senior adviser to the Coalition Provisional Authority, see L Diamond, 'What went wrong in Iraq', *Foreign Affairs*, 83 (5), 2004, pp 34–56.
41 See, for example, M Mann, *Incoherent Empire*, London: Verso, 2003.
42 G Achcar, 'Self-deception and selective expertise', 5 May 2004, at www.counterpunch.org.
43 J Dobbins, 'Iraq—winning the unwinnable war', *Foreign Affairs*, 84 (1), 2005, online edition, at www.foreignaffairs.org.
44 The classic study of Iraq under British hegemony remains Hanna Batatu's monumental *The Old Social Classes and The Revolutionary Movements of Iraq*, Princeton, NJ: Princeton University Press, 1978.
45 For a version of this view by a former adviser to Tony Blair, see R Cooper, *The Breaking of Nations*, London: Atlantic Books, 2003. For a case of disintegration where outside powers played a decisive role in effecting the collapse of the state, see B Rubin, *The Fragmentation of Afghanistan*, New Haven, CT: Yale University Press, 2002.
46 SM Hersh, 'Plan B', *The New Yorker*, 28 June 2004, online edition.
47 Kagan, 'America's crisis of legitimacy'.
48 For example, C Krauthammer, 'A fight for Shiites', *Washington Post*, 26 November 2004.

49 S Negus, 'Iraq's hit-and-run insurgents outsmart under-strength troops', *Financial Times*, 20 November 2004.
50 B Graham, 'Army plans to keep 120 000 in Iraq', *Washington Post*, 24 January 2005. Two sober recent assessments of the guerrilla war in Iraq are A Cordesman, 'The developing Iraqi insurgency: status at end-2004', Center for Strategic and International Studies, working draft, 22 December 2004, at www.csis.org; and T Lasseter & JS Landey, 'Iraq insurgency growing larger, more effective', Knight Ridder Newspapers, 23 January 2005, at www.realcities.com/mld/krwashington/.
51 *National Security Strategy*, p 1.
52 Gowan, *The Global Gamble*, Part 1.
53 Z Brzezinski, *The Choice: Global Domination or Global Leadership*, New York: Basic Books, 2004.
54 D Reynié, *La fracture occidentale*, Paris: La Table Ronde, 2004.

Whither Iraq? Beyond Saddam, sanctions and occupation

TAREQ Y ISMAEL & JACQUELINE S ISMAEL

ABSTRACT *The question of Iraq's future in the wake of 35 years of dictatorship and 13 years of sanctions is a major problem on the global agenda. This question is complicated by numerous factors, not the least of which are military occupation by the world's sole superpower, growing resistance and hostility to the presence of foreign troops and contractors, and the post-occupation influx of international terrorist groups into Iraq. To address the question of 'whither Iraq', this paper represents an effort to identify guideposts to Iraq's future that are manifest in its present. These guideposts are identified as a function of the interplay between national, regional and international political dynamics. Iraq's future is situated in an interaction between history and contemporary political dynamics. The USA's policy of nation-building and state-building in Iraq are examined against two earlier models of political reconstruction there—British and Baathist. Using the guideposts revealed, four scenarios are posited based on different sets of assumptions about the state of state- and nation building.*

The question of Iraq's future in the wake of 35 years of dictatorship and 13 years of sanctions is a major problem on the global agenda. This question is complicated by numerous factors, not the least of which are military occupation by the world's sole superpower and the growing resistance and hostility to the presence of foreign troops and contractors. To address the question of 'whither Iraq', this paper represents an effort to identify guideposts to Iraq's future that are manifest in its present. These guideposts are identified as a function of the interplay between national, regional and international political dynamics. Iraq's future is situated in an interaction between history and contemporary political dynamics. Four future scenarios are posited based on different sets of assumptions about the state of state- and nation building.

Iraq in history

The territory of today's Iraq is relatively geographically consistent with the ancient land of Mesopotamia. The vast bulk of the Iraqi population still lives in the fertile alluvial plain, which is situated between the Tigris and Euphrates rivers. This geographic region is often referred to as the cradle of civilisation as it was the birthplace of writing, which was accompanied by advances in the arts and sciences and the emergence of complex social, political and economic institutions. Ancient Mesopotamia introduced the world to a plethora of 'firsts': the first recorded epic poem, the first stringed musical instrument, the first written code of law, the Prophet Abraham (recognised as the first prophet by Judaism, Christianity, and Islam), the first city-state, and so forth.[1] If the history of this ancient civilization (circa 2600 BC to 500 AD) could be condensed by time-lapse cinematography into a 24-hour documentary, for the first three hours we would be watching Ancient Mesopotamia, and for 90% of the remaining 21 hours, Mesopotamia and Ancient Egypt would dominate the picture. The territory of Iraq, in other words, has been a cohesive historical unit and a catalyst to civilisation since the dawn of history, with a myriad of patterns of interaction interconnecting the diverse people of the area through space and time.

In the medieval period (circa 500 to 1500 AD), Iraq played a central role in the rise of Islamic civilisation. The golden age of classical Islamic civilisation was initiated under the Abbasid Dynasty, which founded Baghdad in 762 AD. From the ninth to the 13th centuries, Baghdad was the centre of extraordinary cultural and intellectual development and the cultural bridge between ancient and modern civilisation. Under the tutelage of the Abbasid Dynasty, Baghdad became a centre of learning and the pursuit of knowledge was championed. In 1184 there were 30 independent schools in Baghdad, in addition to an engineering school and three medical schools. Private and public libraries were established and contained tens of thousands of books and manuscripts. From this wellspring bloomed the multicultural, multi-ethnic mosaic of Islamic civilisation fostered from intellectual diversity and cross-cultural synergy.[2]

Following the Mongol destruction of Baghdad in the 13th century, Iraq moved to the sidelines of world history, first as a backwater of the Ottoman Empire, where it remained until the 20th century, when it became a backwater of the British Empire. On the eve of British occupation in 1917 the territory of present day Iraq consisted of three independently administrated provinces under the Ottoman Empire: Mosul, Baghdad and Basra. Although it had been a nominal part of the Ottoman Empire, Iraqi elements did not play a central role in the machinations of Ottoman politics. Rather, Iraq was politically, socially and economically localised. Congruent with provincialism was the social structure, which was derived from segmented agrarian communities. The communities were differentiated by tribal, ethnic, and/or religious affiliation, and held together by the interlocking patterns of exchange, co-operation and conflict that had evolved through socioeconomic and cultural interaction over the millennia.[3]

With the collapse of the Ottoman Empire after World War I, and the carving up of the Arab world into British and French mandates, Britain occupied Iraq and merged the three provinces into the new state of Iraq under its colonial administration. Direct British rule, the presence of the British military, the British failure to honour their promise to end the occupation, and the exorbitant taxes that were at a much higher scale then than those of the Ottomans,[4] provided the catalyst for the emergence of an Iraqi resistance movement, and precipitated the Revolt of 1920 that cost the British Exchequer up to £56 million.[5] Winston Churchill, then the British Secretary of State for War, introduced the military tactic of blanket bombing of villages as the original 'shock and awe' doctrine, which eight decades later the US military adopted. In ordering the gassing of Iraqi civilians, Churchill said, 'I do not understand the squeamishness about the use of gas. I am strongly in favour of using poison gas against uncivilised tribes.'[6] Whole villages were bombed and gassed. Men, women and children fleeing from gassed villages in panic were mercilessly machine-gunned by low-flying British planes. The Royal Air Force routinely bombed and used poison gas against the Kurd, Sunni and Shi'ite tribes without discrimination.[7] The tenacity of Iraqi resistance, however, demonstrated to Britain the impossibility of ruling Iraq by military might, and Britain nominally transferred sovereignty to a puppet regime and withdrew to military bases.

Britain was the architect of the modern Iraqi state and organised an elected parliamentary system and constitutional monarchy. However, the system was in reality a façade for a puppet administration that had little room for manoeuvring outside British interests. A descendant of the Prophet from the Hashemite line, Faisal, was brought in as the first king. He represented the continuation of Muslim unity which the Ottoman Caliphate had symbolised, and thus enjoyed a modicum of political legitimacy for an otherwise alien political system. The various local power groups—the notables, cultural elite, merchants and land owners, and the Iraqi officers in the Ottoman army—were integrated into the modern bureaucratic machinery of the state, and the elected parliament was designed to place minimal constraints on the Iraqi monarchy. After about three decades of British suzerainty over the modern Iraqi state, local power groups grew increasingly restive with British limitations on Iraqi sovereignty and plundering of Iraq's oil, and Arab nationalist ideology grew increasingly popular among the disenfranchised majority. In 1958 a military coup led by General Karim Kasem put an end to the royal regime and declared Iraq a republic. The emergence of Iraq as a republic ruled by a nationalist military regime placed the country in the fulcrum of regional and international political dynamics and Iraq became a contested zone of Arab nationalist and cold war politics.[8] In this context outside influences from regional and international actors poured into Iraq and a plethora of political groupings struggled for power. A coup led by Ba'athists brought down the Kasem regime in 1963, and was in turn brought down eight months later. It is no longer a secret that the Ba'ath *coup d'état* of 1963 was facilitated by the covert efforts of the CIA. Ali Salih al-Saadi, a Ba'ath leader of the 1963 coup, openly stated 'we came to power on the CIA train'.[9]

The impact of dictatorship (1968–90)

With the help of the USA the Ba'ath returned to power in 1968.[10] And by the time Saddam Hussein assumed the presidency in 1979, the Ba'ath, awash with oil wealth, had already established a totalitarian regime in Iraq through control of a command economy, the army and other sources of coercion, and through total control of the media and other vehicles of communication. What gave the totalitarian Ba'ath state its pervasive and oppressive power was not the fact that it was the largest employer by virtue of ownership of the public sector. It was rather the fact that the state was the producer and the owner of the oil sector. The phenomenal oil price increases in 1974 rendered the state independent of the production capacity of Iraqi society (the primary, secondary and tertiary sectors combined) and hence unaccountable to it. Oil revenue helped the Ba'ath create the political economy of patron–client relations where personal relationships and crony capitalism were the driving forces. This distorted state–society relations by reshaping the business class in the image of the ruling clan class.[11] Unchecked by financial constraints, and inflamed by a toxic combination of geopolitics internationally, heady nationalism regionally and tribal parochialism nationally, the Ba'ath in general, and Saddam Hussein in particular, sought self-aggrandisement of the state through extravagant military expenditures, as reflected in Table 1.

Nationally the Saddam regime achieved virtually total control first of the Ba'ath Party apparatus then of Iraqi society through a combination of ruthless coercion, financial co-optation and a complex web of security agencies spying on the population and on each other. The subordination of civil society and culture to the state sapped these of their vitality and ultimately their viability. Regionally the Saddam regime sought leadership of the Arab world by championing Arab issues, especially the Arab–Israeli question. And internationally, by invading Iran, the Saddam regime sought to fill the geopolitical vacuum created by the collapse of the Shah's regime and the emergence of the Islamic state in Iran. This ignited an eight-year war that not only exposed the superficial vanity and strategic naiveté of the Iraqi military establishment (for all its armaments and manpower), it also exhausted the state financially and bankrupted it ideologically.

The embroilment of Iraq in a lengthy war with Iran (1980–88) seems to have been a successful application of the US strategy of 'dual containment'.[12] Both Iraq and Iran posed a potential threat to Israel for various reasons, and Iran represented a direct ideological challenge to US interests by offering a 'third way' out of the Cold War's global competition between the USA and the USSR for world hegemony. The economies of

TABLE 1 Iraq's public expenditures as a percentage of GNP, 1960, 1987, 1990

	1960	*1987*	*1990*
Health	1	0.8	0.8
Education	5.8	4.6	5.1
Military	7.3	30.2	27.4

Source: RL Sivard, *World Military and Social Expenditures*, 1991, 1993 (Leesburg, VA: World Priorities).

both Iraq and Iran were severely damaged during the war. What aggravated further their economic problems was a 75% decline in the value of petroleum revenue by 1986. The war's economic damage to Iraq was at least US$120 billion, which amounted to more than the total Iraqi oil exports since 1973. In 1988 Iraq incurred a debt of $90 billion, with about $40 billion just to Saudi Arabia and Kuwait. The Iraqi oil revenue for the same year was $13–15 billion; but civilian imports were $12 billion, debt service $5 billion and another $1 billion went on salaries for guest workers.[13] The economic loss was perhaps $644 billion, and its GDP per capita declined from $6052 in 1977 to $2944 in 1988. Iran suffered even greater economic setbacks than Iraq because it financed its war effort internally but, unlike Iraq, Iran emerged without having developed untenable financial obligations to regional economic powers like Saudi Arabia. Drawn into the vortex of military adventurism by the toxic combination (geopolitics internationally, nationalism regionally and parochialism nationally), the Saddam regime hurled the Iraqi state down the path of military adventurism, culminating in the invasion of Kuwait in 1990.

The impact of sanctions (1990–2003)

The Iraqi invasion of Kuwait in August 1990 resulted in the UN Security Council's (UNSC) imposition of the severest international sanctions regime ever imposed on a country. The stated intent of the regime was to force a withdrawal from Kuwait. Resolution 687 called for ending the sanctions when Iraqi compliance was established by the Security Council. However, President Bush (senior) rejected the primary purport of Resolution 687, and barred even the relaxation of the sanctions as long as Saddam was in power. President Clinton later concurred, and Secretary of State, Warren Christopher, announced in 1994 that Iraqi compliance was not enough to lift the embargo, thus changing the substance of the Security Council ruling unilaterally.[14]

While the campaign, dubbed Operation Desert Storm, completely destroyed Iraq's civil infrastructure, it left Saddam Hussein's regime intact. In the immediate aftermath of the war, these appeared as unintended consequences. However, the resolute maintenance of the rigid sanctions regime over the next 13 years supports the contention widely accepted in the Arab world that these were covert objectives, not unintended consequences.[15] Denis Halliday and Hans Von Sponeck have argued that, if the sanctions had been directed against preventing a WMD programme rather than targeting the Iraqi population (because of the way they were administered by the UK and USA), the Iraqis might have been able to send Saddam to the fate of other tyrants, like Suharto, Marcos, Ceausescu, Mobuto, Duvalier, etc.[16]

After the war in 1991 Iraqi per capita income fell from $2279 in 1984 to $627 in 1991 and decreased to as low as $450 in 1995. Numerous surveys and reports conducted by the government of Iraq and UN agencies over the decade following the Gulf war detailed the deepening of the complex humanitarian crisis precipitated by the war and exacerbated by the continuing sanctions regime.[17] The 1999–2000 Report of the UNDP Iraq Country Office summarised the situation as follows.

> Iraq's economy has been in crisis since the imposition of economic sanctions in 1990. Despite the Oil-for-Food program, the country continued its decline into poverty, particularly in the south. Food supplies continue to be inadequate in the centre and south of the country; the prevalence of general malnutrition in the centre and south has hardly changed. Although the rates have stabilised, this happened at 'an unacceptably high level'. In the area of child and maternal health, in August 1999, UNICEF and the Government of Iraq released the results of the first survey on child mortality in Iraq since 1991. The survey showed that under-five child mortality had more than doubled from 56 deaths per 1000 live births in 1984 to 131 deaths in the period 1994–1999. At least 50% of the labour force is unemployed or under-employed; a shortage of basic goods, compounded by a drought, has resulted in high prices and an estimated inflation rate of 135% and 120% in 1999 and 2000 respectively...Most of the country's civil infrastructure remains in serious disrepair. GDP per capita dropped to an estimated US$715 [from US$3508 before the Gulf War], which is a figure comparable with such countries as Madagascar and Rwanda.[18]

Food production and availability were major factors exacerbating the problem of increasing morbidity and mortality in Iraq under the sanctions regime. Fuelled by lavish oil income, in the 1970s and 1980s the Ba'ath had substituted importation of foodstuffs from the international market for domestic development. As a result, agricultural and domestic industrial sectors were not only undeveloped but languished as the market was deluged with imported goods. Under the embargo imposed by the sanctions regime, oil revenue precipitously declined and food importation was seriously curtailed. In addition, replacement parts for repairs to civil infrastructure destroyed by the aerial bombardment and components essential to increase agricultural production in Iraq were embargoed. As a result, dietary energy supply had fallen from 3120 to 1093 kilocalories per capita/per day by 1994–95, with women and children singled out as the most vulnerable members of Iraqi society. Against a UN target of 2463 kilocalories and 63.6 grams of protein per person per day, the nutritional value of the distributed food basket did not exceed 1993 kilocalories and 43 grams of protein. Reflecting the economic impact of war and sanctions on Iraq's economy, the rate of inflation after the imposition of the sanctions regime increased from 18% in 1975 to 2000% in 1992, and the exchange rate of the Iraqi dinar to the US dollar dropped from 1:3 in 1972 to 180:1 in 1993; in other words the dinar was equivalent to 1 US cent.[19]

Before the start of the oil-for-food programme in 1996 the government of Iraq had been distributing 1300 kilocalories per day.[20] The prevalence of malnutrition in Iraqi children under five almost doubled from 1991 to 1996 (from 12% to 23%). Acute malnutrition in the centre and southern regions rose from 3% to 11% for the same age bracket. Indeed, the World Food

Programme (WFP) indicated that, by July 1995, average shop prices of essential commodities stood at 850 times the July 1990 level. While the humanitarian programme in Iraq, initiated in 1996 with the oil-for-food programme, successfully staved off mass starvation, the level of malnutrition within Iraq remained high and directly contributed to the morbidity and mortality rates.[21] In 1999 a UNICEF report estimated that sanctions had caused the death of half a million Iraqi children.[22] The 2003 *State of the World's Children* report, which UNICEF issued, stated: 'Iraq's regression over the past decade is by far the most severe of the 193 countries surveyed'.[23] The impact of the sanctions regime on Iraq was overwhelming and multifarious. While it pauperised the Iraqi people, it also strengthened the grip of the Saddam regime over the population.

Under the suzerainty of the Security Council the Iraqi state lost control of its air space in the north and south; nonetheless, it maintained territorial jurisdiction in the centre and the south, and nominal power in the north where the Kurds enjoyed *de facto* autonomy under US protection. After about a decade of the US protective umbrella the Kurds appear politically to have become US 'clients'. In this aberrant context the Iraqi people, excluding the Kurds, suffered a cynical game of brinksmanship between the Saddam regime and the US – UK led Security Council with regard to weapons of mass destruction. Bombed back to a pre-industrial stage of development by Operation Desert Storm, the people reverted to pre-industrial social patterns for survival in the aberrant socio-political and economic situation of the sanctions regime. Tribal, religious and ethnic bonds of community reciprocity and exchange re-emerged as central institutions bridging personal and social security.

At the regional and international levels, sanctions served to isolate Iraq both politically and economically. The Saddam regime's invasion of Kuwait in 1990 not only exacerbated ideological tensions in the Arab world between the conservative Gulf states, led by Saudi Arabia, and nationalist groups, but also dealt a terminal blow to Arab nationalism as an ideological force in regional politics. The invasion precipitated the collapse of organised Arab opposition to Israel and the acceptance by Arab regimes of US military bases on Arab territory. Until the Gulf war in 1991 the Ba'ath had championed the cause of Arab unity and the Palestinian question, and had kept in the forefront of Arab politics the relationship between the Palestinian question and imperialism. In the face of this collapse Israel's right wing became more politically strident, as reflected in Ariel Sharon's provocative walk on 28 September 2000, to the al-Aqsa Mosque, which initiated the second *Intifada*. The second US military defeat of the Iraqi state (9 April 2003) within 1100 hours of the initiation of the war was traumatic for all Arabs, who perceived it as a reflection of the bankruptcy of Arab regimes after three generations of nation building. The toll of sanctions on the Iraqi people, and the perceived collusion of Arab regimes in the destruction of Iraq fuelled the rise of anti-Western sentiment throughout the Arab world, and inflamed the increasing schism between Arab governments and their populations.[24]

The invasion and occupation of Iraq

The most immediate impact of the invasion was the systematic destruction of a large portion of Iraq's cultural heritage and infrastructure. Represented in the US media as an unintended consequence of an explosion of freedom by an oppressed people, it was portrayed differently in the Islamic world. Rather, the free rampage of organised looting of cultural, educational and health facilities and the wholesale burning of historical records symbolised an intentional policy of cultural cleansing. This was even more prevalent in Iraq than throughout the rest of the Islamic and Arab world, as many Iraqis took great pride in their unique history, where the cultural connection to their locale extended far beyond the Baghdadi Caliphate into the very origins of 'civilisation' itself. The significance of the looting and destruction of Iraq's cultural symbols cannot be overstated. The American forces, while guarding only the Ministry of Oil, watched the burning and the looting of Baghdad indifferently, and even refused to intervene when people requested their help.

'Operation Iraqi Freedom' also reduced the public infrastructure to rubble.[25] The quality of life in Iraq, already seriously compromised by almost 15 years of international sanctions, deteriorated even further under the occupation. Reflecting this, a report conducted by the Fafo Institute for Applied Social Sciences found that acute malnutrition among Iraqi children between the ages of six months and five years had increased from 4% before the US invasion to 7.7% after more than a year of occupation.[26] The death toll of the US occupation on Iraqi civilians was estimated at over 100 000 by a study undertaken by Johns Hopkins and Columbia universities in collaboration with al-Mustansiyah University. Most individuals reportedly killed by coalition forces were women and children. The risk of death from violence in the period after the invasion was 58 times higher than in the period before the war.[27]

In an investigative report from Iraq, Naomi Klein wrote that the Mongolian-like destruction brought about by the US invasion was deliberately allowed and served the neoconservative ideology that dominated the thinking and the implementation of US foreign policy. By applying a pervasive 'shock therapy', and in effect erasing the past, the neoconservatives firmly believed that a new stage could be set to establish a 'utopia' of a free market economy, which would be championed by US transnational and multinational corporations. According to Klein: 'Two months before the invasion the USAID drafted a work order...to oversee Iraq's transition to a sustainable market-driven economic system, and to take appropriate advantage of the unique opportunity for rapid progress in this area presented by the current configuration of political circumstances'.[28]

Paul Bremer, who arrived in Iraq on 2 May 2004, set out to accomplish two goals. The first was to apply free market shock therapy to Iraq's economy. In an apparent effort to jump-start the process, he reduced the number of police and military forces in Iraq. He ousted some 500 000 officers, and thus contributed heavily to a skyrocketing unemployment rate of 60–

70%.[29] His second task entailed banning the Ba'ath party and purging its members from their posts within the government. These two moves resulted in the complete collapse of Iraqi state infrastructure. Bremer's policies created a political and social vacuum, and pre-Ba'ath party social institutions (the tribal, religious and communal formations already emergent under sanctions) were the only agencies left to fill the security vacuum precipitated by the loss of administrative control.

Bremer continued with his agenda and arranged for the largest state liquidation sale of economic enterprises since the collapse of the USSR.[30] While he opened the borders to unrestricted imports with one hand, he closed the door to domestic and Iraqi production with the other by introducing a set of laws in September 2003 aimed at encouraging transnational corporations to move into Iraq and take over the economy. Within these newly introduced laws Order 37 dramatically lowered corporate tax from 40% to 15%; Order 39 permitted foreign companies to own 100% of what had previously been Iraqi assets and allowed investors to transfer internationally all the profit made in Iraq without any stipulation of reinvestment or taxation. This same order also outlined a 40-year lease term for foreign national corporations of Iraqi assets. Order 40 created favourable terms for foreign banks to facilitate foreign capital investment and transfer. Some of the only economically focused laws left untouched were Saddam's laws restricting collective bargaining and trade unions.

The neoconservative agenda that the US occupation was attempting to implement was a major factor in the escalation of armed resistance. In the first four months after Bremer's arrival, 109 US soldiers were killed and 570 wounded. When Bremer's shock therapy took effect in the following four months, the number of American casualties almost doubled.[31] Bremer's policies created half a million jobless people overnight and made resistance to US occupation the only viable alternative to unemployment. In addition, the wholesale plundering of Iraq by US corporations envisioned in the foreign investment laws represented an imminent threat to small business owners, who in turn invested in financing the armed resistance for self-protection. With 67% unemployment the influx of foreign products and workers into Iraq further fuelled the resistance.[32]

The US project for a utopian free market in Iraq, however, was arrested by the belated revelation that international law stipulates that occupation forces can not dispose of the assets of the occupied country in any shape or form. In other words, an independent, government in Iraq would, in the future, have the fundamental right under international law to recapture and nationalise foreign investments and to demand reparations. In an effort to overcome this obstacle Bremer drew up an interim constitution with the commitment that a permanent constitution would be framed by a constitutional assembly appointed by a democratically elected government. Article 126 of the Interim Constitution stipulated that 'for the duration of the interim government the laws, regulations, orders and directives issued by the Coalition provisional Authority...shall remain in force' and could only be changed after general elections were held, which were scheduled for 30 January 2005. According to the US rationale, under the interim constitution investors could buy Iraqi assets and sign contracts that would secure their investments for 40 years. Should any future Iraqi government decide to change the laws, investors could sue for compensation.[33] To facilitate the American corporate usurpation of Iraq's resources in perpetuity, a nominal transfer of sovereignty was hastily arranged. Bremer then dissolved the Iraq Provisional Authority and formed the Iraqi Governing Council, which consisted of 25 hand-picked members. Ayad Allawi—a former Ba'athist and early protégé of Saddam Hussein, who fell out of favour with then Vice President Saddam in the mid-1970s and became a CIA collaborator—was selected as prime minister of the interim government.[34]

Political reconstruction and the resistance

The US Agency for International Development (USAID) appointed the Research Triangle Institute (RTI) as one of a battalion of private contractors attempting to fashion Iraq's legal, economic, political and social institutions so that they would be conducive to US interests. Most of the contracts have been funded by USAID as foreign aid. RTI is recruiting and mobilising expatriate and indigenous Iraqis to reconstruct the institutions of state and civil society.[35] In accordance with their contract with USAID, RTI sought to staff its reconstruction planning venture with 'the most appropriate "legitimate" and functional leaders'—that is, educated Iraqis, particularly expatriate Iraqis who are residents of the USA.[36] The definition of 'legitimate', according to Fritz Weden of the USAID Office of Transition Initiatives, is to 'identify those groups, those leaders that you can work with'.[37] The task of the RTI is to ensure that only the 'legitimate' leaders—those not opposed to US occupation and Iraq's westernisation—prevail, in order to create a base that will support the reconstruction of Iraq according to the neoliberal model. Thomas Carothers, director of the Democracy Project at the Carnegie Endowment for International Peace, said: 'beneath the new interest of the United States in bringing democracy to the Middle East is the central dilemma that the most powerful, popular movements in Iraq are the ones that we are deeply uncomfortable with'.[38]

While the RTI acts as a public recruiting office, the National Endowment for Democracy (NED) and its affiliates were developing the machinery for scores of political formations expected to contest the national elections planned for 30 January 2005 or pack beforehand the scheduled Constitutional Assembly. Various US affiliates set up workshops for teaching a US government-approved perspective on democracy. Larry Diamond, a senior advisor to the Coalition Provisional Authority (CPA) and former co-director of NED, offered a preview of this project in a lecture at Hilla University in January 2004. According to the CPA press release, Diamond told his audience that a basic element of 'democracy' is a 'market economy' and among the most fundamental rights is the right to own property—a view affirmed by USAID. This, in turn, calls for a kind of democracy in which social equality is not a necessary aim and in which inequalities may in fact be necessary.[39]

In Latin America USAID has a long history of cajoling and/or coercing governments to submit to its 'reforms'. However, in Iraq, NED and USAID are attempting institutional reconstruction, not reform. Their point of entry into Iraq was the US occupation, not diplomacy. In this case, 'legitimate leaders' are not to be identified and co-opted, as in Latin America, but to be groomed and primed. Despite the 'transfer of sovereignty' on 28 June 2004, the USA continues to exercise inordinate power over the interim government, especially since Allawi's power base in Iraq is negligible at best and he is totally dependent upon US protection.[40] There is no need to tinker with Iraq's laws because they will be written on a blank slate by the first elected government. All this is possible because of the rare opportunity offered by the occupation. In Iraq the first step was not 'legitimation' or 'constituency building', it was dropping bombs.[41] Despite the appearance of unfettered latitude for action, however, the intensity of the Iraqi resistance has exposed the unpopularity of the USAID and NED project to remodel Iraqi society and left it very uncertain. Reflecting this, in an exclusive interview with *Asia Times* in June 2004, two elite members of the Iraqi resistance declared that the resistance plan had been organised months in advance of the US invasion in March 2003, not to fight the invasion but to expel the occupation that was sure to follow.[42]

An increasing number of popular protests across central and southern Iraq reflected the growing hostility to the occupation. To pacify the growing resistance, in April 2004 the US military moved against Fallujah, a small city in the so-called Sunni triangle about 60 kilometres northwest of Baghdad. On 6 April 2004 the first siege of Fallujah was initiated with intense air and ground assaults. For almost a month a virulent campaign of urban warfare was waged but failed to pacify the city. In the face of intense international pressure and signs of increasing co-operation among Sunni and Shi'ite groups, the US military was forced to pull back and withdrew from Fallujah. But interruption of the occupation's reliance on a military strategy of pacification was only temporary, and attention turned to Shi'ite opposition. Al-Sadr's rejectionist movement had become a lightening-rod of armed resistance to US occupation in the Shi'ite south, and increasing confrontations between US and al-Sadr forces culminated in a three-week siege of Najaf in August 2004 in an effort to crush al-Sadr's movement.[43] This siege also failed to produce a military victory because Ayatollah al-Sistani, the highest religious Shi'ite authority, brokered an agreement between Al-Sadr and the US forces.

> As the dust settled, three parties stood on the ruins of the holy city—Moqtada Al-Sadr, the government and the Hawza...Al-Sadr movement did not accomplish a military victory; and it was not destined to do so, given the balance of power. But they did not lose either. They melted away with a large portion of their weapons and they were not forced to comply with demands to disband...and they are invited, indeed encouraged, to participate in the political process...[44]

Following the resolution of the Najaf siege the US military turned its full attention to the resistance in the Sunni triangle, and in November 2004 the second siege of Fallujah was initiated. But this time the US forces planned the complete elimination of independent news coverage or of any means of communication, such as cell phones,[45] in order to reduce the city to rubble, thus sending a message to quell the spirit of the resistance in preparation for the January election. An estimated 300 000 of Fallujah's 350 000 inhabitants fled as more than 12 000 ground forces sealed off the city, but an estimated 50 000 civilians remained—the elderly, the sick, the young, and those with nowhere else to go.[46] The assault on the city was initiated on 7 November 2004, and by 18 November the insurgency was declared 'broken' by the senior US marine commander in Iraq.[47] However, fighting continued, despite reports that the USA was using napalm and poison gas.[48] As one commentator noted, 'The Falluja police-state strategy represents a sign of weakness, not strength'.[49]

Immediately following the 'successful' siege of Fallujah, which the US had claimed was the heart of the resistance, and from which fighting immediately flared up again following the lifting of aerial bombardments,[50] major attacks were carried out on a Baghdadi checkpoint on 13 and 14 December 2004[51] and on a US military base near Mosul on 22 December,[52] killing over 40 people, including at least 18 US military personnel. In a message to *Asia Times Online* from the Netherlands, Nada al-Rubaiee, a member of the central committee of the Iraqi Patriotic Alliance, a group that is part of the Iraqi national resistance movement both inside and outside Iraq, said: 'Everything in the resistance movement is clear...There is agreement on one issue; that is, getting freedom from foreign occupying forces and their handymen. It is agreed that only Iraqi people would decide the course of government in the post-liberation era.' [53] The continuation of guerrilla warfare and the increasing sophistication of the attacks disrupted US supply lines even to the point where the US military had to resort to air-dropping equipment and supplies into US bases, an incredibly costly venture, in order to reduce the risks incurred by land transport.[54]

The destruction of Najaf and Fallujah provided graphic lessons in collective punishment for the Iraqi population. Even as the Fallujah siege eased the US strategy of military pacification expanded throughout the Sunni triangle, and small-scale assaults were initiated on targeted areas in Mosul, Ramadi, Sammarra and other towns against any manifestation of organised resistance. However, assaults by the Iraqi resistance continued to escalate in frequency, boldness and ferocity. By mid-January 2005 it was clear that the USA could not pacify the Sunni triangle sufficiently to allow for any claim of a democratic election on 30 January. Reflecting the growing discomfort about the elections in the US establishment, on 12 January 2005, the *New York Times* called for its postponement.

State building vs nation building

With the consummation of decolonisation in the 1950s the term 'nation-building' became prominent in liberal discourse to rationalise a Western-sponsored process of decolonisation that favoured the integration of disparate groups and communities of people into facsimiles of liberal democracies. In effect, nation building represented a liberal development strategy in the economic and political context of decolonisation, with nation-states promoted as the agents for transforming pre-modern communities into economically liberal and politically stable entities.[55] While the concept of nation building focused on political process, the corollary concept of state building focused on structure and functions of government. Similarly, Eurocentric state-building theory has roots in classical liberal theory.[56]

Ill-equipped for both nation building (inclusion of disparate social groups in the political process) and state building (the development of a political system of governance), and unabashedly seeking to usurp Iraq's economic assets, US policy in Iraq has created a wellspring of antipathy towards any form of collaboration with US agents, as well as massive support for the growing resistance movement. Iraq's experiences with the two previous models of political reconstruction (nation- and state building) in its modern history provide insight into the challenge of political reconstruction. The first model was undertaken by Britain in the aftermath of its occupation, and therefore presents a relevant comparison with the US effort. The monarchical system of governance established by Britain incorporated an important symbol of cultural legitimacy—Hashemite authority; and embraced all national power groups, not only in the political process but in the political economy of the state, through the creation of a landlord class that cut across traditional tribal and ethnic groupings. This allowed the effective management of the countryside and, through education, the civil service and the military created systems for the national integration of the middle classes. However, it marginalised, dispossessed and impoverished the peasantry, and the urban/rural contradiction manifested in the state's political economy progressively destabilised the state.

In contrast to the British model, the Ba'ath model based its political system on nationalist symbols of legitimacy, and the party apparatus provided the mechanism for inclusion of all social groups in the political process, particularly the urban and rural poor. While the nation-building process was thus more inclusive of social groups than the monarchical system, it attempted to co-opt the already active nationalist groups, or to marginalise them in the event of their opposition or rejection, as was the case with the communists, National Democratic Party and even some factions of the Ba'ath itself. Through the Ba'ath socialist programme many social entitlements, such as health, education, housing, electrification, etc were given to the rural and urban poor. The party apparatus replaced education, the civil service and the military as the system of national integration.

However, under Saddam the command economy was quickly transformed into a type of crony capitalism, and the party apparatus into a personality cult. Thus a complex web of national security agencies emerged to enforce the new cult of personality based on the paternalistic visage of 'Papa Saddam'. A combination of totalitarianism and kinship resulted in vibrant networks of nepotism, and the creation of a 'thick ruling clan-class' deeply embedded in the social structure. This was not just a small elite group, but rather an entire social layer united by blood, as well as by economic and financial ties,[57] which led to the marginalisation of the old social classes and the middle classes of the monarchy.[58] The crony-based economics of Saddam's regime, intensified under sanctions, initiated a process of socioeconomic polarisation of society where the wealthy few contrasted with the pauperised mass of the population.

These two examples serve to illustrate the significance of nation building for political stability. While both models had inherent fault lines, the British model provided relative political stability for almost four decades (1921 – 58), and the Ba'ath model for more than a decade (1968 to about the mid-point of the Iraq – Iran war, we would estimate). How does the US effort compare? With the installation of Ayad Allawi as prime minister of the interim government, the foundation of the US model of nation building was initiated; and, with the 2004 re-election of George W Bush as US president, it appears that no radical change in this outline is likely to occur. Highlighting the significance of the nation-building task is the fact that Allawi is an expatriate who had been outside Iraq for the previous 30 years. He has no popular constituency or support from within Iraq and is therefore directly dependent on the US occupation for his installation and tenure.[59] According to a public opinion poll commissioned by the USA in April 2004, Allawi was the least popular politician and 61% of Iraqi respondents opposed his coming to power. Another poll, taken just before the hand-over of power on 28 June 2004, showed that only 11% of Iraqis had confidence in the US administration, down from 47% in November 2003.[60]

The Interim Governing Council

To establish the Interim Governing Council as a legitimate authority, Allawi, the least popular politician who suffers a serious lack of constituency and is dependent on US support, initiated the Iraqi National Conference, which concluded on 18 August 2004. Heralded as an effort to bestow legitimacy on the interim regime by allowing broader representation in state institutions, instead it widened and deepened political fractures in Iraqi society. In order to enhance the legitimacy of the interim government, the Conference would have had to elect a Council which would be representative of at least some significant segments of Iraq's national political forces. Instead, it incorporated the two main Kurdish political forces of northern Iraq—tribal (led by the Kurdish Democratic Party) and urban (led by the Patriotic Union of Kurdistan)—and marginalised Arab political forces, incorporating in their place the expatriate Iraqis who returned on the heels of the US occupation. National political forces in Iraq's central and southern zones are largely composed of Sunni and Shi'ite Arab rejectionists who oppose the occupation. Within the Arab rejectionist camp, up to August 2004, the Hawza (the Shi'ite religious elite led by Ayatollah al-Sistani) had represented the main Shi'ite body, and the Sunni Muslim Scholar's Association the main Sunni body. In addition to the rejectionist camp, indigenous political forces included a number of smaller civil society groups organised around the interests of ethnic and religious minorities, and tribal leaders who all seek a greater role in the transition. Thus, rather than opting for a policy of inclusion of national forces, the parties that have controlled the transition (the USA and expatriate Iraqis) created the Advisory Council in their image to work with the US occupation and Allawi's regime. This exclusion of significant national political forces from the nation-building process alienated many of the social groupings that would have liked to be a part of the discussion on the future of Iraq and increased the legitimacy of the rejectionist camp among all Iraqis.

In protest of the Fallujah siege the Islamic Party, Iraq's most influential Sunni political group, withdrew from the government, and the Sunni Muslim Clerics' Association urged Iraqis to boycott the planned January elections. Leaders of the Iraqi Islamic Party also cited security as a reason for withdrawing the Sunni party's slate of 275 candidates. Insurgents looked bound to attack election officials, candidates and voters. In addition, in mid-November 2004, 47 political parties and groups had already declared their boycott of the elections, citing that the election plans 'do not express the Iraqi people's will and their demand for sovereignty and independence'.[61] Even in the Kurdish region, support for an early election was modified to assume a middle course between the Sunni demand for delaying the election and the urging of Shi'ites (under Ayatollah al-Sistani's guidance) for no delays. Masoud Barzani, leader of the Kurdish Democratic Party, informed the UN envoy that, 'while we are ready for the election on January 30, we will not oppose its delay...if that will ensure a more comprehensive and inclusive election'.[62] In response, 40 political parties connected to al-Hawza and Ayatollah al-Sistani rejected any delay,[63] in effect reflecting an emerging split along sectarian lines. According to a Knight Ridder report on 27 December 2004, even the Shi'ite bloc was divided as to the form of government. A secular democracy was championed by Al-Sadr and Chalabi, but a more focused religious-oriented government was advocated by the Al-Dawa Party and the Supreme Council for the Islamic Revolution.[64]

As violence continued to escalate in the Sunni triangle and the north, in November and December 2004 17 major political parties called for the elections to be delayed, including the prime minister's al-Wfaq al-Watani party and the Iraqi Islamic Party. Mohsen Abdul Hamid, head of the party, told reporters in Baghdad that 'We asked to postpone the election long ago because we believe the security situation in the country is not suitable to hold elections, and the Iraqis don't understand the elections yet. We need enough time, at least six months, to prepare ourselves because the security issue is very complicated.' [65] Further, the Sunni Muslim Clerics' Association urged Iraqis to boycott the planned January elections.

Outside Iraq the US military tactics were vociferously opposed. The cumulative impact of the Najaf and Fallujah campaigns indicated that the USA was losing the war in Iraq politically. Reflecting the increasing international opposition to the US occupation of Iraq, on 16 September 2004, UN Secretary General Kofi Annan told the BBC that the US-led invasion of Iraq was illegal, and warned that there could not be credible elections 'if the security conditions continue as they are now'.[66] And on 17

November the UN High Commissioner for Human Rights, Louise Arbour, called for an investigation into alleged abuses in Fallujah, including the disproportionate use of force and the targeting of civilians.[67] Additionally, in the Arab world, US policy in Iraq was increasingly compared with Israeli policy in the West Bank and Gaza. An opinion poll commissioned by the Arab American Institute, the University of Maryland and the Zogby Institute in August 2004, reported on the increasing hostility of educated and business elites in the Arab world toward the US occupation of Iraq.[68]

Elections under occupation

The Iraqi election took place on 30 January 2005 under extraordinary circumstances of military occupation, rampant insurgency and insecurity. The process was marked by major irregularities, including the appointment of an incognito election commission by the occupying power, secrecy surrounding candidates' names and a lack of on-site observers. The final vote count was officially announced on 13 February 2005. Sixty million ballot sheets were flown to Iraq days before the election for an estimated 15 million eligible voters. Some 7500 candidates were scattered among 257 lists. Twenty-five Iraqi towns and cities boycotted the elections.[69] According to Reuters news agency, while there were 63 000 polling booths throughout Iraq, there were only 33 763 Iraqi election monitors. Should this have been the case in another country, such as Ukraine, it would have elicited an unmitigated international protest.[70]

On 13 February 2005 the Iraqi Election Commission declared the vote count, and after three days of working out the necessary adjustments in accordance with complex electoral procedures, the final voting was as follows. Out of the 58% voter turnout, the United Iraqi Alliance, which is the list put together by Ayatollah al-Sistani, won 51% of votes and captured 140 seats out of 275. The Kurdish list came second, capturing about 26% of the votes and about 75 seats. The loss of the list of Iyad Allawi was something of a surprise because Allawi had all the advantages of incumbency. According to Juan Cole, professor of history at the University of Michigan, Allawi dominated the airwaves in December and January. He went to Baghdad University and made all sorts of promises to the students there and this was dutifully broadcast, and there were lots of similar such photo opportunities. Allawi's list also spent an enormous amount on campaign advertising. The source of these millions is unknown, since Paul Bremer passed a law making disclosure of campaign contributions unnecessary. Despite these enormous advantages, clear American backing, money, etc, Allawi's list won only about 14% of the votes (40 seats) and he certainly lost all chance of becoming the future prime minister, which is a defeat for the American administration.[71] Other Shi'te lists won 11 seats and minor or unknown parties took the very few seats left.

The 7500 candidates were arranged on lists of about 117 political entities that were swiftly constructed, professing about 117 political programmes, which must have been confusing for the Iraqi voters given the living conditions and the political legacy of dictatorship.[72] According to the Administrative Law drawn up by Bremer, the selection of the president, the two vice presidents, and the prime minister requires a two-thirds majority. The president chooses the prime minister, but this is otherwise a ceremonial position along with the two positions of vice president. However, to the extent possible in law making, the Administrative Law stipulates 'a majority', which the United Iraqi Alliance (UIA) already enjoys. Thus the UIA, which comprises the Supreme Council for Islamic Revolution, led by Abdel Aziz al-Hakim, and the Da'wa Party led by Ibrahim al-Ja'fari, can make laws without any need for coalition. Yet recent reports communicated by Juan Cole suggested that the UIA will enter into coalition with the other small Shi'te parties, like the Sadrists, thus ensuring a safe majority on issues of legislation.[73]

Scenarios for the future of Iraq

What are the prospects for Iraq's future? Four possible scenarios can be outlined from political dynamics within the state and schematised along two dimensions. As Table 2 indicates, we propose that Iraq's future will be determined by the state of two countervailing forces—the regime and the resistance. The state of the regime is represented by two contradictory states of political development—Saddamisation (indicating a heavy-handed dictatorship), or democratisation (indicating the participation of significant national political forces in the processes of governance). As we have discussed, since the US invasion, the state of the regime has been primarily a product of the US occupation, and a deepening dependence of the regime on US military occupation is readily apparent.

In contrast to the dichotomy represented in the state of the regime, the two categories comprising the state of the resistance represent polar end-points on a continuum assessing the degree of cohesion among the political forces of resistance. At one end of the continuum the resistance forces are fragmented and in conflict with each other. At the opposite end resistance forces are consolidated in terms of their objectives and acting in close co-ordination. Sunni and Shi'ite rejectionists represent the main body of the national political forces comprising the resistance, but the resistance as a whole is composed not only of national political forces but also of disparate actors not part of the body politic of Iraqi society, such as foreign agents, fundamentalist zealots and criminal groups; and some may very well have their own self-interested agenda that has nothing to do with the political well-

TABLE 2 Scenarios for Iraq's future

State of regime	*State of resistance Fragmentation*	*Consolidation*
Saddamisation	1	2
Democratisation	3	4

being of the Iraqi people. It is our contention that these disparate actors largely came into Iraq with the occupation, and it will take co-ordination among national political forces to overcome them. In other words, while they are involved in the violence, they do not contribute to the national political dynamics because they are a product of the external forces affecting events on the ground in Iraq. This suggests that the state of the resistance, like the state of the regime, is a product of internal and external forces.

Four major scenarios prevail from the juxtaposition of the countervailing forces. As discussed earlier, under the US model of state building, the state of the regime is moving inexorably in the direction of Saddamisation. Under the occupation, scenarios 1 and 2 reflect the realities of contemporary Iraq. Scenario 1 is posited on the assumption of a polarisation among Kurdish, Sunni and Shi'ite political forces, and on the concomitant segmentation of political dynamics in Iraq into northern, central and southern political divisions. The January 2005 elections appear to be the flashpoint, signalling a widening gulf between Sunni and Shi'ite political forces. Ayatollah al-Sistani's endorsement of the proposed January election reflects a dramatic reduction of tension between the Hawza and the Allawi regime, explained largely by the promise of a Shi'ite-dominated government resulting from the election. However, political dynamics in Iraq are more complex than a simple Sunni/Shit'ite dichotomy suggests. Fragmentation along the Kurdish/Arab fault line cuts across the religious sectarian fault. Ayatollah al-Sistani's rejection in March 2004 of a proposed Kurdish veto in the interim constitution, and Masoud Barzani's approval in November 2004 of a proposed delay to the election, highlighted the political dynamics emerging around the Shi'ite/Kurdish dimension. The Kurds are a predominantly Sunni population, and there is a strong Islamist group that has been marginalised in the alignment of the USA with nationalist forces (Barzani and al-Talabani groups).

The second scenario is posited on the assumption of the increasing convergence of national resistance forces around objectives and strategy. During the first assault on Fallujah and the siege of Najaf there was evidence of co-operation between Sunni and Shi'ite rejectionist groups in general, and in particular among their respective clergies. However, this was dissipated with the settlement of the siege of Najaf, and it is widely believed that Ayatollah al-Sistani cut a deal with the US occupation forces, brokered by Ahmad Chalabi, to forsake support for Sunni resistance in the face of increasing US military action in the Sunni triangle, in exchange for a reduction of US military pressure and presence in Shi'ite communities.[74] Indeed, there was no overt and no reported covert sectarian co-operation in the second siege of Fallajah, and increasing indications of fragmentation around the date for the proposed elections emerged, as discussed earlier. This reflects the inherently unstable and volatile nature of scenario 2. Under the conditions of foreign occupation and Saddamisation of the regime, the various factions of the resistance might be easily played off against each other by the regime, the USA and the plethora of external actors with a vested interest in influencing events on the ground in Iraq.

For each scenario the state of the regime is the primary determinant of the state of the resistance. Thus, scenarios 3 and 4 are dependent on democratisation, and the prospects for democratisation are dependent on the interplay of forces inside and outside Iraq. As a global superpower and occupier of Iraq, the USA is the major arbiter of the state of the regime in Iraq. The USA went to Iraq to stay, which explains the American fervour in building military bases in Iraq.[75] With the re-election of George W Bush to the presidency, the prospects for a dramatic shift in US policy in Iraq were clearly off the horizon. Nevertheless, pressures within the US domestic political economy and pressures on the USA from the international political economy are mounting because of Iraq. Change is imminent, and whether or not these changes can be channelled towards a US policy in Iraq that allows democratisation really depends on the international community.

The completion of elections in Iraq with a relatively high voter turn-out in Kurdish and Shi'ite areas indicates some consolidation of domestic forces along ethnic and sectarian dimensions. Fragmentation of the resistance nationally, and consolidation of political forces at a regional level along ethnic or sectarian dimensions, presents Scenario 3. The prospect that looms in this scenario is the fragmentation of Iraq, with a Kurdish quasi-state in the north, a quasi-Islamic state in the south, and a quasi state of chaos in the centre. The nightmarish regional instability implicit in this scenario has haunted the international public since the first Gulf war in 1990–91. Scenario 4 is the most favourable prospect for the peace and security of Iraq and the region, but its prospects are being overshadowed by Scenario 3.

Notes

This article has been adapted from a forthcoming book.

1 Dick Teresi, *Lost Discoveries: The Ancient Roots of Modern Science from Babylonia to Maya*, New York: Simon & Shuster, 2002.
2 Jacqueline Ismael, Tareq Y Ismael & Raymond Baker, 'Iraq and human development: culture, education and the globalization of hope', *Arab Studies Quarterly*, 26 (2), 2004, pp 55–56.
3 Faleh A Jabar, 'Al-Dawla, al-Mugtam'a al-Madani wa al-Tahawul al-Demokrati fi al Iraq', *Markaz Ibn Khaldoun li al-dirasat al-Inma'iyya*, Cairo, 1995, pp 52–53.
4 Henry CK Liu, 'Geopolitics in Iraq: an old game', *Asia Times*, 18 August 2004, at http://www.atimes.com/atimes/Middle_East/FH18Ak02.html.
5 Jabar, 'Al-Dawla', p 194.
6 Liu, 'Geopolitics in Iraq'.
7 *Ibid.*
8 Jabar, 'Al-Dawla', pp 54–59.
9 Ali Karim Said, *Iraq 8 Shabat 1963 Min Hiwar al-Mafhim ila Hiwar aldm: Muraja'at fi Thakrat Talib Shabib*, Beirut: Dar al-Kunuz al-Adabiyah, 1999, p 291 ft.
10 Abdul Wahab Hamid Rashid, *al-Iraq al-Mu'asir*, Damascus: al-Mada, 2002, pp 164–166.
11 Faleh A Jabar, 'Post conflict Iraq: a race for stability, reconstruction, and legitimacy', *US Institute for Peace—Special Report 120*, May 2004, at http://www.usip.org/pubs/specialreports/sr120.html.
12 Leon T Hadar, 'Letter from Washinton: Pax Americana's four pillars of folly', *Journal of Palestine Studies*, 26 (3) 1998, pp 49–59.
13 Tareq Y Ismael, *Middle East Politics Today: Government and Civil Society*, Gainesville: University of Florida Press, 2001, pp 216–217.
14 Noam Chomsky, *Hegemony or Survival: America's Quest for Global Dominance*, New York: Henry Holt, 2003, p 30.
15 Tareq Y Ismael & Jacqueline S Ismael, 'Cowboy warfare, biological diplomacy: disarming metaphors as weapons of mass destruction', *Politics and the Life Sciences*, 18, (1), 1999, pp 70–78.
16 Chomsky, *Hegemony or Survival*, p 249.

17 T Ismael & J Ismael, *The Iraqi Predicament: People in the Quagmire of Power Politics*, London: Pluto Press, 2004, pp 126–165.
18 United Nations Development Program (UNDP), *1999–2000 Report*, Iraq Country Office, at http://www.iq.undp.org.
19 Jabar, 'Al-Dawla', pp168–169.
20 Office of the Iraq Program, United Nations, 'Oil-for-Food, basic figures', 18 May 2002, at http://www.un.org/Depts/oip/background.
21 *Ibid.*
22 UNICEF, *1999 Iraq Child and Maternal Morbidity Surveys.*
23 Chomsky, *Hegemony or Survival*, p 126.
24 Ismael & Ismael, *The Iraqi Predicament*, pp 9–38.
25 Keith Watenpaugh, Edouard Metenier, Jens Hansse & Hala Fattah, *Opening the Doors: Intellectual Life and Academic Conditions in Post-War Baghdad*, Iraqi Observatory, June 2002, at www.ifla.or/V14/admin/iraq2107.pdf. See also Hala Fatah, 'Iraqi universities and libraries: one year after the occupation', *Middle East Studies Association Bulletin*, 38, (1) 2004, pp 24–27.
26 http://www.fafo.no/english/.
27 Les Roberts, Riyadh Lafta, Richard Garfield, Jamal Khudhairi & Gilbert Vurnham, 'Mortality before and after the 2003 invasion of Iraq: cluster sample survey', *Lancet*, 29 October 2004, at http://image.thelancet.com/extras.
28 Naomi Klein, 'Baghdad year zero: pillaging Iraq in pursuit of neocon Utopia', *Harpers*, September 2004, p 44.
29 Carsten Matthäus, 'Zur Kolonie degradiert', *Der Spiegel*, 26 December 2003, at http://www.spiegel.de/wirtschaft/0,1518,278961,00.html.
30 Klein, 'Baghdad year zero'.
31 *Ibid*, pp 44, 48.
32 *Ibid*, pp 48–49.
33 *Ibid*, p 48.
34 Peter W Galbraith, 'Iraq: the bungled transition', *New York Review*, LI (14), 2004, p 70.
35 Herbert Docena, 'Silent battalions of democracy', 3 September 2004, at http://www.zmag.org/content/showarticle.cfm?SectionID = 15&ItemID = 6159.
36 Quotation marks around 'legitimate' appear in the original contract.
37 Docena, 'Silent battalions'.
38 *Ibid.*
39 *Ibid.*
40 In Iraq Allawi is jokingly referred to as 'the Mayor of Baghdad' as a result of his political impotence.
41 Docena, 'Silent battalions'.
42 Alix de la Grange, 'The liberation of Baghdad is not far away', *Asia Times*, 25 June 2004, at http://www.atimes.com/atimes/Middle_East/FF25Ak07.html.
43 Michael A Weinstein, 'The Iraqi National Conference: legitimation failure', 24 August 2004, at http://www.pinr.com/report.php?ac = view_report&report_id = 200.
44 Abbas Kadhim, 'Comment: Al-Sistani's triumph', *Al-Ahram Weekly*, at http://weekly.ahram.org.eg/print/2004/706/re6.htm.
45 Naomi Klein, 'You asked for my evidence, Mr Ambassador. Here it is', *Guardian*, 13 November 2004, at http://www.guardian.co.uk/comment/story/0,,1366278,00.html.
46 The size of the population varies from 250 000 to 350 000, depending upon the source; and the size of the population remaining in Fallujah when the ground assault was initiated also varies. The figure cited here is the most conservative estimate. According to an article by James Cogan, 11 November 2004, on the *World Socialist Web Site* (www.wsws.org/articles/2004/nov2004), the US military estimated that between 100 000 and 150 000 civilians were still in Fallujah when the ground assault was initiated.
47 *USA Today*, 18 November 2004, at www.usatoday.com/news/world/iraq.
48 See Mike Whitney, 'Firebombing Fallujah', *ZNet*, 1 December 2004, at http://www.zmag.org/content/showarticle.cfm?ItemID = 6772; and Joseph Kay, 'After Fallujah's destruction: US occupation force to reach 150 000', *World Socialist Web Site*, 3 December 2004, at www.wsws.org/articles.
49 Michael Schwartz, 'America's sinister plan for Fallujah', *TomDispatch*, as found on *ZNet*, 17 December 2004, at http://www.zmag.org/content/showarticle.cfm?ItemID = 6877.
50 Borzou Daragahi, 'US bombing marks return of Fallujah's displaced people', *Independent*, 24 December 2004, at http://news.independent.co.uk/world/middle_east/story.jsp?story = 595866.
51 See Rory McCarthy & Osama Mansour, 'Seven killed in repeat suicide attack', *Guardian*, 15 December 2004, at http://www.guardian.co.uk/Iraq/Story/0,2763,1374018,00.html.
52 'US army base hit in Mosul', *Al Jazeera.Net*, 22 December 2004, at http://english.aljazeera.net/NR/exeres/7CFA91E9-FEFB-4724-AAD2-D6F764A21858.htm.

53 Syed Saleem Shahzad, 'Mosul attack "an inside job"', *Asia Times*, 25 December 2004, at http://www.atimes.com/atimes/Middle_East/FL25Ak01.html.
54 Eric Schmitt, 'Cargo flights added to cut risky land trips', *New York Times*, 15 December 2004.
55 For further details on nation-building theories, see Raymond Geuss, 'The state', in Geuss, *History and Illusion in Politics*, Cambridge: Cambridge University Press; Georg Sorensen, *Changes in Statehood: The Transformation of International Relations*, New York: Palgrave, 2001, pp 19–20, 75–80; and Jochen Hippler, 'Ethnicity, state, and nation-building',at http://www.jochen-hippler.de/Aufsatze/Nation-Building/nation-building.html.
56 On state-building theory, see Clifford Geert (ed), *Old Societies and New States: The Quest for Modernity in Asia and Africa*, New York: Free Press of Glencoe, 1963; and Francis Fukuyama, *State-Building: Governance and World Order in the 21st Century*, New York: Cornell University Press, 2004.
57 Faleh A Jabar, 'Formative forces in the development of the modern Iraqi state', US Institute for Peace, 15 April 2004, at http://www.usip.org/fellows/reports/2004/0415_jabar.html.
58 Hanna Batatu, *The Old Social Classes and the Revolutionary Movements in Iraq*, Princeton, NJ: Princeton University Press, 1978.
59 Ehsan Ahrari, 'Iyad Allawi: a premier for all reasons', *Asia Times*, 2 June 2004, at http://www.atimes.com/atimes/Middle_East/FF02Ak01.html.
60 Galbraith, 'The bungled transition', pp 70, 72.
61 *Al-Quds Al-Arabi* (London), 19 November 2004.
62 *Azzaman* (Baghdad), 30 November 2004.
63 *Al-Quds Al-Arabi*, 3 December 2004.
64 Hannah Allam, 'Iraq's Shiite leaders disagree on whether new government should be religious or secular', Knight Ridder, 27 December 2004, at http://www.kansas.com/mld/kansas/news/special_-packages/iraq/10508314.htm.
65 Karl Vick, 'Sunni Party pulls out of Iraq vote as doubts grow', *Washington Post*, 28 December 2004, p A01, at http://www.washingtonpost.com/ac2/wp-dyn/A28323-2004Dec27?language = printer.
66 BBC News, 16 September 2004, at www.bbc.co.uk/2/hi/middle_east.
67 *AlJazeera.Net*, 20 November 2004, at http://english.aljazeera.et/NR/exeres; and *The Command Post*, 17 November 2004, at www.command-post.org/2_archives.
68 Khaled Dawoud, 'Arab opinions', *Al-Ahram Weekly*, August 2004, at http://weekly.ahram.org.eg/print/2004/701/in2.htm.
69 'Iraqis respond to the election: commentary from Imad Khadduri, Tahrir Swift, and Munir Chalabi', 1 February 2005, at http://www.occupationwatch.org/article.php?id = 9106.
70 Rohan Pearce, 'Have the elections saved the occupation?', 9 February 2005, at http://www.zmag.org/content/showarticle.cfm?SectionID = 15&ItemID = 7212.
71 Juan Cole, 'Informed comment', 13 February 2005, at http://www.juancole.com. See also *Al-Jazeera News*, at http://www.aljazeera.net/NR/exeres/A44036F0-5090-4EF8-A8DC-DCA76418260A.htm.
72 Nermeen Al-Mufti, 'Iraq's ticking time-bombs', *Al-Ahram Weekly*, 10–16 February 2005, at http://weekly.ahram.org.eg/2005/729/fr2.htm.
73 Juan Cole, 'Informed comment', 18 February 2005, at http://www.juancole.com.
74 www.alrafidayn.com/Story/News/N_29_08_04_1.html.
75 David R Francis, 'US bases in Iraq: sticky politics, hard math', *Christian Science Monitor*, 30 September 2004.

Iraqi Kurdistan: contours of a post-civil war society

MICHIEL LEEZENBERG

ABSTRACT *Iraqi Kurdistan began the road to reconstruction after it became an autonomous region following the 1991 Gulf war. Although many of the difficulties facing post-Saddam Iraq are similar to those facing Iraqi Kurdistan in the early 1990s, the experience of the North cannot be treated mechanically as a model for the country as a whole. The paper traces political and economic developments since 1991 and concludes that many of the factors which led to destabilisation in the North in the 1990s are present today in the rest of Iraq. These include the use of violence to create ethnic and sectarian tensions in pursuit of political ends, dependence on centralised food distribution, and foreign interference. The 1990s also witnessed the emergence of new clientelist networks, which cut across the distinction between state and civil society. The rehabilitation of the oil industry and a geographically fair division of its considerable revenues may hold out the prospect for a peace dividend, but this is not guaranteed unless issues of security, genuine political participation, massive unemployment and clientelism are addressed.*

At first blush, Iraqi Kurdistan seems the neoliberal success story of post-Saddam Iraq. For decades a poor, underdeveloped and conflict-ridden part of the country, it has emerged as by far the most stable, secure and prosperous region. From 1991 onwards a *de facto* independent area under international protection emerged in the north of Iraq, which, despite external interference and internal infighting, has blossomed economically, especially since the start of the UN oil-for-food programme in 1997.

As much as it had suffered in the decades-long Kurdish insurgency, during the Iran–Iraq war and in the aftermath of the 1991 Gulf war, Iraqi Kurdistan hardly sustained any damage in the 2003 war. The only major battle ground in the Kurdish-held areas was the mountainous terrain near Khurmal on the Iraqi–Iranian border, where American aerial bombardments prepared the way for a ground attack against local positions of the Islamist Ansar al-Islam.[1] These and other operations, however, hardly affected the local population. Even the contested city of Kirkuk fell without much of a fight; moreover, its takeover by Kurdish forces led to neither a much-feared showdown between Kurdish *peshmergas* and Turkish troops, nor to an even more anxiously anticipated outburst of inter-ethnic violence. Subsequently power was transferred to the Americans, and attempts at establishing a pluralist local government have been at least in part successful.

Many of the difficulties facing post-Saddam Iraq are eerily familiar to those facing Iraqi Kurdistan in the early 1990s: attempts to create a stable civilian government, eradicating the totalitarian heritage of three decades, and interference from neighbouring countries, to name but a few. Even economic sabotage of the kind seen in Iraq since the 2003 war (which includes pillaging electricity installations and cutting off water supplies, attacks on truck transport, and sabotage of oil transport) is nothing new to anyone who has followed developments in Iraqi Kurdistan in the 1990s. These developments include relatively successful local elections in 1992, from which two parties, the Kurdistan Democratic Party (KDP) headed by Massoud Barzani and the Patriotic Union of Kurdistan (PUK) led by Jalal Talabani emerged victorious; the steady erosion of the elected bodies by a strict 50:50 division between both parties of parliamentary seats, cabinet posts and other positions; the outbreak of several rounds of increasingly destructive infighting between the PUK and KDP in May 1994, exacerbated by the interference of the Baghdad government and neighbouring states; and, following the end of fighting, the political stabilisation of two one-party statelets under the control of the KDP and the PUK, respectively. Under the oil-for-food deal a remarkably flourishing economy emerged, in spite of the continuing UN embargo against Iraq.

At present Iraqi Kurdistan is long past the reconstruction stage. The rehabilitation of basic infrastructural facilities, which in Iraq as a whole has yet to get off the ground, has made considerable progress in the Kurdish-held north since the establishment of a *de facto* independent entity there in 1991. Today infrastructural facilities, such as schools and health care, though not everywhere of first world quality, are certainly quite good by regional standards. Kurds are reported to have come from neighbouring Turkey to Kurdish-held Iraq for medical treatment because of its superior facilities.

It would therefore be tempting to treat the experience of the north mechanically as a model for Iraq as a whole, and even as grounds for a moderate optimism on this score.[2] There are dangers in overemphasising such parallels, however: the differences between the Kurds and the other parts of Iraq are by no means negligible. First, although they have as much reason to be wary of US intentions as any Iraqi, the Kurds have never been ideologically anti-American. Allied presence and protection was and is far less controversial in Iraqi Kurdistan than in the rest of the country: there has never been an armed resistance against the Americans of the kind now seen further South in Iraq. Further, in the Kurdish north radical political Islam was a relatively minor, though by no means negligible, social factor during the 1990s, and was virtually crushed in the wake of the 2003 war; in Iraq as a whole, however, it seems to be not only the predominant form of political discourse, but also the major vehicle for the articulation of opposition against the US and other foreign troops among the Shi'ite and Sunni Arab population.

In the violent atmosphere of post-Saddam Iraq the question of whether the country can be turned into a liberal democracy under the rule of law is becoming increasingly academic. In the shorter run the question of public security is vastly more urgent; but, even here, the situation is highly volatile and unpredictable. For this reason, I will largely abstain from speculation about what might be plausible scenarios for a future Iraq, and instead restrict my discussion to the enduring or structural features of present-day Iraqi Kurdistan. Specifically, I will discuss whether there are any lasting effects resulting from the decades-long Kurdish insurgency and its suppression, the eight-year Iran–Iraq war, the Gulf war and the uprisings and sanctions regime in its aftermath, and the Kurdish infighting that raged from 1994 to 1997. Iraq Kurdistan had been solidly integrated into Iraq's evolving economy and polity until, and in several respects even after, the 1991 establishment of *de facto* Kurdish self-rule. For reasons of space, I will not discuss pre-1991 influences and post-1991 parallels in detail, but focus on regional developments since the early 1990s.[3]

From Stalinist state to network society?

Affluent oil-producing states have always constituted something of an anomaly for dependency theorists, who tend to depict dependent or peripheral economies as wholly derivative from, and kept deliberately poor by, first world capital. In general, Iraq had an unusual status among developing nations: it had a relatively strong state, an elaborate bureaucracy and a government that because of its expanding oil income was relatively autonomous from society. It thus constituted what conventional Marxist-inspired analyses would call a 'rentier state', as its income derived from foreign capital acquired through the export of non-labour-intensive raw materials rather than from the productive activities of its own working class. The differences between Iraq and other canonical rentier states, however, even regional ones like Egypt and Syria, are as significant as their similarities.[4] In general, traditional political economy approaches tend to represent the economy as a more unambiguously determining force than it is. For example, Faleh Abdul Jabar argues that rentier states are more likely to pursue their foreign policies by aggressive rather than diplomatic means:[5] However, Saudi Arabia and the smaller Gulf monarchies are as much rentier states as was Saddam's Iraq, yet their domestic and foreign policies have been far less violent and destructive than were Iraq's. Iraq's systematic use of violence at home and abroad should be seen not in terms of political or economic necessity or expediency but as a *style* of governing which was articulated in terms of an obsession with sovereignty, treason and espionage, and which was primarily inspired by Stalinist practices.

Likewise, important analyses like Chaudhry (2002) threaten to dissolve the specifics of the Iraqi state in the generalities of the contemporary economic and political order. Chaudhry criticises the widespread assumption that the Iraqi state of the 1970s and 1980s, because of its oil wealth, needed no broad social base. Despite all its repressive apparatus, she argues, the Baathist state was not able to control or regulate the forces of the internationalised market, as it could not, for example, durably attract capital from Iraqi expatriates during the 1990s.[6] According to this analysis, the Iraqi state was at once the only protection against an unbridled capitalism, and a major source of oppression in itself—a paradox she sees as central to the modern state at large (2002: 262).

Inspired by another approach, one could argue that Iraqi Kurdistan, and Iraq as a whole, are part of a 'regional conflict formation' like Afghanistan, the Great Lakes region or the Horn of Africa (cf Rubin, 2003), witness the political and economic spill-over of internal conflicts across state boundaries, the weakening or even collapse of the state, and the emergence of a shadow economy and even shadow state. The notion of a regional conflict formation was introduced as a counterweight to more traditional, state-biased approaches; it seems fruitful for Iraq, but should not ignore some of its rather distinct features. First, the state in Iraq (as in its neighbours Iran and Turkey) has traditionally been strong, well entrenched, and centralised; second, as I will argue below, the infrastructure-dependent but lucrative oil industry in Iraq has in the past been a major incentive for striving towards a stable and state-like polity.

What, then, was the character of the Iraqi state under Saddam? The conventional notion is that it was turned into a Stalinist one-party totalitarian state with a pervasive apparatus of surveillance and repression that remained largely intact even during the 1990s. Unlike Stalin, however, Saddam did not purge all regional and especially clan and kinship ties from the state apparatus: on the contrary, his closer and more distant relatives formed the backbone not only of his regime but also of the core or new economic elites. This style of government has repeatedly been compared to the management of a mafia clan (see eg Perthes, 2002: 278).

There is another way in which tribalism is important in Iraqi power. The absolute concentration of power and the permanent and omnipresent apparatus of surveillance and repression may correspond to the self-image the Baath wished to project, especially in the cities; but the real articulation of power relations was always more complex, especially in the countryside. In the 1980s the regime strengthened, and in part even created, (quasi)tribal structures in the Kurdish north as a means of creating irregular troops for the northern Iraqi countryside rather than diverting military personnel from the war with Iran. In the early 1990s this retribalisation policy, which involved a partial privatisation of the state monopoly on violence, was extended to Iraq as a whole.[7]

Post-1991 Iraq under Saddam developed a form of crony capitalism, where the new economic elites were in part protected by tribal and mafia-like networks that could use violence to protect their markets. In many respects the same situation holds in the north. It would of course be grossly unfair to suggest that the two Kurdish statelets have merely reproduced the Baathist model; life in the Kurdish-held north is incomparably more prosperous and less precarious than it was under Saddam. Nevertheless, the emerging societies and economies do display significant structural similarities.

The relative peace and prosperity of present-day Iraqi Kurdistan are unprecedented; one could even say with some justification that it is this stability, rather than armed conflict and economic underdevelopment, which would seem the anomaly. Since at least the early 1960s the region has suffered severely under successive, and in part overlapping, forms of large-scale armed conflict. The successive stages of insurgency and repression since 1961 have affected the whole region. The 1980–88 war with Iran primarily affected the border areas, but the counterinsurgency operations carried out in its wake led to the destruction of thousands of villages and even several larger cities, like Halabja and Qala Diza. The brutal crushing of the uprising in the aftermath of the 1991 Gulf war caused an enormous (if largely temporary) population displacement and widespread looting; and, finally, infighting between the Kurdish parties between 1994 and 1997 caused further havoc. The questions I will address below include whether the region's current prosperity has developed in spite or rather because of these conflicts; where this prosperity comes from; how it is divided among the population, and how secure the region's current position is.

Given the region's violent past, it makes sense to take open, violent conflict not as a temporary or anomalous deviation from a normal form of society as 'civil', but as a permanent risk or condition of social life. This is not the place for extended theoretical discussion, but in different areas—like ethics and social, political and legal theory—society has been fruitfully conceptualised as based not on the end of conflict as liberal theories would have it, but as irreducibly involving conflict or antagonism of one form or another.[8] In Iraq's highly conflictual recent history the uncritical usage of such apparently neutral liberal oppositions—between the official and the informal economy, between legitimate rule and oppression, between legal trade and smuggling and between state power and crime—may actually lead to the tacit introduction of all kinds of misleading normative assumptions of civility and legitimacy.[9] In such a constellation it may be the stability and legitimacy of any authority that calls for explanation as much as any conflict or shift of power. The legitimacy of, say, the Baath regime or the respective Kurdish regional administrations, not to mention the local predominance of warlords or tribal leaders can always be contested; a central question for conflict approaches is why such challenges emerge only relatively rarely. In this respect, 1990s Iraqi Kurdistan was a fascinating if disturbing laboratory, showing how quickly power relations can reconfigure. In early 1992 civilians could still challenge the authority of armed militiamen or *peshmerga* with relative ease but, a mere two years later, during the party infighting, it had become much more difficult (if not dangerous) to do so openly.

In such an antagonistic constellation, in other words, the main question is not so much when power is challenged, but rather when authority is perceived, or succeeds in presenting itself, as legitimate at all. As an analytical tool, I will therefore employ Charles Tilly's provocative thesis that once one abstracts away from questions of legitimacy, the activities of states and organised criminal gangs do not differ all that much (Tilly, 1986). Analytically, activities like taxation, ie the extraction or extortion of money in exchange for protection against real or imagined dangers (which may in fact be created or imagined by the very agents subsequently offering protection), and the self-arrogated right to wage war or more generally to use or even monopolise violence, are common to both states and criminal gangs. The difference between them lies not in what they are doing, but in whether they are perceived as having the right to do it.

Politics and economics since 1991

The economy of 1970s Iraq, based on Eastern bloc models, was state-driven and quasi-socialist. In the early 1980s Iraq developed a war economy in the classical sense: increased state intervention and industrial production actually strengthened the labour force and encouraged the participation of women, and even unintentionally stimulated the independent trade organisations. However, from 1983 onwards in the agricultural sector, and from 1987 in the urban industries, the regime started a drive to dismantle this state-led economy. Even before the 1990 crisis and the ensuing war the Iraqi welfare state underwent a rigorously and painfully applied economic shock therapy. This shock therapy, however, was but briefly pursued; it was interrupted by the social and economic havoc it caused, and even more by the occupation of Kuwait and the ensuing sanctions and war (cf Chaudhry, 1991; 2002).

The Kurdish-held north was of course an integral (if in some respects 'peripheral') part of the Iraqi economy before the uprising; but, even afterwards, it maintained a kind of symbiosis with it. The 1991 establishment of a Safe Haven along the Turkey – Iraq border contributed to the creation of a juridically anomalous *de facto* independent entity: it was no longer part of Iraq, yet not recognised as distinct; the UN Security Council Resolution 688 that sanctioned it was interpreted as setting a precedent for humanitarian intervention, yet in fact it protected Turkish state interests against Kurdish refugees (cf Leezenberg, 1997). By the summer of 1991 most refugees had returned to their homes, many of which had been looted by government forces. An uneasy balance of power was reached between Iraqi government forces and Kurdish insurgent troops and after several bloody clashes, the Iraqi regime withdrew its military and other personnel from most of the Autonomous Region in October 1991. At the same time, it imposed an economic blockade, gradually reducing oil supplies and centrally distributed foodstuffs.[10]

Next to the temporary dislocations caused by the 1991 war there were more enduring demographic problems, mostly resulting from the conflict between the central government and the Kurdish insurgency. There were not only the *mujamma'ât* or relocation camps, where hundreds of thousands of deported villagers had been reduced to a non-productive life of total dependence on government handouts; there was also a steady influx of Kurds and Turkomans, especially from Kirkuk, as a result of government policies of ethnically based expulsions that went back to the mid-1970s.

Apart from the large numbers of internally displaced persons from Kirkuk, Sinjar and Khanaqin, the Kurdish-held region harboured considerable numbers of refugees from neighbouring countries, notably Iranian Kurds and Fayli Kurds. The latter had been expelled from Iraq in 1971 and 1980 for allegedly having Iranian rather than Iraqi nationality; many of them were forcibly repatriated by Iran to the Kurdish parts of Iraq in the course of the 1990s. Further, in 1993 several thousand Kurds fled Turkey and established a camp at Atrush in Kurdish-held territory, which was subsequently transferred to Makhmur further south.[11] Finally, in some of the more remote mountainous areas there are pockets of remaining—and rather demoralised— PKK fighters. It is relatively unlikely that either Turkey or the USA will mount any large-scale military operation against them; if there were an amnesty perceived as fair, the vast majority of them would probably return to Turkey.

By far the largest flow of refugees during the 1990s, of course, was out of Iraq and towards western Europe. One main route of transportation ran through Turkey and the Mediterranean; another led through the Ukraine and other parts of the former Soviet Union. In 2001 and 2002, just before the American-led war against Iraq, there was a discussion in the Netherlands and other European countries about whether northern Iraq was safe enough for the involuntary repatriation of rejected asylum seekers. The two Iraqi Kurdish administrations did not dismiss these proposals outright, but emphasised that they did not have the financial and other infrastructural means to accommodate returnees without substantial support from abroad.[12]

Apart from these groups the need for emergency relief was relatively short; but it proved a hard task to get from short term-relief to longer-term reconstruction. There were not only political factors like the UN sanctions against Iraq, Baghdad's blockade of the north, and the interference of neighbouring states; there also were structural factors, such as urbanisation and the long-term decline of Iraq's agricultural sector within the international market. It proved difficult to reverse the long-term trend towards urbanisation: for years agricultural activity had been undermined by the Iraqi government's agrarian policies (in part inefficient, in part destructive), and especially by the system of subsidies on basic foodstuffs. Following the imposition of an internal blockade in 1991, transport from local production centres became prohibitively expensive. Misguided policies, protracted conflicts and the international market, not to mention the enticements of an oil economy, have not wholly destroyed the local agriculture; but they have seriously jeopardised the prospect of self-sufficient agriculture, in Iraqi Kurdistan as elsewhere in Iraq.[13] With the industrial sector the situation was even worse. The Kurdish north had never witnessed a degree of industrialisation even remotely comparable to that of the Baghdad area and, following the imposition of sanctions, what industry there was suffered further because of a lack of spare parts.

The emergence of a new regional industrial sector, therefore, was always unlikely; Iraq's oil production was and remained the major source of income. None of the country's major oil fields had come under Kurdish control during the 1991 uprising but a lively and lucrative transit trade in petrol products from Iraq to Turkey developed afterwards, mostly going through the KDP-held Ibrahim Khalil checkpoint. Obviously this form of oil export was officially forbidden by the UN sanctions regime, and ruled out by Baghdad's internal blockade, but it was in fact tolerated if not encouraged by local authorities. Moreover, the petrol trade was increasingly 'privatised': in a sense it replaced the state supplies of oil to the north, at far greater cost to the local population. On the Iraqi side, Saddam's son Uday was in control of this privatised smuggling; on the Kurdish side, Barzani's nephew Nechirwan (who subsequently was to become prime minister of the Arbil-based cabinet) appears to have steadily increased his control over the transit trade. The oil-for-food programme does not seem to have reduced the income generated by this smuggling to any significant degree. More generally, the rapidly expanding (semi-legal) import of luxury goods formed an increasingly visible reflection of rising prosperity. Especially in Duhok, near the Turkish border, huge shopping malls emerged; trade opportunities were so promising that, in June 2004, an Iraqi Kurdistan trade forum was organised in London.[14] The late 1990s also saw the re-emergence of the local tourism sector: the Kurdish region, with its numerous summer resorts in the mountains, had long had, but not yet realised, a promising economic potential in this field. Between 200 000 and 300 000 tourists were expected in the summer of 2004, mostly from the Arab parts of Iraq and from neighbouring Arab countries.[15] Needless to say, however, only a small minority of the local Kurdish population benefited from these new developments: although they did yield increased employment opportunities in construction and services, they primarily led to an enormous increase in income disparities.

At the political level there were significant and serious attempts to create a civilian and pluralist government for the region (especially through the May 1992 elections). These were equally hampered by a lack of international recognition of the elected bodies, and by the emergence of a form of parallel government by the relatively richly endowed foreign (or foreign-funded) ngos.[16] The equal division of both parliamentary seats and government posts between the KDP and PUK provided ample opportunity for corruption, and increasingly for competition between these two parties elected into the regional government.

The revenues of the transit trade in oil were an enormous source of wealth, and hence a potential bone of contention: disagreement over the division of these revenues was one of the main causes of Kurdish infighting. The outbreak of clashes between, primarily, the KDP and PUK in May 1994 should be seen, however, not as a victory of the executive over the legislative, but as a victory of the party politburos over the elected government (cf Leezenberg, 1997). The infighting not only led to the withdrawal of many foreign ngos; it also increasingly affected life in the cities; Arbil especially descended into an ever-greater chaos and anarchy. Fights around the Kesnezan checkpoint led to the repeated shelling, and even the looting, of Arbil's nearby main hospital. Local strongmen could set up their own checkpoints in the city, and kidnappings and other forms of extortion reached a high point.[17]

In this period there was a serious danger of the region sliding into a Lebanon-style social anarchy, in which urban and rural warlords would violently dominate life. The dramatic climax was undoubtedly the KDP's military takeover of Arbil with the aid of the Iraqi army on 31 August 1996; however, somewhat surprisingly perhaps, the fighting abated in the second half of the 1990s. It quickly became clear that the KDP, by taking not only Arbil but also Sulaimaniya, had overstretched its military capacities; the equally rapid recapture of Sulaimaniya by PUK troops and the establishment of a new demarcation line just east of Arbil proved that neither party had the military means to eliminate the other.

Direct and high-level US mediation led to the formal cessation of hostilities in the so-called 'Washington agreement' signed in September 1998. Both party leaders pledged to work towards the re-establishment of the elected regional parliament and government. But nothing of the sort happened. Despite weekly 'normalisation talks' between the two parties from late 1997 to just before the 2003 war, few if any substantial steps (other than the exchange of prisoners of war) were taken towards the reconvening of the regional parliament elected in 1992 and the reunification of the two administrations.[18]

It was not war fatigue or US diplomatic pressure, however, that brought an end to the open conflict and social anarchy of the mid-1990s. Another—and perhaps decisive—factor was the implementation of the oil-for-food agreement from 1997 onwards. Of its revenues 13% were earmarked for the Kurdish-held region. The allocation and implementation processes were slow, inefficient and corruption-prone; nonetheless, the programme proved a strong incentive to ceasing hostilities, especially as it involved lucrative contracts for local distribution and infrastructural projects. Through the new contracting business the two parties further consolidated their positions in the territories under their military control, even though the allocation of resources was not strictly in their hands but in those of the UN officials and even the Iraqi regime.

In retrospect the implementation of the programme appears to mark a turning point for the better; one cannot help wondering whether this reintegration through oil revenues might not constitute an optimistic scenario for the future of Iraq as a whole. It should be kept in mind, however, that whatever the undoubted benefits of the oil-for-food programme, it did not solve any of the underlying structural weaknesses of the regional and national economy. For decades Iraq had had a centralised food distribution system; in October 1991 this system was discontinued in the Kurdish-held north, and by the mid-1990s it was in danger of being discontinued in the rest of the country. Under the oil-for-food scheme it got a new lease of life. In a sense the programme extended the phase of relief aid at the expense of efforts to rehabilitate a self-sufficient economy: to some extent it has actually undermined the rehabilitation of agricultural production. More generally, it has had contradictory aspects and effects regarding state sovereignty: it undermined the Iraqi state's sovereignty over its own population, yet strengthened the regime; it institutionalised the special status of the north, yet gave the Baghdad administration more leverage there.

The institutionalisation of patronage

Despite its distinct course of development, then, Iraqi Kurdistan shares many structural features with the country as a whole. It is therefore worth looking at the character of state–society relations in the region. Contemporary Iraqi Kurdistan has no recognised state, and is not quite a rentier state (or quasi-state) in the classical dependency–theoretical sense of the word, as the wealth generated appears not so much the result of the extraction of non-industrial raw materials, but rather of transit trade. It may be more useful to qualify it as (to coin a term of art) a 'post-civil war society', in which the heritage of domestic conflict has strengthened and even institutionalised patronage relations, primarily through the maintenance of different forms of scarcity. One open question is whether this reflects the more general demise of the state in its classical form, and the concomitant rise of networks. Has Iraqi Kurdistan become a 'network society' (Castells, 1996), reflecting the weakening of the state as a general historical trend of the information age?

The importance of networks of patronage has indeed increased since 1991. In 2003 unemployment for Iraq as a whole was estimated at some 50%; there is little reason to believe that Iraqi Kurdistan was essentially better off. Typical for the region is an extreme economic inequality. According to UN figures, in the summer of 2002 some 50% of households in Iraqi Kurdistan had to survive on the equivalent of US$25 a month; this sub-poverty income was supplemented by a food basket worth $50 every month, financed by the oil-for-food programme.[19] The enduring poverty and dependence of the bulk of the population provided the opportunity structure for widespread patronage and corruption from above. Traditionally anthropological studies describe patronage as informal and perceived as basically illegitimate. The parties' persistent attempts to monopolise, and indeed institutionalise, clientelist networks suggests that the formal–informal distinction, or even the concept of patron–client relations may not be the most useful here.[20] Both regions nominally have multiparty systems; but even the opposition parties are actually on the payroll of the main parties.[21] Apart from the Islamist Yekgirtuy islami or Islamic League, which weakened considerably following the 11 September 2001 assaults, no serious mass opposition movements have emerged. Before 2005 KDP candidates were not allowed to run in local elections in PUK territory, and vice versa.

It may be that this institutionalised patronage has weakened the chances for the emergence of a new social contract, that is, an ultimately voluntary and non-violent form of pluralist political association in the region, and in Iraq as a whole. In Eastern Europe one of the longer- term effects of communist rule was an enduring mistrust of the state and its institutions; where resources are supplied by the state, these tend to be seen as a source of private profit rather than of common good. At present it is hard to say whether and how strongly a similar attitude obtains among the Iraqi population as a whole.[22] In the Kurdish north decades of totalitarian rule, corruption and violent repression may have durably undermined the very idea of state legitimacy as founded on a social contract of sorts. There seems to be a widespread perception that institutionalised clientelism, and having to bribe officials for various kinds of civil services, is, if not the norm for legitimate government, then at least the normal factual state of affairs. People may be dissatisfied with the authorities in power, but they often not only lack the means and the media for voicing their protests; they are also too financially dependent on the parties to engage in any genuine public oppositional activities. In late 2003 a 'referendum movement' emerged which by early 2004 claimed to have gathered the signatures of almost two million Iraqi Kurds, but this movement was at least as much a sign of opposition against the Kurdish leadership as of a wish to secede from Iraq. By early October 2004 the referendum movement had organised massive demonstrations in several major Kurdish cities.[23]

The post-1991 region has witnessed a rapid and relatively smooth reconfiguration of networks and change of elites. The previous generation of local economic elites had emerged in the course of the 1980s; it included tribal leaders like those of the Surchis and the Herkis, who had profited especially from the lucrative contracting business and headed internationalised business empires as much as 'traditional' tribes. Consequently some of the infighting between 1994 and 1997, including the KDP's notorious destruction of the traditional Surchi stronghold of Kilekan just before its takeover of Arbil in the summer of 1996, should not be seen in terms of quasi-tribal conflicts but rather as an attempt to monopolise and secure regional strategic interests (especially the supply lines between the KDP heartlands in the north, the Spilk military base and the city of Arbil).

An analytically distinct but partly overlapping kind of network, in Iraqi Kurdistan as in Iraq at large, is formed by the various organised crime rackets. Not all of these networks are politically or tribally defined, but there is certainly an exchange between them. The convenient self-image of many Iraqis is that, at least until the 1970s, Iraq had a relatively low rate of both common and organised crime. This does not match very well with the well known social anarchy of the late Ottoman age and, of course, smuggling has been a major activity in the Kurdish region as long as there have been international borders. But it is undoubtedly true that the 1970s and 1980s marked a new phase in both the development of an informal economy and the growth of organised crime. A first important factor was the creation in the 1970s of a highly inefficient and corruption-prone Eastern-bloc style state-driven economy, funded by the rapidly increasing oil revenues. Second, the war economy of the 1980s created further opportunities for a shadow economy: the entirely artificial official exchange rate, state controls on food prices and on the import of cigarettes and alcohol made black-market activities all the more lucrative. It was primarily the existing power elites that profited from this situation.

Following the state collapse in the north in 1991 and in the whole of Iraq in 2003, various tribal, political and criminal groups engaged in acts of economic sabotage, or in what Bozarslan (1996) has called 'predation'. However, there were also other, more intrusive and violent forms of crime, like the kidnapping of foreign truck drivers, reconstruction workers, security personnel and even diplomats. In present-day Iraq many of these kidnappings have an ostensibly political motivation, but as often as not they (also) aim at extorting substantial ransoms. Moreover, such kidnappings have been taking place in Iraq on a large scale for over a decade, and even now target rich Iraqi civilians rather than foreigners. In other words, there is a clear overlap between governments or political movements and organised crime in activities, tactics and in part even personnel.

Another, and probably more important, illegal or semi-legal activity is smuggling. In the local context the demarcation between smuggling and regular trade, or between legitimate taxation and illegitimate extortion, becomes problematic. For example, the massive and lucrative oil transports through Habur gate between Turkey and Iraq were in violation of UN sanctions, but the KDP administration regulated and hence legitimised it by imposing customs duties. At first, non-petrol smuggling centred around cigarettes, alcohol, pornography, narcotics and luxury technological goods; in the course of the 1990s, however, there was a steady rise in the trade in passports, exit visas and refugees. At rates of up to $5000 per person, such transports became an increasingly lucrative option, and carried far lower risks of long-term imprisonment for the personnel involved than did drug trafficking, for example.

The large-scale transport of refugees, involving boats carrying hundreds of Iraqis at a time across the Mediterranean, required a high degree of international co-operation. Yet, despite this high degree of internationalisation, the traffickers apparently formed loose networks rather than strictly hierarchical organized criminal gangs. Further, they cultivated good relations with the people they transported, and appeared to be relatively autonomous from other forms of organised criminal activity. Finally, they were strongly intertwined with the legal economy, and with different parts of the state apparatus (especially the police and immigration officials) in the various countries involved.[24]

It seems, then, that the post-civil war economy and the forms of scarcity created before, during and after the different conflicts, have facilitated not only the rise and even institutionalisation of clientelist relations, but also the formation and strengthening of networks which overlap, but by no means coincide, with party hierarchies. In this respect Iraqi Kurdistan is probably atypical of a (post)conflict zone, in that a more-or-less functional state bureaucracy has remained in place or re-emerged, and a strong financial incentive developed against the continuation of large-scale civil conflict.[25] The region has maintained an indirect dependence on Iraq's oil income, and shown a paradoxical rehabilitation of the Iraqi state food distribution system under a UN umbrella.

Conclusion: balance and prospects

Iraqi Kurdistan shares many structural features with the rest of the country. Many of the factors that in the 1990s contributed to destabilisation in the north (protracted foreign interference, a weak elected government, problems with the demobilisation of fighters, economic scarcity, an increase in organised forms of (semi)illegal activities, and a pervasive sense of insecurity among the population) at present also pertain in the rest of Iraq. But can developments in Iraqi Kurdistan since 1991 serve as a model, or at least as a plausible scenario for the post-war reconstruction of Iraq as a whole? Moreover, what will be the future relations between the Kurdish region and the rest of the country? And more generally, are there any broader theoretical implications of the experience of the Kurdish-held north?

First, in the north, conflict has contributed to the creation of the very scarcities and dangers the conflict partners could then offer protection against. Or, to put the point differently, violence has been one of a variety of strategies the parties have used to extend a grip on the territory they wished to monopolise. The current violence in central Iraq may in part reflect a similar struggle for political and economic power.

A second point concerns the relations between the state, society and networks. Iraqi Kurdistan has proceeded rather further on the road towards a market economy, but its continuing dependence on centralised food handouts suggests that the liberalisation of the economy can at most be partial. Moreover, the power elites simultaneously try to monopolise civil society through party patronage, and to restructure the state apparatus through ties of kinship, especially in the higher echelons. These different networks have partly overlapping personnel, but are by no means wholly identical, with the party hierarchies. Thus, economic success in the Kurdish region was and is undoubtedly facilitated by affiliation or friendly contacts with one of the parties or its higher-ranking officials, but does not entirely depend on it: the old economic elites have perhaps lost their privileged status, but they have not wholly disappeared. In short, institutionalised patronage cuts across the familiar state – civil society opposition. Moreover, if the above argument holds, the emergence of clientelist networks is at least as important as the matter of state sovereignty. This renders somewhat theoretical the pervasive talk of Iraqi sovereignty under occupation.

A third point concerns the stereotype of Iraq's fragile inter-ethnic relations. Whatever contemporary ethnic or sectarian tensions there are, they are the result not of primordial sentiments, but of confrontational policies and antagonisms deliberately created or strengthened by political parties, by the Iraqi regime or even by neighbouring states;[26] moreover, they function in a radically transformed privatised economy. Nevertheless, the risk of violent inter-ethnic conflict is increasingly serious, especially in Kirkuk. The root cause of the rising tensions is not so much ethnic antagonism as such, but rather uncontrolled attempts to reverse the legacy of decades of ethnic cleansing, exacerbated by interference from neighbouring states. The Kurdish parties pursue contradictory policies: they have made valiant efforts to contain violent confrontations but, at the same time, they have been trying to create facts on the ground by conducting media campaigns and giving financial rewards to Kurdish families trying to return to their former dwellings (probably as much a sign of continuing KDP–PUK rivalry as of purely ethnic policies).[27] The reverse tendency seems to loom in the Sunni Arab triangle, especially in places like Fallujah, where during the siege of March 2004 rebels appear to have deliberately drawn the fighting towards the Kurdish quarter of town; some Kurds where actually told to leave the city (to which they had been deported under Saddam). Similar reports of ethnic cleansing of Kurdish 'traitors' have emerged from nearby Samarra.[28] Large-scale pogroms or ethnic cleansing of Kurds from Arab-majority areas or vice versa could be a distinct possibility, if Kurdish relations with their Arab and other countrymen were to turn sour; but they are relatively unlikely. First, while the Kurdish parties at times hint at the possibility of secession, this seems to be a negotiation tactic rather than a seriously contemplated option. The actual likelihood of secession of a single Kurdish region is relatively small, given the region's current division in two and the rivalries between the two Kurdish leaders in both the past and the present. Second, ethnic animosity in Iraq more often than not comes from above (and at times even abroad) and relatively rarely starts at grassroots level. Popular sentiments are at times certainly antagonistic, but they are not consistently strong or violent, and can probably be contained if the political will and effort are present among the leadership of the different parties involved.

A final word about the prospects for a new Iraqi social contract. The Kurds, with good reason, distrust the more radical forms of Arab nationalism, and its more recent reappearance in the guise of Sunni or Shi'ite Islamism. But Kurdish nationalist sentiments do not (yet) seem a very potent political factor (as opposed to social sentiment): at the time of writing, it seems unlikely that either Kurdish leader will provide any genuine support for the referendum movement. Given the relative unimportance of constitutional arrangements in Iraq's recent past, it is not very likely that the drafting of a new constitution will in and of itself secure the loyalty of the Kurds, or, for that matter, of any Iraqi population group. It is perhaps more likely that a geographically fair division of oil revenues would contribute to the relative stability and peacefulness of the country. In oil-rich Iraq, as earlier in Iraqi Kurdistan, the dividends of peace are substantially bigger than the profits of war. In this sense, too, Iraq may be unlike other war or civil-war zones. Compare, for example, the continuing instability in the Great Lakes region of Africa, or Afghanistan, where the production or extraction of illegal goods requires little or no industrialised infrastructure. In the past Iraq's oil income has often been a source of conflict and division but, when its distribution is even and institutionally secured, it may also be a source of stability and integration, regardless of whether it takes the shape of a nationalised oil industry or of a shareholder society, as Jabar (2004) has suggested. The increasingly violent insurgents seems to realise this, witness their deliberate targeting of the oil sector. It would be a major error, however, to see the rehabilitation of the oil sector as a panacea for Iraq. As long as public security remains absent, unemployment remains high and genuine political participation remains restricted, there will be a permanent potential for social unrest. The apparent stability of institutionalised patronage relations should not blind us to the many who feel they have been left out, or have received less than their fair share. The post-conflict constellation of Iraqi Kurdistan should not be mistaken for a stable and harmonious liberal, or neoliberal, polity.

Notes

An earlier version of this paper was presented at the international workshop '(Post) Conflict and the Remaking of Place and Space: Economies, Institutions and Networks', Khartoum, 1–2 September 2004. I thank the workshop participants, in particular Hamit Bozarslan, for their comments and criticisms.

1 The subsequent re-emergence of Ansar in other parts of Iraq is not necessarily the return of the same unified and coherent group, but more likely the reconfiguring of a loose and wide coalition of radical Islamic individuals and groups with broadly comparable ideals and tactics. Moreover, as I will argue below, there is a significant overlap between religiously or nationalistically legitimated armed resistance and more strictly economically driven forms of organised crime.

2 Indeed, some Iraqi policy makers are at present looking at the Kurdish experience to learn from its mistakes. Thus, Ghassan Atiyyah (personal communication) informs me that the electoral working group studied the 1992 regional elections in order to avoid repeating its main shortcomings (such as leaving the leaders out of the electoral process, creating a polarising effect because of the high threshold, and different ways of manipulating the outcome) on a nation-wide scale.

3 For an analysis of the social and economic impact of the Kurdish region's long-term integration within Baathist Iraq, see Leezenberg (1997).

4 Likewise, Henry & Springborg (2001: ch 4) describe Saddam's Iraq as a 'bunker state' comparable to Algeria or Syria, ruled by a narrowly based power elite, which out of a lack of legitimacy governs through coercion rather than consent. But not only did the Baathist state in Iraq create a mass base by greatly expanding party membership, its use of violence was also driven by ideology as much as by any perceived lack of legitimacy.

5 Faleh Abdul Jabar, report summary, 'Formative forces in the development of the modern Iraqi state', available at http://www.usip.org/fellows/reports/2004/0415_jabar.html.

6 It is unclear how far the Kurdish region was different in this respect. For much of the 1990s the region saw a massive influx of foreign currency from relatives abroad (in a financial flow that was largely independent of the equally important foreign humanitarian aid), but no precise figures are available on the extent and development of this informal financial traffic.

7 Baram (1997) describes the regime's policies of the 1990s but ignores those of the 1980s. It is not entirely correct, either, to describe the resulting tribal and other clientelist relations as 'primordial', as does, for example, Faleh Abdul Jabar (cf his 'Formative forces in the development of the modern Iraqi state'). Talk of 'primordial' as opposed to 'modern' states proceeds from rather misleadingly unilinear modernisation-theoretical assumptions, and prejudices an adequate understanding of the actual mechanisms at work, which are highly contingent, novel and by no means 'traditional'.

8 Cf, among others, Stuart Hampshire's (2000) view of justice-as-conflict in ethics and Carl Schmitt's (1976) idea of the friend–enemy distinction as the criterion of the political. See also and especially Foucault (2002).

9 Here I will not discuss the question of whether such a provocative, but rather one-sided, conflict model of society fits Iraq in all its complexity; I merely use it as a heuristic tool. Neither should this position be taken as legitimising or trivialising the numerous, and at times horrendous, human rights violations and other acts of violence the region has witnessed in the past few decades.

10 For a table tracing the progressive reduction of state supplies, see Hafeed (1993: 40).

11 Turkey's accusation that this camp tolerated PKK activities is not entirely baseless, as UNHCR repeatedly objected to the open usage of PKK flags and other symbols in the camp. In the wake of the 1995 Turkish invasion the refugees were moved to government-held Makhmur, where they have remained ever since. At the time of writing these refugees are quite unwilling to be repatriated, as camp life is relatively prosperous and allows for education in Kurdish rather than Turkish (see, eg, IRIN-Asia, 12 May 2004).

12 In June 2001 the prime minister of the KDP-led regional government, Nechirvan Barzani, visited the Dutch ministry of Foreign Affairs for talks on these matters.

13 According to the Kurdistan Development Corporation, chaired by KDP veteran Siyamand Banna, annual agricultural production in Iraqi Kurdistan had risen to 736 000 tons of wheat and 375 000 tons of barley by 2002, compared with 142 000 and 44 000 tons, respectively, in 1989. KDC News, 19 March 2004, at www.kurdistancorporation.com. However, these figures may be overly optimistic in the light of the continuing undermining of agriculture by the Oil-for-food distribution of subsidised foodstuffs.
14 Present-day Kurdish business elites are oriented towards, and have a foothold and representatives in, the UK even more than the USA.
15 Nick Birch, 'Tourism thrives in Kurdish north', *Washington Times*, 8 August 2004, at http://www.washtimes.com/world/20040807-112348-1747r.htm.
16 For a more detailed overview of the (partly unintended) consequences of the international humanitarian aid effort, see Leezenberg (2000).
17 Significantly, the mid-1990s also seem to be the period when in government-held Iraq social anarchy reached a high point, and organised crime was at its strongest. Personal communication, local observers.
18 All this renders largely theoretical the widespread talk in the Western media of Kurdish secession and the possibly violent reactions of the rest of the population and especially neighbouring states. The new party-backed elites in the Kurdish north are less interested in establishing an independent landlocked country than in maintaining their existing privileges.
19 Quoted by Jim Muir, 'Kurds grit teeth for US strike', BBC World Service, at http://news.bbc.co.uk/2/hi/world/middle_east/2074787.stm.
20 I have criticized the assumption that patronage is by definition informal in Leezenberg (forthcoming).
21 Interview with local opposition intellectual. Another local informant, a middle-ranking PUK official, unabashedly acknowledged that the cessation of hostilities between his party and the Islamic movement was in part secured by monthly payments to the Islamists.
22 Cf Oxford Research International, *National Survey of Iraq*, February 2004, at http://news.bbc.co.uk/nol/shared/bsp/hi/pdfs/15_03_04_iraqsurvey.pdf.
23 WKI news summary, 8 October 2004. According to other sources, however, the movement started out as a PUK initiative intended to put pressure on the KDP, and subsequently gave both parties increased room for manoeuvre on the national stage.
24 For an overview of refugee trafficking centring around Turkey, see Akinbingöl (2003: esp chs 6–8).
25 Again the comparison with other experiences is instructive. Beatrice Hibou (1999) argues that neoliberal reforms have failed in Africa because they ignored the existence of an informal 'shadow state' as an economic actor. In Iraqi Kurdistan the shadow state has in a sense merged with, or been integrated into, a continuing or rehabilitated state apparatus.
26 Thus, over the past decade, both Turkey and Iran have at different times supported various different actors in Iraqi Kurdistan, such as the KDP, the PUK, various Turkmen groups, the staunchly Sunni Islamic Movement of Iraqi Kurdistan and some of its more radical offshoots (most famously Jund/Ansar al-Islam), and Moqtada al-Sadr's Shi'ite movement. As long as there is no strong and stable government in Baghdad, and in Iraq as a whole, there are few grounds for hope that neighbouring countries will stop interfering in the country.
27 Nawzad Hady, governor of Arbil, confirmed that the Kurdish authorities actually paid families $3500 to return to Kirkuk. J Banbury, 'Rage and danger in Kurdistan', *The Salon*, 22 July 2004. See also the extensive Human Rights Watch report, *Claims in Conflict: Reversing Ethnic Cleansing in Northern Iraq*, at http://hrw.org/reports/2004/iraq0804/.
28 For events in Fallujah, see M Howard, 'Kurds flee Fallujah in fear', *Washnigton Post*, 7 May 2004, at http://washingtontimes.com/world/20040506-110737-5615r.htm. For Samarra, see, for example, George Packer, 'The next Iraqi war', *The New Yorker*, 4 October 2004, at http://newyorker.com/fact/content/?041004fa_fact.

References

Akınbingöl, ÖF (2003) *Knooppunt Istanbul: Mensensmokkel via Turkije* (Amsterdam: Meulenhoff Documentair).

Baram, A (1997) Neo-tribalism in Iraq, *International Journal of Middle East Studies*, 29, pp 1–31.

Bozarslan, H (1996) Le Kurdistan: économie de guerre, l'économie dans la guerre, in: F Jean & J-C Rufin (eds), *Économie des guerres civiles* (Paris: Hachette).

Castells, M (1996) *The Information Age I: The Rise of the Network Society* (Oxford: Blackwell).

Chaudhry, KA (1991) On the way to market: economic liberalization and Iraq's invasion of Kuwait, *Middle East Report*, May–June 1991, pp 14–23.

Chaudhry, KA (2002) Consuming interests: market failure and the social foundations of Iraqi étatisme, in: K Mahdi (ed), *Iraq's Economic Predicament*, pp 233–266 (London: Ithaca Press).

Foucault, M (2002) *Society Must be Defended* (New York: Picador).
Hafeed, S (1993) The embargo on Iraqi Kurdistan, in: F Hussein, M Leezenberg & P Muller (eds), *The Reconstruction and Economic Development of Iraqi Kurdistan: Challenges and Perspectives. Proceedings of the International Conference on the Reconstruction and Development of Iraqi Kurdistan, Zeist, The Netherlands, September 4–6, 1992* (Amsterdam: Stichting Nederland-Koerdistan).
Hampshire, S (2000) *Justice is Conflict* (Princeton, NJ: Princeton University Press).
Henry, CM & Springborg, R (2001) *Globalization and the Politics of Development in the Middle East* (Cambridge: Cambridge University Press).
Hibou, B (1999) 'The "Social Capital" of the State as an Agent of Deception, or the Ruses of Economic Intelligence', pp 63–113, in: J-F Bayart, S Ellis & B Hibou, *Criminalization of the State in Africa* (Indianapolis: Indiana University Press).
Jabar, FA (2004) *Postconflict Iraq: A Race for Stability, Reconstruction, and Legitimacy*, Special Report 120, United States Institute of Peace, available online at: http://www.usip.org/pubs/specialreports/sr120.html.
Leezenberg, M (1997) Irakisch-Kurdistan seit dem zweiten Golfkrieg, in: C Borck *et al* (eds), *Ethnizität, Nationalismus, Religion und Politik in Kurdistan*, pp 45–78 (Münster: LIT Verlag).
Leezenberg, M (2000) Humanitarian aid in Iraqi Kurdistan, *Cahiers d'études sur la Méditerranée orientale et le monde turco-iranien (CEMOTI)*, 29, pp 31–49.
Leezenberg, M (forthcoming) Urbanization, privatization, and patronage: the political economy of Iraqi Kurdistan, in: FA Jabar & H Dawod (eds), *Tribes and the State: The Case of the Kurds* (London: Saqi Books).
Perthes, V (2002) *Geheime Gärten: Die neue arabische Welt* (Berlin: Siedler).
Rubin, R (2003) *The Fragmentation of Afghanistan* (New Haven, CT: Yale University Press).
Schmitt, C (1976) *The Concept of the Political* (Rutgers, NJ: Rutgers University Press).
Tilly, C (1986) War making and state making as organized crime, in: P Evans *et al* (eds), *Bringing the State Back In*, pp 169–191 (Cambridge: Cambridge University Press).

Divisible Sovereignty and the Reconstruction of Iraq

ROLF SCHWARZ & OLIVER JÜTERSONKE

ABSTRACT *Seeking to make sense of conflicting views regarding the continued relevance of the notion of sovereignty, this article argues that there is a discrepancy between international norms and practices. This discrepancy is rooted in conflicting understandings of the term sovereignty. By building on the link between sovereignty, the state of emergency, and the dialectic of* auctoritas *and* potestas, *this article proposes a new reading of sovereignty based on an understanding taken from Hugo Grotius. The argument formulated posits that the current political impasse in Iraq can only be adequately analysed through the lens of divisible sovereignty, and that such a perspective will aid in judging future developments in Iraq and in forecasting the political success or failure of post-war reconstruction there.*

> The notion of sovereignty is not at all a ghost we can exorcise at will. It is a spirit which is very much alive, and very wide awake. Some may regret it, but if they fail to recognize this fact, they abandon the firm foundation of reality.[1]

As an ordering principle in international relations, sovereignty is usually dated back to the Westphalian treaties of 1648. Although growing interdependence through globalisation has led many to argue that states are no longer the central, 'sovereign' actors they once were, sovereignty nonetheless remains the bedrock of the current international system, as a legal as well as a political concept. EN van Kleffens' observations remain on the mark.

With the end of the Cold War and the growing emergence of multilateral interventions in the name of humanitarian principles, the notion of sovereignty has come to be called into question from a different perspective. On the one hand are those declaring that the promotion of human rights 'beyond borders' heralds the end of sovereignty as such; on the other are those who argue that, in order to justify the use of military force in the context of humanitarian disasters and the oppression of parts of the population by the state, sovereignty has become more important, not less.

In line with the work of Stephen Krasner, this article seeks to make sense of these conflicting views by arguing that there is a discrepancy between the international norms and practices of sovereignty. This discrepancy, rooted in conflicting understandings of the term 'sovereignty', is clearly illustrated by the case of contemporary Iraq. Whereas those states advocating the primacy of human rights and the protection of the individual will point to the existence of international 'norms' of behaviour and a duty to adhere to the values inherent in the 'community' of states, those who feel threatened by this universalism will refer to Article 2 para 7 of the United Nations Charter, and tell others not to interfere in their internal affairs. Formulated more theoretically: it is the constructed understanding of what sovereignty means that determines whether there is compatibility between 'imposed' notions of the term.

Though agreeing with Krasner's argument, the authors of this article nonetheless have reservations as to his categorisation of alternative meanings of sovereignty. While the distinction between international legal, domestic and Westphalian sovereignty is undoubtedly a useful one,[2] it will be argued that such a classification misses a crucial element, namely the possibility of dividing sovereign prerogatives among different agents. Indeed, whereas in a natural body it is not possible to have one head (*caput*) for many bodies, the same does not hold true for moral bodies, such as societies or states.[3] Grotius highlights the important distinction between a human assembly (*coetus*), forming a sovereign entity, and the person (or persons) that can be said to be sovereign within that assembly. This distinction has later also been highlighted by Georg Jellinek when he noted that 'the highest power in the state has nothing to do with the highest power of the state. The sovereign organ within the state and the sovereign state are therefore two entirely different things.[4]

Taking the work of Edward Keene as its starting point, the article proposes a new reading of sovereignty based on an understanding of the term derived from the work of Hugo Grotius.[5] Moreover, it takes issue with Krasner's underlying claim that embedded in the different usages of sovereignty is the distinction between authority and control. Using the current situation in Iraq as an illustration, it will be suggested that the crucial distinction is rather the one between *auctoritas* and *potestas*, a distinction, originating out of Roman constitutional law, which, largely because of the rise of totalitarianism and the breakdown of traditional authorities, we no longer seem to be in a position to make.

The US-led military intervention in Iraq in 2003 'suspended' that state's sovereignty by forcing its regime from power.[6] As the Bush administration never tires of telling the world, the ultimate aim is to give sovereignty back to the Iraqi people as soon as the security situation there permits, as soon as Iraqi forces are able to stand on their own two feet, and a legitimate government is in place. All this is meant to highlight the temporary nature of this 'suspension'. In what follows it will be argued that the fact that the 'situation on the ground' is nevertheless not improving—in the eyes of many, it is actually worsening—is the result of conflicting views of sovereignty.

While the US administration subscribes (consciously or otherwise) to a Grotian notion of 'divisible sovereignty', the gradual restitution of sovereignty to the Iraqi people that it entails is perceived (and/or deliberately misinterpreted) by the latter as a form of neocolonialism that must be resisted at all costs, since it is perceived as limited sovereignty. Moreover, the elections held in January 2005 have shown that they are unlikely to change this perception fundamentally, given the way they were conducted and the political constellations they give rise to.

The underlying assumption of the present endeavour is the Gramscian assertion that 'all men are philosophers', and that, consequently, political and legal theory is invariably linked to practice. David Dyzenhaus expresses it well when he writes:

> As Gramsci tells us, all participants in politics are philosophers in that their commitments presuppose a philosophy even if they would not or could not themselves take the time to articulate it. Conversely, even when they deny it, the doctrines of professional philosophers are part of a fabric of ideas which are tied, albeit in very complex ways, to actual experience and practice.[7]

While practice determines what issues we address, practice itself could not be sustained without recourse to theory, be it explicit or implicit. Hence it is only through a sufficient understanding of the latter that the former can be appropriately captured, and this is precisely the point of departure for the following reflections on the concept of sovereignty. While, legally speaking, it may seem clear what is meant by sovereignty (and under which precise conditions it can be curtailed—Article 51, Chapter VII resolutions, etc), the political practices jurists are attempting to assess may contain narratives on sovereignty that do not share the same lucid vision of what the term means. To express it differently, the legal conception of sovereignty may fail to capture a part of the political practice. Yet, as Gramsci points out, even though certain decision makers may not seem to adhere to the legal rules regarding sovereignty (hence the argument that the invasion of Iraq in 2003 was 'illegal'), this does not imply that they were not influenced by theory at all. This article will therefore try to shed light on the discrepancy between norms and practices by attempting to unravel the theory behind the practice—a theory, it will be argued, based on the notion that sovereignty is divisible.

Sovereignty and the project of liberal modernity

> Take up the White Man's Burden –
> Send forth the best ye breed –
> Go bind your sons to exile
> To serve your captives' need;
> To wait in heavy harness,
> On fluttered fold and wild –
> Your new-caught, sullen peoples,
> Half-devil and half-child.
>
> (Rudyard Kipling, 1899)

In the International Relations literature one finds several views on sovereignty, corresponding to different notions of world order. On one end of the spectrum are Realists, who argue that the defining principle in the international sphere is anarchy, and that states find themselves in a perpetual struggle of 'all against all', akin to a Hobbesian state of nature. They will consequently regard state sovereignty as the embodiment of all that matters in such a world: for it is a state's perseverance in a situation of continual animosity that defines its existence, and persevering means asserting one's independence, one's autonomy. At the other end are those who see this insistence on the inviolability of frontiers as heavy-handed, if not downright naive. Without necessarily being idealists, this latter group would point to the community spirit in the international arena, to the role of norms, of shared beliefs and values, and to an ever-growing awareness of the need, in the name of humanity and the rights of the individual, to play an active role, as a collective, in ensuring that these rights are globally respected. Sovereignty, according to this view, places too much emphasis on the primacy of the state, and is thus no longer an adequate concept for the contemporary international order.[8]

In his recent book, Edward Keene proposes a compromise between these conflicting views by exploring the notion of 'divisible sovereignty'. According to Keene, sovereignty should not be conceived as 'indivisibly packaged up in territorial bundles' but rather as a collection of various fragments that may be held by different agents.[9] From Hugo Grotius' legal thought, as found in his major work *De Jure Belli ac Pacis*, as well as in his *Commentarius in Theses XI* and *De Jure Praedae Commentarius*, Keene takes the idea that sovereign rights (ie sovereign prerogatives) are not only held by states in relation to each other, but also by private individuals, who possess rights in the law of nations through their natural rights over their persons and their property. It is this inherent tension between the rights of states and the rights of the individual that Grotius proposes to overcome by introducing the notion of divisible sovereignty.

The concept of sovereignty has usually been regarded as the cornerstone of the Western state system. The first systematic presentation of the concept was formulated by the French scholar, Jean Bodin, in his *De republica* of 1586, in which he defined sovereignty as unlimited power over citizens and subjects, unrestrained by law.[10] This power, Bodin insisted, is by nature absolute, unqualified, perpetual and indivisible. Bodin claimed that sovereignty resides not in the whole state, but in the body of the citizenry in a democracy, in the estate of the nobility in an aristocracy and in the person of the king in a monarchy.

Jean Bodin's conception of sovereignty became prevalent in Europe over the next few centuries, but it was not beyond contestation. The school of political philosophers known as 'Monarchomachs' (the most well known theorist among them is Johannes Althusius) challenged Bodin's absolute view of sovereignty on the grounds that government had come into existence as a result of a written or tacit contract—reminiscent in parts of the later works of Hobbes and Rousseau—between the rulers and the ruled for the mutual convenience of both. In the event of a ruler violating that compact by indulging in despotic misgovernment, his subjects are *ipso facto* released from the obligation of obedience and may engage in revolution. In this reading sovereign power was hence in no way absolute nor supreme, but was limited by the laws of God, the laws of nature, and the terms of the contract with the people, who remained the ultimate and permanent source of sovereignty. Sovereignty, in short, was defined contractually and based on performance.

Hugo Grotius resolved the issue by defining sovereignty as 'that power whose actions are not subject to the legal control of another, so that they cannot be rendered void by the operation of another human will'.[11] Sovereignty (*summa potestas*) is again seen to be limited by certain actions which might be under the legal control (ie the law) of another (*alterius iuri subessent*). Sovereignty might hence be limited by divine law, by the law of nature, by the law of nations, and by the contractual understanding between the ruler and the ruled. It is therefore capable of division and resides *simultaneously* in the government and in the state. In his *De Jure Belli ac Pacis* of 1625, Grotius affirms the overall importance of law-guided behaviour in order to avoid anarchy.[12]

Grotius' ideas on divisible sovereignty are linked to his ideas on the rights of war and peace, and on the equality of states. For Grotius, all sovereign states are equally bound by international law, but they do not possess equal rights and duties. An equal capacity for rights does not mean that there are no differences between states, but rather that differences of great powers are not derived from a legal basis or legal rule.[13] This hierarchical understanding is already reflected in Grotius' understanding of society: society, according to Grotius, is characterised by relations between unequals—relations of father and son, master and slave, king and subject, God and man. Furthermore, Grotius conceived of the state as an association (*consociatio*) not of atomised individuals, but of many fathers (*patres familiarum*) united in one people and one state (*in unum populum ac civitatem*).[14]

Starting from these hierarchical notions of society and state, Grotius considered international relations to be hierarchical as well.[15] In the latter realm even the existence of unequal treaties (*inaequali foedere*) does not automatically render sovereignty obsolete. While it may indeed be the case that some of the contracts imposed by command are highly unequal and unjust—Grotius mentions the example of Rome's treaties with its allies—it also holds true that the inferior party gains from the imposed patron–client relationship. The latter thus retains its sovereignty, provided that the party is 'under protection, not under domination', 'under patronage, not under subjection',[16] and only transfers its sovereignty. In practice such a transfer may, however, lead to some kind of division of sovereignty, because he 'who has the position of vantage in a treaty, if he is greatly superior in respect to power, gradually usurps the sovereignty properly so called'.[17] Then either those who had been allies become subjects, or there is a division of sovereignty (*partitio fit summi imperii*).[18]

With regard to the rights of war and peace, a traditional view at the time of Grotius affirmed that public wars could only be declared by the sovereign, ie by the prince or ruler himself. Grotius argued that private trading corporations could also obtain the sovereign right to declare public wars. His view on this topic can be found in his defence of the East India Company.[19] In *De Jure Praedae Commentarius*, Grotius offered a justification for the seizure of a Portuguese ship, the *Santa Catarina*, by the Dutch. Building on the sovereignty of the King of Johore, a Dutch ally, the right to war (for the Dutch) was acquired *ipso iure* for the East India Company. Warfare was a feature of international society, but was never to be undertaken except to assert rights.[20] Grotius had thus made the claim that a public war could be waged in order to assert the rights of a trading company. This broader view of sovereignty, according to which legal rights could be acquired, partitioned, alienated, or transferred from one entity to another if they so chose—in this case the transfer of sovereignty to a European trading company occurred in exchange for military services—is congruent with Grotius' view of unequal treaties and the exchange of sovereign prerogatives for mutual benefits.[21]

The idea of divisible sovereignty also becomes clear from Grotius' thoughts on the 'Dutch Revolt', when he defended the revolt not by advocating the right of ordinary people to use violence in defence of their natural liberties, a line that was popular in Holland at the time, but on the grounds that it represented a just public war. The crucial proposition in his argument was again that sovereignty is divisible, such 'that it may be possible for some marks [of sovereignty] to reside. . .with persons or assemblies, while others do not'.[22] He illustrated this point by referring to the right of the states of Holland to raise taxes, which had been bestowed upon them by Philip II of Spain. The revolt could then be justified on the grounds that Philip's representative in the Netherlands, the Duke of Alva, had violated his prerogatives by levying taxes on his own initiative, and the Dutch states were hence entitled to defend *their* prerogatives by waging a just public war against the Spanish. Grotius had earlier affirmed that 'a public war ought not to be waged except by the authority of him who holds the sovereign power'.[23] The crucial linkage is that it suffices for someone who holds *a bit* of the bundle of prerogatives and rights which form *summa potestas* (sovereignty) to wage such a war, for 'whoever possesses a part of the sovereign power must possess also the right to defend his part'.[24]

The crucial element in Grotius' legal thought on divisible sovereignty is that, in his scheme, the law of nations was not exclusively a law for nations, but also included rights and duties for individuals and private companies.[25] Grotius' account of sovereignty revolves around the distinction between public and private wars, and between the public rights of sovereigns and private rights of property. While seemingly conservative in its rejection of popular resistance, Grotius still subscribed to a notion of divisible sovereignty according to which individuals or private organisations defended the property of the sovereign and thereby acquired the right to wage public wars to defend this property. His defence of the seizure of the *Santa Catarina* in *De Jure Praedae Commentarius*, and his defence of the 'Dutch Revolt' in *Commentarius in Theses XI*, illustrate his legal teaching on this point. While neither subscribing to an absolutist notion of sovereignty nor to a monarchomachic understanding of popular resistance, Grotius offered a 'third way' by proposing the divisibility of sovereignty.

Though seemingly unorthodox in light of contemporary legal thought, Keene shows how the Grotian notion of divisible sovereignty is nonetheless closely linked to European practices of colonialism and imperialism. In 19th century Europe sovereignty was seen to be inseparably tied to the *ius publicum europaeum*, creating an international order that promoted *toleration* among independent and equal states. Outside Europe, however, international order was supposed to create *civilisation*: 'the fundamental norm governing relations between European states and non-European peoples was that the latter were backward and that some of the sovereign prerogatives of indigenous rulers ought to be held by more advanced Europeans in order to introduce the economic, political and judicial benefits of civilized life'. This was achieved through a division of sovereignty between 'different public authorities and the assertion of individuals' rights to appropriate unoccupied, uncultivated or unimproved land'.[26]

With the rise of 'barbarous' ideologies in European states between 1914 and 1945, and the devastating effects of World War II, Keene argues, these two distinct patterns of international order were merged into one, into a single international system that deliberately moved away from the discriminatory principle of civilised and uncivilised nations and towards a single political and legal order. Yet despite the formal abandonment of the claim that civilisation should be promoted in the international realm, the contemporary (post-1945) international order still embodies two distinct normative principles: that the sovereign independence of states should be respected (*toleration*) and that fundamental human rights should be observed and protected (*civilisation*). Article 55 of the UN Charter states these 'quasi-civilianising' goals at great length:

> the UN shall promote: (a) higher standards of living, full employment, and conditions of economic and social progress and development; (b) solutions of international economic, social, health and related problems; and international cultural and educational co-operation; and (c) universal respect for, and observance of, human rights and fundamental freedoms for all without distinctions as to race, sex, language, or religion.[27]

The formal omission of the discriminatory purpose of the promotion of *civilisation* in the international order after World War II—of which traces can still be found in Article 38 of the Statute of the International Court of Justice, where one reads of the 'general principles of law recognised by *civilized* nations'—without the total abandonment of this normative principle, has thus not alleviated the existing tensions in world politics, but has rather (implicitly) accentuated them. Hence Keene's conclusion that we are either to accept 'perennial instability', or some kind of *de facto* discrimination operating below the official, formal level of international law.

The notion of divisible sovereignty, therefore, is part and parcel of the general project of liberal modernity. As Martti Koskenniemi writes, the story of international law and formal empire in 1870–1914

> is indissociable from the wider narrative of a liberal internationalism that thinks of itself as the 'legal *conscience* of the civilized world' and whose humanitarian aspirations cannot be dismissed as a set of bad-faith justifications for Western domination.[28]

The new international order required a language of equality of nations and states, and just as citizens were educated and taught how best to maintain their fundamental rights, nation-states—the new referent objects of group identity—remained outside the society of civilised states until they had proven their aptness at statehood.[29] The logic of this liberal project of social engineering can today be found in the language of Western governments and international organisations on good governance promotion, civil society, capacity building and democratisation. Entailed is an implicit recognition that there will be no liberal states until there are liberal persons.[30] Reminiscent of this is John Stuart Mill's famous dictum that the principle of freedom cannot require that one should be free not to be free and that hence one may, in the words of Rousseau, be forced to be free—alluding to the inherent *violence* of the project of liberal modernity, in both its domestic and international manifestations.

State reconstruction in Iraq—from exception to normality?

> The CPA is vested with all executive, legislative and judicial authority necessary to achieve its objectives, to be exercised under relevant UN Security Council resolutions, including Resolution 1483 (2003), and the laws and usages of war. (Coalition Provisional Authority Regulation Number 1, 2003)

The notion of divisible sovereignty is central to an understanding of contemporary world order. It encompasses the aims of the liberal project of advocating the rights of the individual through an ethic of human rights—framed in a discourse on human security—that attempts to justify a politics of intervention in world affairs. The Iraqi people are better off without Saddam, the US administration is always keen to point out: ridding a people of its tyrannical dictator creates the conditions for it to join in the liberal project and be part of the 'civilised' world.

Overthrowing a regime, however, necessarily entails the production of a power vacuum, a period in which the territory is controlled by occupying forces and where there is no representative government of any sort. From the point of view of constitutional law, military intervention can be considered as the forceful imposition of a state of emergency: the powers of the regime are suspended (or, in this case, uplifted), and authority is transferred to the intervener-*cum*-occupier. If one follows the logic of Carl Schmitt, that a sovereign is he who decides upon the state of exception,[31] then regardless of how much power the coalition transfers to the Iraqi Interim Government, the latter will not be sovereign in the eyes of the Iraqi people, as the decision to declare a state of emergency still remains with the intervener. The marginalised distinction between *auctoritas* and *potestas* sheds light on this dilemma.

'Men do not wield or submit to sovereignty', wrote FH Hinsley. 'They wield or submit to authority or power':

> Authority and power are facts as old and ubiquitous as society itself; but they have not everywhere and at all times enjoyed the support or suffered the restraints which sovereignty, a theory or assumption about political power, seeks to construct for them.[32]

Indeed, the dominance of the narrative on sovereignty has led to the relationship between authority and power becoming a difficult one to grasp, even more so as the original meaning of *auctoritas* has fallen victim to the project of modernity and the breakdown of traditional authorities—as Hannah Arendt pointed out in her essay entitled 'What is authority?'. 'Practically as well as theoretically', she writes, 'we are no longer in a position to know what authority really *is*'.[33]

Both Bodin and Hobbes were still conscious of the distinction between the concept of *potestas*, corresponding to sovereignty and majesty, and *auctoritas*, which denotes tradition, continuity and *pouvoir légitime*. Derived from the Latin noun *auctor, auctoritas* signified the authority of the Senate in Roman constitutional law, while *potestas* and *imperium* were derived from the people. As Cicero observed, '*cum potestas in populo, auctoritas in senatu sit*'.[34] Likewise, the Roman Pope claimed *auctoritas* over the worldly kings and emperors, while the latter simply possessed *potestas*: '*Duo sunt quibus principaliter mundus hic regitur: auctoritas sacra pontificum et regalis potestas*'.[35] The two magistrates, the Church and the State, both demanded allegiance from their subjects, giving rise to what William Bain has called a 'division of allegiance'. He notes, 'This arrangement aspired to the ideal of a Christian commonwealth conducted by two separate but equal magistrates charged with realising the highest of all possible human achievements—God's kingdom on earth'.[36]

As Giorgio Agamben has attempted to demonstrate, the philological distinction between *auctoritas* and *potestas* may be of importance for understanding the relationship between law and politics. The Western legal system manifests itself in a dual structure of a normative *potestas* and an anomic *auctoritas*: the normative element needs the anomic to be applied, while the *auctoritas* can only assert itself within the context of a validation or suspension of this *potestas* (this suspension being embodied in the concept of *iustitium* in Roman law).[37] A system devoid of this structure displays elements of a 'grey zone' between lawfulness and lawlessness, as exemplified by the prison camps in Guantanamo Bay, where life attains its highest degree of indeterminacy.

It is far beyond the scope of this article to attempt to do justice to the dialectical relationship between *auctoritas* and *potestas*, as this would entail venturing into the realm of anomie and *nomos*, legality and legitimacy, and the discussion Walter Benjamin's notion of the 'force of law' (*Gesetzeskraft*). For now, suffice it simply to assert that *auctoritas* is the name given to the force that accords legitimacy in the dual sense of validating the *potestas* through the people (*auctoritas populi*) and having the means to suspend it (*auctoritas patrum/senatus*).

The above considerations are of particular relevance in the case of post-Saddam Iraq. The highly mediatised hand-over of sovereignty on 28 June 2004 begs two questions: to what degree has sovereignty actually been given back to the Iraqi people and, consequently, what are the long-term implications of this hand-over?

The invasion and subsequent occupation of Iraq by coalition forces in March 2003 resulted in the dismantling of the existing state structures (the Iraqi Army, the Information Ministry, and the Ministry of Defence were all dissolved on 23 May 2003), the installation of a regime of military occupation, and the announcement of the construction of a new liberal and democratic polity under the guise of various Security Council resolutions. From an international legal point of view this was an unprecedented situation, a juridical *unicum*, as Marcelo G Kohen called it.[38]

The situation in Iraq was exceptional for yet another reason. For decades, state-formation in the case of Iraq under Saddam Hussein had been decoupled from the demands of society, and had aimed at a transformation of it. Abundant oil revenues allowed the Iraqi state to pursue this radical transformation of society and the accompanying attempt at nation building, most evident in the omnipresence of the Baath Party. With declining oil revenues in the late 1980s, and especially during the decade of sanctions in the 1990s, this state building project ran aground. The Iraqi state was seriously restricted in fulfilling its most basic functions (welfare, security, representation).

US assumptions about jubilation awaiting allied troops in Iraq were driven by a perception of a fragile Iraqi state. This was most evident in the initial 'decapitation thesis'.[39] Such a perception of a fragile state existed notwithstanding the fact that, since the end of the 1990–91 Gulf war, no successful *coup d'état* attempt had materialised. Despite the curtailment of Iraqi sovereignty during the decade of sanctions in the 1990s, Iraq had maintained a minimal level of statehood and order. Only after the US invasion in March 2003, and only once the Iraqi state institutions had been dismantled by the CPA in May 2003, did Iraq become a collapsed state, where the situation resembled that of a Hobbesian war of all against all.[40] Moreover, the fact that US and allied forces, as well as the new Iraqi Interim Government, can be criticised in their attempts to rebuild a state by radical Islamist groups on the grounds that they are un-Islamic highlights the fact that the scriptural strand in Islamic political thought has gained the upper hand.[41]

While the actual process of state reconstruction was marred by difficulties and characterised by frequent policy changes by the CPA, the formal hand-over of sovereignty to an Iraqi government at the end of June 2004, backed by UN Resolution 1546, was intended to steer this process into calmer waters. The newly established Iraqi Interim Government, however, has only attained (limited) *potestas*, according to our adopted terminology. UN Resolution 1546 limits the sovereign prerogatives of the government to the holding of parliamentary elections in January 2005, while several vague formulations in Resolution 1546 allow the USA to retain control of military and strategic matters. It is also unclear to what extent the new government can reverse previous laws and decrees—especially those from the time of the CPA, such as the Communications Commission established in March 2004, which had received the authorisation to configure the communications sector over five years.[42]

As long as the coalition forces retain military control over the territory, the decision to declare the state of exception remains in any case in their hands, and thus complete sovereignty, defined as the presence of both *potestas* and *auctoritas*, is unattainable. That the Iraqi Interim Government is aware of this is demonstrated by the fact that on 7 July 2004 it immediately passed a law giving it the right to declare martial law in certain parts of the country for a maximum of 60 days. A 'state of emergency' was first decreed on 7 November 2004 for a period of 60 days and on 6 January 2005 prolonged for another 30 days. The paradox remains that a state of exception had already been *de facto* imposed by President Bush in his decision to suspend the sovereignty of Iraq. The missing *auctoritas* of the Iraqi Interim Government, however, can only be attained though the validation of its *potestas*, which is not possible by means of foreign imposition, but only through popular will, as manifested through free and democratic elections.

Since its creation in the 1920s Iraq has never been a stable functioning democracy.[43] The elections held on 30 January 2005 were thus hailed as an indisputable landmark in the history of the country. The reality, however, is far from being that simple. First, and in view of decades of tyrannical rule by Saddam Hussein, Iraq is today devoid of any indigenous civil society that could authoritatively articulate political opinion or institutionalise a nation-wide system of party politics. While the fall of the *ancien régime* has certainly led to political mobilisation, this process remains tentative, unstable and highly fractured. No one individual or party has managed to rally significant support from the population, and scepticism is warranted about whether this will change in the near future.[44] On a technical level the system of single-constituency proportional representation employed in the elections only has the desired outcome if there is a relatively equal voter turnout among the country's ethnic and regional divides—an assumption that is hard to realise given the high level of violence in Sunni-dominated areas. Another potential issue relates to the future role of the Kurdish population and the *de facto* veto power they hold over the eventual adoption of a permanent constitution. Although they only represent some 20% of Iraq's population, the Kurdish minority might bring the entire process to a halt, even if a majority of Iraqis is in favour.

Second, one needs to examine whether the consequences of the elections match stated aims. Whereas the casting of ballots by Iraqis was depicted as the first step in the process of forming an Iraqi polity based on a permanent constitution and a legitimate government, it seems that the actual result of the elections is to give greater international legitimacy to the military occupation—an observation that has aptly been called the 'bait and switch' ploy by one commentator. The 'bait' is the promise to Iraqis that by casting their vote they will make the occupation end quickly, whereas the 'switch' is constituted by the election of expatriate candidates and parties that are backed by the USA, and who are thus likely to 'harken back to previous governing arrangements'.[45] As long as the prosecution of counter-insurgency remains the central aim, coalition forces will retain overall military control and *auctoritas* will remain with the intervener. Iraqis thus find themselves caught in a vicious circle of insurgent violence in the name of a missing *auctoritas* and an externally imposed state of exception that, through its mere existence, retains sole *auctoritas* within itself.[46]

Divisible sovereignty in post-Saddam Iraq manifests itself not only at a vertical level, in the limited nature of sovereignty transferred to the new Iraqi Interim Government, but also at a horizontal level. While it was argued above that security in Iraq is provided by the armed forces of the coalition (state actors), the situation is more ambiguous on the ground, where a multitude of non-governmental actors can be observed. Private groups, subcontracted by the US government, on the one hand, as well as insurgents, terrorists and armed brigades (such as Al-Sadr militias) on the other, challenge the state's monopoly of legitimate violence. While in a traditional Weberian reading such a state of affairs can only be perceived in terms of falling short of a Western ideal of the state—hence the term weak or failed states—this article proposes that this is characteristic of the current US understanding of divisible sovereignty. Divisible sovereignty thereby not only refers to the project of constructing a new and liberal Iraqi polity (Keene's civilisation purpose), but also to the ways and means through which this is to be achieved. Z Laïdi has suggested a 'redistribution of sovereignty' to non-state actors in this context.[47] Indeed, this seems to be the reality in Iraq with regard to the sovereign prerogative of providing internal security.

The focus on divisible sovereignty also draws our attention back to Krasner's assertion that the usages of the concept of sovereignty entail the distinction between authority and control. It is worthwhile to quote him at length on this point:

> Authority involves a mutually recognized right for an actor to engage in specific kinds of activities. If authority is effective, force or compulsion would never have to be exercised. Authority would simply be coterminous with control. But control can be achieved simply through the use of brute force with no mutual recognition of authority at all.[48]

The case of Iraq seems to demonstrate quite clearly the misleading nature of this distinction, for it is becoming increasingly obvious that control cannot be achieved through 'brute force' alone. Rather than talk about control, this article has thus advocated the use of the terms *auctoritas* and *potestas*, the first in order to rehabilitate a more profound meaning of authority, and the second as a reflection of the power vested in the people.

In terms of theoretical understanding, a conceptual rethinking seems necessary to drift away from the classical understanding of sovereignty (as exemplified by Morgenthau, who bluntly asserted that 'the most important of the misunderstandings that have obscured the problem of sovereignty in the modern world—[is] the belief that sovereignty is divisible',[49]) to a constitutional understanding of sovereignty. For in light of the discussion of *potestas* and *auctoritas* above, it seems clear that every polity must be based on the fundamental relationship between law and politics. Only if political rule is grounded in transparent legal arrangements, can political practices such as divisible sovereignty be validated within the project of liberal modernity.

Conclusion

> Sovereignty in foreign affairs is a myth with which fools try to deceive each other.[50]

The question of fools aside, one need not engage in a formal discourse analysis to observe that the spectre of sovereignty continues to haunt us—and, moreover, that exorcism is not a solution. Grapple with the concept we must. The question, then, is how best to come to terms with it. Is the notion of divisible sovereignty outlined here simply a useful lens through which to improve our understanding of the current world order, or does it in fact entail a substantive contribution to the debate on state reconstruction? The authors tentatively claim that there is indeed this substantive element.

This article has not tried to distil a theory of divisible sovereignty from the works of Hugo Grotius. From a contextual point of view this would, in any case, be a futile endeavour. Nevertheless, the article has highlighted elements of Grotius' thoughts on sovereignty to further our understanding of divisible sovereignty. For Grotius, sovereign prerogatives—or in his terminology 'marks of sovereignty' (*actus summae potestatis*)—include, *inter alia*, the right to introduce legislation and to withdraw it, the right to pass judgement and grant pardon, the right to appoint magistrates, and the right to impose taxes on people.[51] In the case of Iraq, the privatisation of certain functions related to war-making and the provision of internal security, such as the subcontracting of civilian firms, is a clear illustration of a division of sovereign prerogatives.

Historically, sovereignty was based on standards of performance in the domestic realm (the provision of security and order according to Hobbes) and standards of civilisation in the international realm.[52] A constitutional understanding of sovereignty would draw upon this insight, and might even offer important policy implications. The violence inherent in the liberal project of modernity can be accommodated by means of an understanding of sovereignty that combines both purposes of promoting civilisation and tolerance, as found in recent contributions on the responsibility to protect.[53] Key in this regard is not the idea that human rights and human dignity have to be protected (somewhat of an emerging international norm today), but that this has to be coupled with *constitutional* principles under international and domestic law. What these elements of an international constitutional sovereignty could look like have been sketched out by Hideaki Shinoda who—drawing on the work of Simeon E Baldwin[54]—proposes a *division* of sovereignty in the international realm based on constitutional principles, just as in the domestic realm: 'Why cannot a division be made on a basis of vesting part of the whole of sovereignty exclusively in one public agency and the rest of that whole in another agency?'.[55]

In his famous textbook *Politics Among Nations*, Hans J Morgenthau dismisses such an idea: 'If sovereignty means supreme authority, it stands to reason that two or more entities . . . cannot be sovereign within the same time and space'.[56] He nonetheless goes on to argue that a division between two officials along functional lines, as exemplified by the mediaeval doctrine according to which supreme authority was divided between emperor and pope, is conceivable. Furthermore, Morgenthau struggles to come to terms with federal systems, such as the USA, when he asserts, in somewhat contradictory manner, that one cannot deny that the federal government is sovereign, nor that it is psychologically impossible to admit that the individual states are no longer sovereign. This culminates in the conclusion that 'constitutional theory simply divides sovereignty' and that it tries to 'reconcile political realities with political preferences'.[57] Morgenthau's obvious unease with the apparent tension in his line of thought points to the changing nature of world politics after World War II, and the subsequent recurrence of interventions justified on humanitarian grounds in the post-cold war era. Although the invasion of Iraq in 2003 can hardly be termed a humanitarian intervention by any stretch of the imagination, it still displays elements of a civilisationary mission, manifested in the intention of constructing a new, liberal and 'democratic' Iraqi polity.

The invasion of Iraq and subsequent 'suspension' of its sovereignty reflects the discriminatory features of the current international order, at times reminiscent of its predecessors in the colonial and imperial period. Despite the formal declaration of the sovereign equality of states, the current international system remains hierarchical in terms of political and legal power. It consequently appears doubtful whether it will be possible to continue to pursue both of the purposes of modern international order (sovereign equality of states, and the promotion of human rights and social progress), as the UN system tries to do, without ultimately being forced to choose between them.[58]

This article has attempted to highlight pathways that might alleviate the contradictions in the present international order, contradictions inherent in the violence of a democratic and liberal vision of modernity. It is precisely because this order only conceives of equality and homogeneity within its own realm, and 'de-civilises' all others, that it nullifies its very claim to universality. Acknowledging and accepting international inequality, as does the theory of trusteeship, cannot be the answer either, however.[59] Without having gone into any great detail at this stage, a constitutional understanding of sovereignty has been proposed that not only furthers our understanding of the current dilemma faced by the coalition in its reconstruction efforts in Iraq, but that also pointed to the root of the problem. In order for the reconstruction of Iraq to succeed, *auctoritas* must be restored to the Iraqi Interim Government. This cannot be procured as an external imposition, but must rather involve an internal process of participatory politics based on 'civilisatory' principles. Such a process must indeed be rule-based and performance orientated (reminiscent of the classical understanding of sovereignty *à la* Grotius), and must be monitored by a separate entity, be this another state, a group of states, an international organisation or even independent societal actors. It is only with such accountability that empirical sovereignty can be restored.

Notes

We would like to thank Peter Haggenmacher for his extensive comments on Hugo Grotius, and Marcelo Kohen, William Bain and the participants of the 2004 Annual Conference of the British International Studies Association in Warwick for constructive suggestions and debate.

1 EN van Kleffens, 'Sovereignty in International Law, Five Lectures', *Recueil des Cours (RCADI)*, 32, 1953, p 128.

2 See SD Krasner, 'Pervasive not perverse: semi-sovereigns as the global norm', *Cornell International Law Journal*, 30, 1997, pp 651–680. His subsequent book, *Sovereignty: Organized Hypocrisy*, Princeton, NJ: Princeton University Press, 1999, adds a fourth meaning of sovereignty, namely interdependence sovereignty, but this usage has no bearing on the present argument.

3 H Grotius, *De Jure Belli ac Pacis*, Book 1, ch 3, para 7.

4 G Jellinek, *Allgemeine Staatslehre* (3rd edition), Berlin: Julius Springer, 1922, pp 457–458. Authors' translation.

5 While Grotius did not develop a theory of divisible sovereignty in its own sense, there are several passages in his work which demonstrate that divisions of sovereignty may occur in practice and in theory. Furthermore, Grotius' understanding of sovereignty was not yet that of state sovereignty—this is first found in Emer de Vattel's *The Law of Nations*—and thus resembles what Krasner has termed 'domestic sovereignty'. See P Haggenmacher, *Grotius et la doctrine de la guerre juste*, Paris: Presse Universitaire de France, 1983, p 540.

6 From an international law perspective, Iraq's sovereignty was of course neither suspended nor did Iraq ever cease to be a sovereign state. Solely the exercise of sovereignty was suspended temporarily. See MG Kohen, 'L'administration actuelle de l'Irak: vers une nouvelle forme de protectorat?', in Karine Bannelier, Théodore Christakis, Olivier Corten & Pierre Klein (eds), *L'intervention en Irak et le droit international*, Paris: Pedone, 2004, pp 299–315, at 301. This distinction between the possession and the exercise of sovereignty was interestingly already highlighted by Hugo Grotius when he affirmed that the 'sovereign power is one thing, the manner of holding it is another'. H Grotius, *De Jure Belli ac Pacis*, Book 1, Amsterdam: G Fritsch, 1735, ch 4, para 10.

7 D Dyzenhaus, *Legality and Legitimacy: Carl Schmitt, Hans Kelsen and Hermann Heller in Weimar*, Oxford: Oxford University Press, 1997, p 5. See also A Gramsci, *Selections from the Prison Notebooks*, New York: International Publishers, 1971, pp 3–23, 323–343.

8 See, for example, JS Barkin, 'The evolution of the constitution of sovereignty and the emergence of human rights norms', *Millennium: Journal of International Studies*, 27 (2), 1998, pp 229–252; ME Keck & K Sikkink, *Activists Beyond Borders: Advocacy Networks in International Politics*, Ithaca, NY: Cornell University Press, 1998; and T Bierstecker & C Weber (eds), *State Sovereignty as Social Construct*, Cambridge: Cambridge University Press, 1996.

9 E Keene, *Beyond the Anarchical Society: Grotius, Colonialism and Order in World Politics*, Cambridge: Cambridge University Press, 2002, p 4.

10 Others had obviously treated the issue of sovereignty before Bodin. Machiavelli, for example, postulated the absolute sovereignty of the territorial state in relation to its neighbours, but did not discuss the location of sovereign power within the state, nor did he analyse the question from a theoretical legal perspective.

11 '*Haec ergo summa potestas quod subiectum habeat, videamus...Summa autem illa dicitur, cuius actus alterius iuri non subsunt, ita ut alterius voluntatis humanae arbitrio irriti possint reddi.*' Grotius, *De Jure Belli ac Pacis*, Book 1, ch 3, para 7. The English translation is taken from FW Kelsey, *De Jure Belli ac Pacis, Libri Tres*, Oxford: Clarendon Press, 1925.

12 '*Verissimum illud, omnia incerta esse simul a iure recessum est.*' Grotius, *De Jure Belli ac Pacis*, Prolegomena 22.
13 H Suganami, 'Grotius and international equality', in H Bull *et al* (eds), *Hugo Grotius and International Relations*, Oxford: Clarendon, 1990, pp 221–240, at p 226. The view that many writers on the law of nations in the formative years of international law did not share Grotius' opinion is brought forward by ED Dickinson, *The Equality of States in International Law*, Cambridge, MA: Harvard University Press, 1920.
14 Grotius, *De Jure Belli ac Pacis*, Book 2, ch 5, para 23.
15 Identical hierarchical notions of society led some Confucian cultures to produce hierarchical conceptions of international relations. See Suganami, 'Grotius and international equality'.
16 Grotius, *De Jure Belli ac Pacis*, Book 1, ch 3, paras 21.2, 21.3.
17 *Ibid*, para. 21.10, translation taken from Kelsey, *De Jure Belli ac Pacis, Libri Tres*, p 135.
18 Grotius, *De Jure Belli ac Pacis*, Book 1, ch 3, para 21.11.
19 R Tuck, *The Rights of War and Peace: Political Thought and the International Order from Grotius to Kant*, Oxford: Oxford University Press, 1999, p 80 *et seq*.
20 RJ Vincent, 'Grotius, human rights, and intervention', in Bull *et al*, *Hugo Grotius and International Relations*, p 244.
21 That sovereignty (*summa potestas*) was seen by Grotius as a right in its own sense, is affirmed by Haggenmacher, *Grotius et la doctrine de la guerre juste*, p 538, where textual evidence for the acquisition, partition and alienation of this right is given.
22 H Grotius, *Commentarius in Theses XI*, ad thesin 4, translation taken from P Borschberg, '*Commentarius in Theses XI': An Early Treatise on Sovereignty, the Just War and the Legitimacy of the Dutch Revolt*, Bern: Peter Lang, 1994, p 227.
23 Grotius, *De Jure Belli ac Pacis*, Book 1, ch 3, para 5.7, translation taken from Kelsey, *De Jure Belli ac Pacis, Libri Tres*, pp 100–101.
24 *Ibid*, ch 4, para 13, translation taken from Kelsey, *De Jure Belli ac Pacis, Libri Tres*, p 158.
25 These rights were limited to specific circumstances which related (a) to private ownership, where lands were still under pre-social communal ownership and hence available for appropriation, and (b) to public purposes of warfare, in the sense that no recourse to public judicial proceedings was available to correct an injustice.
26 Keene, *Beyond the Anarchical Society*, pp 146–147.
27 *Charter of the United Nations and Statute of the International Court of Justice, San Francisco, 26 June 1945*, New York: United Nations, Department of Public Information, 1990.
28 M Koskenniemi, *The Gentle Civilizer of Nations: The Rise and Fall of International Law 1870–1960*, Cambridge: Cambridge University Press, 2002, p 176, (emphasis in original).
29 See T Young, 'A project to be realized: global liberalism and a new world order', in E Hovden & E Keene (eds), *The Globalization of Liberalism*, Basingstoke: Palgrave, 2002, pp 173–190, at 180.
30 *Ibid*, p 184.
31 C Schmitt, *Politische Theologie: Vier Kapitel zur Lehre von der Souveränität*, Berlin: Duncker & Humblot, 1996 (first published 1922).
32 FH Hinsley, *Sovereignty*, London: CA Watts, 1996, p 1.
33 H Arendt, 'What is authority?' in Arendt, *Between Past and Future: Eight Exercises in Political Thought*, New York: Penguin, 1987, pp 91–141, at 92, emphasis in the original.
34 Cited in T Mommsen, *Römisches Staatsrecht*, Vol 3, Part 2, Basle: Schwabe, 1952, p 1034. For the difficulties in deriving a unified definition of *auctoritas*, see also R Heinze, 'Auctoritas', *Hermes*, 60, 1925, pp 348–366; and A Magdelain, *Jus Imperium Auctoritas. Etudes de droit romain*, Rome: Ecole française de Rome, 1990.
35 Cited in C Schmitt, *Verfassungslehre*, Berlin: Duncker & Humblot, 1928, p 75.
36 W Bain, 'Unravelling the Gordian Knot: pluralism, solidarism, and the problem of obligation', paper presented at the Annual Conference of the British International Studies Association, University of Warwick, 20–22 December 2004. In the case of mediaeval Christendom, this understanding of a division of allegiance is, on the whole, comparable with the notion of divisible sovereignty proposed in this article.
37 G Agamben, *État d'exception*, Paris: Seuil, 2003, p 144.
38 Kohen, 'L'administration actuelle de l'Irak', p 304.
39 T Dodge, 'Regime change in Iraq: a step too far in the liberal world order', paper presented at the Graduate Institute of International Studies, Geneva, 9 November 2004.
40 Further examples of state collapse include Liberia, Sierra Leone, Somalia, Congo/Zaire and Albania. See J Milliken & K Krause, 'State failure, state collapse, and state reconstruction: concepts, lessons and strategies', *Development and Change*, 33 (5), 2002, pp 753–774, at 754–755.
41 A Meddeb, *La Maladie de l'Islam*, Paris: Seuil, 2002.

42 Another example of pre-existing laws limiting the Iraqi Interim Government relates to the territorial administration of Iraq and the boundaries of electoral constituencies in the January elections. This has caused serious discontent, particularly in the Al-Tamim province.
43 T Dodge, *Inventing Iraq: The Failure of Nation Building and a History Denied*, Ithaca, NY: Cornell University Press, 2003.
44 T Dodge, 'A sovereign Iraq?', *Survival*, 46 (3), 2004, pp 39–58.
45 C Conetta, 'The Iraqi election "bait and switch". Fault poll will not bring peace or US withdrawal', *Project on Defense Alternatives Briefing Report #17*, 25 January 2005, p 2.
46 Indeed, it is the *external* imposition of emergency rule that is at issue here. *Domestic* imposition is, after all, a common feature of politics in the Third World and, given developments in the USA, might even become the norm in parts of the first. See, for example, D Singerman, 'The politics of emergency rule in Egypt', *Current History*, 651, 2002, pp 29–35, who writes: 'States of emergency have been the norm in Egypt since World War II' (p 30).
47 Z Laïdi, *Adieu Bodin? Souveraineté et mondialisation*, inaugural lectures for the start of the academic year 2002–03, Geneva: Graduate Institute of Development Studies, 2003, p 12.
48 Krasner, *Sovereignty*, p 10.
49 HJ Morgenthau, *Politics Among Nations*, New York: Knopf, 1964, p 325.
50 JHW Stuckenberg, *Sociology: the science of human society*, New York: Putnam, 1903. As cited in van Kleffens, Sovereignty in International Law, p 7.
51 Grotius, *Commentarius in Theses XI*, ad thesin 4; translation taken from Borschberg, '*Commentarius in Theses XI*', p 119. It is worth noticing that Grotius does not mention the right to declare war and to conclude peace, as Jean Bodin had done earlier.
52 GW Gong, *The Standard of 'Civilization' in International Society*, Oxford: Clarendon Press, 1984.
53 International Commission on Intervention and State Sovereignty (ICISS), *The Responsibility to Protect*, Ottawa: International Development Research Centre, 2001.
54 SE Baldwin, 'The division of sovereignty', *International Law Notes*, 3 (26), 1918, pp 57–59; and Baldwin, 'The vesting of sovereignty in a League of Nations', *Yale Law Journal*, 28 (3), 1919, pp 209–218.
55 H Shinoda, *Re-examining Sovereignty: From Classical Theory to the Global Age*, Basingstoke: Macmillan, 2000, p 69.
56 Morgenthau, *Politics Among Nations*, p 326.
57 *Ibid*, p 329.
58 Keene, *Beyond the Anarchical Society*; and M Ayoob, 'Humanitarian intervention and state sovereignty', *International Journal of Human Rights*, 6 (1), 2002, pp 81–102.
59 On the notion of trusteeships, see W Bain, *Between Anarchy and Society: Trusteeship and the Obligations of Power*, Oxford: Oxford University Press, 2003.

Iraq, Imperialism and Global Governance

ERIC HERRING & GLEN RANGWALA

ABSTRACT *The Iraqi state is not representing Iraq in a globalising world: it is representing the globalising world in Iraq. The fact that the USA physically occupied Iraq, installed a government and passed a raft of legislation by decree might suggest almost total US dominance over broader globalising forces and thus that the Iraqi state is almost solely an instrument of US empire. Certainly, Iraq's imperial globalisation from above is* not *primarily decentred in terms of the actors involved or the interests served: US actors and interests are at the forefront. However, other actors have played a significant role, and the actions of the US agents have tended to favour US political power and the US-based fraction of capital less than the fact of occupation would suggest. Furthermore, this advantage has declined over time. In addition, there is a second force for decentred globalisation in Iraq, namely, globalisation from below by means of the workings of the transborder informal economy. Many but not all of the activities of this informal economy are closely related to the insurgency. The interaction of all these forces is generating sometimes competing and sometimes mutually reinforcing effects, and these effects are highly contingent and continue to be contested.*

What has been the relationship between the Iraqi state, on the one hand, and globalising processes and actors, on the other, after the dissolution of the US-dominated Coalition Provisional Authority (CPA) and the installation by the Coalition of the Iraqi Interim Government on 28 June 2004? Most of the debate has focused on a traditionally liberal theme of the locus of sovereignty, that is, final authority exercised effectively and legally by a discrete state apparatus over a bounded territory and citizenry. From this perspective the debate is over the extent to which the Iraqi state has become sovereign. The first position is that the Iraqi state is now *fully sovereign*, as it has had sovereignty transferred to it by an external body, and thus the acts of its government are contingent solely upon the decisions of Iraqis. The second position is that Iraq is *incompletely but potentially sovereign*: the Interim Government remains hemmed in by the restrictions imposed upon it by external powers and by its own limited abilities, both of which are obstacles that can be alleviated through the process of state building and the exclusion of external actors. The third position is that the Iraqi state, like all modern states, will attain at most a *permanently diluted sovereignty*, with its governance shared with benign cosmopolitan forces in a non-hierarchical, globalised network of political institutions.

In this article we argue that the Iraqi state is in many ways not an instrument to represent the sovereign will of the people of Iraq. Instead, the Iraqi state is being reconstituted from above and below to represent a variety of globalising agendas and enforce them in Iraq. The Iraqi state is not representing Iraq in a globalising world: it is representing the globalising world in Iraq. To understand the process of how the Iraqi state is being reconstituted, we draw on literature which considers the relationships between national, international and transnational capital; the institutions of global neoliberalism; and the role of the USA as empire. At one end of the spectrum imperial globalisation is seen as being effectively a *decentred* form of global governance with the US as a state and US capital having lost their leading role.[1] The forces of globalisation are thus arranged hierarchically with regard to the states, economies and societies that they are reconstituting but not hierarchically in relation to each other. Decentred globalisation may be *international* (involving multiple states as the dominant actors) or *transnational* (involving a deterritorialised class which rules by means of states and other institutions). At the other end of the spectrum, globalisation is seen as *US-dominated*.[2] In both cases global governance is not counterposed to imperialism as it is in liberal conceptions of world politics: global governance in its current form is an expression of imperialism, defined in the contemporary period as the formal and informal practices which sustain rule on behalf of capital. While higher living standards and liberal democracy can be functional for capital and can thus be compatible with and encouraged by rule on behalf of capital, where these are perceived to challenge rule on behalf of capital, higher living standards and liberal democracy will be sacrificed if politically feasible. We explore these issues in a number of steps. First, we elaborate upon our critique of the sovereignty debate *per se* and as it relates to Iraq. Second, we assess the management of Iraq reconstruction funds and Iraq's debt and compensation burdens in terms of decentred or US-dominated imperial globalisation from above. Third, we consider the ways in which the transborder informal economy produces effects which work for and against imperial globalisation. Finally, we conclude with a series of observations about the current and highly contingent imperial globalisation of the Iraqi state.

The poverty of the sovereignty debate

Iraq's political trajectory has been mapped and evaluated usually by making the location of Iraqi sovereignty the focus of discussion and inquiry. Coalition governments and agencies have extensively asserted the notion of a transfer of sovereignty in their major statements on the establishment of the Interim Government, the subsequent handing over of power to it, and the accompanying dissolution of the CPA in June 2004. Thus the *Historic Review of CPA Accomplishments*, the end-of-project report, begins: 'On June 30, 2004 Iraq will again become a fully sovereign nation. When this occurs, the Coalition Provisional Authority. . .*will have achieved its primary goal*, and will cease to exist.' [3] After the formal hand-over, Coalition military and civilian personnel may be assisting the Iraqi government in fulfilling many of its domestic functions, but they are there by virtue of the invitation of the sovereign Iraqi government, which acts as the ultimate decision maker. This conception of a hand-over of sovereignty relies upon the change in the legal status of Iraq, a change that relies solely upon a series of formal enactments: Security Council Resolution (SCR) 1546 that proclaimed that 'Iraq will reassert its full sovereignty' upon the hand-over,[4] and a subsequent hurried ceremony in Baghdad.

In contrast, from the gradualist liberal perspective, sovereignty has been incompletely transferred to the Iraqi government. In the international political realm the deliberations that accompanied the negotiation of SCR 1546 hinged on the extent to which the Iraqi government would have to give authorisation for particular armed actions by the Coalition military inside Iraq. Considerable attention was focused on the extent to which the CPA had limited Iraqi sovereignty by leaving behind a series of orders in the tax, banking and media spheres among others, and by creating a set of regulatory institutions that the Iraqi government would not be entitled to dissolve while still in its interim and transitional phases.[5] Full sovereignty, from this perspective, will only return when the Iraqi government has the authority to annul the orders and dissolve the institutions that are a legacy of the occupation. These powers will have been fully restored once a constitution has been ratified and a new Iraqi government elected under it. A stronger version of this argument is adopted by those Iraqis who have taken an oppositional nationalist stance: the hand-over was a façade, real political power remains with the US authorities, and real sovereignty will only return to Iraqis once the US military and political presence departs from the country.

A more developed variant of the gradualist liberal perspective is Toby Dodge's application to Iraq of a standard approach which he draws from the work of Stephen Krasner. Sovereignty, he states, has three 'constituent parts': international legal sovereignty, Westphalian sovereignty and domestic sovereignty.[6] He concludes that Iraq is 'unambiguously' sovereign under international law, involving 'the recognition of a specific state as an independent and legal entity in international diplomacy'. As far as Westphalian sovereignty—the state's ability to exclude external actors from interfering with its capacity to rule within a particular territory—is concerned, he concludes that there is no serious external challenge to Iraq's territorial integrity but that the Iraqi government was not able to 'exclude external actors from interfering with its capacity to rule over its population'. With regard to internal sovereignty—the ability of the Iraqi government to ensure its effective political authority among the population throughout its territory—he suggests that the CPA had failed to achieve this and so it had decided to 'delegate power' to the Interim Government, which may 'gain acceptance and legitimacy from the Iraqi people' since it has 'Iraqis heading the government'. A similar distinction is made by the Council on Foreign Relations, the leading US think-tank on international affairs, in their backgrounder on Iraqi sovereignty: Iraq has 'legal sovereignty' and 'international political sovereignty' (corresponding to Krasner's first two categories), but lacks full 'de facto sovereignty'. This last aspect of Iraqi sovereignty is represented as being 'severely curtailed by the continuing presence of 138 000 US forces in Iraq and the inability of the new Iraqi government to defend itself against armed challenges'.[7]

This gradualist liberal framing, which assumes that self-contained mechanisms of rule are both possible and legitimising and should be developed further, is challenged by liberal cosmopolitans, who argue that globalisation displaces and fractures the modern state as a site of political authority: Iraq is but one particularly stark example of a global transformation. The Iraqi government, according to this view, may still be considered 'sovereign', but it governs in partnership. Thus, transnational and international organisations participate fully alongside the Iraqi state in a multi-layered system of essentially benign governance. Some liberal cosmopolitans have embraced the word 'empire' and insist that US empire is progressive in bringing liberal democracy and freer movement of labour and capital.[8] Other liberal cosmopolitans are deeply uncomfortable with the word empire and the role of the USA. Mary Kaldor manages to survey the evolution of war and governance since the 17th century without mentioning imperialism or empire even once, and has very little to say about the USA.[9] In discussing Iraq, she criticises what she portrays as the British neocolonial preference for doing deals with Iraqi sectional interests and the US neoconservative preference for sweeping all aside in pursuit of their ambitions.[10] Against this, she asserts the need to 'hand over sovereignty to Iraqis', to develop real indigenous 'democratic self-rule' and to locate this within global civil society.

The problem with the liberal cosmopolitan perspective on Iraq is that it overplays sovereignty while misconceiving the role of the state. It asks which capacities remain within the sphere of responsibility of the Iraqi state, and which capacities have been adopted or captured by external and international actors. It thus draws its explanatory potential from a distinction between the role of the state and that of new forces arising out of globalisation. In fact, the apparatus of the Iraqi state itself has been reconstituted to incorporate globalising elements within its structure, including in central decision-making roles, and these constituent elements have been retained largely intact after the formal end of occupation. This is most apparent in the nature of the leading personnel, most of whom are part of a transnational elite. Nearly all leading members of the Interim Government, with the exception of some of its Kurdish members, have lived for substantial parts of their adult life in Western Europe or the USA, and have been socialised into political life in those countries.[11] Their political base thus lies largely outside Iraq, and is often closely entwined with non-Iraqi political agents and organisations in the USA or UK. These individuals were installed by international intervention and the core of their political role has been in channelling international and external power into the Iraqi social arena. Moreover, this power has been crucial in sustaining the Iraqi state after the invasion: without external inputs, the state and its personnel would have largely vanished through the consequences of war and the subsequent insurgency.

The globalising processes which are constituting the Iraqi state from above can be seen clearly in the structure and operation of the institutions established to manage the financial resources for security, reconstruction and the overall budget in Iraq. In the next section of this article, we explore the connections between US-dominated and decentred imperial globalisation in relation to the management of US tax appropriations, Iraqi funds, international funds and Iraq's debt and war compensation burdens.

Reconstruction funds and debt as motors of imperial globalisation

Formally the co-ordination of all international (including US) assistance during and after the formal occupation has been led by Iraqis via the Iraqi Strategic Review Board, the Ministry of Planning and Development Co-operation and the Council for International Co-ordination.[12] The Iraqi Strategic Review Board has responsibility for approving and ensuring proper prioritisation and monitoring of international assistance. Chaired by the Minister of Planning and Development Co-operation, it was composed before June 2004 of Iraq ministry officials, two representatives of the Iraqi Governing Council (IGC) and one CPA representative. The Ministry of Planning and Development Co-ordination is responsible for co-ordinating reconstruction, working with other Iraqi ministries and the CPA's Programme Management Office (PMO) which managed US-funded contracts and, after the transfer of formal sovereignty, its replacement the Project and Contracting Office (PCO). The Council for International Co-ordination is chaired by the Minister of Planning and Development Co-operation and has members from over 23 countries involved in Iraq reconstruction. International tensions over the invasion and occupation are reflected in the fact that, although, according to the US General Accounting Office, this is the main point of contact between US representatives in Iraq and other international donors, it is an information-sharing rather than decision-making body. The characterisation of this system by the Coalition as 'Iraqi-led' ignores the fact that all the Iraqis on these bodies are Coalition appointees and ignores the globalising function of these appointees in decision making.

A more significant role was played by the CPA's Programme Review Board (PRB) which was established in June 2003 by CPA Regulation 3 to recommend allocations of US and Iraqi funds and funding plans prior to final approval by the CPA Administrator, Paul Bremer.[13] The PRB's voting membership was composed of a CPA chair; the CPA economic policy, civil affairs policy, operations and security policy directors; and the director of the US Agency for International Development (USAID) Iraq. Additional voting *ex officio* members were representatives of the Commander of Coalition Forces; the US Departments of Treasury, Defense and State; the UK; Australia; the Chairman of the International Co-ordination Council; and the Iraqi Ministry of Finance. The PRB also had the CPA Comptroller; CPA General Counsel; the Programme Co-ordinator of the Board; and representatives of the US Office of Management and Budget, the US Office of the Secretary of Defense, the IMF and the World Bank as non-voting members. The Special Representative for Iraq of the UN Secretary General and a representative of the International Advisory and Monitoring Board were permitted to attend as observers. Hence the total Iraqi voting membership was one US-appointed person.

Equally, it is important not to see the involvement of Iraqis solely as window-dressing: they are institutionalising, internalising and consolidating the norms and policies of the US and global neoliberal governance into the Iraqi state. This can be seen in more depth by an examination of the management of the three main categories of capital for use in security, reconstruction and debt servicing in Iraq—US appropriations, Iraqi revenues and international funds managed through the UN and World Bank. While it would be very easy to portray the reconstruction process as involving US actors in control of a system which transfers US tax dollars and Iraqi revenues back to US corporations in a simple hierarchical fashion, this would be to lose sight of its important decentred globalising dimensions.

The management of $18.4 billion of US appropriations gives the USA major advantages in its attempts to shape the globalisation of the Iraqi state towards US priorities and US-led capital and pro-US actors. In December 2003 the Department of Defense issued an order, signed by Deputy Secretary of Defense Paul Wolfowitz, which denied countries which had not been part of the Coalition the right to bid to become prime contractors in the award of US funds.[14] The PMO/PCO worked within parameters set by the Appropriations Committees of both the US Senate and US House of Representatives.[15] Another major actor has been the US Department of Commerce, which runs an Iraq Investment and Reconstruction Task Force (IIRTF) to assist US-based companies seeking reconstruction and other business contracts in Iraq.[16] The PMO reported to the CPA, which in turn was mainly responsible to the Department of Defense. The hand-over of June 2004 actually marked a substantial and disruptive shift in power and personnel from the US Department of Defense to the Department of State, in the shape of USAID, its foreign aid arm, and the Iraq Reconstruction Management Office within the US Embassy in Baghdad, headed by John Negroponte. The PCO reports to the State Department and the US Embassy in Baghdad in relation to setting priorities and requirements and to the Departments of Army and Defense in relation to contracting and programme management.[17] A review led by Negroponte resulted in a substantial reallocation of funds, including a shift away from basic services to the security sector and job creation, which then had to be approved by the two congressional appropriations committees.[18] US corporate actors are so deeply involved with the process that they cannot be regarded as simply subordinate to US governmental ones: the PCO itself described the system as a 'hybrid public-private model'.[19] Formally on the top layer is 'the ownership', defined as 'the people of the United States', an ownership which is of course symbolic rather than operational.[20] The next layer down is the overall programme management of over 2000 projects, headed by an American as Director, and with a support office provided by management services company AECOM which is based in Los Angeles. The third layer is sectoral programme management, all headed by Americans, and the bottom layer the sectoral prime contractor or contractors, again with head offices in the USA.[21]

The 'design and build' contractors for each sector are Parsons Delaware of California for buildings, education, health, security and justice; Kellogg, Brown & Root (a subsidiary of Halliburton) of Texas for oil; a joint venture led by Contrack International of Virginia for transportation; Lucent Technologies of New Jersey for communications; Washington Group International of Idaho for electricity and water; and Perini of Massachusetts for electricity. Out of 59 prime contracts awarded from US appropriations in the 2004 financial year up to November 2004, 48 (more than 80%) went to US companies.[22] Several of the remaining 11 contracts were with firms in which US capital had a significant stake, including three with Fluor AMEC, a US–UK joint venture, and one US–Jordanian joint venture, ANHAM. The remaining prime contracts were allocated to Italian, Israeli, Jordanian, Australian, British and Iraqi companies.

This degree of US control of the $18.4 billion does not sit well with the description of it by the PCO as 'a gift...from the American people to the people of Iraq'.[23] However, nor is it simply a gift from the American people to US corporations and back to their shareholders and the American people they employ. This sort of perspective is implied by Iraq Revenue Watch in its observations on Iraq's own resources in the Development Fund for Iraq:

> the CPA awarded US firms 74 percent of the value of the total $1.5 billion in contracts paid from Iraqi funds. When British firms are added to the equation, US and UK companies wind up receiving 85 percent of the value of contracts paid for from Iraqi funds.[24]

Although Parsons operates in 46 US states, it also operates in 37 countries other than the USA.[25] Hence it may be that a substantial amount of the funding is going to branches of the firm in other countries: in other words, global, non-US capital may be benefiting. Furthermore, the order banning bids for prime contracts from companies based in non-Coalition countries was rescinded in summer 2004 and never prevented Coalition prime contractors from using non-US and non-Coalition foreign subcontractors. In September 2004 the PCO claimed to have 76 699 'affiliated' Iraqi employees and 310 Iraqi firms working on reconstruction.[26] Parsons' Iraq infrastructure project is headed by Bechtel of California, and supported by Horne Engineering Services of Virginia, and its implementation plan is co-ordinated with USAID. Parsons has on its team three British companies and it has a commitment to using at least 80% Iraqi labour, purchasing Iraqi materials and equipment where possible and training at least 400 Iraqis for professional and management positions. Parsons' $33.8 million Taji Military Base reconstruction project near Baghdad is virtually complete and used 98% Iraqi labour (2500 people).[27] Bechtel has an outreach programme to

Iraqi subcontractors, with simplified documentation, presentations to Iraqi business associations, translation into Arabic of necessary documentation, waiving insurance requirements, advancing interest-free capital, providing banking services and professional training (including establishing a joint training programme with Baghdad University).[28] By late September 2004 Bechtel had awarded 160 out of 230 subcontracts to 120 different Iraqi companies, had employed more than 40 000 Iraqis and had registered on its supplier and contractor portal over 10 000 companies from 100 countries.[29] Capital is in the business of protecting and extending profit, and therefore has an interest in extending its penetration as far and as quickly as possible in Iraq and in connecting Iraq to its global network rather than merely spending money on expensive US-based employees, although such short-termism and bias against Iraqis is certainly widely believed to have occurred.[30]

The picture of an imperial globalising process, with the US in the primary but not exclusive position is most strongly suggested by an examination of the handling of Iraq's own revenues, except where revenues for the UN Compensation Fund are concerned. The Development Fund for Iraq (DFI) holds funds from Iraqi oil exports, leftover funds from the UN Oil-for-Food programme raised by Iraqi oil exports in the period of sanctions, and income from subsequent Iraqi oil exports and previously frozen Iraqi accounts in at least 10 countries or held by the Bank for International Settlements.[31] Five percent of the revenues from this fund continue to go to the UN Compensation Fund in accordance with SCR 687 (1991) and SCR 1483 (2003) for those individuals, corporations and governments which incurred losses as a result of Iraq's invasion of Kuwait in 1991. The award of claims is decided by the UN Compensation Commission (UNCC), which is a subsidiary organ of the UN Security Council, and the composition of its membership reflects this.[32] It is often pointed out that Iraq has only been allowed to make very limited representations to the Compensation Commission, but the bigger point is that the Iraqi state functions to enforce compensation demands on Iraqi society. The remaining 95% of DFI funds was controlled by the CPA's Programme Review Board (PRB). After the transfer of formal sovereignty, the PRB transferred to the US Embassy in Baghdad. New and unallocated funds from the DFI formally came under the control of the Iraqi Interim Government, while contracts for which DFI funds had already been allocated continued to be managed by the USA.

In order to provide audit oversight of the DFI, the International Advisory and Monitoring Board (IAMB) was established on the basis of SCR 1483 (22 May 2003), and was made up initially of representatives from the UN, World Bank, IMF and Arab Fund for Economic and Social Development. It later included additional representatives from the Interim Government. Nevertheless, throughout its existence, the CPA (and its contractors) had a fairly free hand with Iraq's resources: the IAMB did not actually meet until December 2003 and did not appoint an auditor until April 2004, not long before the CPA was due to be wound up. It reported that oil production was not metered properly so that it was not possible to know how much oil was produced, the award of contracts took place without competitive bidding in

ways that caused concern and required further investigation, and the CPA failed to inform the IAMB of the results of its review of the operation of the State Oil Marketing Organization. The IAMB pointed out that it had raised these issues with the CPA repeatedly, and commissioned two audits from international accounting company KPMG. On the basis of the first audit, for the period up to 31 December 2003, the IAMB concluded that the CPA and Iraqi ministries had failed to track Iraq's money to a degree that it could be confident that it was being spent as intended, although it did not find evidence of fraud.[33] KPMG found that PRB minutes were not a clear record of decisions and reasons for them, that it often took decisions when not quorate according to CPA Regulation 3, and that the Iraqi official only attended two of its 43 meetings up to 31 December 2003. It also noted many other procedural irregularities in the contract awarding process run by the CPA once a proposal had been approved by the PRB and CPA Administrator. These included extremely short timescales for bids which undermined effective competition, lack of clear documentation of award of contracts on a non-competitive basis and award of funds to contractors without adequate monitoring of performance.[34]

The fact that the CPA was spending Iraqi funds allowed it to avoid following many of the procedures and controls that apply to spending US funds and explains why it generally spent Iraqi funds in preference to US appropriations.[35] As of 4 April 2004, 97% of the dollar value of the contracts awarded by the PCO ($0.847 billion out of $1.04 billion) was paid for from Iraqi funds. Furthermore, 73% of the dollar value of contracts paid for from Iraqi funds was awarded as sole-source contracts with no competitive bidding.[36] Not surprisingly, allegations of abuses have been made, such as the claim that US-based company Custer Battles charged $20 million to provide security guards but subcontracted to a Kurdish Iraqi company for the work and pocketed as profit the difference of approximately 95% of the value of the contract.[37] In this case, US government auditors disputed two-thirds and withheld $5 million of the $20 million.[38] At one level, critiques of mismanagement of Iraqi funds by US agencies are important, as the money is then not available to Iraqis for their needs. However, a focus on ensuring that the funds are managed according to the highest procedural standards neglects the bigger issue of their imperial globalising role, mismanaged or not.

The most extensive and institutionalised expression of the decentred imperial globalisation of the Iraqi state in relation to reconstruction funding has taken the form of the International Reconstruction Fund Facility for Iraq (IRFFI). As such, its significance is much greater than is suggested by the small amount of money deposited in it—a mere $0.6 billion as of 26 May 2004, as opposed to the $13.6 billion promised.[39] The IRFFI is made up of two trust funds—the World Bank (WB) Iraq Trust Fund focused on economic transition, governance, public sector reform and poverty and safety net issues, and the UN Development Group (UNDG) Iraq Trust Fund focused on basic services, infrastructure, capacity building, employment generation and community-level rehabilitation. It is managed by a UN–WB

Facility Committee and a Donor Committee composed in May 2004 of 13 major donor countries and the European Commission, with observers from the UN, World Bank and other International Financial Institutions (ifis). These bodies liaise with the Iraqi Strategic Review Board, the Ministry of Planning and Development Co-operation and the Council for International Coordination (CIC) Assembly, which in turn liaise with bilateral contributors and the Ministry of Finance in relation to the national budget. All these bodies in turn liaise with recipients and executing agencies (UN agencies, ifis, ngos, ministries, governorates, municipalities, other elements of the public sector and the private sector). IRFFI monies are allocated in accordance with the priorities in the UN – WB Strategic Transitional Programmes which were in turn based on the October 2003 UN – WB Needs Assessment. Iraqis were integrated into the process of making the Needs Assessment and endorsing the outcome of that process. The Needs Assessment formed the basis of the Madrid donors' conference in October 2003; the institutional system described above generated 700 projects costed at $4 billion for consideration at the international donors' conference in Abu Dhabi in February 2004. Further ideas were proposed for the donors' conference in Doha, Qatar. As of June 2004 there was no centralised tracking of international assistance coming into Iraq or of its co-ordination with CPA activities, although the US State Department and Iraqi ministries were in the process of trying to establish one.[40] Hence the effect of the IRFFI has been to create a system in which there is wide-ranging decentred penetration and globalisation of the Iraqi polity.

The processes of decentred imperial globalisation are also being reinforced by the spread and handling of Iraq's enormous war reparations payments and external debt. Iraq's combined multilateral and bilateral debt inherited from the Saddam era is estimated to be as much as $137 billion. This does not take into account unpaid interest (which could more than double the total) or $30 billion outstanding on reparations awarded by the UNCC and $97.9 billion of claims still to be decided by it.[41] Iraq paid arrears to the IMF of $81 million in order to trigger in September 2004 approval by the IMF of a loan of $436 million in emergency 'post-conflict' assistance. Furthermore, the purpose of the loan is to improve Iraq's fiscal administrative capacity, with the explicit expectation that the increased capacity will be directed towards preparing Iraq for marketisation and debt management.[42] In November 2004 the Paris club of creditor states agreed to write off up to 80% of Iraq's debt to them by 2008, after protracted negotiations between its 19 members, on the condition of its acceptance of an IMF programme.

Formally, Iraq was in a position as a sovereign state to repudiate its debt, and thus reject the IMF programme; its failure to take this alternative is not a mark of its lack of sovereignty, but of its enmeshment in decentred structures of globalisation. Iraq has made its repayment and has accepted the Paris club proposal to mark its acceptance of IMF rules and has borrowed money which it is going to use to reshape itself into the mould desired by the IMF. This commitment to working within the framework of existing rules was an important factor in also allowing Iraq to secure credit from other institutions such as the Islamic Development Bank, which agreed to lend Iraq $500 million for infrastructural and humanitarian projects.[43]

The extent of Iraq's integration into decentred globalisation is displayed by this report of an interview with Ibrahim Bahr al-'Ulum, the minister for oil from September 2003 to June 2004:

> [Bahr al-'Ulum] thought the policies of the interim government are similar to those the IMF would recommend, however he still rejected [IMF] conditionality because of the limitation on Iraq's freedom: 'We are Iraq! We were the cradle of civilisation and I don't want to see anyone controlling our economy by any means.' [44]

The defiance in this statement is wholly undermined by being combined with a commitment to following IMF policies. As the Iraqi state is locked into the neoliberal economic model that is a constituent element of imperial globalisation, external impositions appear unnecessary for it to adopt the consequent policies. A major issue facing the Iraqi state and the actors which are globalising Iraq from above is how to deal with Iraq's informal economy in ways which subsume it within the project of imperial globalisation.

Iraq's transborder informal economy: decentred globalisation from below

Iraq's transborder informal economy is massive, diversifying and contributing significantly to the decentred aspects of the globalisation of Iraq as overlapping networks outwith state regulation increasingly assert their power.[45] Although much of the informal economy is primarily regional, it has many global connections. The informal economy refers to all economic activities for which state regulations exist but are not applied. The term 'informal' is more useful than 'illegal' because goods can be produced legally without violence or illegality but traded in an illegal fashion and because those operating informally are sometimes not trying to evade regulation—with the feebleness of the Iraqi state, the effort to regulate economic activity is distinctly limited. The informal economy can be evidence of the early stages of liberal market economic revival, which can be gradually brought under state and international regulation. However, it can also be effective as an alternative economy outside the control of the state.[46] In the case of Iraq, it is in some respects part of a serious challenge to neoliberal globalisation from above. This is most obviously the case where it is serving insurgents who are overtly aiming to disrupt that process. Economic activity is being fragmented as a host of regional and global networks take control of, and expand, various sources of income.

Of all the many elements of Iraq's informal economy, oil is the most important and is highly decentred and transnational in character. In October 2003 the US and British navies intercepted large numbers of road vehicles and small ships smuggling Iraqi oil, but about 2000 tons of Iraqi oil—10% of Iraq's output at the time—was sold on the black market. The smuggling rings tend to be composed of Iraqis living in the United Arab Emirates (UAE) using tanker lorries or thousands of ships crewed by Ethiopians, Iranians,

Somalis and Syrians.[47] Despite the crackdown, the British military calculated that the amount of oil being smuggled out of Iraq each week to Kuwait and UAE had risen to about 3000 tons in December 2003.[48] Iraqi officials put the illegal export of Iraqi refined oil at up to 25% of output in January 2004.[49] Estimates of how much of Iraq's oil is smuggled go as high as 60%.[50] Although seizures continued, the Iraqi Minister for Oil announced in August 2004 that the country had lost some $2 billion worth of oil income to smuggling and sabotage combined.[51] The Iraqi oil industry lacks proper metering facilities and so the authorities do not even know how much oil Iraq is producing.[52] The failure to meter the oil encourages the growth of the informal economy, not least by encouraging a sense that the state is not actually particularly concerned about where the oil goes. The prosecution of smugglers is rare. During UN sanctions, oil was smuggled out via Syria, Jordan, Turkey, Iran and the Persian Gulf, and there was tacit UN approval of the barter of Iraqi oil for Jordanian goods outside the UN Oil-for-Food Programme. Whereas the profits tended to go to Saddam's regime in the past (with some officials at all levels managing to skim money off for themselves), they now go to the smugglers and their allies. Coalition military commanders assume that they will never have the resources to catch most of the smugglers, and the US government is unwilling to push hard on an issue which would probably implicate some of its Gulf allies.

Oil smuggling, ironically, receives direct subsidies from the state, and the extent of oil theft indicates that smuggling must receive substantial assistance from state officials. Before the invasion, petrol, diesel and heating oil were subsidised to the point that their cost was almost negligible, and those subsidies have continued for fear of the political cost of charging real prices. The effect is to allow individuals with large vehicles—nicknamed *Bahara* (sailors)—from Iraq and other countries to fill up with subsidised Iraqi petrol for resale in neighbouring countries at 10 times the price for which they bought it and to make around $20 profit per trip.[53] It has also acquired a significant new transnational dimension in that much of the petrol which is being smuggled will have been imported into Iraq in the first place because of problems with the production and refining of Iraqi oil caused by Coalition policy and the insurgency. Smugglers have been found to be re-exporting fuel using tanker trucks stolen from the Ministry of Oil's huge fleet.

Many other elements of the decentred transnational informal economy are not only present but appear to be growing in significance. With imports into Iraq this is a form of economic power that originates with US attempts to create a consumer boom—it results from the high salaries paid. But some of the import routes are now managed by the paramilitaries of al-Anbar province, who take goods and resources from traders to allow those routes to function. With oil exports the productive power originates with the US orienting its technological assistance and planning to the oil sector, but it thereby funds those smuggling the oil out, who are insurgents or who ally with insurgents to obtain and protect their resources. Other examples are the significance of personnel and resources from the US-funded security apparatus within the insurgency; and how the Coalition's reinvigoration of

Iraq's religious significance has led to paramilitaries seeking control over pilgrimage routes and shrines. In the early days of the occupation, the significance of looting was played down by Coalition officials, in the expectation that it would cease quickly. However, it soon became apparent that the looting had merged with smuggling, and was being carried out by insurgents as well as criminals. In addition, a common practice in the earlier part of the occupation was the theft and melting down into bars of high-tension copper electrical cables, which has been a major factor inhibiting improvements in electricity supply.[54] In April 2004 the CPA published rules for licensing the export of scrap metal and penalties for violating those rules, but hundreds of flatbed trucks and semi-trailers leave Iraq each day, loaded with new components imported for the reconstruction, old military vehicles, scrap of all kinds and even entire dismantled building complexes from former military-industrial sites.[55] While this smuggling may have a military-related dimension, it is probably primarily non-military in nature. Iraq is being integrated more deeply into world informal trading in weapons, pornography and illegal drugs, including heroin, hashish, cocaine, tranquillisers, anti-depressants and other medications, with drugs looted and stolen from hospitals and pharmacies or entering via Iran, Afghanistan, Saudi Arabia and Syria and being sold openly.[56] Smuggling of Iraqi ancient artefacts is another widespread practice to service the global art market centred around Geneva, Tokyo, New York and London.[57] Iraq is also being integrated into the global sex industry. Iraqi and Egyptian human traffickers kidnap and sell Iraqi women into prostitution slavery, sometimes moving them overland to Syria and flying them to brothels in Yemen.[58] Iraq's prostitutes now have a major client base in the form of hundreds of thousands of dollar-rich foreign civilian and military personnel. The economies that result from drug, artefact and person trafficking complement those of oil smuggling in linking Iraq closely into transnational networks that have considerable power in reordering the form of Iraqi society, and thus have a high degree of tenacity.

Overall, it can be seen that Iraq's informal economy has regional and global dimensions. Some of them provide challenges to the imperial reconstitution of the Iraqi state, some of them operate alongside that reconstruction and some of them even reinforce that imperial reconstruction: thus they allow for the penetration of Iraqi society by global criminal networks or by channelling Iraqi oil into the global oil market by the back door. The overall relationship between these complex forces in the imperial globalisation of the Iraqi state is considered in our conclusion.

Conclusion

To understand the mechanism of rule in Iraq and its trajectory, it is important to look at how the apparatus of the Iraqi state is being continuously constituted by globalising forces. It is not a case that there is an Iraqi government that somehow stands outside globalising forces, which act as limitations upon that government's actions. Instead, globalising forces have largely shaped the preferences of the Iraqi government, its mode of assessing the methods to realise those preferences, its mechanisms for implementing those methods, its choices of which preferences to prioritise, and its ways of assessing whether those preferences have been realised. These forces remain present not simply by permission of the Interim Government, but have become deeply embedded into the structure of the economy. We have explored in this article various aspects of Iraq's rearticulation to capital: there are many other aspects of that issue (such as privatisation and the operation of private military companies) and many other issues (such as the political networks and practices of liberal democracy) which also influence the imperial globalisation of Iraq and which require further exploration. Understanding of the competitive, complementary and mutually constitutive relationships between US-dominated aspects of globalisation, decentred aspects of globalisation (international and transnational, from above and from below), and Iraq's social forces also needs further theoretical and empirical development. The formal hand-over of 28 June 2004 served the purpose of putting an Iraqi face on imperial globalisation and providing much greater legal cover for it than was available under formal occupation. Ironically, one of the most important exercises of what might be called popular 'sovereignty' in Iraq is one not generally represented as such—the direct privatisation of Iraq's oil industry has been prevented thus far by a belief that an attempt to do so would produce political disquiet on a scale that would render the US presence in Iraq untenable.

The fact that the USA physically occupied Iraq, installed a government and passed much legislation by decree might suggest almost total US dominance over broader globalising forces and thus that the Iraqi state is almost solely an instrument of US empire. Certainly, Iraq's imperial globalisation from above is not primarily decentred in terms of the actors involved or the interests served: US actors and interests have been at the forefront. However, the actions of US actors have tended to favour US political power and the US-based fraction of capital less than the fact of occupation would suggest: actions by the USA are not necessarily actions on behalf of the USA.

Furthermore, this advantage has declined over time. The USA has experienced considerable tension between trying to retain freedom of manoeuvre through retaining control over decision making and seeking to consolidate its position through the establishment of effective co-opted Iraqi decision making and the involvement of other international and transnational actors. It has sought to square this circle by a gradual shift to an emphasis on the second approach, dangling the prospect of more access to contracting and subcontracting in the hope of attracting more political and military support, and by permitting Iraqi appointees more decisions over the allocation of Iraqi resources. Other states have positioned themselves to maximise their corporate penetration of Iraq and debt and compensation repayment by Iraq while letting the USA bear the costs of facing the insurgency. In addition, there is a second force for decentred globalisation in Iraq, namely, 'globalisation from below' by means of the workings of the transborder informal economy. Many but not all of the activities of this informal economy are closely related to the insurgency. The USA, neoliberal institutions and the actors in the informal economy are generating sometimes competing and sometimes mutually reinforcing effects. This globalisation from below demonstrates that Iraq is not merely the passive object of globalisation from above. The globalisation of Iraq from above and from below is proceeding in a highly dynamic fashion, resulting in and as a product of a considerable level of unpredictability. For example, the USA has repeatedly changed its plans for Iraq, and international actors such as the UN, World Bank and IMF have been forced to operate at arm's length from outside Iraqi territory. Further major changes of direction—and even reversals of aspects of imperial globalisation—are easy to imagine as the contest over Iraq is played out.

Notes

Thanks to Anne Alexander for superb research assistance, to Doug Stokes and Sultan Barakat for comments on an earlier draft and to the ESRC for financial support. This article is adapted from material in our forthcoming book *Iraq in Fragments: The Occupation and its Legacy* (London: Hurst, 2006).

1 See especially M Hardt & A Negri, *Empire*, Boston, MA: Harvard University Press, 2001; and WI Robinson, *A Theory of Global Capitalism: Production, Class, and State in a Transnational World*, Baltimore, MD: Johns Hopkins University Press, 2004.
2 See especially N Chomsky, *Hegemony or Survival: America's Quest for Global Dominance*, London: Penguin, 2004; T Barkawi & M Laffey, 'The imperial peace: democracy, force and globalization', *European Journal of International Relations*, 5 (4), 1999, pp 403–434; M Laffey & J Weldes, 'Representing the international: sovereignty after modernity', in J Dean & P Passavant, *The Empire's New Clothes: Reading Hardt and Negri*, London: Routledge, 2003, pp 121–142; R Biel, 'Imperialism and international governance: the case of US policy towards Africa', *Review of African Political Economy*, 93, 2003, pp 77–88; and D Stokes, 'The heart of empire: theorising US empire in an era of transnational capitalism', *Third World Quarterly*, 26 (2), 2005, pp 217–236.
3 *An Historic Review of CPA Accomplishments*, Baghdad, nd, p 2, emphasis added. A prospective example is found in the speech of L Paul Bremer, CPA Administrator, 24 March 2004, 'One hundred days to a sovereign Iraqi government', at http://www.cpa-iraq.org/transcripts/20040324_Bremer_100.html.
4 Operative Paragraph 2, Security Council Resolution 1546 (8 June 2004). The text of the resolution, together with its short annex, refers to the sovereign nature of the new Iraqi government 16 times.
5 For example, NJ Brown, 'Leaving a trail of legislative "orders" behind in Iraq', *Daily Star* (Beirut), 30 March 2004.
6 T Dodge, 'A sovereign Iraq?', *Survival*, 46 (3), 2004, pp 39–58.
7 Council on Foreign Relations, *Iraq: The Sovereignty Issue*, 25 May 2004, at http://www.cfr.org/background/background_iraq_sovereignty.php, accessed 16 October 2004.
8 N Ferguson, *Colossus: The Rise and Fall of the American Empire*, London: Allen Lane, 2004.
9 In Kaldor's *New and Old Wars: Organized Violence in a Global Era*, Cambridge: Polity Press, 1999, there is a single, passing reference to 'colonial wars' on p 15.
10 M Kaldor, 'Iraq: the democratic option', 13 November 2003, at http://www.opendemocracy.net/debates/article.jsp?id = 2&debateId = 95&articleId = 1579.
11 Examples are interim Prime Minister Iyad Allawi, resident in the UK from 1972 to 2003, Foreign Minister Hoshyar al-Zibari, resident in the UK from 1979 to 2003, and Minister of Defence Hazim Sha'lan, resident from 1985 in the UK, where he managed a real estate firm. US examples are provided in Farah Stockman and Thanassis Cambanis, 'As Iraq seeks own way, many involved have US links', *Boston Globe*, 10 June 2004.
12 This system was established via CPA Regulations 5 (June 2003) and 7 (5 December 2003). US General Accounting Office (GAO), *Rebuilding Iraq*, June 2004, pp 22–24.
13 Programme Review Board, CPA, at http://www.iraqcoalition.org/budget/program_review_board.html.
14 P Finn & P Baker, 'US decision on Iraq contracts irritates excluded war critics', *Washington Post*, 11 December 2003.
15 PCO, at http://www.rebuilding-iraq.net/.
16 http://www.export.gov/iraq/.
17 PCO press release, 'PCO transition of authority', 15 August 2004, at http://www.rebuilding-iraq.net/pdf/Main_Story_press_release_filter.htm.

18 M Curtius & P Richter, 'State Dept criticizes focus of Iraqi effort', *Los Angeles Times*, 22 July 2004; and US Department of State, 'Transcript: US increases spending in Iraq for security, election preparations', 14 September 2004.
19 PCO, 'PCO transition of authority'.
20 PCO, 'Programme Management Office concept of operations', at http://www.rebuilding-iraq.net/portal/page?_pageid = 35,74115&_dad = portal&_schema = PORTAL, accessed 21 September 2004.
21 For a survey of all US firms with Iraq-related contracts, see the Windfalls of War project of the Center for Public Integrity, at http://www.publicintegrity.org, accessed 1 October 2004.
22 'FY2004 reconstruction contracts and grants', US Department of Commerce website, Export.gov/Iraq, at http://www.export.gov/iraq/market_ops/contracts04.html, accessed 6 November 2004.
23 PCO, 'PCO transition of authority'.
24 Iraq Revenue Watch (IRW), *Disorder, Negligence and Mismanagement: How the CPA Handled Iraq Reconstruction Funds*, Report No 7, September 2004, p 2. See also P Chatterjee, *Iraq, Inc: A Profitable Occupation*, London: Seven Stories Press, 2004.
25 Parsons, at http://www.parsons.com/about/default.asp, accessed 21 September 2004.
26 http://www.rebuilding-iraq.net/portal/page?_pageid = 35,62867&_dad = portal&_schema = PORTAL, accessed 21 September 2004.
27 Parsons, 'Taji Military Base renovation, Iraq', at http://www.parsons.com/about/press_rm/potm/09-2004/index.html, 21 September 2004.
28 Bechtel Corporation, 'Bechtel's outreach to Iraqi subcontractors', at http://www.bechtel.com/sample_iraq_supplier_information.htm, accessed 5 October 2004.
29 Bechtel Corporation, 'US government's Iraq infrastructure reconstruction program', at http://www.bechtel.com/iraq.htm, accessed 5 October 2004.
30 International Crisis Group (ICG), *Reconstructing Iraq*, 2 September 2004, pp 11–15, 17–18.
31 IAMB, at http://www.iamb.info/. See also GAO, *Rebuilding Iraq*, pp 27–35.
32 UN Compensation Commission, at http://www.unog.ch/uncc/.
33 IAMB, 'Statement: release of the KPMG audit reports on the Development Fund for Iraq', 15 July 2004, at http://www.iamb.info/auditrep/pr071504.pdf.
34 KPMG Audit and Risk Advisory Services, *Development Fund for Iraq, Appendix*, June 2004, at http://www.iamb.info/auditrep/r123104.pdf.
35 IRW, *Disorder, Negligence and Mismanagement*, p 8.
36 *Ibid*, pp 3, 7; and CPA Office of the Inspector General, *Coalition Provisional Authority's Contracting Processes Leading Up to and Including Contract Award*, 27 July 2004, p 3, at http://www.cpa-ig.com/pdf/cpaig_audit_cpa_contracting_processes.pdf.
37 IRW, *Disorder, Negligence and Mismanagement*, pp 2–3, 8.
38 N King & YJ Dreazen, 'Amid the chaos in Iraq, tiny security firm carved out opportunity', *Wall Street Journal*, 13 August 2004.
39 UN–WB International Reconstruction Trust Fund Facility for Iraq, at http://www.uniraq.org/donors/irffi.asp, accessed 1 October 2004; GAO, *Rebuilding Iraq*, pp 17–26; and ICG, *Reconstructing Iraq*, pp 24–26.
40 GAO, *Rebuilding Iraq*, pp 18, 23.
41 Jubilee Iraq, at http://www.jubileeiraq.org/debt_today.htm, accessed 10 October 2004.
42 IMF, 'IMF Executive Board approves US$436.3 million in emergency post-conflict assistance to Iraq', Press Release No 04/206, 29 September 2004, at http://www.imf.org/external/np/sec/pr/2004/pr04206.htm.
43 Islamic Development Bank, 'IDB allocates US$500 million for Iraq reconstruction', 7 January 2004, at http://www.isdb.org/english_docs/idb_home/content.htm?content = include/iraqpress.inc.
44 Jubilee Iraq, at http://www.jubileeiraq.org/iraqiviews.htm, accessed 22 November 2004.
45 These themes are explored with regard to cases other than Iraq by M Pugh & N Cooper with J Goodhand, *War Economies in a Regional Context*, Boulder, CO: Lynne Rienner, 2004.
46 MA Centeno & A Portes, *The Informal Economy in the Shadow of the State*, Working Paper #03-06, Center for Migration and Development, Princeton University, February 2003, at http://cmd.princeton.edu/papers/wp0306.pdf.
47 R Collier, 'Black market drains Iraq oil: Pentagon out to stop ships plying booming trade', *San Francisco Chronicle*, 22 October 2003.
48 J Cole, 'Basra: massive drug, petroleum smuggling; Christians, musicians harassed', *Informed Comment*, 31 December 2003, at http://www.juancole.com/2003_12_01_juancole_archive.html.
49 'Oil Ministry cracks down on smugglers', *Iraq Press*, 14 January 2004, at http://www.iraqpress.org/english.asp?fname = ipenglish%5C2004-01-14%5C0.htm.
50 I Wilkinson, 'British troops hunt night oil raiders who are bleeding Iraq', *Daily Telegraph*, 13 July 2004.
51 Xinhuanet, 'Iraq confiscates ships for smuggling oil', 21 August 2004.

52 J Cox, 'Audit finds US lax on control of oil money', *USA Today*, 15 July 2004.
53 E Eckholm, 'On Iraq's border, sailors of the desert smuggle subsidized gasoline', *New York Times*, 21 August 2004.
54 UN Information Service, 'Organized crime to be a growing problem in Iraq UNODC fact-finding mission reports', UN Office on Drugs and Crime, 27 August 2003, UNIS/CP/445, at http://www.unodc.org/unodc/press_release_2003-08-27_1.html.
55 J Glantz, 'Not all scrap metal leaving Iraq is junk', *New York Times*, 27 May 2004.
56 For example, A Janabi, 'Drugs trade thriving in Iraq', *Aljazeera.Net*, 29 March 2004.
57 Z Bahrani, 'Days of plunder', *Guardian*, 31 August 2004.
58 V Firmo-Fontan, 'Abducted, beaten and sold into prostitution: a tale from Iraq', *Independent*, 26 July 2004.

Corruption, Reconstruction and Oil Governance in Iraq

PHILIPPE LE BILLON

ABSTRACT *With the world's second largest oil reserves, Iraq is potentially a very prosperous country. Like many other oil-dependent countries, however, Iraq's recent history points to a pattern of authoritarianism, corruption and violence. The US administration has portrayed its occupation of Iraq as an effort to break with this pattern and ensure democracy, security and a shared prosperity for Iraqis. This article engages with the challenges of oil governance and reconstruction in Iraq, focusing on the role of corruption and the record of the Coalition Provisional Authority. Iraq's political legacy, oil dependence and transition under US occupation suggest that the new Iraqi regime may once again rest on corruption-based patronage; but of a type more accommodating to US interests.*

> *This is George W Bush, the President of the United States. At this moment, the regime of Saddam Hussein is being removed from power...and we will not stop until Saddam's corrupt gang is gone...You deserve better than tyranny and corruption. ('President's Message to the Iraqi People', 10 April 2003)*

> *The people have awoken from their stupor, they realise the degree of corruption and tyranny which [Saudi rulers] use to rob them of their rights. Muslims in the country of the two holy mosques insist on regaining their rights at any cost. (Osama Bin Laden, audio-tape, December 2004)*

The 'corruption' of Saddam Hussein's regime has provided the US administration with one of its main official justifications for military intervention in Iraq. Although the Bush administration initially focused on weapons of mass destruction (WMD) as a threat resonating with the US public, it emphasised corruption and human rights abuses to legitimise a forceful regime change in the eyes of the Iraqi public (quickly extending this justification to the Western public as there were no WMD to be found).[1] Ironically, the statements of the White House on corruption and the justification of a forceful change echoed those of Islamic 'terrorist' groups seeking to bring down 'corrupt regimes' in the Middle East, from Hamas in Palestine to Hezbollah in Lebanon or Al-Qaeda in Saudi Arabia. Of course, the US did not invade Iraq *simply* to end the corruption of the regime of Saddam Hussein (or to replace it by a more favourable one, as discussed below). Nonetheless, concept of corruption plays an important role in the US intervention in Iraq and vision of its broader impact on the politics of the Middle East, opening up questions regarding the role of corruption in political transition and reconstruction processes.[2]

Corruption is a concept which is difficult to define, even in the context of orderly political regimes.[3] It seems even more slippery when the legitimacy of rule, as in the case of Iraq, is openly and violently contested. As Johnston remarks, the most important issue 'may not be what the term "corruption" means, but rather who gets to decide what it means, and how widely those decisions will be accepted'.[4] Corruption has long been a 'taboo' issue in the international arena of governments and development agencies, often being justified by geopolitical agendas and portrayed as relatively benign. With the end of the Cold War major donors and international agencies have redefined corruption as a central tenet of the 'good governance' agenda. Anti-corruption reforms have proliferated and have targeted a vast number of countries, many of them in the midst of major political and economic transition. As discussed below, many of these initiatives fail to take into account the multiple forms and roles of corruption, thereby potentially undermining transition processes.

This article engages with the challenges of oil governance and reconstruction in Iraq, focusing on corruption and the transition process initiated by the US/UK invasion of March 2003. With the world's second largest oil reserves and a population of 25 million people, Iraq is potentially a very prosperous country.[5] However, Iraq's recent history, like that of many other oil-dependent countries, suggests that the frequent confluence of oil wealth and authoritarianism is particularly prone to high levels of political corruption. The US administration has showcased the military ousting of Saddam Hussein's regime in March 2003 as providing a historic opportunity for Iraq to depart from this pattern. Against the backdrop of Saddam Hussein's abuses and in the absence of WMD, the US administration has increasingly justified the occupation of Iraq in terms of a transition to democracy, security and probity for Iraqis.

Although it is too early to assess the long-term impact of the initial phases of the transition, the US-dominated Coalition Provisional Authority (CPA) in charge of the occupation of Iraq has failed in many respects to set propitious conditions for such a transition.[6] Misguided US policies have been violently confronted by the realities of local and regional power networks and powerful discourses of resistance. Reconstruction has been slow, costs have spiralled above initial estimates, and early priorities were wrongly placed on large infrastructure projects awarded to a handful of US companies. In turn, the absence of tangible economic benefits and improvements in living conditions for most Iraqis has fuelled resentment, and contributed to both political and economic violence. Iraq's own repatriated funds and oil revenues, rather than US or international funds, have financed most of the initial reconstruction efforts, leaving the new Iraqi authorities in a tight fiscal position. As a key asset for the country, the oil sector has proved a vulnerable economic target for insurgents opposing the US, with massive disruptions in the flow of oil and the rehabilitation of infrastructures. Oil also remains a widespread reason for distrust of the US and its ultimate motives. As a result, Iraq faces the prospect of continued reliance on limited oil revenues and donor handouts, rather than a windfall peace dividend, which in any case many feared would have mostly benefited foreign investors if the CPA's liberal economic policies had been implemented.[7]

The results of the national elections in January 2005 marked a strong departure from the patterns of Iraqi politics and the dominance of Arab Sunni minority groups that should strongly shape the future of Iraq. Whatever the outcome of a lengthy and violent transition process, oil dependence and corruption are likely to remain major challenges in Iraq. In this article I first briefly discuss the so-called 'resource curse' affecting many resource-dependent countries, before turning to the case of Iraq. I then examine the recent specific risks and opportunities that corruption-based patronage represents in the current period of intense political and economic transformation in Iraq.[8] Finally, after examining the record of the Coalition Provisional Authority in matters of oil governance, reconstruction and corruption, I outline some suggestions to help Iraq (and the US) to extricate itself from the current pattern of violence and underdevelopment.

Contextualising corruption

The end of the 'corruption taboo' in the international arena is to be welcomed when considering the devastating economic, social and political costs of corruption, in particular those of Cold War-era complicity with corrupt but 'friendly' regimes. There is little evidence, however, that this shift has reduced the overall level of corruption (in a domain notoriously difficult to measure) even if it has affected some of the forms that corruption takes (eg electoral corruption in democracies).[9] Critics point out that the anti-corruption agenda reflects in part a post-Washington consensus seeking to reinvigorate regulatory institutions while maintaining the blame for the failure of development on governments in the South.[10] Much of the 'good governance' agenda has concentrated on combining economic liberalisation and democratisation with a crackdown on bureaucratic corruption, a strategy that often overlooked the privatisation of political corruption during structural adjustments and transition to a 'market' economy, the pauperisation of (former) civil servants, and the motivating and facilitating role of a globalised capitalist economy. In many economically weak countries the transition to democracy has been marred by conflicts, with corruption generally shifting from monopolistic patronage–clientelism ensuring a degree of relative stability to more competitive and disintegrative patterns of corruption.[11] Anti-corruption initiatives also remain selectively applied by most governments and corporations that prioritise their self-interest rather than international norms and instruments.

Anti-corruption reform programmes over the past decade have also been criticised for consisting of 'wish lists' lacking contextualisation that often have little positive impact. Johnston argues in this regard that corruption is strongly contextualised by two key variables: the character of political institutions; and the source of wealth.[12] According to Johnston, political institutions can be relatively open to competition, as in the case of democracies and countries in political transition, or on the contrary be relatively closed and autonomous, as in the case of authoritarian regimes. Wealth opportunities can be located in the 'economic' realm (ie the private sector), or within the 'political' realm (eg through fiscal rents such as the control of the oil sector). Depending on the source of wealth and political institutions involved, different forms of corruption can be expected to be dominant. For example, in a context of open political institutions and economic wealth opportunities, corruption generally takes the shape of bidding between different private interest groups to gain political influence. This form of corruption is often institutionalised, as with the US example, with major energy corporations influencing political decision making through the provision of large electoral funds to political parties, the movement of senior corporate executive leaders to high-level political postings, anonymous participation in the design of official national energy policy, and recommendation for the privatisation of public sector activities leading to legal non-bidding allocation of major public contracts.[13] If, in contrast, political institutions are open to competition but political avenues are the most important wealth opportunities, insecure and rival elite groups compete to build and discipline personal followings through handouts and promises of future rewards. This pattern of 'fragmented clientelism' is characteristic of countries in transition, such as Russia in the 1990s.

Alternatively, in the case of highly autonomous institutions, 'elite hegemony' tends to dominate when economic opportunities are greater than political ones, with entrenched elites exchanging scarce political access for wealth. If, on the other hand, political opportunities are greater than economic ones, the pattern is that of 'patronage machines', with political monopoly allowing for a clientelisation of the population (through its poverty or lack of economic alternative, as in many oil dependent countries). Johnston's typology indicates that distinct patterns of corruption arise from different political and economic contexts. Acknowledging the heterogeneity of corruption which may not only assist with the tailoring of reforms to specific situations, but also expose more fundamental barriers to developments.

Oil wealth and the resource curse

Resource-dependent countries like Iraq are comparatively more prone to poor economic growth, corruption, authoritarianism and high levels of poverty.[14] Not all resource-dependent countries are equally exposed to the economic, political and military risks of this so-called 'resource curse'. A country's specific history, economic and institutional development before resource exploitation, and its leadership are all significant factors that come into play. As noted by an Angolan journalist jailed for denouncing the war and corruption fuelled by oil and diamonds in his country: 'It's fashionable to say that we are cursed by our mineral riches. That's not true. We are cursed by our leaders.' [15] No doubt one can similarly point to the responsibility of Saddam Hussein in the case of Iraq. But beyond his individual responsibility also lies a complex array of factors, one of which is the context of oil wealth.

Resource dependence is associated with a number of economic, political and security problems. First, economic growth has been comparatively slower in most resource-dependent countries since the 1970s; a pattern that also affected most oil exporters after the end of the oil boom in the mid-1980s. Second, resource dependence has been associated with poor governance, high levels of corruption and (often incompetent) authoritarianism. Governments in resource-dependent countries tend to be more corrupt as a result of the discretionary control of large rents generated by resource exploitation. Resource-dependent states also often exhibit extreme levels of institutional conservatism and inertia, with government stability relying on fiscal transfer rather than statecraft.[16] Third, many resource-rich governments prioritise security spending, while oil exporting countries in particular face a higher risk of armed conflict.[17] Extremely high levels of resource revenues have allowed some governments to maintain stable autocracies by buying social peace, co-opting political opponents and funding effective security agencies. In most cases, however, a concentration of power by factionalised ruling elites, poor governmental legitimacy, as well as foreign vested interests present major challenges to peace in resource-dependent countries. The consequences of the 'resource curse' for the population are often paradoxical as it finds itself 'hostage' to an omnipotent state, source of both hope and frustration when facing conditions of poverty, inequalities and human rights abuses.[18] Although the state may pursue populist policies by redistributing resource wealth, the state is ultimately insulated from the population through the independent tax base that the resource wealth provides. In such contexts the risk of institutionalised political corruption—which will vary according to the type of political regime in place—is high.

Political transition and reconstruction

Political and economic transitions are particularly prone to corruption, and transitions in conflict-affected countries are no exception.[19] Corruption is often one of the key concerns of local populations in conflict-affected during reconstruction, along with insecurity and unemployment.[20] Many Iraqis, fear that reconstruction monies will be squandered in the midst of a culture of corruption and favouritism reminiscent of Saddam Hussein's regime.[21]

Several factors help to explain why corruption (and its perception and political instrumentalisation) is such a prevalent problem in conflict-affected countries. First, corruption often predates the conflict—sometimes having contributed to it—and is frequently entrenched during hostilities. Armed factions often justify corruption by the context or goals of war, using it to strengthen their hold on power. For lack of an alternative ordinary people resort to corruption and illegal economic activities to cope with the hardships of war or economic sanctions.[22] Although war generally aggravates corruption, ideals and strict discipline have significantly limited corrupt practices among some armed movements.

Second, in the context of a transition to peace, 'national reconciliation' often results in politically driven distribution of state assets and positions, with a tacit agreement on corruption included in peace accords. Transition to democracy period also represents a critical moment in terms of political party financing. A shift from overtly coercive modes of political control to more democratically savvy forms of patronage and vote buying may aggravate political corruption in the form of illegal (or dubious) political donations and economic activities, misappropriation of public funds, or abuse of state resources.[23] Eager not to 'jeopardise the peace', international donors often turn a blind eye to such practices or even portray them as a 'normal route to capitalist development and stability'.[24] There is therefore a high risk that a transition to democracy increases political corruption in the absence of formal instruments of party financing.

Third, the transition to a market economy that characterised many post-conflict reconstruction processes in the 1990s offers major corruption opportunities that post-conflict institutions may be unwilling or unable to address. Immediate private gain is attractive when facing the uncertainties and opportunities of the transition from war to peace, while personal financial wealth also becomes a greater symbol of social status in a peaceful era. International donors also generally invest massive sums in reconstruction. Although most of these funds are directly administered by foreign aid agencies, some have a significant impact on the probity of institutions. Local politicians frequently attempt to capture such windfalls, economically or politically. Reconstruction contractors frequently jockey for a share, which may lead to corrupt practices. Embezzlement and wastage can be staggering. Distrust of public institutions and donors is often rife among victimised populations following delays, aid shortages, misallocation and setbacks. The presence of aid agencies, as well as that of large numbers of foreign troops, often leads to highly inflated local prices and salaries setting an economic context propitious for corruption.

Corruption, oil wealth and political regimes in Iraq

The creation of a 'modern state' in Iraq by the British in the 1920s—ironically driven by a similar mix of military dominance, commercial interests, and contempt for 'corrupt Oriental despotism'–maintained an unequal society with entrenched Sunni Arab elites oversseing patronage networks. This pattern of institutionalised corruption was part of the rationale motivating the *coups d'état* against the Hashemite monarchy in 1936, 1941 and 1958. The

1958 coup, led by Brigadier Abd al-Karim Qasim, was successful and set in motion a reshaping of patronage consolidating his military rule. This attempt largely failed, however, as demonstrated by a succession of counter-coups and violent purges by competing groups of military officers characteristic of a situation of fragmented clientelism.[25] Successive regimes, including that of Saddam Hussein after the Ba'ath party seized power in 1968, continued to ensure dominance through patronage and coercion.

The oil windfall of the 1970s made populist economic policies more affordable to the Ba'athist regime and consolidated the patronage machine of the regime through a broadened politics of redistribution. The oil sector had played a growing role in Iraq during the 20th century, ranging from the colonial 'invention' of the country by British interests seeking to control potential oil fields, to domestic economic and political life and contemporary geostrategic importance.[26] Economically, Iraq greatly benefited from the two oil booms of the 1970s, having nationalised its industry a few years before. Annual economic growth averaged 14% in the 1970s and by 1979 Iraq was the second largest OPEC oil exporter behind Saudi Arabia. This new wealth was used by the Ba'ath party for a massive arms build-up and served the private interests of the Ba'ath party regime's cronies. It also benefited much of the population through a rapid rise in living standards. Iraq's costly war with Iran between 1980 and 1988 and falling oil prices after 1981 resulted in a drastic turnaround. Negative growth averaged 6% per year during the 1980s. This growth collapse was further aggravated by the imposition of economic sanctions after Iraq's invasion of Kuwait. By 1994, when the sanctions regime was still applied in full force, Iraq's per capita real GDP was estimated as close to that of the 1940s.[27] This situation improved with the oil-for-food programme. By the time of the 2003 US-led invasion, however, the country still faced staggering financial obligations estimated at $383 billion, a devastated economic and public service infrastructure requiring an estimated $53 billion investment, and a largely destitute population.[28]

Although the economy was marked by spectacular growth in the 1970s, opportunities remained within the political realm as the state controlled oil revenues and most economic sectors. Oil revenues consolidated the hegemony of the elite by providing it with massive financial resources to strengthen its patronage and coercive capacity, including at a regional level through a massive arms build-up motivated by military ambitions and facilitated by Western and Soviet interests.[29] Even though oil allowed the regime to extend the reach of its patronage and security apparatus, it nevertheless proved relatively ineffective at building a consensual national politics and a strong economy. Rather, as Iraqi academic Isam al Khafaji remarks, the oil windfall benefiting the Ba'athist regime until the early 1980s allowed it to forcibly impose:

> a destructive concept of unity among Iraqis...atomis[ing] the population and linking the individuals directly to the state...marginalizing and suppressing entire communities and regions...political, family and clannish cronyism deprived Iraqis from any autonomy and enhanced a perception among them

> that the state does not owe anything to the people. Rather it was they who owed their living to the state.[30]

Although the war launched against Iran in 1979 provided the Iraqi regime with a powerful nationalist discourse and project, it bankrupted the country and demonstrated the limits of Iraqi military power. A progressive tightening of the politics of 'national' patronage—initially conducted under a 'bullet and butter' policy seeking to insulate the population economically from the conflict—led to focusing patronage on the officer corps as the war with Iran dragged on. The defeat against US-led forces in Kuwait in 1991 and the imposition of UN sanctions in 1990 further increased this shift towards nepotistic and competitive corruption. The control of smuggled goods and kickbacks from oil sales became the central economic focus of the regime as its formal tax handle on the oil sector drastically weakened. In continuity with the fiscal austerity measures of the 1980s the regime whittled down its politics of favouritism while strengthening its command of the rationing programme and the 'illegal' economy on which the population depended. Increasingly nepotistic forms of corruption that benefited 'Saddam's faithful' (*umana' Saddam*) replaced the 'national' politics of patronage extended through the state. The educated middle class that had once constituted the main power base of the Ba'ath party was broadly marginalised. The regime was cautious, however, to maintain personalised rewards with several thousand selected individuals in all walks of life, thereby sustaining a link with most groups and communities. Oil trafficking also allowed the regime to maintain political and economic channels of influence, both regionally and internationally (see below).

The situation with regard to corruption was more one of fragmented clientelism, with competing groups in Saddam Hussein's entourage controlling smuggling by clamping down on competing sanctions busters.[31] The concentration of wealth within the ruling family was certainly not exceptional in the region, although the level of neglect and abuse of the population certainly was. Saddam Hussein's first son, Uday, accumulated at one point close to 30 official positions and supervised both 'legal' and 'illegal' economic activities, most notably oil smuggling during the sanctions regime.[32] Protected by their political connections, the 'embargo cats' (*bazazine al hisar*) came to constitute a heterogeneous and docile *nouveau riche* class. The control of part of the 'informal' market and the official control of the rationing programme enabled the government of Saddam Hussein to strengthen its 'dictatorship of force' with a 'dictatorship over needs' targeting the mainstream population.[33] Yet widespread corruption among impoverished civil servants demonstrated the weakness of the regime, opening spaces of negotiation with the state and enabling some transgression of rules.

Petty or administrative corruption increased within the civil service in the context of minimal wages and a *de facto* 'privatisation' of the state. From 1997 onwards the regime officially engaged in a user-fee financing policy for public services. Access to administrative, health or education services, as well as to justice, had to be paid for. The purchase and falsification of official documents became widespread, while theft and the sale of government property sharply increased. As a result, the capacity of the state collapsed and a large portion of the population lost its access to key public services. This 'state failure' led the regime to ensure its tenure through 'shadow state' politics overseeing the illegal economy.[34] As the state withdrew from many basic social and economic services, non-state institutions once again asserted their social importance. Beyond turning to the 'informal' economy, the regime also eschewed some of its ideology and turned to Islam, tribal ethos, as well as national mobilisation against western aggression, and Saddam's personality cult to ensure social regulation and order.[35]

Unsurprisingly there was even less respect for 'state' property after the fall of Saddam Hussein. The looting and appropriation of state assets had long taken place under the sanctions regime. This practice was brutally amplified and extended to the former elite's assets immediately after the US military took over Baghdad, constituting a form of 'popular redistribution' after years of deprivation. Many political parties also took advantage of this power vacuum. They seized funds, buildings, vehicles and arms to consolidate their power through private militias and patronage networks.[36] Interim Iraqi authorities have also faced widespread allegations of corruption, many of these appearing politically motivated. Bureaucratic corruption was also reported to be on the rise, with average monthly civil service salaries around only $60.[37]

The oil-for-food programme

In operation between 1996 and 2003, the oil-for-food programme generated $69 billion dollars from Iraqi oil sales, of which $38 billion were allocated to humanitarian purchases for Iraq. Following the imposition of comprehensive economic sanctions on Iraq, the regime of Saddam Hussein had refused a humanitarian programme on the grounds of sovereignty, preferring in effect to have control over a smaller illegal import/export sector. In 1995 the Iraqi regime agreed with the UN Secretariat to a revised programme providing it discretionary control over oil pricing and the selection of purchasers of oil exports and humanitarian (and oil industry spare parts) imports. Illicit Iraqi income from surcharges on oil sales and kickbacks on humanitarian purchases would represent between $268 million and $7.5 billion according to different estimates. Beyond consolidating the formal patronage capacity of the regime domestically, the oil-for-food programme was also politically manipulated internationally, with the regime extending its reward system overseas through oil vouchers provided as gifts, commissions for services, or in payment for goods to foreign companies and influential individuals.[38] Many of the voucher recipients lobbied for an end to sanctions and normalisation of relations with Iraq.

Although there remains much debate about the nature and political impact of the oil-for-food programme at the time of writing, the overall picture appears to be one of political opportunism (or 'realism') on the side of UN Security Council members, and political aquiescence on the side of the UN Secretariat managing the programme itself. To maintain the sanctions regime in place, the

US and UK appear to have turned a blind eye to over-invoicing so that the interests of countries on the Security Council could be in part addressed through the oil-for-food programme. In other words, some members of the Security Council would have allowed corruption for the sake of pursuing a sanctions-based security agenda while others financially benefitted from the regime of Saddam Hussein. Beyond the case of the oil-for-food programme, Security Council members also *de facto* tolerated Iraqi illicit revenues from oil smuggling (outside the programme) estimated at between $5.7 and $13.6 billon between 1997 and 2002.[39] Again political 'realism' played out in this attitude, with the USA in particular seeking to avoid a confrontation over smuggled oil with 'friendly regimes' such as Jordan and Turkey. In other words, the US administration under President Clinton appears to have accommodated corruption in the sanctions regime for the sake of 'keeping Saddam Hussein in a box', and despite massive humanitarian costs.

The UN Secretariat itself did not tackle the problem of illicit revenues, considering it a political issue to be addressed by the Security Council. Allegations of bureaucratic corruption by the head of the programme, Benon Vahe Sevan, also appear to be true, while the exact role and possible gains of UN Secretary General Kofi Annan's son Kojo—who was affiliated to a Swiss firm at the time it received the programme's inspection services contract—had not yet been clarified at the time of writing. The official investigation into the programme—led by Paul A Volcker—has recognised the political interference of Security Council members in the running of the programme, but it has also strongly criticised the failure of the UN Secretariat to challenge this interference and to observe its 'own rules of fairness and accountability'.[40] What the Volcker commission may be missing here, or be prevented by its limited mandate from saying, is that it is the sanctions regime itself that failed to follow these rules. From the perspective of a high-ranking UN official, the programme had turned into a 'Frankenstein' escaping the control of its creators.[41] From the perspective of the Iraqi people, sanctions were anything but fair and accountable.

The US Coalition Provisional Authority and its legacy

Oil has been a major driving force behind foreign interests, balance of power, and territorial conflicts in the Persian Gulf. As a result of the terrorist attacks of 11 September 2001, debates on oil and the US security agenda in the Gulf region have significantly shifted. On one side of the debate those opposing US military intervention argue that the 'war on terror' has provided yet another convenient cover for a renewed 'imperialist oil grab' in the region.[42] Others have justified intervention in terms of the dismal record of human rights abuses under Saddam Hussein, continued regional instability, and the threat of state-sponsored and oil-funded political violence. Among these, the US administration has portrayed its foreign policy on Iraq and the Persian Gulf as going beyond ensuring free access to oil for the world market to ensuring that oil is supporting 'freedom' in Iraq and the region.[43] Accordingly, the US has justified its control of the Iraqi oil sector in light of the welfare and political stability requirements of the country. Despite opposition to the Iraq war, UN Security Council members largely back this vision, provided that the right of the Iraqi people to 'control their own natural resources' be recognised, and that the management of oil revenues by occupying forces 'benefit the Iraqi people' and be adequately audited.[44]

Budgetary arrangements under the CPA marked a strong departure from those under Saddam Hussein's regime, when public disclosure was a criminal offence; and to a lesser degree from those of the oil-for-food programme, when information on individual expenditure contracts was not publicly accessible. The CPA oversaw two main sources of funding: US appropriated funds and Iraqi funds, with the Security Council-approved Development Fund for Iraq (DFI) centralising Iraqi oil revenues and repatriated funds.[45] Many of the failings of the CPA can be accounted for by the massive challenges that it faced, although policy orientations, shifting timetables largely dictated by US domestic political priorities, bureaucratic infighting and red-tape, as well as high staff turnover and lack of experience also contributed in major ways.[46] Key failures by the CPA under the budgetary and oil governance rubric relate to: Iraqi policy ownership, funding sources, allocation of benefits and auditing.[47]

Before the war, the US State Department had undertaken a policy planning exercise with more than 200 Iraqi exiles through 17 thematic 'Future of Iraq Project' working groups, including 'anti-corruption measures' and 'oil and energy'.[48] Once the war began, however, this planning and policy ownership effort was 'virtually ignored by [US] decision-makers'.[49] The CPA and prime contractors only conducted very limited consultation with Iraqi experts or representatives (with, in turn, many Iraqis unwilling to interact with the occupying powers). Iraqi control over oil revenues was non-existent until 28 June 2004 except once fiscal transfers had been executed to individual Iraqi ministries. The Iraqi Governing Council did not provide a legitimate or effective mode of 'shared sovereignty' with the CPA, which nominated its members. Iraqi people were also 'represented' in the Program Review Board, which recommended budgetary expenditure in occupied-Iraq. Yet coalition-affiliated and CPA-nominated members held all voting rights and pro-consul L Paul Bremer III made ultimate budgetary decisions.[50] If some Iraqis exercised any 'sovereignty' over the oil sector during the CPA era, it was through illegal practices such as theft and sabotage.

Reconstruction policy was similarly driven from Washington and the CPA office and based on a strong pro-market ideology emphasising the need for immediate and widespread privatisation (leaving aside the oil sector), as well as free trade and lax foreign direct investment rules.[51] This set of policies was not only illegal under international law, given the CPA's status as an occupying power, it was also broadly criticised as an untimely and inappropriate 'fire sale' transferring wealth and market opportunities to foreign hands.[52] The resulting stalemate was such that state companies were not privatised, but neither did the US reconstruction programme assist them despite huge needs following more than a decade of war, sanctions and looting. Several state companies, in fact, had their accounts frozen or inventory sold to replenish Iraq's budget, their market monopoly revoked, or their managers and technicians fired following the CPA's blanket de-Ba'athification.[53] In turn, the controversy over and impacts of the CPA's reconstruction policy contributed to political and economic violence.

The second shortcoming of the CPA has been the fast and opportunistic disbursement of Iraq's public funds compared with that of US-appropriated funds. By the end of June 2004, 88% of the $23.4 billion Iraqi funds (DFI) had been expended or obligated by the CPA, leaving only $2.8 billion for the new Interim Iraqi government.[54] In contrast, only 56% of the $24 billion appropriated by the US Congress for relief and recovery activities in Iraq had been obligated, with only $3.7 billion actually expended.[55] Furthermore, out of the $13 billion pledged by other international donors in September 2003, only about $2 billion had been allocated. This imbalance between domestic and international funding drastically curtailed the future financial independence of the Iraqi government and opened the road to a pro-cyclical management of oil revenues.[56] It also allows for future US aid leverage over the Iraqi authorities, without having to ask for more money from Congress.[57] Such financial leverage may be used by the US and other donors to push the Iraqis to open up the Iraqi oil sector to international oil companies, given that nearly all Iraqi oil revenues will probably remain committed to recurring expenditures and prevent the Iraqi government from massively investing in national oil companies. Furthermore, most of the almost three billion dollars allocated to the US military commanders on the ground to fast-track reconstruction as an effective way to 'win hearts and minds' came from DFI.[58] In short, the US sought to buy Iraqi friends with Iraqi money, leaving little behind for the future Iraqi government to buy friends of its own.

The contracting of reconstruction also disproportionately benefited well connected US companies, rather than local Iraqi firms and people. The value of contracts awarded by the US government without competition represented two-thirds of the total in 2003, a proportion that sharply declined in 2004 following a widespread outcry. 'Indefinite-delivery, indefinite-quantity' contracts and 'cost-plus' budgeting limited competition while increasing overpricing, wastage and 'mission-creep'. Most criticised among prime contractors was Halliburton, which boasted up to $11 billion in potential revenues, given its former CEO, US Vice-President Richard Cheney, and several allegations of corruption and fraud.[59] Foreign workers have frequently been hired instead of qualified Iraqi people, and Iraqi firms have been relegated to menial sub-contracting jobs. As stated by a board member of the American Iraqi Chamber of Commerce: 'If you take $10 million from the US government and sub the job out to Iraqi businesses for a quarter-million, is that business, or is that corruption?'.[60] For critics US reconstruction funds, rather than providing a windfall, have only trickled through because of bureaucratic and legal hold-ups, and the diversion of half of the disbursed funds 'to security and insurance costs, corruption, profits for US companies and US administrative needs'.[61] Reconstruction funds have also sustained an import-driven economy, rather than helped rebuild local production capacities crippled by economic sanctions (again with the exception of the petroleum sector).

The final shortcoming of the CPA which will be discussed here has been the delay in, or inadequate provision for, auditing. Reconstruction in Iraq was deemed by the CPA to be 'the single most audited program in our government's history...[backed by]... severe punishments for corrupt behavior on the civilian as well as the government side'.[62] Yet auditing and sanctioning measures proposed by US Senators were rejected by the US administration and the number of CPA and Department of Defense auditors was deemed insufficient.[63] In the meantime, staff from implementing agencies on the ground complained of a lack of flexibility as well as bureaucratic delays and formalities in funding projects. The US Inspector General noted 'severe inefficiencies and poor management' in the CPA's management of Iraq's national budget process and oversight of Iraqi funds, which the CPA justified in part by the high level of insecurity, poor accounting practices by the Iraqi bureaucracy, and the need to keep civil servants and 'young armed men' employed.[64] International oversight fared even worse. The International Advisory and Monitoring Board for Iraq (IAMB), created to independently monitor the Development Fund for Iraq, was created five months after the UN Security Council requested its establishment. The IAMB had its first briefing by the CPA only about a year after the US-led forces took control of Baghdad.[65] Auditing by the IAMB revealed poor oversight by the CPA over Iraqi oil sales, poor accounting practices, and non-competitive bidding for contracting (with contracts not made available to IAMB). Despite a broad mandate, the IAMB had no power of subpoena or impose sanctions against the CPA.

From this perspective the CPA era leaves at best a mixed legacy to the Iraqi people in terms of oil governance and fiscal management. Although the CPA did somewhat improve financial transparency, it is doubtful that serious accountability measures will address the many shortcomings and abuses identified by auditors, not to mention the overall economic interests that partly motivated the invasion of Iraq in the first place.[66] In terms of legislation the CPA issued an executive order to protect government whistleblowers.[67] In terms of institution building it established a 'Commission on Public Integrity' only in January 2004, and its first Commissioner had to be directly appointed by Bremer as the Interim Governing Council failed to agree on a candidate.[68] The CPA also 'reconfirmed' the role of the Board of Supreme Audit Law created under Saddam Hussein and nominated its president, who was assassinated shortly after.[68] The CPA also trained Iraqi inspectors general to operate in all Iraqi ministries. More generally, the CPA and Iraqi Governing Council also initiated moves towards democracy, including the election of local governing councils (in part to correct previous US nominations that were criticised locally).

There is little doubt that the US will seek to maximise its influence on future Iraqi authorities well beyond the national elections to be held in

2005.[70] Whether that influence, and reactions to it, will end up benefiting the Iraqi population as a whole remains to be seen. An unintended legacy of the CPA in this regard could well turn out to be the consolidation of sectarian politics. In search for 'democratic' representation the US used sectarian lines to apportion Iraqi representatives within the interim Iraqi authorities. This choice did not happen in a vacuum, but it did not reflect the diversity and relative character of identities and interests in Iraqi society. This choice exacerbated sectarian politics, and could increase corruption and conflicts over oil revenue allocation.

Conclusion

Saddam Hussein's regime was not an aberration, but rather the caricature of a pattern of power that has long prevailed in Iraq. As historian Charles Tripp remarks, the combination of restricted elite circles, primacy of military force, and oil wealth created in Iraq a dominant political perspective marked by authoritarian leadership, and through which politics have been understood as discipline and participation as conformity.[71] This state-centred and 'hegemonic' conception of power has been repeatedly confronted by groups of Iraqis through coups, insurrections or exile. Using a clannish and personalised system of favouritism in which ruthlessness and corruption played a major part, Saddam Hussein succeeded in staying in power for nearly three decades. Divisive politics of mutual dependence sustained his rule, while leaving individual clients and communities at the mercy of economic exclusion and violence from a state rendered 'omnipotent' by the oil windfall. Later faced by the financial constraints of bankruptcy and economic sanctions, the Iraqi regime retained power by placing 'the arbitrary, the blurring of borders between the tolerated, the accepted, the legal and the illegal at the heart of the political and aim[ing] at "breaking" possible economic and political rivals'.[72] Despite officially being the target of the 'international community', the divisions, economic interests and security 'realism' of its members in effect sustained Saddam Hussein's regime until it was brought down by a more hawkish US administration.

Two years after Saddam Hussein's removal from power, Iraq's transition to an inclusive democracy and shared prosperity remains elusive. Continued insecurity, economic reliance on weak oil revenues, trickling international assistance on the ground, and sectarian political violence represent major challenges for the new Iraqi authorities. There remains a risk that the new Iraqi regime will fall back on coercion and patronage to assert political order. Corruption-based patronage, however, may not achieve sufficient legitimacy and broad coverage to end political violence. Unable to translate its huge oil wealth into fiscal revenues in the short-term, the Iraqi state is unlikely to regain a hegemonic position through populist policies of wealth redistribution. Rather than populist benevolence, it may have to rely on selective patronage and political corruption. However, some insurgent and other opposition movements may seek to bolster their political legitimacy and popular appeal by denouncing corrupt practices (real, perceived or fabricated) by Iraqi authorities to claim the moral high ground. Corruption-based patronage thus risks prolonging armed resistance and instability. A key challenge for the new Iraqi authorities will be to strengthen its legitimacy without the use of such double-edged corruption. Without much room for manoeuvre financially, the Iraqi state will also remain dependent upon foreign donors and companies—a situation that some of them may cynically perceive as increasing their leverage over political, geostrategic or commercial interests. A second challenge for the legitimacy of the new Iraqi regime will rest on the management and perception of this relationship of relative dependence, most notably in terms of a security.

Major and rapid progress is required in a number of domains, starting with the consolidation of democracy and diversification of the economy. The governance of the oil sector is crucial to both dimensions. Oil governance will reflect on the political objectives and quality of the Iraqi government, as well as on the 'ulterior motives' of the US that many have suspected of being oil-related. Greater transparency in oil governance should start with oil flow metering, a public consultation on oil policy, and the publication of all revenues derived from the oil sector. Strong accountability mechanisms are also required, through independent media, auditing and judiciary. Similar measures on the fiscal expenditure side should complement these to minimise loopholes facilitating embezzlement. Direct disbursement to the Iraqi population of some of the oil revenues could also insulate it from the risk of mismanagement by the state and provide a form of 'individualised sovereignty' over the expenditure side of oil governance.[73] Such a radical departure from past practices could strengthen a sense of national community and tangible peace dividend, although the new Iraqi government is unlikely to follow these suggestions, given its weak fiscal position.[74]

At the international level the UN Security Council is prolonging the depositing of proceeds from oil export sales of petroleum to the DFI and the mandate of the IAMB until the constitutionally elected government takes control by the end of 2005.[75] This measure should constitute a basic safeguard against embezzlement and political manipulation of oil revenues by interim Iraqi authorities, but no mechanism of accountability has been incorporated. Finally, foreign governments and companies should take adequate measures—such as implementing the OECD Anti-Bribery Convention and the UK's Extractive Industries Transparency Initiative—in order to curb corruption and improve transparency in their dealings with Iraqi partners.[76] Similar imperatives and demands apply to the governance of reconstruction funds.

Coming back to the US vision of delivering Iraqis from 'corruption', Iraq long followed a pattern of elite hegemony under British and military rule, while oil windfalls enabled a patronage machine. The country is now facing a situation of fragmented clientelism as a result of the UN sanctions regime and US intervention. The consolidation of democratisation and economic liberalisation of Iraq would be expected to move the pattern of corruption in Iraq towards interest-group bidding, with private wealth accessing a competitive and open political system, a move that would, arguably, better serve US interests, both in terms of political influence and economic rewards. Open markets and democracy provide rules and a level playing field that are more amenable to US political influence and corporate activities. In contrast, authoritarian regimes present a much higher political risk, as demonstrated by the preference given to Russian, Chinese and French oil companies by Saddam Hussein's regime. Yet the US is also obviously not operating in a political and social vacuum. Despite the violent backlash of 9/11, the US administration and oil interests may seek to collaborate with religious forces and participate in the consolidation of a US-dependent Islamic regime, as they have done elsewhere in the region.[77] Ultimately, the questions remain as to what sort of corruption the US will come to accommodate in Iraq, and at what costs for the Iraqi population.

Notes

1 See 'Wolfowitz interview with Sam Tannenhaus, Vanity Fair', United States Department of Defense, 9 May 2003; and US Presidential addresses dated 10 April 2003, 9 February 2004, 10 April 2004 and 1 May 2004 from the US Office of the Press Secretary, at www.whitehouse.news/releases.

2 GW Bush, 'Freedom and the future', speech at the American Enterprise Institute, 26 February 2003; and PH Gordon, 'Bush's Middle East vision', *Survival*, 45 (1), 2003, pp 155–165. On the US geopolitical discourse linking oil and 'freedom', see P Le Billon & F El Khatib, 'From free oil to "freedom oil": terrorism, war and US geopolitics in the Persian Gulf', *Geopolitics*, 9 (1), 2004, pp 109–137.

3 See R Williams, 'New concepts for old?', *Third World Quarterly*, 20 (3), 1999, pp 487–489. Corruption is defined here as the 'abuse of public office or entrusted power for private gain'.

4 M Johnston, 'Corruption and democratic consolidation', paper presented at the conference on 'Democracy and Corruption' Shelby Cullom Davis Center for Historical Studies, Princeton University, 12 March 1999 (revised June 2000), p 6.

5 Iraq has estimated proven oil reserves of 112.5 billion barrels and probable reserves of 200 billion. M Radler, 'Worldwide reserves increase as production holds steady', *Oil & Gas Journal*, 100 (52), 2002, pp 113–145.

6 See R Chandrasekaran, 'Promises unkept: the US occupation of Iraq', *Washington Post*, 19 June 2004.

7 I Warde, 'L'Occupation Américaine en échec: Irak, l'eldorado perdu', *Le Monde Diplomatique*, May 2004; and N Klein, 'Baghdad year zero. Pillaging Iraq in the pursuit of a neocon utopia', *Harper's*, September 2004, pp 43–53.

8 Corruption-based patronage can be defined as the illegitimate use of state assets to serve and protect the interests of specific groups in order to consolidate a political rule. See M Johnston, 'The political consequences of corruption: a reassessment', *Comparative Politics*, 18 (4), 1986, pp 459–477.

9 A review of the different forms of corruption falls beyond the scope of this paper. See S Rose-Ackerman, *Corruption and Government: Causes, Consequences, and Reform*, Cambridge: Cambridge University Press, 1999; and AK Jain, 'Corruption: a review', *Journal of Economic Surveys*, 15 (1), 2001, pp 71–121.

10 E Brown & J Cloke, 'Neoliberal reform, governance and corruption in the South: assessing the international anti-corruption crusade', *Antipode*, 36 (2), 2004, pp 272–294; H Marquette, 'Corruption, democracy and the World Bank', *Crime, Law and Social Change*, 36, 2001, pp 395–407; and T Polzer, 'Corruption: deconstructing the World Bank discourse', *DESTIN Working Paper no 01-18*, December 2001, London School of Economics.

11 A relationship of causality is to be noted between the two as the long-term impact of stable patterns of corruption-based patronage often contributed to the (violent) downfall of these regimes. See P Bardhan, ' Corruption and development: a review of issues', *Journal of Economic Literature*, 35, 1997, pp 1320–1346; C Freeland, *Sale of the Century: Russia's Wild Ride from Communism to Capitalism*, New York: Crown Publishing, 2000; and P Le Billon, 'Buying peace or fuelling war: the role of corruption in armed conflicts', *Journal of International Development*, 15, 2003, pp 413–426.

12 Johnston, 'Corruption and democratic consolidation'. As Johnston and many authors suggest, the context is not limited to these two dimensions and also includes for example socio-cultural factors. See, for example, JP Olivier de Sardan, 'A moral economy of corruption in Africa', *Journal of Modern*

African Studies, 37 (1), 1999, pp 25–52. A discussion of the cultural embeddedness and social norms influencing corruption in Iraq falls beyond the scope of this paper.

13 L McQuaig, *It's the Crude, Dude: Big Oil, and the Fight for the Planet*, Toronto: Random House, 2004.

14 On the 'resource curse' affecting many oil-dependent countries, see R Auty, *Resource Abundance and Economic Development*, Oxford: Oxford University Press, 2001; ML Ross: 'The political economy of the resource curse', *World Politics*, 51, 1999, pp 297–322; Ross, 'Does oil hinder democracy?', *World Politics*, 53, 2001, pp 325–361; and Ross 'Extractive sector and the poor', Oxfam America Report, October 2001. For a counter-argument, see GA Davis, 'Learning to love the Dutch disease: evidence from the mineral economies', *World Development*, 23 (10), 1995, pp 1765–1779.

15 R Marques, cited in P Salopek, 'CEOs of war bleed Angola', *Chicago Tribune*, 2 April 2000.

16 C Leite & J Weidmann, 'Does mother nature corrupt? Natural resources, corruption, and economic growth', *IMF Working Paper WP/99/85*, Washington, DC: IMF, 1999; MD Shafer, *Winners and Losers: How Sectors Shape the Development Prospects of States*, Ithaca, NY: Cornell University Press, 1994; TL Karl, *The Paradox of Plenty: Oil Booms, Venezuela, and other Petro-states*, Berkeley, CA: University of California Press, 1997; and Ross, 'Does oil hinder democracy?'.

17 Evidence of a higher likelihood of war affecting resource-dependent countries is still disputed. See P Collier & A Hoeffler, 'Greed and grievances in civil war', WPS/2002-01, Oxford: Centre for the Study of African Economies, 13 March 2002; J Fearon, 'Primary commodity exports and civil war', *Journal of Conflict Resolution*, forthcoming; and P Le Billon, 'The political ecology of war: natural resources and armed conflicts', *Political Geography*, 20 (5), 2001, pp 561–584.

18 Ross, 'Extractive sector and the poor', p 16.

19 See Le Billon, 'Buying peace or fuelling war'.

20 See, *Global Corruption Report 2005*, Berlin: Transparency International, 2005, pp 19–32.

21 International Crisis Group (ICG), *Reconstructing Iraq*, Middle East Report 30, ICG, Brussels, 2 September 2004.

22 D Keen, *The Economic Functions of Civil Wars*, Adelphi Paper 320, Oxford: Oxford University Press, 1998.

23 M Walecki, 'Political money and corruption', *Global Corruption Report: Political Corruption*, London: Transparency International and Pluto Press, 2004.

24 J Hanlon, 'Do donors promote corruption? the case of Mozambique', *Third World Quarterly*, 25(4): 2004, pp 747–763, 'Towards a New Political Economy of Development', University of Sheffield, 3–4 July 2002.

25 C Tripp, *A History of Iraq*, Cambridge: Cambridge University Press, 2000, p 281; T Dodge, *Inventing Iraq. The Failure of Nation Building and a History Denied*, London: Hurst, 2003; and AS Hashim, 'Military power and state formation in modern Iraq', *Middle East Policy*, 10 (4), 2003, pp 29–47.

26 H Mejcher, *Imperial Quest for Oil: Iraq 1910–1928*, London: Ithaca Press, 1976; P Sluglett, *Britain in Iraq 1914–1932*, London: Ithaca Press, 1976; and D Gregory, *The Colonial Present. Afghanistan, Palestine, Iraq*, Oxford: Blackwell, 2004.

27 A Alnaswari, *The Economy of Iraq: Oil, Wars, Destruction of Development and Prospects, 1950–2010*, Westport, CT: Greenwood Press, 1994; and J Amuzegar, *Managing the Oil Wealth: OPEC's Windfalls and Pitfalls*, London: IB Tauris, 1999.

28 Financial obligations included debt ($127 billion), war reparations ($199 billion) and pending contracts ($57 billion). This amount did not include about $100 billion of war compensation claims by Iran. See 'A wiser peace: an action strategy for a post-conflict Iraq. Supplement I: background information on Iraq's financial obligations', Washington, DC: Center for Strategic and International Studies, 23 January 2003.

29 A Friedman, *Spider's Web: The Secret History of How the White House Illegally Armed Iraq*, New York: Bantam Books, 1993; and P Mantius, *Shell Game: A True Story of Banking, Spies, Lies, Politics and the Arming of Saddam Hussein*, New York: St Martins Press, 1995.

30 'Statement by Dr Isam al Khafaji before the US Senate Foreign Relations Committee', 24 September 2003, p 2, at http://foreign.senate.gov/testimony/2003/KhafajiTestimony030924.pdf.

31 ICG, *Iraq Backgrounder: What Lies Beneath*, Middle East Report 6, ICG, Brussels, 1 October 2002.

32 Abdul Jabbar Mandeel, 'Corruption in Iraq', *Iraq Press Online*, at www.iraqpress.org, accessed 24 August 2004; and PJ Luizard, *La Question Irakienne*, Paris: Fayard, 2002.

33 Kurdish communities were in part protected through a special quota allocated from the oil-for-food programme. Tripp, *A History of Iraq*; and F Rigaud, 'Irak: Le temps suspendu de l'embargo', *Critique Internationale*, April 2001, p 15.

34 On the concept of the 'shadow state', see W Reno, *Corruption and State Politics in Sierra Leone*, Cambridge: Cambridge University Press, 1995. On its application to Iraq, see Tripp, *A History of Iraq*; and Dodge, *Inventing Iraq*.

35 F Rigaud, 'Irak'; and A Baram, 'Neo-tribalism in Iraq: Saddam Hussein's tribal policies 1991–1996', *International Journal of Middle East Studies*, 29 (1), 1997, pp 1–31.

36 Among the most controversial—and most widely reported in the Western press—were the access of cleric Moqtada al Sadr to pilgrims' donations to the shrine of Imam Ali in Najaf, and accusations against Salem Chalabi—the director general of the Iraqi special tribunal for crimes against humanity—concerning the murder a Ministry of Finance official reporting on government property illegally seized by the party of Chalabi's family, the Iraqi National Congress. See B Whitaker & M Howard, 'Wanted for murder of finance official', *Guardian*, 10 August 2004.
37 R Rageh, 'Iraqis: corruption still exists in Iraq', Associated Press, 10 August 2004.
38 A list of 270 names was initially published in the Iraqi newspaper *Al Mada*, 25 January 2004. See also 'Friends of Saddam' website, at http://www.acepilots.com/unscam/.
39 See Interim Report of the Independent Inquiry into the United Nations Oil-for-Food Programme, 3 February 2005; C Rosett, 'The oil-for-food scam: what did Kofi Annan know, and when did he know it?', *Commentary Magazine*, 16 April 2004; and C Rosett, 'Sources of revenue for Saddam and sons: a primer on the financial underpinnings of the regime in Baghdad', Washington, DC: Coalition for International Justice, September 2002.
40 Interim Report of the Independent Inquiry into the United Nations Oil-for-Food Programme, p 4.
41 Interview with anonymous UN official, New York, 2000.
42 See anti-war coalitions' websites, at www.socialistworker.co.uk and www.stopwar.org.uk; and M Renner, 'Post-Saddam Iraq: linchpin of a new oil order', *Foreign Policy in Focus*, 1 January 2003.
43 Le Billon & El Khatib, 'From free oil to "freedom oil"'.
44 United Nation Security Council, Resolution 1483, 21 May 2003, approved by all members except Syria (abstained).
45 Cash inflow into the DFI since its inception on 28 May 2003 represented close to $20.6 billion; half of that amount came from oil sales, the rest coming from transfers of the now defunct oil-for-food programme and repatriated funds from the Saddam Hussein regime. 'Development Fund for Iraq: financial reporting matrix', *Coalition Provisional Authority*, at http://www.cpa-iraq.org/budget/DFI_26jun2004.xls.
46 ICG, *Reconstructing Iraq*.
47 Budgets were considered highly confidential under the regime of Saddam Hussein; the oil-for-food programme failed to provide public accounts of the contracts involved. Rosett, 'The oil-for-food scam'.
48 'Duty to the future: free Iraqis plan for a new Iraq', at http://usinfo.state.gov/products/pubs/dutyiraq/dutyiraq.pdf, posted April 2003. For a critique of 'pre-war reconstruction', see R Mac Ginty, 'The pre-war reconstruction of post-war Iraq', *Third World* Quarterly, 24 (4), 2003, pp 601–617.
49 See ICG, *Reconstructing Iraq*.
50 Coalition Provisional Authority Regulation No 3, 18 June 2003.
51 This policy, however, was not extended to the oil sector—at least in public declarations by the US government—probably for fear of confirming Iraqi public opinion that the US and UK had invaded Iraq for its oil. See Section 6.1, Coalition Provisional Authority Order No 39, 19 September 2003.
52 Employees of state companies fearing lay-offs and Iraqi businessmen fearing foreign competitors also resented it (although many welcomed the facilitation of foreign investment). For a review of criticisms, see R Looney, 'Neoliberalism in a conflict state: the viability of economic shock therapy in Iraq', *Strategic Insights*, 3 (6), June 2004; S Mulugeta, 'Reform concerns: changes have Iraqi workers nervous' *Newsday*, 14 December 2003; and Klein, 'Baghdad year zero'.
53 Besides the 400 000 people who lost their Iraqi army job, up to 30 000 high-ranking Ba'ath party members were initially fired from public jobs, with about 12 000 subsequently re-hired. J Steele, 'US decree strips thousands of their jobs', *Guardian*, 30 August 2003; and ICG, *Reconstructing Iraq*.
54 If about $9 billion were allocated to the 2004 budget of Iraqi ministries (with much controversy about their lack of accountability), close to $2 billion were committed in the last six weeks of CPA administration to special projects. 'Iraqi fire sale: CPA giving away oil revenue billions before transition', Briefing Paper 7, Iraq Revenue Watch, New York, June 2004; and Regulation no 11 (CPA/REG/18 June 2004) seeking to secure outstanding contracting liability under the DFI beyond 30 June 2004, at the CPA website, accessed 18 August 2004. At least an additional $1.1 billion in frozen Iraqi assets held by non-US UN members could be released to the Iraqi government.
55 SR Weisman, 'US is quietly spending $2.5 billion from Iraqi oil revenues to pay for Iraqi projects', *New York Times*, 21 June 2004.
56 Arguably the Iraqi budget will benefit from a continued oil revenue stream, while donor commitments are bounded in time (2003–07/08).
57 For example, Deputy Defense Secretary Paul Wolfowitz emphasised to Congress that: 'There's a lot of money to pay for this [reconstruction] that doesn't have to be US taxpayer money, and *it starts* with the assets of the Iraqi people'. House Committee on Appropriations Hearing on a Supplemental War Regulation, 27 March 2003, emphasis added.

58 Only $140 million had been budgeted from US appropriated funds for this purpose and the Commander's Emergency Response Program was essentially financed by Iraqi funds.

59 J Chaffin, 'Focus on Halliburton masks deeper problems with Iraq contracts', *Financial Times*, 30 March 2004; Windfalls of War project, Center for Public Integrity, at www.publicintegrity.org; and TF Armistead, 'Halliburton reveals $6-million overcharge in alleged Iraq corruption', *Engineering News-Record*, 23 January 2004.

60 E Kubba, cited in N Klein, 'Risky business in Iraq', *The Nation*, 5 January 2004, p 11.

61 B Crocker, 'The economy: with money comes power', *Washington Times*, 20 June 2004. See also N Klein, 'Shameless in Iraq', *The Nation*, 24 June 2004.

62 'US aid package for Iraq cracks down on corruption', *Daily Star*, Beirut, 4 May 2004.

63 M Shapiro, 'Spoils of war', *MarketPlace, Center for Investigative Reporting*, 21 April 2004; and B Crossette, 'No simple place to pin blame for Iraq oil-for-food problems', *UN Wire*, 10 May 2004.

64 L Margasak, 'Audit: $9 billion unaccounted for in Iraq', Associated Press, 31 January 2005.

65 The delay in its creation was the result of sharp disagreement over the extent of its mandate between the CPA and IAMB members (the UN, World Bank, IMF, and Arab Fund for Economic and Social Development). Press releases from http://www.iamb.info/pressrel.htm; and 'Racing the deadline: the rush to account for Iraq's public funds', *Revenue Watch 6*, Open Society Institute, April 2004.

66 Many fear that only administrative sanctions will be taken against offenders and that contracted companies will only undertake minimal repayment for over-pricing and other frauds.

67 Coalition Provisional Authority Order No 59, 1 June 2004.

68 D Haynes, 'New watchdog to sniff out corruption in Iraq', Agence France Press, 20 June 2004; and ICG, *Reconstructing Iraq*.

69 Coalition Provisional Authority Order No 77, 18 April 2004. This move was seen by some as a delaying mechanism to protect the reputation of the UN from the oil-for-food programme scandal until UN-supervised elections could be undertaken. See B Pisik, 'Iraq oil probe to take many months', *Washington Times*, 28 May 2004; and M Rubin, 'The growing gap. Bremer has alienated Iraqis', *National Review Online*, 21 May 2004.

70 Many critics question the 'sovereignty' of interim Iraqi authorities, pointing to continued reliance on US security, policy advisers and funds. The interim prime minister, Ayad Allawi, has long had connections with the CIA and MI6, and purveyed some of the (dubious) intelligence upon which the war on Iraq was justified by the USA and Britain. See press reports at www.sourcewatch.org.

71 Tripp, *A History of Iraq*.

72 Rigaud, 'Irak', p 19, translation by the author.

73 J Thierney, 'The struggle for Iraq: Iraq's wealth; a popular idea: give oil money to the people rather than the despots', *New York Times*, 10 September 2003; and TI Palley, 'Combating the natural resource curse with citizen revenue distribution funds: oil and the case of Iraq', *Foreign Policy in Focus Special Report*, December 2003. On the viability of direct aid disbursement to individuals, see J Hanlon, 'It is possible to just give money to the poor', *Development and Change*, 35 (2), 2004, pp 375–383.

74 Critiques of this 'oil-for-the-people' option point out that the current public service could not be relied on to distribute the money honestly. See 'Oil revenue accountability in Iraq: breaking the resource curse', *Briefing 5*, Iraq Revenue Watch, New York, 2003.

75 The Transitional Iraqi Government (post-elections in early 2005) can request the UN Security Council to review this policy. UNSC S/RES/1546, 8 June 2004.

76 See Convention on Combating Bribery of Foreign Public Officials in International Business Transactions, 21 November 1997; and www.eitransparency.org/.

77 See T Mitchell, 'McJihad: Islam in the US global order', *Social Text*, 73, 20(4), 2002, pp 1–18.

Iraqi Transitions: from regime change to state collapse

TOBY DODGE

ABSTRACT *This paper focuses on the US occupation of Iraq from the seizing of Baghdad in April 2003 until the official hand-over of sovereignty to the Iraqi government in June 2004. It seeks to explain the reasons for the failure of US forces to impose order on and then stabilise the country by examining the political and sociological legacy of Saddam Hussein, US planning before and after the war and how the occupation set about trying to build political structures in post-Saddam Iraq. Ultimately it argues that the most important reasons for the failure of the occupation have been ideological. US administrators charged with planning for and then occupying the country fundamentally misunderstood the size and nature of the task they were about to undertake. They set out to apply neoliberal measures of state reform only to find that the state had collapsed and they were now involved in a prolonged exercise of state construction. They then applied a primordial understanding of Iraqi society, exacerbating a divisive and potentially violent sectarianism into Iraqi politics.*

Introduction: from regime change and governmental reform to administrative collapse and state building

In aftermath of 9/11 the US government strove successfully to convince its electorate that the unilateral deployment of America's military dominance was the key to ensuring that a new form of asymmetrical warfare did not come to haunt the world's remaining superpower. In the 2002 State of the Union Address, and then more clearly in *The National Security Strategy of the United States*, published in September of that year, the issues of rogue states, weapons of mass destruction and terrorism were amalgamated into one homogeneous threat to the continued security of the American people.[1] The dangers of instability and violence were described as coming primarily from the periphery of the international system. President Bush's new 'grand strategy' identified the location of these threats in the weaker creations of decolonisation: states in the developing world. Their 'right' to sovereignty was now only to be granted when these states had met their US defined 'responsibilities' to the international community.[2] These responsibilities concerned the suppression of all terrorist activity on their territory, the transparency of banking and trade arrangements and the disavowal of weapons of mass destruction. All necessary means, diplomatic, financial and military were to be deployed to convince the ruling elites of errant states that it was in their interests to conform to these new demands. However, this new doctrine faced two types of problem states, the failed and the rogue; those that were either too weak to impose new responsibilities on their populations or states that simply refused to be coerced.

As the Bush administration set about applying this new doctrine in the aftermath of 9/11, the Baathist regime in Baghdad provided the vehicle for uniting a set of previously disparate problems. The Iraqi government was accused of sponsoring terrorism and developing weapons of mass destruction. It appeared to offer a prime target for 'offensive defence' but also a comparatively easy one.[3] Regime change as a key concept in the Bush doctrine could be sold to the American people through the easy toppling of an undoubtedly rogue governing elite. In the years that followed the invasion of Kuwait in 1990, Saddam Hussein's regime had become a potent symbol of a defiant third world state. Throughout the 1990s, despite a partial invasion, continuous bombing and a decade of the harshest sanctions ever imposed on a country, it had steadfastly rejected the demands of the USA and the international community. By 2001 it had become a powerful example for those governing elites of a rebellious disposition that state autonomy could be defended in a world dominated by a single hegemon. Internationally, by engineering regime change in Baghdad, Washington was setting out to signal clearly its commitment to the Bush doctrine, as well as the lengths it would go to achieve its core foreign policy goals.[4] Domestically, by promoting the invasion of Iraq as a limited exercise in terms of time and cost, the Bush administration was selling offensive defence to its population on the cheap.

Against this background the ambitious nature of their undertaking in Iraq was not apparent to those in Washington who launched it. In the space of two years, because of invasion and then state collapse, Iraq went from rogue, the first category of problematic state, to the second, collapsed. Although military intervention into failed or rogue states has become increasingly common since the Cold War, it has to date been largely unsuccessful.[5] The two definitive reports on international intervention take many hundreds of pages to say how intervention should be carried out with greater technocratic efficiency, without detailing how government institutions can be built and, more importantly, how they can gain acceptance among the populations they are meant to rule over.[6] There is, at the moment, no successful or indeed evolving blueprint on post-intervention state building. The evidence from post-cold war interventions is hardly inspiring. The Cambodia mission, the first large-scale United Nations attempt at root and branch political reform, failed to deliver meaningful change.[7] Intervention into Somalia resulted in the ignominious exit of US troops and the collapse of the UN mission. As events in early 2004 proved, direct military intervention in Haiti to facilitate regime change achieved nothing, in the long term, to alter the underlying political dynamics of that country. In the cases of Bosnia, Kosovo and Afghanistan the ongoing and very mixed outcomes of intervention mean that it is too early to draw any firm or positive conclusions about the lasting successes or failures of each mission.

However, US intervention in Iraq was not perceived by its planners in Washington or sold to the US electorate as state building.[8] It was to be a limited exercise in regime change and then state reform. The agenda of state reform shaping the plans for post-war Iraq had its heritage in over 20 years of neoliberal policy towards the post-colonial world. This approach was born of the 'Washington consensus' developed in the 1980s. The International Monetary Fund and the World Bank set about applying the 'wisdom of market reliance' to developing countries in economic difficulty. They demanded, in return for loans, not only free trade, but also the liberalisation of their capital and financial markets.[9] By the middle of the 1980s structural adjustment loans accounted for more than 25% of World Bank lending and came to be seen by both the World Bank and the IMF as a precondition for further lending.[10] These loans had a large number of policy conditions attached to them that were specifically designed drastically to reduce the state's role in the economy. It was this neoliberal model of limited state reform not maximum state building that guided policy development aimed at stabilising post-war Iraq.

However, the almost complete collapse of the existing institutions of the state in the aftermath of victory gave rise to more sustained problems that neoconservative ideology did not offer solutions to: the rebuilding of structures of government throughout the country. The immediate problem that dogged the Coalition Provisional Authority (CPA) and still haunts the Iraqi government is their inability to impose and then guarantee law and order on Iraq. However, the provision of order is intimately linked to the much longer-term project of building a sustainable, efficient and representative state.

US war aims in Iraq were primarily about change, the removal of Saddam Hussein's regime and its replacement with one less prone to diplomatic defiance, violent adventurism and domestic repression. However, once the institutions of government had collapsed, the task facing the occupation became much more complex and potentially contradictory. The building of a new political order would ultimately mean guiding Iraq towards a government that was in broad agreement with US foreign policy aims. This would certainly involve minimising the role of former members of the old regime but also identifying and marginalising other political forces that might destabilise a pro-US agenda. This had to be done in conjunction with the labour-intensive task of building a nation-wide system of government. Finally, in recognition of liberal justifications for regime change, that government had to have a degree of legitimacy, in the international community but, even more importantly, in Iraq itself. This would involve, at some stage, not only giving the government back to Iraqis who were deemed suitable in Washington, but back to an Iraqi governing elite that was either electable or who could, at least, mobilise a significant section of Iraqi popular opinion to support its rule.

Following the US military's seizure of Baghdad in April 2003, the sense of relief among the vast majority of the Iraqi population was clear; 35 years of tyranny had come an end. By July 2003 this new space for political action had given rise to at least 140 different interest groups and political parties mobilising popular opinion and lobbying the occupying authorities. In addition, 170 daily, weekly and monthly publications had sprung up, giving a platform to the diversity of views that could now be openly expressed in post-Saddam Iraq.[11] But the initial relief that greeted the seizure of Baghdad quickly dissipated, with a growing suspicion of and resentment focusing on the occupying forces. Iraqi popular opinion and the resulting political mobilisation were fractured and diffuse, with no single group or party able to rally popular support. However, as the CPA failed to deliver law and order or rejuvenate the infrastructure, a groundswell of support began to emerge for 'Iraqi ownership' of the state-building process. The US was faced with a dilemma: public opinion was demanding that it build government institutions that were stable, efficient and sustainable but this was matched with increasing calls that it should primarily be Iraqis who managed this process. But which Iraqis should fill this role and how they should be chosen was not at all clear.

The legacy of Saddam Hussein

The momentous task now facing the Iraqi government, a task that the US occupation made precious little headway in achieving, is largely conditioned by the legacy that Saddam Hussein's period in power left Iraq. US planning for post-war Iraq was based on a fundamental misperception about what that legacy was.

Iraqi regimes, because of their perceived domestic and international vulnerability, have with varying degrees of success sought to maximise their autonomy from society. This process has forced them to become dependent upon funding generated from outside Iraqi society. These resources were first supplied in the 1920s and 1930s by British government aid and since 1958 by increasing oil revenues. This means that Iraqi regimes have never had to rely on tax revenues or become beholden to organised domestic interest groups, economic or civic. This in turn gave governments increasing autonomy to control society. This process reached its apex under the Baathist regime built by Hasan al Bakr from 1968 and consolidated under Saddam Hussein after 1979. The two men built a powerful set of state institutions through the 1970s and 1980s. These managed successfully to reshape society, breaking organised resistance to their rule and effectively atomising the population.

Although figures for the amount of oil revenue going to the Iraqi government remain contested, it is safe to say that, after the oil shock of the early 1970s, vast sums of money began to flow into the government's treasury. Estimates put average annual oil revenue at US$600 million from 1970 to 1972. By 1976 this figure had jumped to $8.5 billion and was up to

$26 billion by 1980. This had the effect of greatly increasing the influence that the Iraqi government had over society, with 21% of the active workforce and 40% of Iraqi households directly dependent on government payment.[12] The shifting base of the political economy of Iraq in the 1970s delivered massive and unprecedented power to those who controlled the state. The government funnelled some of its new resources into a social security system, new housing projects and investments in health and education.

By the 1970s Iraq's population was increasingly linked on an individual basis directly to the largesse of state institutions well funded by oil wealth. It was these state structures, built during the 1970s and 1980s, that were central to the US government's post-war plans for Iraq. US forces hoped to seize the institutions of Saddam Hussein's strong state and use them to control Iraqi society. It was only after order had been re-imposed that the USA would then start to reform the structures of the state it was ruling through.

However, US planners had deployed a very partial reading of contemporary Iraqi political history. The 1980s and 1990s saw the transformation of the Iraqi state that was crucial to US plans. The eight-year war with Iran, the 1990–91 Gulf war and finally the imposition of draconian sanctions changed the Iraqi state and with it Saddam Hussein's strategy of rule. From their application in 1990 until 1997, when UN-supervised oil revenues began to arrive, sanctions on Iraq proved to be extremely efficient. They restricted the government's access to large-scale funding, which meant economic policy became largely reactive, dominated by the short-term goal of staying in power. From 1991 until 2003 the effects of government policy and the sanctions regime led to hyperinflation, widespread poverty and malnutrition. The historically generous state welfare provision that had been central to the regime's governing strategy disappeared overnight. The large and well educated middle class that had grown in the years of plenty to form the bedrock of Iraqi society was impoverished. The story of Iraq from 1991 until 2003 is of a country suffering a profound macroeconomic shock.[13]

With this drastic reduction in state resources Saddam Hussein was forced to concentrate his energies on keeping alive the informal networks of patronage and the security services that underpinned his rule. As sanctions began to take effect after 1991, there was a rapid decline in the official and visible institutions of the state. The government in Baghdad was forced to cut back on the resources it could devote to the armed forces and police.[14] Before 1990 the bureaucracy of the Iraqi state had been complex and all-pervasive. During the 1990s the effects of 'self-financing' meant these institutions were hollowed out. Bribery became commonplace, as civil servants' official wages were almost valueless. State employees, teachers and medical staff had to manage as best they could, extracting resources from the impoverished population that depended upon their services. The 1990s saw many professionals leaving public service, to take their chances in the private sector or flee into exile.

It was the power of these state institutions, forged in the 1970s and 1980s, which the USA assumed it would inherit once its forces reached Baghdad. To quote Condoleezza Rice: 'The concept was that we would defeat the army, but the institutions would hold, everything from ministries to police forces'.[15] Through them, US forces planned to stabilise the country. Once order had been achieved, the occupiers would then move to reform and liberalise the state. However, the state that the US had hoped to inherit was, by April 2003, on the verge of collapse. The third war in 20 years and three weeks of looting in its aftermath pushed it over the edge. Civil servants did not return to work after the ceasefire, instead opting to protect their families and property as best they could. Their offices across the country, but especially in Baghdad, were stripped by looters and burnt.[16] The combination of war, sanctions fatigue and rampant criminality led to a complete state breakdown. In the aftermath of regime change, the Iraqi state failed to exist in any meaningful form.

The collapse of the Iraqi state dramatically changed the nature of the USA's role in Iraq. Regime change had been perceived by the neoconservatives promoting it in strictly liberal, 'Washington consensus', terms. The Iraqi state was to be seized by invading US troops who would use the indigenous institutions to rule the country. This would negate the need for a large number of foreign troops, the deployment of large-scale US resources or indeed an extended occupation. It is this vision of post-Saddam Iraq that allowed Donald Rumsfeld at the Pentagon to budget for such modest post-war expenditure and to claim on the eve of invasion that US troops would only have to be in the country for a short time. After the complete collapse of the state the need was for an extended exercise in state building to stabilise Iraq. The creation of a state, not its reform, was philosophically at odds with the forward-leaning anti-state rhetoric of the neoconservatives. It has also been far more costly and has required much greater expertise and resources than the Pentagon had anticipated or indeed could supply.

US planning before and after the war

The false assumption that US forces, upon entering Baghdad, would be able to utilise the functioning institutions of the Iraqi state was one of a series of miscalculations that undermined the coalition's approach to state building. The combination of an ideologically charged understanding of post-war Iraq and the lack of preparation and sustained research into the country before the invasion resulted in its catastrophic aftermath. It can be argued that influential neoconservatives at the heart of President Bush's administration spent a great deal of their time in opposition during the late 1990s planning Saddam Hussein's removal from power. However, when they returned to government, they appear to have devoted little time to substantive planning about what they would do with Iraq after he was gone. The dominant assumptions about Iraq that shaped thinking, the nature of the experts consulted and the interaction between key governmental institutions were all driven by faulty perceptions about the nature of the mission and resulted in the flawed pre-war planning.

In the years before the invasion the civilians in charge at the Pentagon had developed a long and close association with one of the key exiled opposition parties, the Iraqi National Congress (INC). This had profound implications for the post-war political settlement. The small number of cadres who formed the INC were seen as the nucleus of a government in waiting, the pro-US elite who were to run post-Saddam Iraq. The INC's Ahmed Chalabi and his senior aides supplied the US government with information not only on Iraq's supposed weapons of mass destruction programme but on all other aspects of Iraqi government and society. The legitimacy of INC data and more importantly their analysis came from the spurious claim that INC's information originated from a widespread underground network of supporters in the country.[17]

The head of the INC, Ahmed Chalabi, was a key promoter of the 'decapitation thesis' that was placed at the heart of plans for post-war Iraq. Utilising a broadly liberal understanding of dictatorship, this argued that Saddam Hussein's government was extremely vulnerable and unstable. The ruling regime, it was argued, had no ideological or institutional roots within Iraqi society but instead depended on a small number of people for its hold on power and organisational coherence. Under this rubric a limited military strike aimed at the leadership would force the government to collapse, leaving the institutions of the state in place for US forces to utilise. Those in charge at the Pentagon and White House accepted this assessment, along with excessively optimistic predictions about the celebratory welcome US troops would receive once they reached Iraq.[18] Under this approach, the need for major occupation forces or detailed planning was negated. US troops would be welcomed as liberators and high-level Iraqi participation in government would be provided by INC cadres.

The lack of substantive planning in the run-up to the war can also be explained by the internecine ideological battles that came to be a hallmark of the first presidential term of George W Bush. As war became likely the State Department's Bureau of Near Eastern Affairs began technocratically to plan for the invasion's aftermath. Under the stewardship of Thomas S Warwick, the 'Future of Iraq Project' assembled a broad selection of Iraqi exiles in April 2002. The results provided a series of plans for dealing with the problems that did in fact arise in post-war Iraq. However, by January 2003, after the president had signed a National Security Policy Directive, the government centralised the planning process in the Pentagon. Given the antipathy, both personal and ideological, between the senior politicians running the Pentagon and those of the State Department, it was not surprising that the work done by the Future of Iraq Project was disregarded in the run-up to and the immediate aftermath of the invasion. Warwick himself and other senior Middle East experts at the State Department were then stopped from going to Baghdad in the aftermath of the war.[19]

The civilian responsibility for post-war Iraq was then assigned to the Office of Reconstruction and Humanitarian Assistance (ORHA), run by a retired General, Jay Garner, under the authority of the Pentagon. Before the invasion Pentagon planning focused not on the political institutions of the state but instead on developing a capacity for disaster management, the ability to cope with mass movements of displaced people, widespread food shortages and the consequences of WMD use. None of these planning scenarios happened. Ultimately, because of the dominance of the 'decapitation thesis' and the assumptions underpinning planning more generally, the civil arm of the invasion did not have the capacity to play the role required of it in the aftermath of war. To be effective it should have had the ability to function as a parallel state, running the essential services of government. Instead ORHA staff, mainly made up of retired diplomats and senior military figures in tune with neoconservative aims, did not have the numbers or knowledge to handle the task assigned to them. In addition they were constrained by the military's rules of engagement, which did not let civilian staff move around Baghdad without military escorts.

The failures of ORHA and the obvious shortcomings in pre-war planning resulted in a major shake up in the way that the occupation was run. ORHA was dissolved into a new body, the Coalition Provisional Authority and Ambassador Paul Bremer replaced General Garner in May 2003. This marked a recognition that the assumptions that had shaped pre-war planning had now been proved by post-war events to be hopelessly optimistic. The suspicious and muted welcome that US troops received on entering Baghdad and the collapse of the state in an upsurge of post-war lawlessness meant that the 'decapitation thesis' and a neoliberal approach to state reform were not a sustainable basis to the new task of state building. However, the legacies of the Pentagon's pre-war approach to Iraqi planning continued to haunt the new organisation and its new head.

As with pre-war planning, one of the main problems hampering the occupation was the acute lack of knowledge about the country. The occupation authorities took up residence in the old seat of government, the Republican Palace at the heart of the secure 'green zone' in the centre of Baghdad. With almost no expertise on the country or indeed the wider Middle East, the coalition became worryingly dependent upon the same small group of Iraqi exiles that had advised it before the invasion. This core group was meant to act as a conduit between US forces and the Iraqi population. Despite an absence from the country of many years, it was also supposed to provide reliable advice for American administrators struggling to rebuild the country. Finally, and most importantly, it was still hoped that it would become the basis of the new political elite and form the core of Iraq's new governing classes.

However, this reliance created a set of distinct problems. The Iraqi parties allied to the INC, dominated by the Kurdish Democratic Party and Patriotic Union of Kurdistan, brought with them a distinctive view of Iraqi society. They argued that Iraq was irrevocably divided between sectarian and religious groupings, mobilised by deep communal antipathy. This 'primordialisation' of Iraq clearly influenced the way the first governing council was formed, but it bore little resemblance to the real state of Iraqi society in 2003–04.[20]

Second, the heavy reliance on organisations like Ayad Allawi's party, the Iraqi National Accord (INA) and the INC further exacerbated the divide between Iraqi society and US forces. Despite setting up numerous offices around Baghdad, publishing party newspapers and spending liberally, the two main exile groups found it difficult to rally any popular support. A series of interviews conducted by the author with a cross-section of Iraqis, rich and poor, religious and secular, in Baghdad in May 2003, revealed at best indifference and more usually anger towards the returned exiles, especially the avowedly secular INC and INA.[21]

The Iraqi politicians who returned with US troops had expected to be welcomed as those who had worked hardest for regime change. Instead they found a population generally suspicious of their close links to the US government and resentful that they had remained outside the country during the harsh conditions of the 1990s; they were seen as opportunistic 'carpet-baggers'. Off the record many of the more candid formerly exiled politicians admitted that they had been surprised by the difficulties they faced after returning. Instead of being welcomed they found a sullen and suspicious population who have largely refused to offer political loyalty to the newly returned parties.

The whole US planning process for the aftermath of the Iraqi invasion was undermined by the ideologically driven assumptions that underpinned it. The neoconservatives proselytising for regime change saw the whole exercise through a neoliberal paradigm. This was to be a limited exercise in state reform. The 'decapitation thesis' sold to those in the Pentagon by the exiles of the Iraqi National Congress delivered the policy programme needed to enact the paradigm. Saddam Hussein's regime, the neocons argued, had built a set of strong institutions but was itself narrowly based and entirely separated from society. The small ruling elite could be 'surgically' removed from the apex of the state, leaving in place the institutions that could be used to rule over a gratefully liberated population. Although the appointment of Paul Bremer heralded the recognition that these planning assumptions had been hopelessly inaccurate, the US government was at a loss to replace them with a more coherent approach to state building.

Building political structures in post-Saddam Iraq

Against this background of ideological incoherence, state collapse, increased violence and insecurity, plans for rebuilding the political and administrative structures in Iraq went through a series of distinct phases. As the size and nature of the task began to dawn on the CPA, administrators faced a series of potentially competing needs. The role of former Baathists in the government had to be minimised. This was deemed necessary not only to pursue the ultimate goal of regime change but also to create a space within which a new pro-American ruling elite could be nurtured. However, the policy objective clashed with the demands of the Iraqi population, who in the aftermath of victory held high expectations. If the USA could remove Saddam Hussein, then surely they could restore order and government services with equal speed and efficiency? The political decision to pursue de-Baathification and expel many former administrators from the civil service delayed the technocratic goal of restoring services. Finally the CPA faced a highly mobilised society vocally expressing its new-found political freedom. Against this background, the CPA was committed to the close management of political transition and elite participation in governing structures. This had to be balanced against a commitment to democracy and the need for the nascent political structures to be seen as both Iraqi and legitimate. As policy changed to meet each of these pressing and potentially contradictory factors little attention was paid to the consequences of each new initiative.

General Garner's approach to state building and self-government appears to have been influenced by his close relationship with both the formerly exiled parties influential in pre-invasion Washington and the main Kurdish parties, the KDP and PUK. His inclinations were to meet the legitimacy deficit head on and place as much responsibility in the hands of these Iraqis as quickly as possible. He would manage the transition by promoting Iraqi politicians familiar to the USA, those who had recently returned to the country.[22]

To this end, two meetings were held during spring 2003 to form a body which would act as a forum for Iraqi political opinion. The meetings held at Ur near Nassariyah on 15 March and in Baghdad on 28 April were designed to draw together Iraqis in some form of representative assembly. Given the speed with which these meetings were convened it was no surprise that the Ur meeting was dominated by Iraqis recently returned from exile. Its legitimacy was challenged by a large demonstration held outside, which highlighted the small number of delegates (80) and the dubious nature of their claims to be representative of anything more than themselves. Although the turnout in Baghdad was larger at 300, it did not reach the 2000–3000 predicted in advance.[23] The fact that over half the attendees were again exiles pointed to a larger problem of confidence in the US occupation and the dangers of alignment with it. The whole process was plagued by an awareness of the rising unpopularity of the US presence in the country. Potential politicians, believing the occupation to be temporary, chose to eschew involvement in government institutions, political and administrative, until the situation became clearer and the risks of political involvement fewer.

One of Paul Bremer's first decisions upon arriving in Baghdad in May 2003 was to delay moves towards delegating responsibility to a leadership council largely composed of the exiled parties. This was recognition that the building of a credible government, after the collapse of the state, was going to take a great deal longer than had been anticipated. Bremer's approach was designed to bring managerial coherence to the organisation of the occupation, while slowing down the delegation of power to Iraqis until it was clear which group or groups could rally any significant proportion of the population. By implication this meant that the 'decapitation thesis', the swift disposal of the old regime and a transfer of power to the exiled Iraqis as the new governing elite, had been postponed. The appointment of Bremer indicated a realisation in Washington that state building was going to be much more complicated than pre-war plans had assumed.

This incremental but unrepresentative approach was set aside with the arrival of the UN Special Representative for Iraq, Sergio Vieira de Mello. As an international diplomat with many years' experience, the primary issue for Vieira de Mello was not the security vacuum or the pressing need to increase governmental efficiency, but the lack of a sovereign body that could represent the aspirations of Iraqis to the international community. To that end he persuaded Bremer that a governing body of Iraqis should be set up to act as a repository of Iraqi sovereignty.[24] Given the societal legacy of political atomisation left behind by Saddam Hussein, the rising Iraqi suspicion and resentment directed at the occupation and the increasing politically motivated violence, any sovereign body was bound to be dominated by formerly exiled politicians.

The CPA, in conjunction with the United Nations, set up the Iraqi Governing Council (IGC) in July 2003. This body was chosen by Paul Bremer after extended negotiations between the CPA, Vieira de Mello and the seven dominant, formerly exiled, parties. This highlighted the distinct problem of how to select a body that could claim to be representative in Iraq's highly fluid political arena. The CPA promoted the IGC as 'the most representative body in Iraq's history'. The representative nature of the IGC could not come from the method of its formation, negotiations between Paul Bremer, Sergio Vieira de Mello and a small number of recently returned politicians. Instead the CPA focused on the supposedly 'balanced' nature of its membership. The politicians it had chosen were believed to represent the divided ethnic make up of Iraq: 13 Shias, five Sunnis, a Turkoman and a Christian. The forced and rather bizarre nature of this arrangement was highlighted by the inclusion of Hamid Majid Mousa, the Iraqi Communist Party's representative and indeed the then avowedly secular Ahmed Chalabi himself in the 'Shia block' of 13. Such sectarian mathematics were also used to expand the number of cabinet portfolios to 25, so that the spoils of office could be divided up in a similar fashion.

It was clear from the way that the IGC had been selected that the primordialism of the Iraqi exiles had come to dominate the way US officials running the occupation perceived the Iraqi population. This was in stark contrast to the reception the IGC got from Iraqi society. The manner of its selection caused a great deal of consternation across Iraqi political opinion. Criticism focused on the divisive nature of the selection process, arguing that it had introduced an overt sectarianism that had previously not been central to Iraqi political discourse.[25] Intriguingly, debate also centred on the possible damage such a selection process would do to government efficiency, with complaints that council members should have been chosen for their technical skills, rather than their party, sectarian or religious affiliations.

The council's inaugural meeting was in July 2003, but by early November Paul Bremer and senior US officials in the CPA had already become disillusioned with its inability to deliver either strategic leadership or any widespread support from the Iraqi population. In a series of co-ordinated leaks and off-the-record briefings to the press the council was described by US administrators as a central part of the problem then undermining the occupation. Bremer noted that 'at least half the council is out of the country at any given time and that at some meetings, only four or five members show up'. Senior American CPA officials argued that 'the council has been seriously remiss in oversight of its own ministers' and most seriously had been 'inept at outreach to its own people'.[26] For those in the CPA trying to stem the continually rising tide of violence sweeping Iraq, a new approach was needed; as a senior occupation official said at the time, 'it is unlikely that we will want to make a provisional government out of a council that has been feckless'.[27]

The negative international press campaign focusing on the shortcomings of the Iraqi Governing Council, combined with the rising numbers of casualties among coalition forces, resulted in Paul Bremer's hasty recall to Washington for consultations that led to the 15 November 2003 agreement. Faced with increasing pressure from the UN Security Council for sovereign power to be delegated to an Iraq governing body, the increasing alienation of the Iraq population from the CPA and a rising tide of political violence, the more cautious and incremental construction of Iraq's administrative and governing institutions was abandoned. The Bush administration set 30 June 2004 as the deadline for transferring sovereignty to Iraq.

The plan endorsed by the IGC on 15 November 2003 envisaged the drafting of a 'fundamental law' by the end of February 2004. This was to have been followed by the creation of a transitional assembly of anything between 200 and 500 delegates. This assembly was to select a cabinet and leader for Iraq and guide the country to elections, then scheduled for spring 2005. Although hopes for 'Iraqi ownership' of this truncated process rested with the transitional assembly, it was not to be directly elected. Instead a series of indirect caucuses, or 'town hall meetings' were to be held.

This rather complex, if not obscure, method of securing the backing of the Iraqi population for the new political settlement drew immediate criticism from several sectors of Iraq's newly emergent civil society. Most importantly, the senior Shia cleric Marja Ayatollah Ali al-Sistani publicly set himself against the 'caucusing' approach, restating his long-held position that a constitutional assembly should be elected by universal suffrage. Sistani, painfully aware of Iraq's history and the tendency of 'temporary' unelected governments to transform themselves into permanent dictatorships, demanded that any future sovereign government be directly elected. Sistani's ability to influence events and the highly mobilised nature of the Iraqi polity were highlighted by the 100 000 people who demonstrated in Baghdad in January 2004 to convince the CPA that their objections could not be ignored.

With the apparently intransigent opposition of Ayatollah Sistani, the US government came face to face with the contradictions inherent in its position. With increasing Iraqi opposition to the occupation, the CPA had to delegate real power to Iraqis. However, it felt for both administrative and political reasons that it was not possible to hold nation-wide elections to choose that new sovereign body. Faced with the seemingly irreconcilable demands of powerful local actors and the forthcoming US presidential elections, it was to the UN and specifically Lakhdar Brahimi that the White House turned.

Brahimi, fresh from his mission to stabilise Afghanistan, appeared to be the only mediator who could move the process forward.

Lakhdar Brahimi's plan was designed not only to tide Iraq over from the hand-over of sovereignty until the earliest possible date for elections in January 2005, but also to dissipate the tensions between managing the transition to a new government and building administrative capacity to establish legitimacy. It accepted Sistani's demands that only a democratically elected government should be given sustained political power by opting for an interim administration with a clearly defined time limit and restricted authority. It also acknowledged the results of opinion polls, which indicated widespread mistrust of the politicians involved in the Governing Council and a popular desire to be ruled by those appointed for their skills and qualifications.[28]

Brahimi proposed a new caretaker government comprised of technocrats, chosen for their experience rather than their party political allegiances. They would manage the government during the interregnum before elections. Crucially, he called on those appointed to disavow party politics. This would have guaranteed that the powers of the nascent state were not used to benefit any one of the parties competing for power. In creating a technocratic elite committed to government service rather than politics, the Brahimi plan could have established the basis of an apolitical civil service. Finally by excluding political parties from government, Brahimi was forcing them out of the green zone into the country. The parties that dominated the Governing Council had found it very difficult to create national party networks that could mobilise popular support and deliver it to the ballot box. By demanding that these parties switch their energies from government to society, Brahimi hoped that they would act as channels for public opinion, linking the polity to its government.[29]

The American authorities' treatment of Lakhdar Brahimi on his third and final trip to Baghdad indicated the limits of any future role for the UN and the self-imposed restrictions on the USA's intervention in the Iraqi polity. Brahimi's influence over personalities and events was not based on Security Council resolutions or the institutional commitment of the UN to a sustained role. Instead, Brahimi's position rested on personal assurances he had been given from the highest levels in Washington. The logic of his approach was underpinned by an assumption that US political weight would be brought to bear to impose his plan. The core of his approach, the disbanding of the Governing Council and its member's ejection into Iraqi society to vie for election, was very unpopular with the formerly exiled political parties dominating the council. However, it would have helped institutionalise the democratic process and build much-needed links between the government in Baghdad and the rest of the country. But Brahimi's assumption that the CPA would be willing to forcibly intervene in the political process and face the limited problem of Governing Council animosity for the much greater benefits of democratic elections proved to be wrong.

Brahimi's third trip to Baghdad came at the end of the worst period of violence that the coalition had then faced. US forces were fighting revolts on two fronts, one centred on the siege of Fallujah and the other driven by the radical Shia cleric Muqtada al Sadr. Brahimi's arrival was also greeted with an upsurge of negative coverage in the Baghdad press dominated by the parties of the Governing Council.[30] Relations between the Governing Council and Brahimi were described by one council member as 'war'.[31] Against this background Brahimi did not get the help he was expecting from the CPA, or indeed from Washington. Involved in increasingly acrimonious negotiations and with little support, Brahimi raised the spectre of his resignation, but in the end retreated to New York and let the Governing Council and the CPA dictate the terms of the new interim government.[32]

The Interim Government of Iraq that was handed sovereignty on 28 June 2004 was the very antithesis of the Brahimi plan. Far from being dominated by technocrats who had disavowed any involvement in politics, the new government was full of formally exiled party placemen. The most senior figure, Ayad Allawi, is the leader of Iraqi National Accord, the vice president, Ibrahim Jaafari, is the head of the Al Dawa Party, one of the two main Shia parties. The other vice president, Rowsch Shaways, is a senior member of the Kurdish Democratic Party. Ministerial posts were liberally divided among the other parties that dominated the old Governing Council. It appears that the CPA opted for the expediency of co-opting key members of the Governing Council rather than the aim of guaranteeing the impartiality of the electoral process. After describing council members as 'feckless' and incapable of reaching out to the wider Iraqi population in November 2003, the CPA brought these very same people back into government. It entrusted them and their parties with the creation of Iraq's new administration. This decision indicated the nature and limitations of the US commitment to state building in Iraq. The initial decision to invest in the individuals and party organisations who attained prominence in exile came to dominate the whole approach to reconstituting the government. This had the benefit of allowing for a closely managed transition from the Baathist regime to a new governing elite. However, the administrative capacity of this new elite has proved to be extremely limited. It has also had difficulty working efficiently and harmoniously with the remnants of the old civil service, police and army. Finally and most importantly, its ability to build a base of support within Iraqi society, to mobilise a significant quota of public opinion and bring legitimacy to the new government is highly questionable.

Conclusions

The most important task for the new Iraqi government elected on 30 January 2005 is to establish some form of domestic sovereignty. Unlike the international sovereignty granted to Iraq in June 2004, domestic sovereignty, 'the organisation and effectiveness of political authority' is based on the quality and depth of the relationship between the governed and the governing.[33] This is clearly both institutional and ideational; governments must not only be seen to be ruling over their people but their actions must be felt to be in the interests of those people. For a new government in Baghdad to be successful it will have to try and make substantive progress in engendering a degree of legitimacy and administrative capacity in addition to the most pressing need to re-impose order on the country. It will have to convince a sizeable proportion of the Iraqi population that it is ruling in their interests, furthering their collective ideas of what Iraq is and what it is to become.

The US occupation of Iraq failed spectacularly to build even the foundations of the infrastructural power needed to achieve this. The main reasons for this failure are ideological. They involve the Bush administration's approach to international relations and to the domestic politics and sociology of Iraq. In the international sphere the Bush administration's militant unilateralism clearly made the road to war far more straightforward and easy to travel. However, when the aftermath of regime change proved to be much more complex and costly than Washington had predicted, the support and expertise that the international community could have deployed was not available. The treatment meted out to the UN representative Lakhdar Brahimi in Baghdad was proof, for those who needed it, that the USA was still wedded to a unilateralism that precluded any substantive influence for the international community.

Even more damaging to the long-term stability of Iraq was the way in which the planners in the Pentagon perceived of their post-war mission in the country. Using neoliberal policy prescriptions developed under the 'Washington consensus' the task of US administrators was understood to be very limited—the reform of state structures, certainly not an extended mission of state building. The benefit of this post-war vision was that regime change could be sold to the American electorate on the eve of war as a comparatively limited and cheap foreign policy option. But after Baghdad had been seized and the Iraqi state had collapsed it meant that the Coalition Provisional Authority charged with running Iraq was woefully unprepared to undertake the task of rebuilding the state from the ground up.

The final and most destructive discursive mistake made by US administrators once on the ground in Baghdad was the primordialisation of Iraqi society. Influenced by the former opposition parties, principally the Iraqi National Congress, the Kurdish Democratic Party and the Patriotic Union of Kurdistan, Iraqi society was perceived as irrevocably divided along ethnic and religious lines. By using this understanding to create the Interim Iraqi Governing Council, by deploying a very rough and ready consociationalism, the CPA has encouraged a sectarian dynamic that may yet come to dominate Iraqi politics. This certainly had the advantage of allowing its formerly exiled allies to pose as the representatives of Iraqi communalism, but its long-term ramifications may well be to leave a series of unrepresentative politicians at the head of a new Iraqi state, increasingly reliant on attempts at sectarian mobilisation as the only possible way to rally any support to their cause.

The result of this failure is the security vacuum that casts a shadow over the south and centre of the country and dominates the Iraqi population's everyday lives. This originated in the series of profound mistakes made by the CPA during the occupation. For Western news coverage this vacuum is personified by the suicide car bombs that daily rock Baghdad and the danger that foreigners will be kidnapped and beheaded by Islamic militants. For ordinary Iraqis, from Basra in the south to Mosul in the north, this all-encompassing insecurity is fuelled by the crime wave that greeted liberation. This means that their lives are haunted by the very real possibility of car jacking, house breaking and kidnapping for ransom or prostitution. Given the pervasive violence in Iraq today it is highly doubtful that a multinational effort to save the country from collapse is possible. But successful state building in Iraq would need the resources, expertise and neutrality that only the UN might possibly be able to deliver. If this help is not forthcoming, if US domestic politics or a divided Security Council stops a multilateral attempt at state building in Iraq, then the country is destined to continue on its journey from rogue state to collapsed state.

Notes

1 See Robert S Litwak, 'The new calculus of pre-emption', *Survival*, 44 (4), 2002–03, p 53; and *The National Security Strategy of the United States of America*, September 2002, at http://www.whitehouse.gov/nsc/nss.html. This was made even more explicit in the President's 2003 State of the Union address: 'Today, the gravest danger in the war on terror, the gravest danger facing America and the world, is outlaw regimes that seek and possess nuclear, chemical, and biological weapons. These regimes could use such weapons for blackmail, terror and mass murder. They could also give or sell those weapons to terrorist allies, who would use them without the least hesitation.'

2 See 'Remarks by the President at the 2002 Graduation Exercise of the United States Military Academy West Point, New York', 1 June 2002; *The National Security Strategy of the United States of America*, pp 1–2; Richard N Haass, Director, Policy Planning Staff, 'The 2002 Arthur Ross Lecture, Remarks to Foreign Policy Association New York', 22 April 2002; and G John Ikenberry, 'America's imperial ambition', *Foreign Affairs*, September/October, 2002, p 52.

3 Paul Wolfowitz at Camp David on 15 September 2001, while assessing the potential use of US troops in the aftermath of 9/11, said 'Iraq was a brittle, oppressive regime that might break easily. It was doable.' Quoted in Bob Woodward, *Bush at War*, New York: Simon and Schuster, 2002, p 83.

4 See Nicholas Leman, 'After Iraq: the plan to remake the Middle East', *The New Yorker*, 17 February 2003.

5 For the number of post-cold war interventions, see James Dobbins, John G McGinn, Keith Crane, Seth G Jones, Rollie Lal, Andrew Rathmell, Rachel Swanger & Anga Timilsina, *America's Role in Nation-building: From Germany to Iraq*, Washington, DC: Rand, at http://www.rand.org/publications/MR/MR1753/MR1753.pref.pdf.

6 See Lakhdar Brahimi, *Report of the Panel on United Nations Peace Operations*, UN document A/55/305S/2000/809; and *The Responsibility to Protect, Report of the International Commission on Intervention and State Sovereignty*, IDRC, 2001.

7 See Steve Heder, 'Cambodia (1990–98). The regime that didn't change', in Roger Gough (ed), *Regime Change. It's Been Done Before*, London: Policyexchange, 2003.

8 Indeed, President Bush was, after 9/11, avowedly against using US troops for state building, '" I don't want to nation-build with troops," Bush said yet again.' Quoted in Woodward, *Bush at War*, p 229. See also the 'no foreign policy as social work' campaign message delivered by Condoleezza Rice, 'Campaign 2000: promoting the national interest', *Foreign Affairs*, January/February 2000, pp 47, 53–54.

9 Michael Mastanduno, 'Models, markets and power: political economy and the Asia–Pacific, 1989–1999', *Review of International Studies*, 26 (4), 2000, p 499.

10 David Williams, 'Aid and sovereignty: quasi-states and the international financial institutions', *Review of International studies*, 26 (4), 2000, p 568.

11 See Faleh A Jadar, *Postconflict Iraq. A Race for Stability, Reconstruction and Legitimacy*, US Institute of Peace Special Report, No 120, May 2004, p 14.

12 See Isam al-Khafaji, 'The myth of Iraqi exceptionalism', *Middle East Policy*, 4, 2000, p 68.

13 See Peter Boone, Haris Gazdar & Athar Hussain, 'Sanctions against Iraq: costs of failure', paper delivered at the 'Frustrated Development: the Iraqi Economy in War and in Peace' conference,

University of Exeter, Centre for Gulf Studies in collaboration with the Iraqi Economic Forum, 9–11 July 1997.

14 A visit to any government institution during the 1990s was a sobering event. In the middle of May 2001 I secured an interview with a provincial governor in an area of southern Iraq where the government was feeling particularly vulnerable. On entering the building I had to step over a pool of raw sewage to reach his office door. Clearly the power of the state was not residing in this building.

15 Quoted in Michael Gordon, '" Catastrophic success": the strategy to secure Iraq did not foresee a 2nd war', *New York Times*, 19 October 2004.

16 'So massive was the looting that, just three days after the US secured the capital, computers were selling for as little as $35 in the thieves' market'. Mark Fineman, Robin Wright & Doyle McManus, 'Washington's battle plans: preparing for war, stumbling to peace', *Los Angeles Times*, 18 July 2003.

17 See David L Phillips, 'Listening to the wrong Iraqi', *New York Times*, 20 September 2003.

18 Kanan Makiya and two other Iraqi exiles visited the president in the Oval Office in January 2003. They told President Bush that US troops would be greeted with 'sweets and chocolate'. See George Packer, 'Kanan Makiya, dreaming of democracy', *New York Times Magazine*, 2 March 2003. This theme was also promoted by the influential Washington pundit Fouad Ajami in 'Iraq and the Thief of Baghdad', *New York Times*, 19 May 2002. Ajami's predictions were in turn quoted by Vice President Cheney in a speech in Summer 2002.

19 See Fineman *et al*, 'Washington's battle plans'; David Rieff, 'Blueprint for a mess', *New York Times Magazine*, 2 November 2003; and George Packer, 'Letter from Baghdad: war after war', *The New Yorker*, 24 November 2003.

20 See Isam al Khafaji, 'A few days after: state and society in a post-Saddam Iraq', in Toby Dodge & Steven Simon (eds), *Iraq at the Crossroads: State and Society in the Shadow of Regime Change*, London and Oxford: International Institute for Strategic Studies and Oxford University Press, 2003.

21 This finding was supported by an opinion poll carried out on 9 June by the Iraq Centre for Research and Strategic Studies which found that 'that only 15.1% of Iraqis polled in Baghdad said that the political parties in Iraq represented their interests. Approximately 63% of those surveyed preferred a technocratic government, rather than one based upon political parties'. See Puneet Talwar & Andrew Parasiliti, 108th [US] Congress, 1st Session, Committee Print, 'Iraq: meeting the challenge, sharing the burden, staying the course, a trip report to members of the Committee on Foreign Relations, United States Senate', p 9.

22 See International Crisis Group (ICG), *Governing Iraq*, Middle East Report No 17, Baghdad/Washington/Brussels: ICG, August 2003, p 11.

23 The US organisers acknowledged that the meeting was 'not sufficiently representative to establish an interim authority'. Jonathan Steele, *Guardian*, 29 April 2003.

24 These issues dominated the thinking of senior UN civil servants that I interviewed in New York in May 2003. See Jonathan Steele, *Guardian*, 21 August 2003; and Edward Mortimer, 'Iraq's future lies beyond conquest', *Financial Times*, 22 August 2003.

25 See Rend Rahim Francke, 'Iraq democracy watch: on the situation in Iraq', September 2003, at http://www.iraqfoundation.org/news/2003/isept/26_democracy_watch.html, pp 8–9.

26 Quoted in Robin Wright & Rajiv Chandrasekaban, 'US ponders alternatives to Iraq Governing Council', *Washington Post*, 9 November 2003.

27 Daniel Williams, 'Iraqi warns of delay on constitution vote', *Washington Post*, 10 November 2003.

28 See, for example, the results of polling carried out by the Iraqi Centre for Research and Strategic Studies, which has consistently indicated that Iraqis would prefer a technocratic government 'at least until elections can be held'. 'Factions tussle for post of Iraqi president', *Financial Times*, 31 May 2004.

29 On the Brahimi plan, see 'Statement of the Special Adviser to the Secretary-General, Lakdhar Brahimi, to the Security Council on the political transition process in Iraq', 27 April 2004; and 'Briefing of Special Adviser to UN Secretary-General, Lakdhar Brahimi, to the Security Council on the political transition process in Iraq', New York, 7 June 2004.

30 For a selection of this coverage see http://www.iwpr.net/index.pl?iraq_ipm_index.html.

31 See Roula Khalaf, Nicolas Pelham & James Drummond, 'UN envoy arrives in Baghdad as storm brews over government', *Financial Times*, 6 May 2004.

32 On Brahimi's threats of resignation, see Polly Toynbee, 'Blair's perversity does him harm and Iraq no good', *Guardian*, 12 May 2004. For the unfolding of the process, see Jonathan Steele, 'How honest broker was defeated—and with him hopes of credibility', *Guardian*, 3 June 2004.

33 See Stephen Krasner, *Sovereignty: Organized Hypocrisy*, Princeton, NJ: Princeton University Press, 1999, p 12.

The Prospects for Democracy in Iraq: challenges and opportunities

ADEED DAWISHA

ABSTRACT *There are many challenges to the development of democracy in Iraq: the many decades of authoritarian rule; ethno-sectarian divisions; lack of security; and the hegemony of the state over the national economy. But the right policies could transform these challenges into opportunities. Opinion makers should strive to resurrect into the collective memory of Iraqis the relatively liberal political practices of the 1921–58 period. Federal arrangements should bridge the ethno-sectarian divide, and an economy that shifts radically to the private sector should lessen middle class dependence on the state, thereby further eroding the centralisation of state power. The mushrooming of liberal and civil society institutions since April 2003 is an encouraging development.*

The forcible removal of Saddam Hussein's totalitarian regime was achieved with such relative ease that it engendered great hopes for a swift transformation in the political order. The public commitment of the US administration to democracy, coupled with the alienation of the majority of Iraqis from Saddam's brutal dictatorship engendered hopes that robust and sustainable democratic structures would be built in post-Saddam Iraq. And while it took somewhat longer than had been anticipated to put the process in place, 2005–06 should be the time-frame in which elections will be held and a constitution sensitive to the democratic vision written.

Juan Linz and Alfred Stepan offer the following criteria for democracy:

> legal freedom to formulate and advocate political alternatives with the concomitant rights to free association, free speech, and other basic freedoms of person; free and non-violent competition among leaders with periodic validation of their claims to rule; inclusion of all effective political offices in the democratic process; and provision for the participation of all members of the political community, whatever their political preference.[1]

Deconstructing this definition we can conclude that democracy can be observed and assessed in two main areas: political rights and civil liberties. The former allows citizens to choose their government through fair and free elections in which two or more individuals or political parties compete. The latter mandates that, through the rule of law, citizens are protected from arbitrary government, and their rights to free speech, belief and association are protected. Thus, what we should expect to see in Iraq is the following: the passing of a liberal constitution in which the rights of everyone, including women and ethnic and religious minorities, are guaranteed; elections that are reasonably fair (some harassment may occur, but are not widespread or consequential); a parliament that acts as an effective watch-dog over government; political parties that represent a broad voter choice, including opposition parties that are not curbed into perpetual submission, thus giving rise to what Lawrence Whitehead calls 'apostolic succession', whereby new presidents emerge constantly from within the ruling party, often through coercion;[2] and independently owned and operated media. If, by adhering to these criteria, Iraq can straddle Freedom House's 'free' and 'partly free' categories,[3] say by the middle of 2006, with future expectations pointing to the former, then the country could be deemed to have achieved a successful political breakthrough towards democratic transformation.

Is Iraq's history a liability for democratic transformation?

Since the demise of Saddam's dictatorship, leading writers on democratic transformation, as well as observers of Arab and Middle East politics, have tended to belittle the chances of democratic transformation in Iraq, dismissing these as mere wishful thinking. One main reason for this pessimism is the alleged lack of liberal and democratic traditions in Iraq's political culture and historical experiences.[4] Yet it can be easily illustrated that the country and its people do not necessarily suffer from an immutable democratic deficit. Periods of liberal attitudes and practices in the pre-Republican era testify to existing traditions of political pluralism and experience with representative government.

In the monarchical era, 1921–58, Iraq adopted a parliamentary system modelled on the British political system.[5] The constitution (known as the Basic law), which was promulgated and passed by the constituent assembly in 1924, provided for the right of free expression, publication and assembly, and the forming and joining of political parties within the law. Indeed, political parties were in existence from the early days of the country's birth. Of course, a number of these were defenders of the status quo, particularly as it pertained to Iraqi–British relations. Others, however, were vigorous opposition parties with impressive mass followings. Hizb al-Istiqlal (Independence Party) and al-Hizb al-Watani al-Dimuqrati (National Democratic Party) were well known in the 1940s and 1950s for their vitriolic and ceaseless onslaught on the British and their policies at a time when the Palace and Iraq's main political figures were umbilically tied to British interests in the country. For example, the two parties were at the forefront of those who opposed the 1947–48 negotiations between the Iraqi and British governments over revisions to the 1930 Anglo-Iraqi treaty. Indeed they ended up playing a vital role in the eventual rejection of the treaty.[6]

It is undoubtedly true that parliamentary life and the multiparty system did not constitute a true liberal democracy when judged by modern-day

Western standards. There were of course cases of rigged elections, harassment of opposition parties, institution of emergency laws, and the like. But the fact remains that the political system under the monarchy was for long periods sufficiently open to allow for a multiplicity of political opinions and orientations. This was evident in parliamentary debates that were at times particularly vigorous yet generally imbued with a civility that testified to the respect which members accorded to the institution. And, on the whole, parliamentarians who argued and voted against the government did so without fear of retribution.[7] While the palace and cabinet dominated the political process, parliament was by no means without the capacity to influence the executive.

This nascent political pluralism was also evident in the case of the press. In the 1940s and 1950s, for example, over 20 independently owned newspapers were published in Iraq's three major cities, Baghdad, Mosul and Basrah. A number of these newspapers belonged to various opposition groups and parties and as a rule were relentless, at times unrestrained, critics of governmental policies.[8] Every now and then the government would ban a newspaper for a particularly virulent attack, but the ban typically would last for a short period and the paper would duly reappear, sometimes under a modified name. For example, the leading opposition newspaper, *al-Ahali* (the People), would be banned and reappear as *Sawt al-Ahali* (Voice of the People), be banned again and reappear again as *Sada al-Ahali* (Echo of the People), and so on.

Iraq's democratic experience in the period 1921 – 58 did not approximate to the ideal of a Jeffersonian democracy, but neither was it the 'mock democracy' claimed by the sceptics.[9] Here, we need to recognise that historical recollection is not necessarily linear or cumulative. For instance, in the treatment of the 'frontier' in US history, particular narratives that at one time had been forcefully asserted, were then forgotten, and later rediscovered.[10] Indeed, especially in the realm of politics, historical memory is often the subject of reinterpretation by those searching for a 'usable past' by which to legitimise public policy.[11] For those thinking about, and hoping for, a democratic future for Iraq, the 1921 – 58 period could certainly be utilised as that usable past.

The possibility of democratic transformation in Iraq, therefore, is not hostage to historical or cultural liabilities. The problem is not so much in the past, but in present conditions. Saddam's malevolent dictatorship promoted political decay, socioeconomic stagnation and ethno-sectarian sensitivities, and was followed by war and foreign occupation. Thus present conditions for democratic peace are brittle, constituting major challenges to robust and sustainable democracy. Yet by no means are they insurmountable, and they could be alleviated by judicious and prudent policy. The success or failure of democracy will depend on whether the new political institutions take into consideration the country's existing social and communal imperatives.

Communal divisions and federalism

The two consequential fissures in Iraqi society, which were greatly intensified by Saddam's blatantly ethno-sectarian policies, are those of Arab against

Kurd and Sunni versus Shiite. It is important to note that the two schisms are not symmetrical.[12] They differ contextually as well as in their essence. The ethnic divide between Arab and Kurd has the greater potential for undermining Iraq's social and political unity. Of a different ethnic stock, demographically concentrated in the self-contained mountainous north, and speaking an Indo-European language, the Kurds, who comprise some 20% of Iraq's population, have a fully developed sense of nationhood. Their 12 years of virtual independence under the no-fly zone arrangements, and Kurdish tranquillity in the post-war period, which contrasted sharply with the chaos that ravaged the rest of the country, only served to cement nationalist, and perhaps separatist, sentiment. So far Kurdish leaders have been careful not to advocate separation, more a result of recognising geostrategic realities than eschewing nationalist aspirations. But this might change if the central government in Baghdad continues to be weak and is perceived to be subject to influence from other Iraqi groups, particularly the Shiites, who are not necessarily swayed by Kurdish demands.

On the other hand, the communal divide between Sunnis and Shiites is a conflict between Arab and Arab, and thus lacks the intensity of ethnic particularisms. The Shiites have never demanded autonomy, let alone political independence; they simply wanted a shift in the political and economic balance which, since Ottoman days, has been heavily in favour of the minority Sunnis. While they have been demographically concentrated in the south, the expansion of modern transportation and communications throughout the 20th century brought about increased communal interaction, which has been exemplified in the dramatic growth of multi-communal cities. This was augmented by the spread of secular education, which emphasised the 'oneness of Iraq' and the 'Arab' rather than the sectarian characteristics of the Iraqi population. Thus Iraq's sectarian sensitivities do not carry the same conflict potential that characterises the Arab–Kurdish divide.[13] In short, Shiite identity is subsumed within the wider Iraqi identity. Nevertheless, Shiite grievances against the Sunnis are genuine and plentiful, and were sharpened by the pervasive fear and mistrust engendered by the clannish rule of Saddam Hussein.

The sudden demise of Saddam's regime brought about a dramatic shift in political fortunes. This was emphatically demonstrated by the results of the January 2005 elections, in which the Arab Sunnis, for so long the holders of power and privilege, were marginalised. A minority of Sunnis took up arms against the new order, mounting a sustained insurgency that has undermined the security and stability of the new order and paralysed economic development. And, while the majority of Arab Sunnis did not resort to violence, neither did they seem ready to accept their reduced political status. The ensuing political conflict has resulted in sharpening societal fissures along potentially destructive vertical communal lines.

It is hardly surprising that such communal divisions have been perceived as an impediment to political stability and democratisation. Antagonisms among the ethno-sectarian communities could indeed undermine the prospects for sustainable democracy in Iraq. Yet, by the same token, the innate interest of each community to limit the power of the other could in fact provide the checks and balances that are so essential to the promotion of democracy at the expense of rigid communal particularism. Transforming Iraq's communal diversity from a dislocative force to an agent for positive change will depend on working out constitutional arrangements and political institutions sensitive to Iraq's social and cultural mosaic.

For democracy to take root and be sustained, a federal system has to be created and constitutionally enshrined where both centre and regions are designated equal guardians of the constitution. Keeping both in their assigned constitutional space is the responsibility of a strong federal judiciary, with constitutional amendments occurring only with the concurrence of both houses of the legislature, the head of state and all federal units. Moreover, the distribution of revenues has to be the responsibility of both centre and periphery. Central revenues would be used to redistribute resources from rich to poor regions, whereas local revenues would support local economic and cultural initiatives. Revenue-sharing arrangements are critical: power follows resources, and if the centre denies to regions the right to raise and spend revenue, it is tantamount to denying them power. Revenue sharing between the centre and regions also decreases the temptation for one ethnic group to either capture the state or seek separation. However, given the country's present debilitated economy, the power to control exploration and distribution of petroleum needs to reside with the centre, at least for an initial period of some years.

The federal system in Iraq has to be territorially, not ethnically, based. Otherwise, in the long term, a sociopolitical environment may be created in which citizens' commitment to the 'general good' is gradually transferred to the 'good' of the narrower community. This is a recipe for civil breakdown, even for state collapse. The case of Lebanon is instructive. The confessional system guaranteed the political rights of each of Lebanon's diverse communities in the expectation that, by alleviating intercommunal suspicion and mistrust, the various groups would remain committed to the larger entity of Lebanon. What happened instead was an entrenchment of community-based attitudes and loyalties so great that the country ended up losing a quarter of its lifespan to a catastrophic civil war.

A variant of the Lebanese system has in fact been tried in Iraq. Four months after the fall of Saddam, the Coalition Provisional Authority (CPA) appointed an Iraqi Governing Council, whose membership consisted of 13 Arab Shiites, five Arab Sunnis, five Sunni Kurds, a Christian and a Sunni Turkoman. Two months later the Governing Council itself appointed a cabinet in which portfolios were allocated to reflect precisely the ethnic and sectarian make-up of the council, and supposedly the country.

Apparently deemed successful, this practice was extended to district and council elections in communally heterogeneous Iraqi cities and towns. The CPA would determine the number of representatives for each community according to its demographic weight and then invite members of that community to vote for their representatives. The northern city of Kirkuk was the most pertinent example: its elected city council consisted of Kurds, Sunni

Arabs, Sunni Turkomans, and Christian Assyrians. The CPA would tout Kirkuk's democratic experiment as one of its major successes in Iraq.

Yet the experiment quickly foundered. The multi-ethnic council was beset with so many divisions that it hardly functioned. Within a few months, the mayor was demanding the relocation of hundreds of thousands of Kurds to the city, which prompted the Arab deputy mayor to demand a new election. The Turkomans on the council consistently threatened to boycott council meetings, demanding that the mayor remove Kurdish flags from various areas in the city, an issue which precipitated armed clashes. The Christians complained about being under-represented, and Arab Shiite clerics arrived in Kirkuk to 'protect' the small Shiite Turkoman community, which was unrepresented in the council.[14]

It is thus absolutely crucial to recognise that institutionalising such ethno-sectarian and Lebanese-style confessional arrangements, say in the constitution, would be hugely deleterious to Iraq's future, since it would ingrain and legitimise particularistic identities, creating notions of 'exclusiveness' that inevitably would exacerbate dislocations among the country's various communities. Such an entrenchment of ethnic and sectarian attitudes would inevitably lead to a spectrum of highly undesirable outcomes ranging from ethnic cleansing to inflexibility in political bargaining among the federal units and between them and the centre.

This is not the path that Iraq should follow. The goal is to de-emphasise particularistic attachments to ethnicity or sect, while simultaneously assuaging the fear that one group might come to power and, through strong central government, impose its interests and goals on the other groups. Thus a federal system that is decentralised on the basis of territory, not ethnicity or sect, where local governments have responsibility for all citizens in their areas, not just for ethnic or sectarian co-nationals, is the best alternative for sustainable democracy in Iraq.

Of all the Iraqi groups the Kurds are likely to be the most resistant to the above prescription. This was evident in the debate that preceded and followed the publication of the 'Basic Law' in March 2004. Article 61 C was included upon the insistence (and the threat of walking out) of the Kurds, and states that the constitution will be vetoed if two-thirds of three Iraqi provinces vote against it. As the three provinces of Sulaymaniya, Irbil and Dahouk are overwhelmingly Kurdish, this provision was the Kurds' guarantee that their rights not be compromised. Yet inevitably it was met with bitter opposition from other Iraqis, particularly the Shiites, who saw this manoeuvre as giving the Kurds disproportionate powers.

Iraq's democratic path is intimately linked to the progress (or otherwise) of harnessing the country's various groups, especially the Kurds, into a workable and equitable federal system. Some compromise on Kurdish identity, such as allowing for a Kurdish parliament, is possible within the general parameters of territorial federalism. However, the Kurds have to be persuaded to accept some modifications to article 61 C in order to pre-empt future constitutional deadlocks, which would be disastrous for democratic progress in Iraq. Indeed, the Kurds should understand that, with the erosion of Sunni political power, article 61 C could play into the hands of the Arab Sunnis as well, as they too could utilise their large demographic majorities in the three provinces of Anbar, Salah al-Din and Diyala to create constant constitutional crises. One possible compromise on the issue would be to give provinces veto powers over legislation that directly affects the provinces, but not over all the provisions in the constitution.

Socioeconomic conditions

Economic performance and its impact on people's lives are key prerequisites for the success or failure of democratic transformation. The more prosperous the country, the more likely it is to be democratic.[15] According to Samuel Huntington, 'in poor countries democratization is unlikely; in rich countries it has already occurred. In between there is a political transition zone; countries in that particular economic stratum are most likely to transit to democracy...As countries develop economically and move into this zone, they become prospects for democratization.' [16] Rising living standards and availability of work opportunities are the hallmarks of countries boasting stable democratic political orders.

Prosperity is also associated with a thriving middle class, and writers on democratic theory agree that an independent and self-sustaining middle class creates the basis for democratic civil life.[17] Looking back at the second half of the 19th century, one is struck by the contrast in the democratic experiences of Britain and Germany. Democracy was rapidly being incorporated into the British body politic through a series of parliamentary acts that not only expanded the electorate, but also placed ever increasing limitations on the power of the monarchy and aristocracy. In Germany's Second Reich, however, political elites dominated by the nobility ruled through a strong authoritarian regime in which the chancellors and their cabinets were in no way answerable to the Reichstag (the German parliament). It is no coincidence that Britain's progress towards democracy was spurred by an entrepreneurial middle class largely independent of the state. In Germany, however, the economy continued to be connected to the state, and the industrialisation of the country occurred as a result of the alliance between the state and the traditional elites. The lack of an independent, self-sustaining middle class was a major reason for the authoritarianism of the Second Reich.

Iraq too suffers from this 'democratic deficit'. Mirroring the role of the middle class in other Arab countries, much of Iraq's middle class has been directly dependent on the state, primarily through employment in the bureaucracy, in state-owned industries, in military and security agencies and in Ba'thist political bureaus.[18] In fact, the problem goes deeper, for even the 'independent' private sector has shown little inclination to promote democracy. As long as it was allowed, indeed aided, by the authoritarian state to 'make money', it was content to leave politics alone. This is because Iraq, like other Arab oil-producing countries, is a 'rentier state',[19] where government revenue has come mainly from oil sales rather than taxation.

Thus, with virtually no taxes to pay, citizens in a rentier state are 'far less demanding in terms of political participation. The history of democracy owes its beginning…to some fiscal association (no taxation without representation). The government's budget in the oil states remains a one-sided document, an expenditure program, a promise to spend money and distribute benefits to the population with virtually no levy on them in terms of taxes or similar impositions.' [20] This relationship between government and citizenry, which existed for over half a century in Iraq, and which was accentuated under Saddam, simply added to the political docility of Iraq's middle class.

The process of nurturing democracy in Iraq must have as one of its cornerstones a commitment to transferring resources from the public to the private sector. Stimulating entrepreneurship and strengthening the free market will have an enormous political pay-off, for it will develop a self-sustaining middle class that will become more proactive in promoting democratic values and institutions. Moreover, a proper taxation system should gradually be introduced, for only then will the middle class discard its traditional deference and demand accountability from the government. Iraq's middle class needs to be told, and should itself realise, that there can be 'no representation without taxation'.

A major hope for post-Saddam Iraq was that the country would enter a period of economic rejuvenation, in which the economy would quickly grow. Great strides towards this end could be made by giving Iraqi companies a chance to participate vigorously in the reconstruction of their country. Awarding contracts to Iraqi firms would pump capital into the private sector, thus allowing it to assume a greater share of the country's economic growth and giving it the financial capacity to acquire many of the publicly owned industries. This would stimulate entrepreneurship and strengthen the middle class. Even more crucially in the initial period, it would put people to work. All this would nurture democratic attitudes and practices.

Alas, none of this has come to pass, at least not in the first two years that followed the collapse of Saddam's order. Economic growth in Iraq by spring 2005 was stagnant at best, reconstruction was progressing at a snail's pace, unemployment remained at an unacceptable 40% and services, such as electricity, water treatment and public health, were woefully inadequate.

One of the major problems was the lack of expenditure. The World Bank has estimated that Iraq needed $17.5 billion simply to restore infrastructure and basic services to pre-war levels.[21] US Congressional approval in autumn 2003 of allocating $18.4 billion to Iraq was an admission not just of the country's dire and immediate needs, but also of the political and security dimensions of these needs. Yet, a full 12 months later, less than $1 billion had been dispersed, and about half of that was spent outside Iraq.[22] There is no doubt that poor planning, confusion in the disbursement of funds and the lack of purposeful vision were partly to blame. After all, the much trumpeted privatisation initiative undertaken by the CPA in summer 2003 turned out to be a major fiasco that smacked of the complete absence of prior study and planning. And, when projects were awarded, they were generally given to US contractors, who relied excessively on foreign subcontractors, who in turn generally brought with them their own workers.[23] This was happening in a country which had large numbers of highly trained, yet unemployed, structural, civil, mechanical and electrical engineers![24] On the rare occasion when Iraqis took charge of a construction project, they delivered quality products that put the meandering large US corporations to shame. And let us not forget that it took Saddam's regime a mere six months to erase all manifestations of the devastation that befell Baghdad in the first Gulf war. That work was done *entirely* by Iraqis. What was the need for high-priced foreigners when Iraqis could do a better job at a fraction of the price?

The lack of planning and confusion over priorities, coupled with a strangely anaemic understanding of local conditions by the coalition undoubtedly contributed to the economic stagnation of the first two years of post-Saddam Iraq. At a minimum this would slow the progress of democracy in Iraq. After all, at a very basic level, people who are out of work do not as a rule place democracy as their highest priority.

The security challenge

Beyond the shortcomings of the coalition, a major, perhaps even heftier, impediment to economic reconstruction has been the incessant violence in the country. The abduction and murder of foreign workers and contractors has played a big role in dissuading companies from investing and working in Iraq. It had been anticipated that by summer 2004 Iraq's oil production would surpass the pre-war level of 2.3 million barrels a day. Indeed, this was achieved ahead of time, but sabotage of pipelines continued to reduce production by more than one million barrels a day. No sooner was a damaged pipeline repaired than another was sabotaged. The same is true of electricity. Repairing electric grids and building power generators was a major priority since the Iraqis lived the nightmare of four hours per day of electricity in the 120° heat of summer 2003. The hope was for doubling electric production to 7000 megawatts by summer 2004. Again, in the face of persistent sabotage, electric production hovered around 5000 megawatts.[25] But perhaps the most discouraging statistic is to be found in the area of building construction. The CPA had promised that by summer 2004 no fewer than 2300 construction projects would be fully under way, yet, consumed by the security crisis, it was able to deliver on only 140 projects.[26] Sadly but understandably, to confront the deteriorating security situation, the US administration converted $3.2 billion that had been earmarked for economic and infrastructural projects to spending on security. Nisrin Berwari, Iraq's Minister of Municipalities and Public Works, lamented that this would have an undoubted negative impact on her ministry's projects, which included 'water sanitation and other services that [had] a direct connection to the life of the Iraqi citizen'.[27] Thus the promise of alleviating social and economic adversity, which, as we have seen, is a critical prerequisite for democratic transformation, became hostage to the deteriorating security situation.

Regardless of the economic consequences, no political order, including one based on democratic principles, would be accorded legitimacy if it was incapable of providing basic security for its citizens. Yet, if one thinks of Iraq in the two years following the forcible removal of Saddam's regime, the image that comes to mind first is one of bedlam and anarchy. Law and order that come either from a societal social contract that engenders a universal respect for the law, or from a strong regime that imposes on the population its own set of rules and regulations, were totally lacking. Some resistance to the new political order was to be expected, but the intensity and longevity of the campaign were the main surprises of the post-Saddam era.

Even so, supporters of democracy should not be too disheartened. The perpetrators of violence have a narrow support base. In the two years that followed the collapse of Saddam's regime, resistance to the new political order has come from two main sources: the armed militia of the young Shiite cleric, Muqtada al-Sadr, and the Sunni insurrection, the heart of which is located in the area that became known as the Sunni Triangle. The former was contained through the use of the stick and carrot approach. First, Sadr's fighters were battered mercilessly in the Shiite holy city of Najaf by a combined US–Iraqi force. Defeated, with nowhere to go, remnants of the militia holed themselves up in the venerated Imam 'Ali Mosque. But they were to quickly recognise the narrowness of their support base when hundreds of thousands Shiites under orders from Grand Ayatollah, 'Ali Sistani, the most senior Shiite cleric, marched to the mosque and literally expelled the few hundred fighters.

Sadr's eventual defeat was predictable. Recognising their demographic majority, the Shiites understand that a peaceful transformation works in their favour. It was hardly surprising that Sistani became the most committed advocate of elections and parliamentary representation. So it was only a matter of time before the Shiites would stand up to the self-obsessed upstart who was making a personal grab for power.

Undermining Sadr further would occur through economic revitalisation and job creation, since the motivation to join his militia was on the whole determined less by religious or nationalist fervour than by socioeconomic deprivation. The Iraqi interim government, backed by the Americans, embarked on a policy for the reconstruction of Najaf and the Baghdad Shiite slum of Sadr City, and compensated those damaged by the fighting.[28] The expulsion of Sadr's fighters had to be rewarded, and the rewards had to be physically visible for everyone to see. This would not only broaden support for the new political order, but would also put unemployed men to work and encourage dead-end youth to attend schools, thereby limiting Sadr's recruitment base. In all this, Najaf and Sadr City would become the shining examples of what co-operation with the authorities could bring to a particular locale. The calculation was that money spent on these two projects would have a political pay-off, since the Shiite population was deemed to have little ideological antipathy to a new democratic political order, and would co-operate fully if it saw government making resources available to improve the socioeconomic status of their community. The political pay-offs were demonstrated in the January 2005 elections with the large voter turnout in Najaf and Sadr City, as well as in other predominantly Shiite areas.

The 'Sunni triangle' presented a more menacing challenge. The resistance there was ideational and unwavering. Constituting the backbone of Saddam's security and intelligence forces, the towns of the triangle had no stake in the new order in which their political and economic status would inevitably and considerably suffer. Additionally, certain towns in the triangle, especially Fallujah, had become a haven for militant Salafi sheikhs even in the days of Saddam Hussein. These clergy not only radicalised the Islamic culture in the town, but also attracted extremist Islamists from abroad after the demise of Saddam's regime. The result was an alliance of convenience between two uncompromising groups, committed Sunni members of the old regime and psychotic Islamists bent on fighting *al-Salibiyeen* (the crusaders).[29] If there is an obdurate hostility to the new order and its democratic purpose, it resides in this area.

The recalcitrance of Sunni areas must not be allowed to derail the admittedly ambitious timetable that has been set for the momentous constitutional and institutional changes culminating in the general elections that are scheduled for December 2005. Security issues will undoubtedly present problems, but they should not be allowed to derail the democratic process. In the words of Britain's Defence Minister, 'security is vital to elections, but elections are equally vital for security'.[30] Interestingly enough, this sentiment was echoed by the Shiite senior clergy, who, in their insistence that elections should not be postponed, argued that 'lack of security should not be used as an excuse, because security is linked to elections'.[31] In any case, elections have been held in other countries where the lack of security has been an issue. Northern Ireland, Colombia, El Salvador, Sri Lanka, Kashmir and Algeria come to mind.

Democratic developments

As we have seen, democratic ideas and institutions are not alien to Iraq. The relatively liberal 1921–58 era boasted a parliamentary system, opposition political parties and an independently owned press that did not shy away from vigorous criticisms of the government. But it is also true that any semblance of democracy was obliterated in the post-1958 Republican period, particularly during Saddam's totalitarian rule, and this might have fostered attitudes disdainful of democracy. However, even if that has indeed happened, as in post-World War II Germany and Japan, and in many post-communist transitions, democratic political institutions can themselves over time, and sometimes surprisingly quickly, change such attitudes, promoting a democratic mind-set.

In fact, there is much that is encouraging about the prospects for democratisation in Iraq. After all, in an environment of persistent insecurity, which as a rule fosters authoritarian attitudes, Iraqis have made impressive strides in embracing and fostering democratic and civil society attitudes and institutions. This is particularly the case at the level of local government and civil society. Shortly after the collapse of Saddam's regime, most Iraqi towns and cities, including the major urban areas, acquired governing councils that were chosen through consensual processes, often involving elections. The case of genuine 'grassroots democracy' in Baghdad is especially instructive. Suffering from widespread lawlessness, the city was still able in autumn 2003 to form 88 neighbourhood councils, which then in turn elected a 37-member council for the whole city.[32] In the face of persistent threats from anti-democratic forces, the council continued to hold public meetings and formulate policy.

The mushrooming of local self-government councils proved to be one of the major success stories of the occupation. Even those councils that were not elected were selected through peaceful and relatively consensual means, and provided forums for unprecedented amounts of open debate and citizen participation. As such the 'selected' councils too represented strong signs of progress, and would eventually be brought under the electoral principle without fundamental disruption.

At the national level, the unitary and all-encompassing Ba'th Party was replaced by a plethora of political parties. These ran the ideological gamut from left to right, and represented secular as well as religious concerns. Organisationally some developed a national reach with offices in more than one city, while others focused on building support on narrower ethnic or tribal bases. A number of these parties proceeded to build alliances, coalescing around a common policy or political demand. One example was the co-ordination among leftist parties in highlighting the plight of the unemployed. Another was the effort by various, politically disparate, groups to work out coalitions of parties opposed to the interim government of Iyad Allawi.[33] This expression of opposition peacefully and within the democratic 'rules of the game' is the kind of sign one would hope to see if democracy in Iraq is to be sustained.

At the level of civil society many important professional syndicates representing journalists, physicians, engineers, lawyers, writers, university professors, pharmacists and others have ousted the old leaders that Saddam forced on them and elected new ones in their place. These newly modelled syndicates not only called for the institution of a democratic political system, but were also eager to partake in the political life of the new Iraq. On the preparatory committee of the physicians' syndicate, for example, sat doctors who also held memberships in 14 of the new political parties.[34] Additionally, large numbers of literary and artistic groups put on productions and festivals that celebrated freedoms they had not enjoyed for more than four decades.

Particularly encouraging was the resurgence of women's groups into the public sphere. Spurred by a resolution of the Iraqi Governing Council (IGC) in 2003, which would have transferred key provisions of personal and family status law from civil to clerical administration under Shari'a law, women planned public meetings, held street protests and demonstrations, and threatened boycotts. The IGC was forced to retract the resolution. Simultaneously, women established a number of organisations to protect their rights, and were successful in securing 25% of the seats of the national assembly in summer 2004.

Perhaps the most spectacular change in culture that has occurred in Iraq has been the proliferation of independent, privately owned newspapers. In Saddam's Iraq only five daily newspapers were published. The prose may have differed from one paper to the other, but the strict robotic rendition of governmental policies and directives defined all of them. In 2004 over 160 newspapers were sold on the streets of Baghdad alone. They represented all kinds of organisations and all shades of opinion.

Conclusion

These are encouraging achievements particularly in light of the uncertain security situation. They are indicators that a palpable, indeed innate, proclivity for democratic, pluralist and civil society practices exists at almost all levels of Iraqi society. What is noticeable is the sheer frequency with which key democratic terms, such as elections, parliament, human rights, press freedoms, minority rights and the like, are entering the daily lexicon in Iraq. In the wide-ranging discourse over the country's future, there is hardly any dissent from the proposition that Iraq needs parliamentary life. When it comes to the electoral process, there may be debates over the timing as well as the exact method and institutions to be adopted, but a clear majority harbours no doubt that elections are the necessary road to governance.[35]

Even the senior clergy insist on elections as crucial to the legitimacy of any government or constitutional arrangement. This is particularly the case with the religious leaders of the majority Shiite population. In the words of Grand Ayatollah Sistani: 'the voting booth is the medicine that will cure all of Iraq's problems'. In the same proclamation he added that he would fully support the people's choice for president whether the person was 'Sunni, Shiite, Christian, Kurd, or from any other Iraqi denomination, as long as he ruled in accordance with the law and guaranteed everyone their freedoms and beliefs'.[36] In a similar vein Grand Ayatollah Ishaq al-Fayadh urged all sectors of Iraqi society to vote, saying that 'elections would determine the people's political, social and economic destiny, [allowing them] to attain their legitimate rights'.[37] While Sunni clerics have been more circumspect than the Shiites or Kurds about the feasibility of fair elections, they too have nevertheless publicly supported the notion of representative government and the electoral process.

Opinion survey polls have consistently confirmed this propensity. They have shown time and again that a majority of Iraqis support multiparty, parliamentary democracy over centralising presidencies and Iranian-type clerical government.[38] What is particularly encouraging about these figures is that the strong residue of pro-democracy sentiment is held at a time of extensive frustration with lawlessness, lack of services, and considerable unemployment—conditions that traditionally have oriented people's attitudes toward strong centralising institutions.

Iraqis' preference for democratic transformation was dramatically and emphatically demonstrated in the January 2005 elections. In the face of widespread threats and intimidation by insurgents, Iraqis came out in their millions to elect representatives for a national assembly and provincial councils. That seminal event gave the lie to the proposition that Iraqis, having been numbed by over half a century of authoritarian and personalised rule, have acquired a structural passivity to electoral and democratic processes.

These attitudes and proclivities should fortify the resolve of those who are planning the country's democratic transformation. In all probability Iraq will end up with something less than a 'Jeffersonian democracy'. But if, at the end of the road, the rights of all citizens, including women and minorities, are preserved, and citizens are able to choose their representatives, who in turn act as a watch-dog over governmental policies without intimidation, then Iraqis will come to believe that the undertaking was well worth all the uncertainties and sacrifices.

Notes

1 Juan J Linz, *Crisis, Breakdown, and Reequilibrium*, Baltimore, MD: Johns Hopkins University Press, 1978, p 5.

2 Lawrence Whitehead, *Democratization: Theory and Experience*, Oxford: Oxford University Press, 2002, p 207.

3 For an explanation of the criteria and a ranking of various countries in 2003, see Adrian Karatnycky, 'The 2003 Freedom House Survey: national income and liberty', *Journal of Democracy*, January 2004, pp 82–93. In fact, the criteria used here do not much differ from the 'minimum requirements for democracy' suggested by Larry Diamond & Leonardo Morlino, 'The quality of democracy: an overview', *Journal of Democracy*, October 2004, pp 20–31.

4 For instance, see *San Francisco Chronicle*, 13 April 2003; *Middle East Institute Brief*, 3 May 2004; *Hoover Digest*, Spring 2003, p 2; and *Washington Post*, 8 April 2003.

5 For a more detailed analysis, see Adeed Dawisha, 'Democratic attitudes and practices in Iraq, 1921–58', *Middle East Journal*, 59 (1), 2005, pp 11–30.

6 'Adel Ghaffouri Khalil, *Ahzab al-Mu'aradha al-'alaniya fi al-'Iraq, 1946–1954* (The Public Opposition Parties in Iraq, 1946–1954), Baghdad: al-Maktaba al-'Alamiya, 1984, pp 155–170; 'Abd al-'Aziz al-Qassab, *Min Dhikrayati, 1888–1960* (From My Memoirs, 1888–1960), Beirut: 'Uwaidat Pyblications, 1962, p 316; 'Abd al-Amir Hadi al-'Akam, *Tarikh Hizb al-Istiqlal al-'Iraqi, 1946–1958* (History of the Independence Party, 1946–1958), Baghdad: Dar al-Shu'un al-Thaqafiya al-'Amma, 1986, p 219; and Kamel al-Chadirji, *Mudhakarat Kamel al-Chadirji* (Memoirs of Kamel al-Chadirji), Cologne: al-Jamal Publications, 2002, p 193.

7 'Abd al-Karim al-Uzri, *Dhikrayat fi Tarikh al'Iraq, 1930–1958* (History in the Memoirs of Iraq, 1930–1958), Baghdad: Dar al-Shu'un al-Thaqafiya al-'Amma, 1988, p 77; and Mir Basri, *A'lam al-Siyasa fi al-'Iraq al-Hadith* (Political Personalities in Modern Iraq), London: Riad al-Rayyes li al-Tiba'a wa al-Nashr, 1987, pp 82–83.

8 See, for example, Muhamed Mahdi Kubba, *Mudhakarati fi Samim al-Ahdath, 1918–1958* (My Memoirs at the Heart of Events, 1918–1958), Beirut: Dar al-Tali'ah, 1965, p 227. Faiq Butti, a journalist who was a virulent critic of governmental policies, says that the press was instrumental in 'fostering democratic attitudes' in Iraq. Faiq Butti, *Sahafat al-'Iraq: Tarikhuha wa Kifah Ajyaliha* (Iraqi Press: Its History and the Struggle of its Generations), Baghdad: Matba'at al-Adib, 1968, p 122.

9 James Dobbins *et al*, *America's Role in Nation-Building: From Germany to Iraq*, Santa Monica, CA: Rand Corporation, 2003, p 191.

10 See Frances FitzGerald, *America Revisited: History Schoolbooks in the Twentieth Century*, New York: Vintage, 1980, pp 76–77, 90–91, 130–131.

11 S Frederick Star, 'A usable past', *The New Republic*, 15 May 1989.

12 See Adeed Dawisha, 'The assembled state: communal conflicts and governmental control in Iraq', in Leonard Binder (ed), *Ethnic Conflict and International Politics in the Middle East*, Tallahassee, FL: University Press of Florida, 1999.

13 *Ibid*, pp 65–66.

14 *Daily Star* (Beirut), 2 January 2004.

15 Seymour Martin Lipset, *Political Man: The Social Bases of Politics*, New York: Doubleday, 1960, pp 45–76. Larry Diamond, however, doubts whether this is a universally accurate statement. While he

concedes that 'richer countries fare better', he still argues that 'today, almost a third of the countries with "low human development" (according the UN Development Program) are democracies'. See Diamond's reply in the exchange entitled 'Was Iraq a fool's errand?', *Foreign Affairs*, November/December 2004, pp 130–133.

16 Samuel Huntington, *The Third Wave: Democratization in the Late Twentieth Century*, Norman, OK: University of Oklahoma Press, 1991, pp 59–72.

17 For a sampling of this literature, see *ibid*, pp 66–68.

18 See John Waterbury, 'Democracy without democrats? The potential for political liberalization in the Middle East', in Ghassan Salame (ed), *Democracy Without Democrats? The Renewal of Politics in the Muslim World*, London: I B Taurus, 1994, p 27.

19 Hazem Beblawi & Giacomo Luciani (eds), *The Rentier State*, London: Croom Helm, 1987.

20 Hazem Beblawi, 'The rentier state in the Arab world', in *ibid*, pp 53–54.

21 International Crisis Group (ICG), *Middle East Report*, 30, p 2.

22 *Ibid.* See also *al-Sharq al-Awsat* (London), 9 September 2004; and the interview in *cfr.org* with Anthony Cordesman, 16 September 2004.

23 ICG, *Middle East Report*, 30, p 17; and *New York Times*, 1 July 2004.

24 The Minister of Planning, Mahdi al-Hafidh, alluded to the necessity of actively including indigenous Iraqi companies in the construction process at the meeting of donor countries held in Japan in October 2004. See *al-Sabah* (Baghdad), 25 October 2004.

25 *Al-Sharq al-Awsat*, 13 September 2004.

26 *Daily Star*, 6 July 2004.

27 *Al-Sharq al-Awsat*, 7 October 2004.

28 See *al-Zaman* (Baghdad), 9 October 2004; *al-Sabah*, 16 September 2004; *al-Sharq al-Awsat*, 7 October 2004; and *al-Sabah*, 25 October 2004.

29 'Crudsader' has been secularised in the English language, and in no way conveys the real meaning it carries in Arabic. *Al-Salibeyeen* literally means 'Those of the Cross'. The reference is utterly unambiguous.

30 See *Al-Zaman*, 18 September 2004.

31 This statement was made by Grand Ayatollah Ishaq al-Fayadh. See *al-Sabah*, 9 October 2004.

32 Thomas L Friedman, 'The least-bad option', *New York Times*, 12 October 2003.

33 *Al-Zaman*, 29 July 2004; *Al-Sharq al-Awsat*, 30 September 2003; *al-Sabah*, 25 October 2004.

34 *Al-Wifaq* (Baghdad), 7 September 2003.

35 For example, a spokesman on behalf of Grand Ayatollah Ali Sistani expressed the Ayatollah's reservation that the utilisation of a party-list, proportional representation method in the January 2005 elections was 'not appropriate for a country like Iraq'. Nevertheless he said that he would still 'urge popular participation' in the elections and the democratic process. See *al-Hayat* (London), 18 October 2004.

36 *Baghdad*, 8 September 2004. In another instance, this time in a Friday sermon, a spokesman for Sistani said that abstaining from voting was tantamount to 'treason and is punished by hellfire'. *Al-Zaman*, 10 October 2004.

37 *Al-Sabah*, 9 October 2004.

38 See for example, *al-Wifaq*, 9 September 2003; *Washington Times*, 5 October 2003; *al-Sharq al-Awsat*, 24 October 2003; *The Economist*, 1–7 November 2003; *al-Zaman*, 16 February 2004; *al-Sabah*, 21 July 2004; and *al-Sabah*, 9 September 2004.

Reconstructing Gender: Iraqi women between dictatorship, war, sanctions and occupation

NADJE AL-ALI

ABSTRACT *This article explores the role of Iraqi women in reconstruction processes by contextualising the current situation with respect to changing gender ideologies and relations over the past three decades. Before discussing the Iraqi case specifically, I provide a brief theoretical background about the significance of gender in reconstruction as well as nation-building processes. A historical background aims to shed light on the changing gender ideologies and relations during the regime of Saddam Hussein. The article focuses particularly on the impacts of the early developmental–modernist discourses of the state and the impacts of war (Iran–Iraq war 1980–88, Gulf wars 1991, 2003) as well as on the comprehensive economic sanctions regime (1990–2003). The latter involved wider social changes affecting women and gender relations but also society at large because of the impoverishment of the well educated middle-class, wide-scale unemployment, an economic crisis and a shift towards more conservative values and morals. It is against this historical background that contemporary developments related to ongoing conflict, occupation and political transition affect women and gender relations.*

Despite the common rhetoric of democratisation, women's rights and inclusion, Iraqi women might turn out to be the biggest losers in the current and future political and social map of Iraq. Having already suffered from the steady erosion of socioeconomic rights, which had been gained in the early years of the Saddam Hussein regime, women and gender relations have been particularly hard-hit by economic sanctions (1990–2003), as well as by the recent war in 2003 and its ongoing violent aftermath. UN resolution 1325, calling for the mainstreaming of gender in all aspects of reconstruction and political state building, has taken on a tragic twist: to start with, the question of reconstruction appears premature at a time when the increasing levels of violence and conflict prevent any serious development projects and processes. Second, there has been the danger of a backlash against women's rights and gender relations as the call for the mainstreaming of gender is being linked to the wider issue of foreign occupation, neocolonial configurations and an interim government that lacks widespread credibility among the Iraqi population.

This political dilemma should not, however, prevent political debates and academic analyses that put gender on the map. Without doubt the differentiation and relative positioning of women and men is an important ordering principle that pervades systems of power and is sometimes its very embodiment:

> Gender power is seen to shape the dynamics of every site of human interaction, from the household to the international arena. It has expression in physique—how women and men's bodies are nourished, trained and deployed, how vulnerable they are to attack, what mobility they have (Cockburn, 1999: 3).

Gender also has expression in prevailing ideologies and norms, in laws, in citizenship rights, in political dynamics and struggles and, of course, in economics—how money, property and other resources are distributed between the sexes. However, what is important to point out here is that gender does not necessarily constitute the most significant factor. Economic class, ethnic and religious differentiation, sexual orientation and political affiliation also shape power hierarchies and structure political regimes and societies. And these differentiating factors, in turn, are gendered and are part of the specific constructs of men/masculinities and women/femininities.

In this article I will first provide a brief theoretical background to the significance of gender in reconstruction and nation-building processes before exploring the role of women and changing gender relations in contemporary Iraq. A historical background aims to shed light on the changing gender ideologies and relations during the regime of Saddam Hussein. I will focus particularly on the impacts of the early developmental–modernist discourses of the state and the impacts of war (Iran–Iraq war 1980–88 and Gulf war 1991), as well as on the comprehensive economic sanctions regime (1990–2003). The latter involved wider social changes affecting women and gender relations but also society at large, eg impoverishment of the well educated middle class, wide-scale unemployment, an economic crisis and a shift towards more conservative values and morals.

It is against this backdrop that the impact of the latest war (2003), the occupation and reconstruction attempts need to be analysed. In addition to the most immediate effects of the current situation (lack of security and mobility, humanitarian crisis and political marginalisation of women), the article will explore more long- term issues related to the issue of mainstreaming gender.

Nationalism and national identities: gendered perspectives

One of the key issues in delineating gender differences is the relationship between nationalism and gender, that is, the ways in which nationalism and the nation-state are gendered as well the as various ways in which women participate in or challenge nationalist processes. Case studies of women in a variety of geographical and political contexts substantiate the theoretical model sketched out by Yuval-Davis and Anthias (1989: 7) to describe the various ways in which women can and do participate in ethnic and national processes:

1. as biological reproducers of members of ethnic collectivities;
2. as reproducers of the boundaries of ethnic and national groups;
3. as actors in the ideological reproduction of the collectivity and as transmitters of its culture;
4. as signifiers of ethnic and national groups;
5. as participants in national, economic, political and military struggles.

The most 'natural' way in which women participate in national and ethnic processes is the 'biological reproduction of the nation', which corresponds to the notion of *Volksnation*, a nation of common origin, common 'blood and belonging' (Yuval-Davis, 1997: 66). The relationship between cultural reproduction and gender relations can be articulated in terms of a *Kulturnation*. Here, gender relations are at the centre of cultural constructions of social identities and collectivities, where women tend to constitute their symbolic 'border guards'. Being constructed as carriers of the collectivity's 'honour' and the intergenerational reproducers of its culture, specific codes and regulations delineate the 'proper women' and 'proper men' (Yuval-Davies, 1997: 67). Often women are perceived to be both biological and cultural reproducers of a nation. In Iraq, for example, women were asked by the regime of Saddam Hussein to 'produce' future soldiers, while they were also increasingly being used as symbols for the honour and stamina of the nation. In post-Saddam Hussein Iraq, women are increasingly being used as symbols against the previous, largely secular regime as well as against Western cultural and political imposition.

Cockburn (1999) argues convincingly that the more primordial the rendering of people and nation, the more are the relations between men and women essentialised:

> 'Women are reminded that by biology and by tradition they are the keepers of hearth and home, to nurture and teach children "our ways". Men by physique and tradition are there to protect women and children, and the nation, often represented as the "motherland"' (p 8).

This process can also be observed in Iraq, where the increasing significance of primordial ethnic and religious identities goes side by side with more conservative and restrictive gender ideologies.

Gender and post-conflict periods

Peace for women does not mean the cessation of armed conflict. Women's security needs are not necessarily met in 'post-conflict' situations, as gender-based violence still remains rampant in reconstruction periods (Gervais, 2004). Enloe's definition of peace is 'women's achievement of control over their lives' (Enloe, 1987: 538). Peace, as defined by Enloe, would require not just the absence of armed and gender conflict at home, locally and abroad, but also the absence of poverty and the conditions which create it (Kelly, 2000: 48).

In reality women often experience a backlash in post-war situations when traditional gender roles inside the home or outside are evoked. Violence against women is often endemic in post-war situations, partly because of the general state of anarchy and chaos but also as an element of heightened aggression and militarisation, and prevailing constructions of masculinity promoted during conflict. An extreme example of this situation is contemporary Iraq, which, despite the official ending of military conflict, is extremely violent and insecure. As a matter of fact, the level of every-day experienced violence is even greater now than during the period of formal military intervention. Women have particularly suffered from the chaos, lawlessness and lack of security and have been subject to increased harassment and abductions, as well as sexual abuse and rape.

For women at home and within the diaspora it often seems as if the challenges posed to traditional gender ideologies and roles during times of war have become too great for patriarchal societies to accept in peace. Women often have less political space to challenge gender relations and to contribute to political processes in the aftermath of conflict. According to Pankhurst (2004):

> The ideological rhetoric is often about 'restoring' or 'returning' to something associated with the *status quo* before the war, even if the change actually undermines women's rights and places women in a situation that is even more disadvantageous than it was in the past. This is often accompanied by imagery of the culturally specific equivalent of the woman as 'beautiful soul', strongly associating women with cultural notions of 'tradition', motherhood, and peace (p 19).

Historically women rarely sustain wartime gains in peacetime. Societies neither defend the spaces women create during struggle nor acknowledge the ingenious ways in which women bear new and additional responsibilities.

Absence of women in formal reconstruction processes

In many post-conflict settings women have been sidelined or marginalised from formal peace initiatives, political transitions and reconstruction efforts. Formal peace negotiations among warring parties and their mediators serve to define basic power relations and to identify priorities for immediate post-war political activity (Sorenson, 1998). Traditional militarised gender regimes tend to endow men with the power in politics and locate women's importance within the family (Cockburn & Zarkov, 2002). However, women within conflict-ridden societies as well as within diasporic communities do find ways to work for peace and reconciliation through grassroots activism. Women from all walks of life participate in this informal peace-building work, but their activities are often disparaged as 'volunteer', 'charitable' or 'social', even when they have a political impact (Ferris, in Sorenson, 1998).

Despite UN Resolution 1325 passed in October 2000 stating the importance of the inclusion of women and mainstreaming gender into all aspects of post-conflict resolution and peace operations, the reality of post-conflict situations is often quite different. If acknowledged at all, UN Resolution 1325 is frequently translated into adding a few women into governments and ministries. However, the mainstreaming of gender would involve the appointments of women to interim governments, ministries and committees dealing with systems of local and national governance, judiciary, policing, human rights, allocating funds, free media development—all economic processes. It also aims at encouraging independent women's groups, NGOs and community-based organisations.

In some post-conflict settings, especially with respect to Muslim societies, the stress on UN resolution 1325 is perceived to be part of a Western plot to destroy a society's traditional culture and values. This is particularly the case in contexts of US-led military intervention, such as in Afghanistan and Iraq. Paradoxically, people who might otherwise be sympathetic to issues pertaining to women's rights and women's equality could express strong opposition to women's inclusion in post-conflict reconstruction if this is made one of the aims of the occupying powers. The political involvement or even return of diaspora women might evoke resentment and a backlash from local women's rights activists. This trend has been particularly evident in the Iraqi context, where the diaspora has played a disproportionate role in the new Iraqi leadership supported by the USA. Diaspora women have tried to put their mark on emerging women's organisations within Iraq, but have frequently been perceived as patronising and being part of a Western ploy.

It is important to point out that Iraqi women have been very much part of the 'public sphere' until a decade or so ago. Despite the context of general political repression by the Baath regime of Saddam Hussein, Iraqi women were among the most educated in the whole region. They were part of the labour force and visible and active on almost all levels of state institutions and bureaucracy. These days, however, women are prevented from leaving their houses by fear and a great sense of insecurity. Violent burglaries, mafia-like gangs that roam the cities at night, increased sexual violence, including rape, as well as militant resistance and US snipers have pushed women into the background. The demise of women's gains during the 1970s and early 1980s was already evident before the war in 2003. Aside from the most obvious effects related to the atrocious humanitarian situation, there have been changes in gender relations and ideologies in the context of wider social changes related to war, sanctions and changing state policies.

Even before this last war, because of sanctions, there was a massive deterioration in basic infrastructure (water, sanitation, sewage, electricity) that severely reduced the quality of life of Iraqi families, who often had to get through the day without water and electricity. High child mortality (about

4000–5000 per month), rampant malnutrition and increased rates of leukaemia, other forms of cancer, epidemic diseases, and birth defects were among the most obvious 'side-effects' of the sanctions regime. However, everyday lives changed not only with respect to the drastic deterioration in economic conditions and basic infrastructure: the social and cultural fabric of Iraqi society has also been affected.

Iraqi women have experienced a number of profound social and cultural changes linked to gender relations and ideologies. These changes are not easily quantifiable and visible to an outside observer. But when war and economic hardship are brought to a civilian population, women suffer in various ways. Data on war and conflict-ridden countries such as Iraq tend to conceal gender-specific forms of hardship. In this article I focus on a number of social and cultural changes that have had an impact on women and gender relations. It is too early to address with certainty the impact of this last war, occupation and the ongoing conflict in Iraq, but some trends are already evident.

More long-term and quantitative research would be needed to provide statistical information and evidence, so I can only provide a broad sketch of certain trends and transformations. My findings are based on observations during my own visits to Iraq (the last two were in 1991 and 1997), interviews with Iraqi refugee women in the UK and Germany who have recently left Iraq, discussions with my parents and friends who have been visiting Iraq more regularly, phone contact with relatives, and discussions with my PhD student who has been doing fieldwork in Iraq.

Historical context

An analysis of the impact of economic sanctions and war on women in Iraq must be prefaced by a brief historical background addressing the general situation of Iraqi women before the sanctions regime came into place in 1990. Despite indisputable political repression in the 1970s and early 1980s, a large part of the Iraqi population enjoyed high living standards in the context of an economic boom and rapid development, which were a result of the rise of oil prices and the government's developmental policies. These were the years of a flourishing economy and the emergence and expansion of a broad middle class. State-induced policies worked to eradicate illiteracy, educate women, and incorporate them into the labour force. The initial period after the nationalisation of the Iraqi oil industry in 1972 was characterised by economic hardship and difficulties. But the oil embargo imposed by OPEC countries in 1973, known as the 'oil crisis', was followed by a period of boom and expansion. Oil prices shot up and oil-producing countries started to become aware of their bargaining power *vis à vis* Western countries' dependence on oil.

In the context of this rapid economic expansion the Iraqi government actively sought out women to incorporate them into the labour force. In 1974 a government decree stipulated that all university graduates—men and women—would be employed automatically. In certain professions, such as those related to health care and teaching, education itself entailed a contract with the government, which obliged the students to take up a job in their respective professions.

Policies of encouraging women to enter waged work cannot be explained in terms of egalitarian or even feminist principles, however, even though several women I interviewed did comment positively on the early Baathists' policies of the social inclusion of women. The initial ideology of the Baath party, the ruling party of Iraq, was based on Arab nationalism and socialism. It is beyond the scope of this article to explore in detail the specific motivations and ideology of the Baathist regime with respect to women's roles and positions. What can be said is that human power was scarce and that, as the Gulf countries started to look for workers outside their national boundaries, the Iraqi government also tapped into the country's own human resources. Subsequently, working outside the home became for women not only acceptable but prestigious and the norm. Another factor to be taken into account was the state's attempt to indoctrinate its citizens—whether male or female. A great number of party members were recruited through their workplaces. Obviously it was much easier to reach out to and recruit women when they were part of the so-called public sphere and visible outside the confines of their homes.

Whatever the government's motivations, Iraqi women became among the most educated and professional in the whole region. How far this access to education and the labour market resulted in an improved status for women is a more complex question. As in many other places, conservative and patriarchal values did not automatically change because women started working. Furthermore, there were great differences between rural and urban women, as well as between women from different class backgrounds.

During the years of the Iran–Iraq war (1980–88) women's increased participation in the public sphere to replace male soldiers coincided with the further militarisation of society and a glorification of certain types of masculinity, ie the fighter, the defender of his nation and the martyr. Women were simultaneously encouraged by the state to replace male workers and civil servants, who were fighting at the front, and to 'produce' more Iraqi citizens and future soldiers. The glorification of a militarised masculinity coincided with the glorification of the Iraqi mother.

Only two 'peaceful' years were followed by the invasion of Kuwait (August 1990) and the Gulf war (January–March 1991). The latter was particularly traumatising, as night after night of heavy bombing not only disrupted sleep and family lives but left many in deep shock and fear. Iraqis invariably have vivid memories of the Gulf war and, even before the latest war, many Iraqis spoke about ongoing nightmares, a sense of anxiety and a great sensitivity to certain noises that could only remotely be mistaken for bombs. Unlike in other war-torn countries, eg Bosnia-Herzegovina, 'post-traumatic stress syndrome' has not been a recognised medical condition in Iraq. And even if it were acknowledged, lack of resources and expertise make systematic treatment impossible.

Impact of wars and economic sanctions

Despite common generalised depictions of Iraqis as either culprits or victims, a closer look at Iraqi society reveals the obvious fact that Iraqi women as well as men are not a homogeneous group and have been affected by sanctions and war in different ways. Among the numerous differentiating factors are place of residence (urban versus rural), ethnic (Arab or Kurd) and religious (Shi'a, Sunni, Christian) backgrounds and, perhaps most important, social class. However, the previously existing class system itself has been inverted, most notably through the impoverishment of a previously broad and stable educated middle class and the rise of a class of war and sanctions profiteers. The latter group tended to be closely related to the Iraqi regime and to constitute political and economic networks of privilege. Another extremely significant factor affecting the ways sanctions and war had an impact on daily lives is the existence of relatives or close friends in Western countries. Remittances sent by relatives from all over the world, but most notably from northern Europe and the USA, often made the difference between misery and coping.

For women of low-income classes in urban areas or poor women living in the countryside sheer survival became the main aim of their lives. There is no doubt that it was particularly the poor mothers whose children were more likely to become yet another statistic in the incredibly high child mortality rates or who suffered from disease and malnutrition. Yet even for educated women who were part of the broad and well-off middle classes of Iraq feeding their children became the major worry and focus. Hana', who left Iraq in the late 1990s and now lives in London, recalls:

> I would feed my children and my husband before eating anything myself. Often I would stay hungry. I would also feed my children before visiting anyone. Before the sanctions people were very generous. You would always serve tea and biscuits if not a meal when a visitor came. Now people stopped visiting each other so that they do not embarrass each other.

During the time of sanctions about 60% of the population was dependent on the monthly food rations given out by the government and paid for by the oil-for-food programme. In the aftermath of the downfall of the regime, most of the Iraqi population have become dependent on food aid, which currently needs to be distributed by the occupying forces (UNICEF, 2004). Sanctions and war have led to massive impoverishment and insecurity, which have subjected women of various social backgrounds to considerable material strain. Household management in the context of electricity cuts and water shortages has been time-consuming, exhausting, and frustrating.

Widespread unemployment, high inflation, and a virtual collapse of the economy have affected most women in their daily lives. For a population used to plenty and abundance—one oft-quoted example are the well-stocked home freezers—scarcity has come as a shock. Many women have had to revert to or learn homemaking skills practised by their grandmothers. For example, bread had been too expensive to buy on the market and many Iraqi women had no choice but to bake their own bread on a daily basis, using the flour ration distributed by the government. Furthermore, for many women, especially those living in the countryside or in the south of Iraq, food storage has been largely impossible because of the frequent electricity cuts.

Aside from the more obvious effects related to basic survival strategies and difficulties, the sanctions and war have also left their mark on the social and cultural fabric of Iraqi society. Without doubt Iraqi women have lost some of the achievements gained in the previous decades. They can no longer assert themselves through either education or waged employment, as both sectors have deteriorated rapidly.

The breakdown of the welfare state had a disproportionate effect on women, who had been its main beneficiaries. Women were pushed back into their homes and into the traditional roles of being mothers and housewives. From being the highest in the region, estimated to be above 23% before 1991, women's employment rate fell to only 10% in 1997 (UNDP, 2000). Monthly salaries in the public sector, which, since the Iran–Iraq war, had increasingly been staffed by women, dropped dramatically and did not keep pace with high inflation rates and the cost of living. Many women reported that they simply could not afford to work anymore. The state withdrew its free services, including childcare and transportation.

There has also been a sharp decrease in access to all sectors of education for girls and young women because many families have not been able to afford sending all children to school. Illiteracy, drastically reduced in the 1970s and 1980s, rose steadily after the Iran–Iraq war and grew between 1985 and 1995 from 8% to 45%. The drop-out rate for girls in primary education reached 35% according to the United Nations Development Fund for Women Report of 2004 (UNIFEM, 2004). According to UNICEF, 55% of women aged 15–49 are illiterate.

The deterioration of the general education system was already evident in the early 1990s.Wadat, an educated middle-class woman in her late forties, had worked as a teacher in a high school until 1995. She told me:

> We did not feel it so much during the first years of the sanctions, but it really hit us by 1994. Social conditions had deteriorated; the currency had been devalued while salaries were fixed. Many women started to quit work. Some of my friends could not even afford transportation to the school. Before the sanctions, the school made sure that we were picked up by a bus, but all this was cut. For me, the most important reason was my children. I did not want them to come home and be alone in the house. It has become too unsafe. And then, I know from my own work that schools have become so bad, because teachers have quit and there is no money for anything. So I felt that I have to teach them at home.

Because of the bad conditions in schools as a result of the lack of resources and teachers, many parents have felt that they had to contribute to their children's education.

Higher education has virtually collapsed and degrees became worthless in the context of widespread corruption and an uninterrupted exodus of university professors in the 1990s. Monthly salaries in the public sector, which had paradoxically become increasingly staffed by women, had dropped dramatically and did not correspond to high inflation rates and the cost of living. During the period of economic sanctions even the few academics who were still employed were often not paid their salaries. In the current post-Saddam period salaries have risen considerably. However, unemployment rates are still very high and, because of the lack of security, women are extremely reluctant to take up work again. There have also been numerous reports of absolute chaos at universities, looting of libraries, professors being forced to step down; many have been threatened to be killed by students as they were perceived to be Baathist.

Working women like Wadat suffered from the collapse of their support systems. One previous support system, funded by the state, consisted of numerous nurseries and kindergartens, along with free public transportation to and from school and to the women's workplaces. The other major support system was based on extended family ties and neighbourly relations, which helped in childcare. Ever since the sanctions regime, women have become reluctant to leave their children with neighbours or other relatives because of the general sense of insecurity.

Crime rates have been on the increase since the Gulf war in 1991. Many women reported that before the imposition of sanctions they used to keep all their doors open and felt totally secure. During the sanctions regime there were numerous accounts of burglaries—often violent ones. And, in the current situation of occupation, looting, burglaries, killings and rape are widespread. With mafia-like gangs roaming the cities at night, most Iraqis do not want to hand in the weapons they have as they feel they have to protect themselves and their families. In light of the failure by US and UK soldiers to protect hospitals, museums, libraries, etc the only people perceived to have provided security in a systematic way are the religious authorities, especially local imams at the mosques.

Changing family and gender relations

Although Iraqi families used to be very close-knit and supportive of each other, family relationships have been strained by envy and competition in the struggle for survival. In the past children grew up in the midst of their extended families, often spending time and sleeping over at the houses of their grandparents, uncles and aunts. These days nuclear families have become much more significant in a context where people have to think about themselves and those closest to them first.

Some women reported that they had stopped visiting their relatives, as they did not want them to feel embarrassed because they could not provide them with a meal. Hospitality, especially where food is concerned, is a very important aspect of Iraqi culture. During the sanctions period most Iraqi families could not provide their guests with full meals because of widespread unemployment and low salaries. The same holds true in the current context of chaos, lack of security and widespread unemployment during occupation.

This has had a damaging impact on family and social life in contemporary Iraq. Aside from sadness, depression and sometimes anger, Iraqi women and men of all ages have become remarkably fatalistic and have built up an incredible resistance to deal with pain and suffering.

The loss of loved ones has become a common aspect of the pool of experiences of Iraqi women. Three wars, political repression, widespread disease, malnutrition and a collapsed health system account for the great number of deaths occurring in Iraq. According to UNICEF 4000–5000 children were dying each month since 1991 from malnutrition and water-borne diseases, but also from various forms of cancer, which have been related to the impact of depleted uranium.

The demographic cost of two wars, political repression and the forced economic migration of men triggered by the imposition of international sanctions accounts for the high number of widows and female-headed households. In Basra up to 60% of all households were female-headed in 2003, according to the October 2003 UNICEF report. The Human Relief Foundation estimates that there are roughly 250 000 widows in Iraq. A recent UNDP-commissioned study on widows in Baghdad found that, in one small district of Al-Sadr City (Hai'our), almost every multi-family household had one widow. It is not only widows who find themselves without husbands, but also women whose husbands went abroad to escape the bleak conditions and find ways to support their families. Other men just abandoned their wives and children, being unable to cope with their inability to live up to the social expectations of being the provider. During the 1990s female-headed households, rural areas and poor households had the highest rates of infant and child mortality. While those whose husbands were killed in battle have received a small government pension, those whose husbands were killed by the former regime for political reasons have received no benefits and have been left to fend for themselves.

But even those women who still have husbands alive are struggling: the difficult economic and political situation seems to have taken its toll in terms of relationships between husbands and wives. There are no concrete figures, but it seems that the divorce rate has increased substantially. A caseworker working with Iraqi refugees in London reported that there is a very high divorce rate among couples who have recently come from Iraq. About 25% of Iraqi refugees in the UK are either separated or divorced. A few women stated that their husbands have become more violent and abusive during the past decade. Widespread despair and frustration and the perceived shame of not being able to provide the family with what is needed evokes not only depression but also anger. Women are often at the receiving end of men's frustrations.

Family planning has become a big source of tension and conflict between husbands and wives. Before the Iran–Iraq war all kinds of contraception were available and legal. During the war contraception was made illegal as the government tried to encourage Iraqi women to produce a great number of future citizens to make up for the loss of life during the war. Many incentives were given, such as the extension of paid maternity leave to a year, of which six months were paid. Baby food and articles were imported and subsidised.

After the Gulf war in 1991, contraceptives were still not available, but women's attitudes towards children had changed because of the material circumstances and the moral climate. There has also been fear of congenital diseases and birth defects, which have been incredibly high since the war. Unlike in previous times, Iraqi women are now reluctant to have many children. Abortion is illegal so many women risk their health and their lives to have illegal abortions in back alleys. The director of an orphanage in Baghdad stated in 1997 that a new phenomenon had emerged in Iraq: women abandoning newborn babies on the street. These babies may be a 'result' of so-called illicit relationships, but, according the director, they are often left by married women who just can't face not being able to feed their children.

Despite the overall strain on marital relationships, some women state that their relationships with their husbands have improved. Aliya, a housewife in her late thirties, says:

> My husband never did anything in the house before the sanctions. He used to work in a factory outside of Baghdad. Ever since he stopped working, he helps me to bake bread and to take care of the children. We get along much better than before because he started to realise that I am working very hard in the house.

While families and marriages are affected in multifarious ways, many Iraqi women can only dream of marriage and having their own families. One of the numerous consequences of the current demographic imbalance between men and women is the difficulty for young women to get married. Polygamy, which had become largely restricted to rural areas or uneducated people, has been on the increase in recent years. There is also a growing trend among young women to get married to Iraqi expatriates, usually much older than they are. This is largely for economic reasons, as most Iraqi men will not be able to provide for a new family. According to some respondents there are numerous cases of women who have not been able to cope with living abroad, and who feel totally alienated from their husbands and the new environment in which they find themselves. Others are being married off to older men within Iraq, often to settle a debt within the family.

A further common phenomenon is what one Iraqi woman called 'marrying below one's class'. Iraq has traditionally been a very class-oriented society where one's family name and background might open or close many doors. Now one can detect greater social mobility and less rigid class barriers. This is partly because of the uneven demographic situation between men and women but it also relates to the radical inversion of class structures mentioned above. The impoverishment of the previously well off middle classes goes side by side with the emergence of a *nouveau riche* class of war and sanctions profiteers.

While the majority of the Iraqi population has been impoverished and has suffered greatly from the policies of its own government as well as war and sanctions, a small percentage of people have actually managed to profit from the situation. These people are mainly working in the black market economy, engaging, for instance, in smuggling goods across the Jordanian, Syrian, Iranian or Turkish borders. These profiteers used to have close ties to the Iraqi regime. Living in luxury in the midst of widespread suffering and poverty asks for envy and contempt. But it also guaranteed greater marriage prospects and access to social circles previously exclusive to the educated middle and upper middle classes.

Islamisation and increased conservatism

At the same time that marriage has become a relatively difficult undertaking, young women in particular feel pressured by a new 'cultural' environment that is marked simultaneously by a decline in moral values like honesty, generosity and sociability and an increased public religiosity and conservatism. Many women I interviewed concurred with one of my female relatives in Baghdad when they spoke sadly about the total inversion of cultural codes and moral values. I will never forget when one of my aunts told me: 'You know, bridges and houses can easily be rebuilt. It will take time, but it is possible. But what they have really destroyed is our morale, or values.' She, like many other Iraqi women I talked to sadly stated that honesty was not paying any more. People have become corrupt and greedy. Trust has become a very rare word and envy even exists among closest kin.

Young Iraqi women frequently speak about changes related to socialising, family ties and relations between neighbours and friends. Often a parent or older relative was quoted as stating how things were different from the past, when socialising was a much bigger part of people's lives. Zeinab, a 15-year-old young woman from Baghdad, spoke about the lack of trust between people. She suggested the following as an explanation for the change in dress code for women and the social restrictions she and her peers experience constantly:

> People have changed now because of the increasing economic and various other difficulties of life in Iraq. They have become very afraid of each other. I think because so many people have lost their jobs and businesses, they are having loads of time to speak about other people's lives, and they often interfere in each other's affairs. I also think that because so many families are so poor now that they cannot afford buying more than the daily basic food, it becomes so difficult for them to buy nice clothes and nice things and therefore, it is better to wear *hijab*. Most people are somewhat pressured to change their lives in order to protect themselves from the gossip of other people—especially talk about family honour (Al-Ali & Hussein, 2003).

In addition to increased responsibilities and time restrictions related to economic circumstances, teenage girls in particular complain about the increasing social and movement restrictions. While the parents of the predominantly middle-class young females who were interviewed used to mingle relatively freely when they were the age of their children, today's young Iraqis find it increasingly difficult to meet each other. Schools are often segregated, but even in co-educational schools interaction between boys and girls has become more limited. Girls are extremely worried about their reputation and often avoid situations in which they find themselves alone with a boy. These fears may have been aggravated by the not uncommon occurrence of so-called 'honour killings' during the past decade. Fathers and brothers of women who are known or often only suspected of having 'violated' the accepted codes of behaviour, especially with respect to keeping their virginity before marriage, may kill the women in order to restore the honour of the family. Although this phenomenon is mainly restricted to rural areas and uneducated Iraqis, knowledge of its existence works as a deterrent for many female teenagers.

Others may be less worried about the most dramatic consequences of 'losing one's reputation'. For educated middle-class women from urban areas it is not so much death they fear as diminished marriage prospects.

The most obvious change that has taken place over the past decade or so is the dress code for young women. Aliya (16 years old) is clearly unhappy about the changes:

> I do think that our life was much more easy and happy in the past than it is now. My father used to be so open and believe in women's freedom. He would let my mother go out without covering her hair when they visited our relatives in Baghdad. We only had to wear the *abbayah* in Najaf because it is a holy city.[1] Some years ago, he started to change his attitude to many things. And lately he has become so conservative that he thinks covering the hair is not enough, and he demanded that my mother wear *abbayah* everywhere outside the home. He said that I also should keep the cover on my hair when I go to Baghdad. I am now not even allowed to go out with trousers outside our home. My mother and I have to wear long skirts with a long wide shirt covering the hips when we go outside our home (Al-Ali & Hussein, 2003.).

As much as Aliya detests the imposed dress codes and her father's new conservatism, she understands the underlying reasons. She explains:

> I know why my father is doing this and I am not angry with him. I discussed this issue with him many times, and I really do not blame him for this change in attitude. I think it is not only my father who is doing this, but that it may be all fathers in Iraq. They are doing the same in order to protect their daughters from the risks of becoming victims of bad rumours. (Ibid)

These days there are numerous reports of unveiled women being harassed on the streets by Islamists who demand that all women wear a headscarf or *abbayah*.

Increased social conservatism and the threat of gossip that would tarnish one's reputation are a common complaint among young Iraqi women. Girls especially suffer in a climate where patriarchal values have been strengthened and where the state has abandoned its previous policies of social inclusion with respect to women.

Economic hardships have pushed a number of women into prostitution—a trend that is widely known and subject to much anguish in a society where a woman's 'honour' is perceived to reflect the family's honour. In the mid-1990s the government condemned prostitution and engaged in violent campaigns to stop it. In a widely reported incident in Iraq in 2000 a group of young men linked to Saddam Hussein's son Uday singled out about 300 female prostitutes and 'pimps' and beheaded them.

The drastic increase in female prostitution does not stop at the Iraqi border, however. Most of the female prostitutes in Jordan, for example, are Iraqi women. The imposition by the government of the *mahram* escort for females leaving Iraq did not succeed in stopping this trend. This law does not allow women under 45 to leave the country unless they are accompanied by a male first of kin. It was enforced after the Jordanian government complained to the Iraqi government about widespread prostitution by Iraqi women in Amman.

Men often feel compelled to protect their female relatives from being the subject of gossip and from losing the family's honour. The increasing social restrictions imposed on young women have to be analysed in the context of wider social changes, particularly with respect to the increase in prostitution, significant numbers of female-headed households, rampant unemployment, the appropriation of Islamic symbols by the Iraqi government under Saddam Hussein, the general religious revival within Iraqi society and the rise of Islamist forces in contemporary Iraq.

Processes related to Islamisation of society and Islamist politics are not only leading to increasing conservatism in gender relations, but are also dominating Iraqi political power struggles in the post-Saddam era. One example of the increased impact of Islamist tendencies was the attempt in December 2003 to scrap secular family laws in favour of *sharia*-based jurisdiction (Islamic Law) by the Iraqi Governing Council under its then chairman Abdel Aziz al-Hakim, head of the Supreme Council for the Islamic Revolution in Iraq. The secular code established in 1959 was once considered the most progressive in the Middle East, making polygamy difficult and guaranteeing women's custody rights in the case of divorce. Although unsuccessful, the attempt to change the law and the discussion around it reveals the current climate and the possible dangers lying ahead. This is particularly important in a context where women's rights and equality are perceived to be part of Western agendas to impose an alien culture and morals. Many Iraqis, who under different circumstances might have been sympathetic to or even supportive of women's rights, view women's roles and laws revolving around women and gender relations as symbolic of their attempt to gain independence and autonomy from the occupying forces.

Many women in Basra, for example, report that they have been forced to wear a headscarf or to restrict their movement in fear of harassment from men. Female students at the University of Basra say that, since the war ended, groups of men began stopping them at the university gates, shouting at them if their heads were not covered. These reports are symptomatic of wider conservative trends and various ways in which women are being used in

Iraq—as in many other societies—to demarcate boundaries between 'us' and 'them'. Islamicisation here fulfils two objectives: a break with the previous secular regime of Saddam Hussein and resistance to the occupying forces.

Women's political participation

Although Iraqi women have a history of some political participation and activism before Saddam Hussein came to power, their autonomous political participation came to an end in the 1970s. Women were encouraged to join the Baath party and to run for the rubber-stamp parliament. Scores of Iraqi women contested elections in 1980 and 16 won seats in the 250 member Council. In the second Baathist parliamentary elections in 1985, women won 33 Council seats (13%). But even this sponsored participation was reduced towards the end of Saddam's regime, as shown by the reduction in successful women candidates to 8% of members elected to the parliament in 2003.

The major vehicle for women's participation was the General Federation of Iraqi Women (GFIW) founded in 1969. It had branches all over Iraq and it is estimated that about one million Iraqi women were members. Despite the fact that the Federation was a branch of the ruling party and lacked political independence, the government's initial policies of social inclusion and mobilisation of human power did facilitate a climate in which the Federation could play an implementation role in promoting women's education, labour force participation and health, as well as providing a presence in public life. The role of GFIW changed drastically in the 1990s when the state abandoned its policies of social inclusion and began to promote women's traditional roles. The GFIW then concentrated on humanitarian aid and the provision of health care.

At the same time as Iraqi women were loosing state support in terms of socioeconomic rights, semi-autonomy in Iraqi Kurdistan allowed women there to establish civil society associations and become involved in party politics. While only two of the 20 ministers in the Kurdistan Regional Government were women in 2003, women gained employment in the civil service. But it is also the case in the Kurdish areas that women's initiatives and political participation have been opposed by conservative male political actors. Women activists campaigning against widespread honour killings in the north have been subject to harassment and a newly established women's shelter for victims of domestic violence had to close down because of political opposition.

Since April 2003 women's organisations and initiatives have been mushrooming all over Iraq. Most of these organisations, like the National Council of Women (NWC), the Iraqi Women's Higher Council (IWHC), the Iraqi Independent Women's Group or the Society for Iraqi Women for the Future, for example, have been founded either by members of the Iraqi National Council (IGC) or by prominent professional women with close ties to political parties. While mainly founded and represented by elite women, some of the organisations have a broad membership and have branches throughout the country. Their activities revolve around humanitarian and practical projects, such as income generation, legal advice, free health care and counselling, etc, as well as political advocacy. The two main issues that have mobilised women of mainly educated middle-class background throughout Iraq are 1) the attempt to replace the relatively progressive personal status law governing marriage, divorce and child custody with a more conservative law (Article 137); and 2) the issue of a women's quota for political representation. Although women were unsuccessful in obtaining a 40% quota in the transitional constitution, they managed to negotiate a 25% quota.

However, the actual long-term status of the transitional constitution and the decision of the Iraqi Governing Council, as well as of the Coalition Provisional Authority remain to be seen. In recent months women's organisations have been seriously impeded by the security situation, which often stop women from leaving their houses altogether. This has also prevented many women from running for elections in January 2005.

Lack of security

The fact that only a relatively small number of women have expressed their political dissent and wishes, is not only the result of the lack of democratic political culture within Iraq. It is also because the biggest problem for women in Iraq today is the lack of security. Aside from the more recent threat of militant resistance and suicide bombings, of which Iraqis have been the main victims so far, women suffer from gender-specific threats and violence. 'This violence is still a daily occurrence, especially on the streets of Baghdad, without attracting the least attention of the soldiers', Yanar Mohammed, Director of the Baghdad-based Organisation for Women's Freedom, told the press some time ago.

A Human Rights Watch Report published in November 2003 bears witness to numerous reports of sexual violence and abduction of women and girls (Human Rights Watch, 2003). Medical practitioners, victims, witnesses and law enforcement authorities have documented some of these crimes. However, many cases go unreported and uninvestigated. Some women and girls fear that reporting sexual violence may provoke honour killings and social stigmatisation. For others the obstacles of filing and pursuing a police complaint or obtaining a forensic examination that would provide legal proof of sexual violence prevent them from receiving medical attention and pursuing justice. Whatever the reason, both documented and rumoured stories of sexual violence and abduction are contributing to a palpable climate of fear:

'Women and girls today in Baghdad are scared, and many are not going to schools or jobs or looking for work', said Hanny Megally, executive director of the Middle East and North Africa division of Human Rights Watch. 'If Iraqi women are to participate in post-war society, their physical security needs to be an urgent priority' (Human Rights Watch, 2003).

According to Human Rights Watch (2003: Summary), many of the problems of addressing sexual violence and abduction against women and girls 'derive from the US-led coalition forces and civilian administration's failure to provide public security in Baghdad. The public security vacuum in

Baghdad has heightened the vulnerability of women and girls to sexual violence and abduction'. This resonates with the Organisation for Women's Freedom in Iraq, which chided coalition forces for their failure to protect women in post-war Iraq, asserting that over 400 had been raped since the end of the war.

Since the police force is considerably smaller now and relatively poorly managed, there is limited police street presence. This has become worse during recent months as the newly established Iraqi police have been frequently targeted by militant resistance. The insecurity plaguing Baghdad and other Iraqi cities has a distinct and debilitating impact on the daily lives of women and girls, preventing them from participating in public life, in reconstruction processes, in the labour force and in shaping the political future of Iraq.

Conclusion

The rather bleak picture I have sketched out only touches upon some aspects of the numerous ways war, sanctions and occupation have affected women and gender relations in contemporary Iraq. I have tried to point to the social and cultural phenomena that have emerged during recent years and which have to be viewed as mainly triggered by the sanctions regime and the government of Saddam Hussein. It is too early to be able to grasp fully the complex and multifarious ways the recent ongoing war and occupation is affecting daily lives as well as wider gender ideologies.

What can be said about the current situation, however, is that, so far, women have been pushed even more into the background and back into their homes. They are suffering both in terms of a worsening humanitarian situation and an ongoing lack of security on the streets. Aside from the fact that basic needs (including water, electricity, medical care, and food) as well security are not addressed adequately, a more long-term issue is the lack of women's representation in the various political parties and emerging political constituencies. It remains to be seen whether the women's quota of 25% will actually be implemented or whether a push for women's political participation during the period of occupation might eventually backfire.

What needs to be emphasised is that involving women in the reconstruction of Iraq will not simply be a matter of ' just add women and stir'. What is missing is a gender perspective in line with UN Resolution 1325 passed in October 2000, which acknowledges the importance of the inclusion of women and mainstreaming gender into all aspects of post-conflict resolution and peace operations. Research and political experiences within other conflict areas and post-war situations, such as Northern Ireland, Bosnia Herzegovina, Cyprus and Israel/Palestine, demonstrates that women are often more able to bridge ethnic, religious and political divides and play a significant role in peace making. To my mind any future peace can only be achieved by confronting and working through Iraq's past with the help of a truth and reconciliation committee that would be sensitive to all kinds of human rights abuses, including gender violence.

The mainstreaming of gender would have to involve the appointment of women to interim governments, and to all ministries and committees dealing with systems of local and national governance. Women would also have to be present and active in the judiciary, policing, human rights monitoring, the allocation of funds, free media development, and all economic processes. There should be encouragement to create independent women's groups, NGOs and community based organisations.

Comprising both the majority of the population as well as an increasingly vulnerable and marginalised group, it is of ultimate importance to support women's political participation. However, as women are perceived to be symbols and markers of cultural boundaries and 'authenticity', any insensitive promotion of women's rights and women's equalities as part and parcel of 'liberation' will strongly backfire in the current context of occupation, as well as in its aftermath. Western feminism is negatively identified with the imposition of Western values and the eradication of indigenous culture and morals not only in Iraq, but in most other countries in the region and the Muslim world. Any women's rights initiatives and organisations promoted by the occupying forces or the Iraqi Interim Government will not only be short-lived, but will also negatively affect locally initiated women's organisations and gender roles and ideologies more generally. Similarly, Iraqi women's organisations and activists based abroad lack legitimacy and credibility among the majority of the population and should not be used either to represent or to short-cut locally based initiatives.

At the same time it is important to point out that Iraq, like other countries in the region and the Muslim world, has a history of indigenous women's rights struggle and women's movements. There are many, mainly educated middle class women, who are already involved in humanitarian assistance as well as in political lobbying and advocacy related to social justice with respect to women and gender relations. It would be detrimental for Iraqi women if they were not given special support in the process of reconstruction and political transition.

One way to sensitively support women is to change the language from a feminist rights approach to one emphasising education, training and participation in reconstruction, thereby appealing to a modernist–developmental discourse. The other major strategy is to link women with organisations, experts and initiatives in other countries in the region or in the Muslim world. Based on research I carried out among women's organisations in Egypt, for example, I found that women felt much more empowered by the exchange of experiences and training with non-Western women activists.

The current situation in Iraq leaves doubt about the intentions of the USA in terms of good governance, its commitment to human rights and democracy building. Especially where women and gender relations are concerned, I personally do not expect too much from the occupying forces, considering Bush's record of conservative policies towards women in the USA. The case of Afghanistan is a sad example of the US government paying lip service to women's rights but not actually seeing it through in the aftermath of the war. In fact, Afghanistan is an example of how not to do it, as the mere appointment of a women's minister without resources (who subsequently had to resign) was a cynical token towards a human and women's rights agenda.

Let me finish this article on a slightly brighter note. It is very important to say that Iraqi women are not just passive victims. And here I am not talking about those women who were implicated in the previous regime or are now made token women in the current political structures. I am talking about ordinary women of various social backgrounds. Contrary to common media representations of oppressed Arab women, in many ways Iraqi women have been more resourceful and adaptable to the changing situation than Iraqi men. Small informal business schemes, such as food catering, mushroomed during the period of economic sanctions. Skills in crafts and the recycling of clothes and other materials have demonstrated an incredible creativity. In the post-Saddam period women activists have defied simple ethnic, religious and political party divisions and have pulled together to lobby around several issues. Any analysis of women and gender relations in Iraq needs to pay tribute to the dignity, humanity and courage of women despite ongoing hardship and struggle.

Note

1 *Abbayah* is the traditional black garment worn by Iraqi women. Najaf, a holy city south of Baghdad, is the location of the main Shi'a cemetery in Iraq.

References

Al-Ali, N & Hussein, Y (2003) Between dreams and sanctions: teenage lives in Iraq, in: A Mahdi (ed), *Teenagers in the Middle East* (Westport, CT: Greenwood).

Cockburn, C (1998) *The Space Between Us: Negotiating Gender and National Identities in Conflict* (London: Zed Books).

Cockburn, C (1999) Background paper: gender, armed conflict and political violence, presented to the World Bank Conference on Gender, Armed Conflict and Political Development, Washington, DC.

Cockburn, C & Zarkov, D (eds) (2002) *The Postwar Moment: Militaries, Masculinities and International Peacekeeping* (London: Lawrence & Wishart).

Enloe, C (1987) Feminist Thinking about War, Militarism, and Peace, in B Hess and M. Ferree (eds) *Analyzing Gender* (Newbury, CA: Sage).

Enloe, C (1998) All the men are in the militias, all the women are victims, in: L Lorentzen & J Turpin (eds), *Women & War Reader* (New York: New York University Press).

Gervais, M (2004) Human security and reconstruction efforts in Rwanda: impact on the lives of women, in: H Afshar & D Eade (eds), *Development, Women, and War: Feminist Perspectives* (Oxford: Oxfam).

Human Rights Watch (2003) Climate of fear: sexual violence and abduction of women and girls in Baghdad, press release 15 (8), July.

Kelly, L (2000) Wars against women: sexual violence, sexual politics and the militarized state, in S Jacobs *et al, States of Conflict: Gender, Violence & Resistance* (London: Zed Books).

Pankhurst, D (2004) The 'sex war' and other wars: towards a feminist approach to peace building, in H Afshar & D Eade (eds), *Development, Women, and War: Feminist Perspectives* (Oxford: Oxfam).

Sorenson, B (1998) Women and Post-Conflict Reconstruction: Issues and Sources', *Occasional Paper*, No. 3, the War-torn Societies Project, Geneva, UN Research Institute for Development.

UNDP (2000) *1999–2000 Country Report*, Iraq Country Office, June.

UNICEF (2004) Iraq: facts and figures, at http://www.unicef.org/media/media_9788.html, accessed 22 April.

UNICEF (2001) UNICEF Humanitarian Action: Iraq Donor Update, 11 July 2001.

UNIFEM (2004) Gender profile, Iraq, at http://www.womenwarpeace.org/iraq/iraq.htm

Yuval-Davis, N (1997) *Gender and Nation* (London: Sage Publications).

Yuval-Davis, N & Anthias, F (1989) *Gender, Nation, State* (London: Sage Publications).

Reconstruction of Infrastructure in Iraq: end to a means or means to an end?

RICHARD H BROWN

ABSTRACT *Infrastructure reconstruction in Iraq was planned as a project-driven straight-line activity. The USA prepared for it for many months on the back of its planned invasion of Iraq. It was predominantly devised as a top-down operation with an assumption of derived benefits to the economy and the population. The plan appeared to be based on the assumption that peace would quickly be restored. The reality was different—rising insurgency led to a slowed rate of reconstruction, thus leading to increasing ambivalence by the Iraqi populace towards the Coalition Provisional Authority as progress fell far short of its expectations. Sustainable infrastructure was perhaps never a prime objective, but the unexpected level of post-war violent conflict saw rebuilding infrastructure as a prime means for creating short-term employment and visible effect, with the intention of diffusing anti-Coalition momentum. This paper will explore the dilemma of facilitating reconstruction for short-term aims and whether in these circumstances it is possible to maintain a long-term vision. It will also analyse to what extent the Iraqi people have genuinely participated in reconstruction plans and whether the eventual outcomes might have been different if a truly participative approach had been taken.*

This article draws heavily on the experience of the author while working as an engineer for Coalition Forces in Basrah and in Baghdad between September 2003 and September 2004. While accepting that solutions for post-war reconstruction will always be contingent to each particular situation, it does nevertheless try to reference policies and strategies formulated for Iraq against developed theory and practice.

The theory against which recent reconstruction policies in Iraq are benchmarked in this paper is based upon the assumption that the eventual objective should be the development of sustainable infrastructure throughout Iraq. However, the author has not encountered strong evidence to suggest that this was ever a prime objective for Iraq; indeed, in hindsight the application of policies would suggest that there was a mandate to reconstruct not develop. Yet, without sustainable solutions, economic growth falters, leaving open the possibility of renewed conflict.

Mac Ginty (2003: 605–609) describes how the US authorities anticipated the course for the post-war reconstruction of Iraq with very substantial pre-war planning. No doubt, this was as a result of acute awareness of previous deficiencies in early planning from previous conflicts.[1] The second Gulf war was a long time coming and it is this perceived responsibility for a complete solution that drove the USA to lead the way in this early planning for reconstruction in Iraq. One might therefore suppose that the chances for success in reconstruction would have been that much greater. So why was there a shortfall? This paper will attempt to answer this question with particular reference to the reconstruction of infrastructure and, as ever, with the benefit of hindsight.[2]

Background to infrastructure in Iraq

Iraq is blessed with an abundance of natural resources, especially oil. Its geography is such that a very substantial infrastructure is needed to exploit these resources as well as to support its population, the large majority of which straddles the length of its two largest rivers, the Tigris and the Euphrates and their confluence channel and estuary, the Shatt-al-Arab. The country is mountainous in the North but flat desert in the West and South.

The primary industrialisation of Iraq took place from the 1960s through to the mid-1990s with the construction of oil refineries, pipelines, power stations, power lines, water and wastewater treatment plants, highways, railways, airports, seaports and a range of production facilities such as cement factories. All these were state-controlled and funded from oil revenues rather than taxation, as in a rentier state, with decision making concentrated at the relevant ministries in Baghdad, supported by a number of state-owned enterprises, including large technically proficient contractors.

Much of the linear infrastructure is orientated in north–south corridors. In the case of oil, this is to link the main oilfields in Kirkuk in the north and Rumailah in the South with oil refineries in Baiji, Baghdad and Basrah, with export lines to Turkey and with the main offshore export terminals in the Persian Gulf (near Al Faw). Power lines (400KV) redistribute the imbalance of electricity generation (in the north and south) with demand (in the centre—Baghdad). Water flows from north to south, with early regulation through dams and reservoirs in the north; in the south canals are used to draw water from the main rivers upstream and deliver it to major cities in the south in order to pre-empt water quality degradation. Principal railways and highways link the major cities on a north–south axis, ultimately serving the two key ports of Khor Az Zubayr and Umm Qasr on the Persian Gulf.

This huge infrastructure (both point and linear) would have required substantial annual expenditure on maintenance and renewal for long-term serviceability.[3] However, Graham-Brown (1999: 157–161) describes the poor state of the infrastructure between the two Gulf wars, particularly in water and sanitation. Indeed, the condition of much of the infrastructure as observed by the author in 2003 would suggest that there were substantial shortfalls in expenditure on renewals and few attempts at technological update through investment. There were many similarities to the situation pertaining in Kosovo in 1999, where the state of the infrastructure reflected the neglect exercised since its loss of autonomy in 1989. And, as in Kosovo, the reconstruction effort would be focused on making good these long-term deficiencies, with the effects of the armed intervention itself being much less of a factor.

The relatively short duration of the 'war' phases of the conflicts in Kosovo and Iraq limited the scale of direct physical damage to infrastructure, although in the case of Kosovo institutional attrition was substantial. Contrast this with the much longer war in Bosnia–Herzegovina, where infrastructure was widely attacked, looted and wrecked. Failing infrastructure can often be a warning indicator of impending armed conflict, and its reconstruction/development should not necessarily be described as purely 'post-war'. In Iraq, to be accurate, reconstruction of infrastructure was only 'post-war' in its timing and by association. It was not really 'post-conflict' either since the conflict endured; however, both continue as convenient designations that threaten to perpetuate global misunderstandings at the geopolitical level as to what reconstruction is all about. Critically, as we shall see, given a true development perspective it had the potential to be part of the solution to the conflict, if not to the war.

It was the imposition of international sanctions that played the main contributing role in the degradation of infrastructure in Iraq. This caused a severe reduction in annual maintenance and renewal expenditure and the curtailment of importation of spare parts for critical infrastructure in the oil and power sectors on the pretext of indirectly having a military use. Sanctions removed government control of state revenue and thus the ability to utilise high spending on public utilities and services as a means of retaining public support for the regime. Saddam Hussein was forced to rely on the use of rule and repression through a paternalistic web of privileged groups, henchmen and an extensive internal security network.

The political manipulation in the use of infrastructure practised by Saddam's regime guaranteed Baghdad plentiful electrical power and potable water while much of the rest of the country experienced shortages, particularly in 'hours of power'. At the planning stage, the US authorities were acutely aware that 'liberation' would release intense frustrations over inadequate essential services. They would have a little time to assuage these frustrations, but not long—hence the publicly stated mission to 'Rebuild Iraq'.

The first Coalition Provisional Authority (CPA) reconstruction plan had four 'pillars': justice, security, governance and infrastructure. For infrastructure it involved big money being poured into hundreds (and eventually thousands) of projects. The concept was that, with a repaired infrastructure, the economy would recover and grow naturally. However, its chief weakness lay in its lack of connection with the Iraqi people and in particular their livelihoods. Although there was a determination to emphasise that Iraqis would be involved in the reconstruction process, the adoption of top-down imposed reconstruction (sometimes known as 'umbrella reconstruction') meant that Iraqi participation was inevitably going to be somewhat haphazard rather than defined as a fundamental principle.

Three key themes

Experience from previous successful post-war reconstructions suggests that the need for a clear *vision* for recovery is essential (RGS, 2003: 3). Within this vision, reconstruction is recognised as being primarily a *development challenge* and this means it is more about 'how' than 'what'. Included in this challenge are objectives for growth, inclusiveness, stability and sustainability; of these, it is *sustainability* that is the crucial factor in forming a vision for infrastructure.

From this standpoint, since participation is a key component of development strategy, it must also be crucial to sustainability within reconstruction. As Goulet (1995: 98–101) describes, it performs three vital functions:

(a) instilling dignity;
(b) mobilising people as problem solvers in their own social environments;
(c) facilitating access to higher arenas of decision making.

A participatory approach will bring development alive and ensure that initiatives lean towards being people-focused rather than just project-focused and therefore sustainable rather than finite.

Sustainability is also linked to human security. Cockell (2000: 24–26) describes the four categories of human security that can be threatened at times of internal conflict—economic, personal, political and community. Clearly, sustainable infrastructure can be a significant contributor to economic security and hence human security (a critical element for establishing durable peace). It is this link that must be exploited to the full in designing infrastructure programmes.

Sustainable infrastructure in post-war areas

Before expanding on the vision for recovery with reference to sustainable infrastructure and its influence on reconstruction policies for Iraq, it is pertinent to seek a deeper definition of sustainable infrastructure and its development.

Sustainability suggests a 'capacity for continuance' (Parkin, 2000: 3–8). Sustainable infrastructure, in the context of the post-war environment, may be defined as follows:

> Physical assets which provide net benefits to a community, its neighbours and the environment on a long-term basis. (Brown, 2001: 41)

Sustainable infrastructure forms part of a larger socioeconomic model and is a critical function in facilitating the development of other basic structures in society such as business, education and health. There are some major administrative functions that contribute to its sustainability (Özerdem, 1998) and these can be summarised into three generic elements (Brown, 2001: 41–42, 54).

An appropriate specification and level of technology

The design of the system must take account of available materials and technologies as well as available or potential expertise for operation and maintenance. A trade-off must be struck between using modern technology to best advantage and simplicity of operation and maintenance. A strong focus should be applied to the involvement of local people as much as possible.

An environmentally-positive (or at least neutral) physical portfolio

The system must not produce environmental benefits in one community at the expense of negative outcomes in a neighbouring community. Thus, an holistic approach must be taken for planning, specification and design.

An appropriate organisation to plan and manage its design, construction, operation and maintenance

This requires the early selection of local people with the potential to master the skills necessary to undertake these activities. Mentoring from external or higher agencies may be necessary for some considerable time. There must be sensitive human resource management and development plans that are impartial to all groups and facilitate focused training for the job in hand. There must be robust financial arrangements that project towards sustainability.

These principles can be applied universally. However, programmes need to be designed according to the particular post-war situation. They will be particularly demanding where the population has suffered repression over a protracted period, but less onerous with more technologically advanced states.

Policies for Iraq

Taking the above model and applying it to Iraq and its infrastructure as the situation pertained in early 2003 would suggest the following:

- The infrastructure was developed, albeit outdated and in need of renewal. However, materials and technology were only available to a certain basic level. Advanced materials and technology would be subject to import (sanctions permitting). Because, or in spite, of state ownership, the infrastructure was largely operated and maintained by Iraqis who had strong basic technical skills and were good at prolonging the utility of assets that were well beyond their normal life.

- There was almost no consideration of the effects on the environment from infrastructure—a situation exacerbated by the impacts of two major conflicts before 2003 (UNEP, 2003). Particularly apparent were, for example, the staining of large areas of the desert by irregular oil discharges, widespread oil contamination of surface water and groundwater and the destruction by draining of the Mesopotamian Marshlands in the South (and the consequent displacement and migration of the Madan (Marsh Arabs)). Environmental planning was almost non-existent (and there was no ministry with direct responsibility for the environment).
- The organisations to plan and manage infrastructure had long existed, and although the staff generally had solid technical skills these were not up-to-date because of little international information exchange, and business and project management skills were underdeveloped. There were inadequate or non-existent charging mechanisms to consumers (public and private) for electricity and water, and consequently no incentives for consumers to be prudent with usage, and no direct ways of funding operational and maintenance expenditure.

This is the reference baseline that might have been used to develop a comprehensive strategy for reconstruction and development of infrastructure with an objective of achieving sustainability for the main elements of key infrastructure.

Reconstruction of infrastructure: April 2003 to December 2004

The outline plans for 'rebuilding Iraq' were largely developed by the White House, US government agencies and the US Department of Defense (with the Pentagon appointed as authority for reconstruction on 20 January 2003). The US Department of State, which allegedly had experts knowledgeable about Iraq, the Arab world and post-war reconstruction, was generally sidelined until the lead-in to the re-establishment of the US Embassy in Iraq on 29 June 2004. The task of reconstruction by any comparison was always going to be huge—the major factor being the long-term neglect of infrastructure throughout the country; the sheer scale led to an early project-led focus with prime contractors being appointed to specify, plan, programme, design and oversee the projects. Overall co-ordination was to be undertaken by the CPA based in Baghdad, but key agents for reconstruction were to be the CPA itself, the US Agency for International Development (USAID) and the US Army Corps of Engineers (USACE), the latter bringing its extensive experience of civilian construction in the water sector from the USA.

Each project had to have a clear technical purpose but that was about as far as it went. There was no consistent strategy for considering the key environmental considerations (political, economic, sociological, technological)—especially links with industry—and no systemic approach to reconstruction. Moreover, there was no overarching strategic picture and therefore no legitimate basis for prioritising projects. Finally, there was no plan for developing Iraqi involvement with the reconstruction programme (other than communicating with the various ministries in Baghdad) and therefore, ultimately, no plan for sustainability. There were, however, single-purpose strategies. For example, a very high priority was given to the reconstruction of the strategic 400KV transmission lines on the basis that this would facilitate fairer distribution of power in Iraq (see Box 1). The rehabilitation of certain key generation plants was also prioritised (with total output targets in MW) but the renewal or restoration of fragile distribution systems in some key cities did not feature anywhere, despite the fact that generation, transmission and distribution are all equal parts of the electricity supply system that ultimately keeps the lights on in homes and the machines running in factories.

Despite the extensive reconstruction plans, a significant degree of misplaced complacency built up in relation to the robustness of the infrastructure in the months following the armed intervention, the focus of the Coalition centering on humanitarian relief. Just how fragile the infrastructure networks were was brought home in August 2003 when, after a combination of coincident factors—loss of production at Basrah oil refinery, looting of transmission lines, failures at electricity substations—outputs in oil, power and water foundered in various cities in Southern Iraq. The resulting lack of water and electricity, with daytime temperatures reaching 52°C and humidity at 90%, led to civil riots in Basrah. From this was born the Emergency Infrastructure Plan (EIP), a regional initiative that comprised a $127 million programme of relief and reconstruction works in oil, power and water, funded by US and UK government agencies with uncharacteristically high levels of financial authority delegated to the regional level.[4]

Reconstruction of Electricity Transmission Lines in Southern Iraq

The transmission grid in Iraq comprises 400KV lines forming strategic north–south links and 132KV lines forming regional networks. Sabotage and looting had left much of the grid unserviceable. Early reconstruction initiatives were to be focused on the strategic network, leaving the regional networks to later programmes. However, civil disturbance in Basrah in August 2003 resulting from multiple failures in essential services illustrated the potential folly in not taking a systemic approach to reconstruction.

Reconstruction of the regional network in Southern Iraq formed a major part of the Emergency Infrastructure Plan (EIP). Recognising that the Transmission Directorate in Basrah had a significant capability in power line construction and repair, it was decided to pass the responsibility for reconstruction to the respective Director-General (DG), giving him international technical and management support where appropriate. It soon became apparent that given the right materials and equipment required for the job, the DG was quite capable of achieving the project objectives. The project proceeded on this basis and all the planned work of erecting towers and stringing cables was completed as scheduled by 1 May 2004. The cost per kilometre was a fraction of that of projects where work was supervised by international management contractors, primarily because local construction techniques were utilised, labour and plant costs were much lower, and security costs were minimal. The Iraqis acquired full ownership of the programme, thus contributing to sustainability. But it should be noted that the whole concept was nearly stonewalled by indirect interference by the Ministry of Electricity and the CPA in Baghdad. This was relatively straightforward reconstruction of linear infrastructure; reconstruction of complex point infrastructure such as major electricity substations, however, generally required input from specialist companies.

Box 1.

EIP did not seek to be any type of development plan, although there were traces of development within it, especially on the water side. However, it did try to embody a participative approach while at the same time achieving rapid tangible effect. Although project definition had to be undertaken quite quickly, there was considerable consultation with Iraqi utility directorates at regional level. Participation continued throughout the six months that EIP was active. Of particular note were weekly meetings of the Infrastructure Projects Review Board (IPRB) in Basrah where Iraqi Director Generals (DGs) played an equal part in the decision-making process.[5] EIP was an exceptional initiative, however, and not typical within the national reconstruction effort.

The general approach to the management of major projects throughout Iraq was, on the contrary, well centralised. US procurement rules and short timescales appeared to leave little opportunity for a truly participative approach. This is best illustrated by reference to the process for implementation of projects associated with the $18.44 billion Supplemental Grant appropriated by the US Congress in November 2003; this grant wholly supported the Iraq Relief and Reconstruction Fund (IRRF) which was the principal vehicle for reconstruction in Iraq.[6] Initially there was a token consultation process back to regional level for the definition of projects; however, regions effectively ended up with one week to decide on the composition of a list of millions of dollars-worth of projects to be proposed. This was quite inadequate, especially since Iraqi utility directorates were (by custom) required to consult with their respective ministries in Baghdad before submitting any proposals. As a result, the lists were subjectively defined, lacked ownership from key Iraqi authorities and took no account of the availability of materials and resources. At about the same time a new agency was established in Baghdad to administer these projects, known as the Program Management Office (PMO). This move reinforced and formalised the centralised, top-down style that was a key feature of the Coalition civil administration in Iraq. Initially, the PMO had no formal Iraqi involvement built into its organisational structure, although many informal links were established with Iraqi ministries and directorates at various levels.

In mid-2004, at about the time that authority for reconstruction passed from the US Department of Defense to the US Department of State, following the appointment of the Iraqi Interim Government and formal transfer of sovereignty,[7] the PMO (now renamed PCO—Iraq Project and Contracting Office) dispersed more authority to its regional offices and they in turn set up more formal participative arrangements with regional Iraqi directorates. (There was, however, little evidence that the ministries were, in parallel, devolving more authority to their regional/governorate DGs). By the end of 2004 an organisation known as the Reconstruction Operations Center (ROC) had been established in Baghdad with the objective of co-ordinating and deconflicting all physical reconstruction projects in Iraq—especially in relation to security—but also charged with incorporating Iraqi ministry representatives into key management positions within itself and therefore levering more control over to Iraqi administration. However, arguably the damage was already done—the early emphasis on projects rather than people (developing, operating and benefiting from projects) had probably irrevocably compromised any objectives that might have embraced the inception of a sustainable infrastructure.

Barakat and Chard (2002: 828) describe how budgets and accountability can be a barrier to effective development. In administering the IRRF the requirement to utilise inflexible and highly regulated US procurement procedures that were designed to limit fraud (thereby protecting US taxpayers) frustrated attempts to break away from centralised project control. The rules were complex and were only really understood by a few in critical posts in Baghdad who had no interest in devolving any control. Iraqi companies were initially barred from seeking nomination as prime contractors, thus ensuring that contract administration at the primary level was always going to be very expensive. This, combined with the very high cost of providing private security for all international staff, meant that project overheads were eating up a substantial element of the IRRF (estimates vary between 20% and 50%). Providing best value did not seem to be a principal objective (whether by meeting strategic intent or by meeting project goals such as speed of construction or employment of local labour)—measurement of output was primarily by dollars spent! There was no accountability to the 'beneficiaries' for the outcomes, one of the conditions of best practice as related by Barakat and Chard.

There are two other barriers that Barakat and Chard (2002: 828–829) describe which have particular significance for Iraq: those of donor conditionality, and competence and political will. For Iraq the principal donor was the US government and, as we have seen, it determined the terms and conditions of its aid. Indeed, such was the will to reconstruct from the centre, that one-way conditionality was taken as read. In order to achieve a development perspective, it would have been necessary to employ staff for the implementation team who had appropriate training and empathy. However, nearly all the staff employed by PMO/PCO were from engineering, finance and project management backgrounds who were then given spend and timeline objectives. This was the political will. Had the will been one of development, then staff profiles would have needed to have been much wider—a very demanding objective in itself given the scale of reconstruction.

Lack of comprehensive strategic planning became apparent in other areas, namely project deconfliction and project co-ordination. In the early months of the intervention, many international organisations clambered to identify 'worthy' projects. The beneficiary organisations would often welcome interest from several bodies on the basis that one of them might just succeed in taking forward the project—however, confliction was the scourge of funding managers who, because money was involved, might pull out rather than risk accusations relating to project duplication. Management of different agency projects at the same sites was also often unco-ordinated until too late, with the result that reconstruction was not optimised.

The contradictions between what the international community preaches as paradigms for developmental processes and the administrative culture of its own institutions seem to be recurring themes in post-war recovery, especially in relation to capacity building (Barakat & Chard, 2002: 818). The difference in Iraq's reconstruction is that a truly developmental approach for infrastructure, as funded by the IRRF, initially never even reached the starting blocks. Had it done so, an onerous unadapted procurement philosophy would have ensured that it ran out of steam very quickly.

The realisation that local participation at the primary level was essential in order to lever Iraqi strengths came too late, but when its importance was eventually recognised it was evident from some initiatives that procurement procedures could be adapted as appropriate. The 'Local Fielding Initiative' (later known as the 'Rapid Construction Initiative') was the first attempt in this direction. In this programme prime contractors were appointed (after open national and international competition) to oversee the construction of road, water and electricity projects throughout Iraq using subcontractors appointed through a conventional tendering process. The successful prime contractors were usually of Iraqi origin, demonstrating the advantages that Iraqi companies have in bidding for straightforward construction.

An example of a successful participatory approach (but outside PMO/PCO responsibility) was the construction of a 100 km missing link in the main north–south highway in Iraq. The Iraqi state-owned contractors originally appointed during Saddam Hussein's regime had become bogged down by security and material-supply problems. The US Army's initial proposal to complete the road was for its engineers to take over construction management. However, after careful reappraisal, a supportive approach was adopted whereby military engineers helped to alleviate particular problems, so allowing the contractors to restore the level of construction activity and complete the main elements of the project—the highways directorate remained in control and thus project ownership by it was retained. The material supply problems for highway construction are described in Box 2.

Livelihoods and basic services

The failure by the early planning teams to focus on human security and, in particular, the restoration of livelihoods as a key theme had widespread repercussions. The reconstruction plan did not target areas with poor basic infrastructure, leaving these areas to fester with high unemployment and unfulfilled dreams of receiving even the most basic of essential services in power, water and sanitation. (Food shortages were not such a problem because supply networks had been well established under the UN's oil-for-food programme.) These areas then became easy recruiting grounds for disaffected youth by rebel groups such as Moqtada al-Sadr's Mehdi Army. It took almost one year from the start of the Coalition's intervention in Iraq for this failure to be fully appreciated and action taken (but too late). Every city needed early development in these areas, but perhaps nowhere more than the Sadr City area of Baghdad, where over two million people lived in squatter conditions; development programmes planned to alleviate many of the severe water and sanitation problems there are only now underway.

Materials for Highway Construction

While raw materials required for road and bridge construction and repair are plentiful in Iraq, years of neglect and conflict left manufacturing and processing facilities in a high state of disrepair. There were particular shortages of bitumen (which is a petroleum-based ingredient in asphalt), mineral filler (which is a very fine substance used to decrease air voids in asphalt) and cement (which is essential for concrete production). These shortages were expected to peak between November 2004 and June 2005 in parallel with high levels of construction activity; the problem would be mitigated by black market supplies and imports (accounting for up to 80% in the case of bitumen) but costs would substantially rise in an over-heated market. Material supply had clearly been an afterthought in planning infrastructure reconstruction—lack of early investment in renewing key processing facilities would lead to delayed reconstruction and another missed opportunity for boosting employment.

Box 2.

Neither did the reconstruction plan target heavy industry, rendered very ineffective by years of neglect and extensive looting during the early months of intervention. The consequence of this was threefold—poor economic recovery, severe shortages of key materials (such as cement and bitumen) to supply infrastructure reconstruction projects and, of course, further unemployment.

The UK's Department for International Development (DFID) set out its response to the increasingly transparent shortcomings in reconstruction policy in its *Interim Country Assistance Plan* (DFID, 2004) in which it set out three strategic objectives:

- to promote rapid, sustainable and equitable economic growth;
- to encourage effective and accountable governance;
- to promote social and political cohesion and stability.

Much of the support required to achieve these objectives was to be in the form of technical assistance, thus attempting to shift the balance in moving the focus from projects to people. However, in pure financial terms DFID's contribution was relatively minor and therefore its potential impact would be limited in the overall scheme of things.

Administrative structures

A comprehensive overview of local governance structures in Iraq is set out in ICG (2004: 4–13).

A crucial component in effective implementation of reconstruction strategies is the organisation of government, whether transitional or permanent. Reconstruction and development require a strong strategic framework to ensure that sustainable programmes are devised. The tendency with imported administrations (and indeed many national governments) has been to over-centralise decision making, leaving outlying districts as pariahs with economic and social peripherality. On the other hand, Barakat (1993: 102–103) finds that, 'total decentralisation is almost impossible, particularly in places where centralisation is a strong culture' and advocates 'controlled decentralisation' as a half-way solution.[8]

In the Saddam era decision making was certainly very centralised in Iraq—for example, each ministry would determine the content of governorate work programmes, and authorities for almost any expenditure were exercised in Baghdad.[9] This centralist approach became strongly instilled in the organisational culture. Such an institutionalised way of life is always going to be hard to change for whatever reason and there was a number of factors that worked against such change taking place after the intervention in Iraq.

As we have seen, the project management structures introduced by the CPA for major expenditures tended to mirror the existing centralised political and organisational structures in Iraq. Convenience was the chief factor: it was considered opportune to maintain strict control in Baghdad so that the demanding procedures necessary to comply with US funding rules could be adhered to correctly in the required timeframes. Indeed, there were some within the CPA administration who believed that a strong centralised administration was so institutionalised within Iraq that any other approach would probably fail.

Yet at governorate level there were some individuals in most of the Iraqi technical directorates who were well motivated and, with suitable international support, quite capable of leading reconstruction programmes. The conclusion must be that the low priority given to institutional strengthening and capacity building in the early months of reconstruction was demonstrative of the lack of commitment to finding sustainable solutions to reconstruction.

Mills (2004: 4) encapsulates the dilemma:

> Critical in the security–reconstruction mix is the need to decentralise funding to local level for councils and communities to make changes for the benefit of their own people. This is a foreign concept to virtually the entire population, having lived only in a highly centralised, command economic and political Ba'athist Party model. But without empowering these communities, it will be nigh impossible for leadership to gain credibility among a people used to a cocktail of party patronage, inefficiency in state delivery and extreme repression.

Thus, the key to future stability has to be through the strengthening of local governance structures. Political empowerment would support community enablement, for which the utility directorates would form a large enabling component.

Insecure environment

With the benefit of hindsight we can say that the conflict definitely had not ended in May 2003 as perhaps the politicians had optimistically proclaimed.

This is the case with most wars—latent conflicts persist for long periods after public pronouncements declare war is at an end. What was so different in the case of Iraq was the scale of continuing violent conflict and also the targeting of the international community.

Such were the threats and attacks against international civilians that many organisations stayed away from Iraq. This was particularly noticeable in the case of international NGOs, less so with international organisations (IOs) although the family of UN organisations was absent.[10] IOs had more opportunity to utilise the general umbrella of international military security than NGOs. This was especially true in the establishment of organisational HQs etc, where IOs often made use of common military/civilian protected areas such as the Green (International) Zone in Baghdad and the International Airport in Basrah. NGOs may not have been so welcome at these locations and indeed might have felt intimidated within them; they usually preferred to stay completely independent.

The substantial risks that civilian organisations perceived in operating in Iraq may partly explain the heavy direct role that military organisations played in the reconstruction process—the distinctions in roles were sometimes blurred or overlapping—and IOs were quick to take advantage of available military personnel with appropriate knowledge for the job (often reservists with expertise in civilian professions) when civilian recruitment or secondment failed to meet the requirement. Indeed, military personnel showed themselves to be particularly strong as enablers and at creating initial momentum. For example, the EIP had been an initiative promoted by DFID; however, early drive came from military engineers (supported by civilian consultants). Also, Governorate Support Teams were usually made up of military personnel co-ordinating civilian projects in each governorate (of which there are 18 in Iraq). Military personnel, given the opportunity, can be surprisingly adept at managing reconstruction and development work, particularly in the engineering sector.[11] The question that seems to tax some of those involved in the development arena is whether this extension of military influence has some more sinister political motive. Perhaps, however, this is a diversion and the more pivotal challenge is to establish optimum strategies for sustainable development at the outset of reconstruction.

Meanwhile, the insurgency was effective at slowing down the pace of reconstruction by frustrating movement of ground transport and by targeting those involved in the reconstruction process—this also drove up the cost of reconstruction. Organisations responded in different ways—the ones who assessed and managed the risks on a local basis using intelligence from all available sources were those that were most effective in limiting the threat effects and maintaining reconstruction targets.

Existing infrastructure suffered targeted attacks over a long period from April 2003. Linear installations such as oil pipelines, power lines, highways and railways were hit most, causing temporary disruptions to supplies and some loss of commercial continuity. Rapid repair techniques mitigated the impacts, although intelligent targeting by insurgents at locations having multiple infrastructure systems led to compounded infrastructure failures.

Elements of linear infrastructure feeding Baghdad were a particularly target.

Following the partial destruction of several cities in central Iraq, the international and Iraqi administrations sought to use rapid reconstruction of infrastructure as an influential tactical instrument in persuading the populations that life was really going to get better and so to diffuse anti-Coalition momentum in what the administrations viewed as a 'window of vulnerability' leading up to the planned January 2005 elections. This was not easy since, as inferred earlier, the initial reconstruction programmes lacked strategic purpose and intelligent prioritisation. They also lacked the flexibility necessary to make easy programme changes to accommodate emerging situations (such as the conflict within Najaf in mid-2004). The availability of AIRP and CERP funds, however, mitigated this shortcoming.[12]

Nonetheless, despite the continuing violence, it should be registered that a huge amount of physical reconstruction activity has been achieved in the oil, electricity, water, sanitation, transport and buildings sectors—although using the amount of money dispersed as an indicator of progress is inappropriate, since the nature of engineering contracts means there is a lag in payment for work done and, anyway, as described earlier, it fails to record value. A peak of activity in construction was anticipated from 2004 to 2006, creating a large amount of temporary Iraqi employment; however, there was no plan for successive employment as construction activity tailed off.

A statistical analysis of projects undertaken by the PCO in mid-2004 revealed that 86.9% of all projects had a cost of under $5 million and that these projects accounted for 11.4% of the infrastructure element of the IRRF, while 13.1% had a cost of over $5 million and accounted for 88.6% of the infrastructure element of the IRRF. What this suggests is a scarcity of middle order projects—ones perhaps particularly suited to Iraqi management.

In summary, there never was a long-term vision for sustainable infrastructure founded upon people-centric strategies, adequate investment in technology, effective lifecycle renewal and efficient planned pre-emptive maintenance (rather than reactive maintenance). But there was a medium-term top-down 'straight-line' plan for infrastructure reconstruction that was selectively realigned by the perceived need to use rather unwieldy infrastructure programmes to facilitate short-term aims in cities subjected to sustained attack and destabilisation by insurgents. Time will tell whether the two time horizons can satisfactorily co-exist within the same programmes. This top-down plan was exactly the type that Barakat & Chard (2002: 826) had in mind when they described the fixed-term pre-planned project culture that characterises most donor-funded interventions and that allows no space for people-led solutions.

A solution (in retrospect)

The scale of post-war reconstruction activities anticipated at the time of the military intervention in March/April 2003, combined with the need to meet popular expectations as best as possible, meant that the process was inevitably going to be complex. But proper process and planning based on academic referencing as well as on the actual situation as it was should have been a prerequisite, even if it meant deferring implementation, with relief mechanisms taking the strain in the meantime.

If we accept from the earlier arguments that a development challenge is more likely to succeed than a purely engineering challenge, that development is a means to extend local capacities and restore livelihoods and that it contributes significantly to the achievement of durable peace, then the defining task (as described in 'Three Key Themes') should have been to develop a clear vision for recovery, incorporating reconstruction as a development challenge with sustainable outcomes. A focused contribution to the vision could have been made through the adoption of the following phrase: 'Restoring livelihoods through development of people, infrastructure and industry.'

From this could have been developed a guiding set of principles based around the concepts of Iraqi participation, at least to governorate level, and intelligent mobilisation of available Iraqi resources in the reconstruction process. The gaps (of which there would have been many), by agreement, could then have been filled utilising international resources. Clearly, driven by lack of necessary capacity in the Iraqi directorates and the urgency to reconstruct, much of the heavy and complex work would have fallen to international/local supervision and international/local contractors, but it would have done so with support and participation from national, regional and governorate DGs. There would also have been great opportunity for capacity building in technical directorates and local companies through partnering arrangements, exchange employment and training programmes—the greatest needs being to improve business and project management skills.

The strategic planning for reconstruction of infrastructure and industry could have been undertaken by joint regional boards co-ordinated by a joint national board (the latter would have been able to inject national strategic needs into the planning process). In this way, identification and prioritisation of popular and national needs in terms of attaining a basic level of economic security would have been more easily facilitated and a better understanding of the holistic effect of a project's or system's construction would have also been possible. The basic requirements to aim for sustainability could have been built in to the process so that projects would have incorporated the most appropriate technology, would have been environmentally friendly and would have had well-trained people to plan and manage their design, construction, operation and maintenance as part of a whole systems approach to utility provision.[13]

Many of these principles reflect the doctrine that underpinned the EIP, described earlier.

Conclusions

To quote Barakat & Chard (2002: 818), 'it is the understanding of best practice in development that must underpin responses to the plight of war-torn countries'. The lack of a developmental approach to infrastructure reconstruction in Iraq threatens the sustainability of outputs from the huge reconstruction programme currently underway throughout the country. Conversely, the opportunity to use development as a device for securing peace in Iraq has all but been squandered in the race for physical results.

The lessons emerging from infrastructure reconstruction in Iraq demonstrate, as in previous contexts, the supreme importance of early planning, with flexible contingency arrangements to cater for strategic change in meeting sustainable horizons. Pre-war reconstruction planning has its merits but, after the armed conflict has notionally ended, a period of regrouping to undertake strategic assessments and reconsider reconstruction policies will pay a handsome long-term dividend. Parallel relief and stabilisation mechanisms must be designed to sustain popular consent until the benefits from sustainable reconstruction and development kick in. The importance of equitable local participation in all aspects of reconstruction planning and implementation overrides often-inflated debates over whether the development intervention should be civilian or military in nature. In insecure environments extended military involvement may be the only option and the culture of the military will need to adapt to align with the professional knowledge of its reservists as it moves into the development world.

> I've tried to stay away from driving-by-the-rear-view-mirror. I frankly don't have a lot of time to go back and study pre-war planning. I'm sure there's a wonderful PhD thesis to be written about the pre-war planning and how it did and it didn't—I'll look forward to reading that after I retire! (Media Briefing by Ambassador L Paul Bremer III, CPA, 26 September 2003)

Notes

1 Mac Ginty (2003: 602–603) lists five reasons why there has been a stronger emphasis on post-war activity in the post-cold war era: 1) peacekeepers can only effectively operate after violent hostilities have largely ceased; 2) perception of novelty in modern conflicts; 3) sheer number of post-conflict situations; 4) need to absorb lessons-learned in reconstruction; 5) global impression of insecurity reinforced by global terrorism.

2 Such is the public criticism of US policy over post-war reconstruction that some commentators now report that the US government failed to plan for Iraq's reconstruction, rather than failed to plan for contingencies during reconstruction.

3 Statistics from military sources indicate that in Iraq there are, for example, some 11 000 km of power transmission lines, 43 power generation plants, 7000 km of fuel pipelines, 2200 wellheads, 800 major oil locations, 2400 km of railway and 110 railway stations.

4 UK funds channelled through DFID effectively levered US funds channelled through the CPA.

5 The IPRB had an unexpected additional benefit—it brought together DGs from different but inter-related technical directorates in a formal setting allegedly for the first time.

6 There were many other sources of funds for reconstruction; of particular note were funds generated from 'Iraqi Seized Assets' which had much looser rules for disbursement.

7 According to certain legal opinion (including the House of Commons Library in the UK), the 'transfer of sovereignty' is an erroneous expression in this case; belligerent occupation only involves the assumption of sovereignty where the country in question is annexed into a parent state.

8 In 2004 Nasiriyah power station in southern Iraq was a key strategic generating node in the national power network. It also provided substantial local employment and the selective distribution of its notional 800MW output was controlled by its own DG who, along with the city's population, appeared to view the station as a regional asset rather than a national asset. Fiercely defended by the local media, his position was almost continually under threat from the Ministry of Electricity in Baghdad, which wanted more power redirected northwards in order to balance out 'hours of power' throughout the

country. This was a classic dilemma between the conflicting interests in respecting national strategic needs and in promoting regional empowerment.

9 Baghdad Municipality (Amanet), however, had a special status, enjoying the unique privilege of its own budget and an appointed mayor with ministerial rank (ICG, 2004: 9).

10 About 400 people, mostly representing Iraqi NGOs, attended the first national NGO conference in Baghdad on 4–5 August 2004.

11 For example, Coalition (UK and New Zealand) military engineers facilitated the construction of new spinal water distribution systems in several village suburbs in Basrah and other cities in southern Iraq. Local residents were encouraged to 'legally' tap into these water mains with special pipe and connection kits.

12 AIRP = Accelerated Iraq Reconstruction Program; CERP = Commander's Emergency Response Program.

13 To include the development and implementation of utility pricing structures and charging procedures.

References

Barakat, SZ (1993) Reviving war-damaged settlements: towards an international charter for reconstruction after war, unpublished DPhil thesis, University of York.

Barakat, SZ & Chard, MA (2002) Theories, rhetoric and practice: recovering the capacities of war-torn societies, *Third World Quarterly*, 23 (5), pp 817–835.

Brown, RH (2001) Towards sustainable infrastructure: an adaptable model for post-war areas in the Indonesian archipelago, unpublished MA dissertation, University of York.

Cockell, JG (2000) Conceptualising peacebuilding: human security and sustainable peace, in: J Whitman (ed), *Regeneration of War-Torn Societies: Global Issues*, pp15–34 (Basingstoke: Macmillan).

Department for International Development (DFID) (2004) *Iraq: Interim Country Assistance Plan*, London: DFID.

Goulet, D (1995) *Development Ethics: A Guide to Theory and Practice* (London: Zed Books).

Graham-Brown, S (1999) *Sanctioning Saddam: The Politics of Intervention in Iraq* (London: IB Tauris).

International Crisis Group (ICG) (2004) *Iraq: Can Local Governance Save Central Government?*, Middle East Report No 33 (Baghdad/Amman/Brussels: ICG).

Mac Ginty, R (2003) The pre-war reconstruction of post-war Iraq, *Third World Quarterly*, 24 (4), pp 601–617.

Mills, G (2004) *A Bit Pregnant? Searching for Peace and Governance in Iraq* (London: Royal United Services Institute).

Özerdem, A (1998) An approach to sustainable recovery of urban water supplies in war-affected areas with specific reference to the Tuzla region of Bosnia and Herzegovina, unpublished DPhil thesis, University of York.

Parkin, S (2000) Sustainable development: the concept and the practical challenge, *Journal of the Institution of Civil Engineers*, 138, (Nov), pp 3–8.

Royal Geographic Society (RGS) (2003) *Post-war Reconstruction: Forever Re-inventing the Wheel?* (London: RGS).

United Nations Environment Programme (UNEP) (2003) *Desk Study on the Environment in Iraq* (Nairobi: UNEP).

Overcoming Dilemmas Created by the 21st Century Mercenaries: conceptualising the use of private security companies in Iraq

KJELL BJORK & RICHARD JONES

ABSTRACT *In the past private security companies have taken responsibility for protecting reconstruction and aid activities during and after conflict. In Mozambique, Angola and Afghanistan such companies have played various roles in providing security for the reconstruction effort and delivery of humanitarian aid. However, the extensive private sector involvement in the reconstruction of Iraq, in addition to expanding aid activities, means that the use of private security companies is at an unprecedented level. Consequently the boundaries between civilian and military activities are becoming blurred, which creates new dangers for humanitarian assistance. Despite the increased number of private security companies in operation, their role is poorly conceptualised, discussed only as part of the overall security response rather than as a vital component of the delivery of aid and of the extensive private sector-led reconstruction programme. To conceptualise the protection of private sector reconstruction and NGO activity, the article examines three interrelated perspectives—the confusion between military intervention and humanitarian aid, the advent of the armed humanitarian and the need to understand the perceptions of the local population. The article provides typologies of local perceptions as a starting point for organisational analysis. It examines the implication of these typologies for reconstruction using Slim's questions: how do we look? What is most visible? Who is looking? The article confirms the link between the use of private security companies for reconstruction and NGO activities and the exacerbation of conflict. Therefore NGOs and organisations working in the private sector need to differentiate their efforts from the military campaigns which by doing so limits the violent consequences of negative perceptions.*

Despite the fact that Iraq's new republican constitution outlaws the privatisation of key state assets, and prohibits foreigners from owning Iraqi firms, privatisation of some of Iraq's major state companies is underway.

Barakat (2004: 2) claims that, as a result of the so-called shock therapy for economic reform introduced by the Coalition Provisional Authority (CPA) and endorsed by the Iraqi Governing Council on 19 September 2003 (Order 39), the first round of privatisation is affecting about 200 of the most successful enterprises. The same order decreed that foreign firms can retain 100% ownership of Iraqi banks, mines and factories, and allows these firms to move 100% of their profits out of Iraq (Klein, 2003).

Klein (2003) claims that under the Hague Conventions of 1907 and the Geneva War Convention of 1949, an occupying power 'shall be regarded only as administrator and usufructuary of public buildings, real estates, forests and agricultural estates belonging to the hostile state, and situated in the occupied country. It must safeguard the capital of these properties, and administer them in accordance with the rules of usufruct.' Bouvier's Law Dictionary defines 'usufruct' as an arrangement that grants one party the right to use and derive benefit from another's property 'without altering the substance of the property'. But 'What could more substantially alter the substance of a public asset than to turn it into a private one?' (Klein, 2003).

The rationale of such an approach to recovery is that economic development within Iraq must be based on the neoclassical lines of market regulation. As such Cannadi and Dollery (2004: 14) state that privatisation is necessary as it eases the public borrowing requirement—a key concern to a recovering nation when needing to spend large sums on welfare provision. In addition the more standard arguments of the greater efficiency and innovation in the private sector, and cheaper prices as a result of competition all have some resonance with the economic reconstruction of Iraq. However, a totally free market in a chronically weak economy exposes the most vulnerable before they have time to re-establish viable livelihoods, while increasing the opportunities for those 'with capital', who benefited from the previous regime, to enrich themselves further and entrench the polarised status quo. It also makes it difficult to target resources to redress uneven development, which perpetuates and exacerbates differences between the south and north of the country, rich and poor, urban and rural, Sunni and Shi'a. Duffield (2001) contends that strategic actors, including politicians of powerful states, officials of donor organisations and even international interests can facilitate violence either by tolerating the war by their actions or making conditions conducive to conflict.

Many of these reforms in Iraq are considered illegal. Worse still, an externally devised model of 'liberal democracy' may mask the continuing domination of existing power elites,[1] exacerbating poverty and giving further grievance to those who target foreigners for 'robbing their country', 'continuing imperialism' and 'impoverishing the country'.[2] Thus there is a strong link between the private sector-led reconstruction effort and the surrounding security apparatus and the Iraqi population's perception of socioeconomic exploitation and crusaderism. In the eyes of the local Iraqi population there are blurred boundaries between a) foreign armies (who are in Iraq to enforce security); b) international private contractors (who are in

Iraq working to a more humanitarian mandate to facilitate post-war recovery); and c) the private security companies who work for both the occupying army and foreign private contractors. As Hansen (2004: 4) observes, this has led to confusion between humanitarian development actions and the peace enforcement activities of the foreign armies. As a consequence, many non-military foreigners have been deliberately targeted, kidnapped, held for ransom, killed or injured. In turn, the likelihood of a violent response from coalition forces increases and more emphasis is placed on security: security itself becomes self-fulfilling and part of the conflict. This, Duffield (2001) claims, causes international organisations to ask how they can improve livelihoods without exacerbating conflict. In Iraq, as in post-war Afghanistan and Bosnia, Shaw (2002: 449) adds that the situation is exacerbated by criminal activities, where gangs and mafias take advantage of an unstable situation to escalate conflict for their own short-term financial and psychological gain. This adds validity to Duffield's (2001) argument that humanitarian and development organisations engaged in war or post-war assistance create alternative institutions that allow some to accumulate power and wealth through violence and thereby help to sustain the conflict.

Diamond (2004: 43–44) and Barakat (2004: 1) confirm that insecurity remains the main threat to Iraq's post-war recovery and that one of the main reasons for the highly volatile situation in Iraq lies with the US decision to dissolve not only the defeated Iraqi armed forces but also the police and all functions of the Ba'ath party in May 2003. For, as von Hippel (2004) explains, when Iraq's regular law enforcement capacity and large parts of the civil administration were shut down, a gap between Saddam's Iraq and the newly occupied Iraq was created. In the absence of law and administration, resistance to the occupying forces as well as organised armed criminal elements began to evolve to fight and/or exploit the chaotic and insecure conditions to gain enrichment through criminal activity. Thus the threat to Iraqi civilians, coalition forces, civilian contractors and humanitarian organisations was and remains very real and very high.

The violence and lawlessness in Iraq has lead to the increased use of private security firms to protect reconstruction and NGO activities. The subsequent blurring of military and civilian roles has increased attacks against military and non-military targets. Much of this blurring results from a lack of understanding among external actors of the perceptions held by significant sections of the Iraqi population. To reduce attacks on non-military civilians, humanitarian and development organisations need to understand how they are viewed and revise strategies accordingly.

The USA has repeatedly identified Al-Qaeda and foreign fighters as responsible for attacks on Coalition forces. However, as Malla (2004: 6) notes the extent of the attacks bears testament to substantial local support. The Coalition forces have failed to provide adequate security for international organisations, companies and government representatives in Iraq, and for the Iraqi public in general. In the absence of public security many international companies and also governmental institutions have turned to private security companies for protection. The *Observer* (2004) states that even international organisations such as the UN and humanitarian NGOs have engaged private security companies for their protection.

As Shawcross (2000) observes, the use of government military forces as well as commercial contractors for reconstruction has increased drastically since the 1990s.[3] Barakat (2004: 14) cautions that the privatisation of reconstruction is increasingly paralleled by the privatisation of war.[4] The post-war amalgamation between an occupying force, foreign contractors and increasing numbers of private security companies to deliver aid provide security and undertake the reconstruction of a state has for some, like Mac Ginty (2003: 610–611) and Barakat (2004: 10), come to characterise all that is wrong with the reconstruction of Iraq, a reconstruction in which the Iraqi people seem to have little influence on their country's post-war development.

To conceptualise the protection of private sector reconstruction and NGO activity, this article examines three interrelated perspectives—the confusion between military intervention and humanitarian aid; the advent of the armed humanitarian; and the need to understand the perceptions of the Iraqi population and their implications for reconstruction.

First, the article establishes how mercenary-type companies are re-emerging as private security companies. Although such companies are used to support reconstruction and aid, they can, as Shaw (2002: 450) confirms, be a cause of conflict. Building on the work of Duffield (2001) the article establishes that the increasing interaction of privatised networks of state and non-state actors has led to a confusion of military intervention and humanitarian aid. Against the background of increasing levels of violence, coalition governments are reluctant to send more troops, wary as ever of Shawcross's (2000: 65) Mogadishu Line. Private security companies are, as Whyte (2003: 590) confirms, filling a gap with the tacit acceptance of the Iraqi government, and more especially of the coalition governments.

Second, the article conceptualises the role of the armed humanitarian. The increasing levels of violence caused by the blurring of military intervention and humanitarian action exacerbated by the lack of a proper regulatory framework, has led to the creation of the armed humanitarian. This phenomenon creates more barriers between the local communities and international agencies, reinforcing misperceptions of 'the other'. Ispen (1999) maintains that in an environment such as Iraq, the institutional values of neutrality and the necessity of being unarmed are severely compromised. However, as Van Brabant (1998: 122) argues, by being armed, an organisation is more likely to be considered part of the 'aggressive foreign occupation' and may be tempted to forgo the community liaison so vital to the success of reconstruction projects. Doing so may in turn also increase the risk being of attacked.

Third, the article offers core typologies of perception among Iraqi attackers, characteristic of the violent targeting witnessed in areas of central Iraq, which have implications for reconstruction. Understanding such typologies as part of an organisational analysis, combined with strategies for providing adequate information to beneficiaries, tailoring operational style to the situation, maintaining a belief in organisational values and ensuring a participative approach, are all crucial to overcoming mistrust and misperceptions when exploring Slim's (1997: 9–10) questions: how do we look? What is most visible? Who is looking?

Finally the article concludes that the link between the use of private military companies to provide security for the private sector reconstruction and NGO effort and the exacerbation of conflict means that humanitarian/ civilian organisations need to do more to differentiate their efforts from military campaigns.

The emergence of private security companies: confusing military intervention and humanitarian aid

Muthien and Taylor (2002: 19) claim that the authority of the traditional state is increasingly replaced or affected by the authority of alternative powers and, in many instances, the enforcement of security is deemed most effective when such alternative powers have direct control over security. Todaro (2000: 39–42) confirms that 'global market forces are giving authority to private enterprises to effect state policy'. Todaro continues (578–579) that international organisations and global corporations are assuming an increasing role in affecting both national and international policy. As Hall and Biersteker (2002) maintain, in the developing or conflict-affected country, the unofficial authority is often the transnational corporation.

Reno (2004: 1–2) argues that in post-conflict situations the political power which would otherwise be weak can be exercised through transnational corporations. Such political strategies create distinctive social contexts in which militarised forms of clandestine commerce and other rent-seeking activities enjoy support from key state officials. Authority is not based on conventional notions of legitimacy or administration through bureaucratic institutions but on cliques which use control of markets, especially of natural resources such as oil, to enhance their power and to manipulate other people's access to economic opportunities. Worse still, such a strategy depends on eliminating autonomous economic opportunities, which also means limiting the autonomy of other social solidarities outside the influence of this political network (Reno, 2004: 2).

Despite the instability, the privatisation of reconstruction can be lucrative for both elite Iraqis and foreign companies, hence the importance placed on extensive security provision.[5] Such private security contractors are working in a regulatory vacuum and, although not formally part of the military, can nonetheless kill and injure those whom they consider a threat. Many of these companies have been characterised by Barakat (2004: 18) and Harding (2005: 1) among others, as little more than mercenary outfits who, according to Duffield (2001), have real conflict-producing potential. Such mercenary companies are re-emerging as private security companies where international corporations have a need for physical control over areas. Abdel-Fatau and Fayemi (2000: 4) state that these companies are becoming the muscle for the transnational companies directly, or are hired by the national authority guaranteeing contracts.

Hansen (2004) claims that the use of private security companies to protect reconstruction and commercial activities blurs the boundary between civilian and legitimate military targets. The private security companies are presented as civilian security providers, offering risk management consultants and safety personnel that will enable governmental and humanitarian organisations to be well protected.[6] However, Duffy (2004: 28) cautions that, in reality, private security companies have little to do with civilian security. The approach provides armed protection to individuals and sites, rather than a civilian constabulary where respect for law and public safety is the primary aim. Duffy (2004: 28–29) reiterates that such organisations are in reality military and respond to military emergencies. This is confirmed by Simons (2004: 68), who states that 'the manner in which private security companies protect their clients' activities is primarily based on military philosophy'. This gives rise to a contradiction: the employees working for private security companies protecting reconstruction efforts base their work on a military philosophy of security provision. However, when such people are killed or kidnapped, the media report deaths of civilian contractors,[7] and their loss is lamented as such. Interestingly, as discussed below, the fact that they were targeted may be because they and the people they are protecting were viewed as part of the exploiting foreign military intervention. Nevertheless, Ipsen (1999) clarifies that, technically, armed security staff are civilians, like the contractors working with reconstruction, even if they do so on behalf of an occupying force. But it is the background of the personnel of the private security companies that points to the organisational philosophy behind them, many being former soldiers.[8]

One of the best known mercenary companies was Executive Outcomes (EO). The company was formed in South Africa in 1989 and banned there in 1999. It provided the first corporate army in modern history. EO commanded over 2000 South African veterans and even had its own air force unit. It provided fighting forces for the governments in Angola and Sierra Leone.[9] Although EO has officially been closed, Bunker and Marin (1999) add that other companies, such as Lifeguard and Saracen, were created to continue EO's operations around the world; these includes providing security in Iraq.

It is not hard to find direct links between the mercenary operations of the 1990s and today's private sector reconstruction business in Iraq. Sandline provides one of the more public examples. According to Chatterjee (2004: 1), in May 2004 the CPA issued a $293 million security contract to Aegis Defence Services (Sandline was its predecessor company), enabling its president and founder, Tim Spencer, to form the largest private army in the world. The primary task under this contract is the protection of contractors conducting US-funded activities in Iraq today.[10]

However, when used to protect reconstruction and the delivery of aid, private security companies can also be a cause of conflict. Shaw (2002: 450) states that the privatisation of security is a cause of conflict and hence an impact on development. The increasing use of private security guards and intelligence, and private soldiers/mercenaries within complex emergencies is aimed at organisational enrichment rather than the result of any concern for peace and stability. Shaw (2002: 450) argues that the selling of statutory forces to regain control of resource-rich areas such as in Cambodia, Congo and Sierra Leone is self-serving. Such private armed assistance, in addition to payments from international agencies or governments, can be financed through the exploitation of the resources in areas they have neutralised, to the detriment of the local population (Cilliers & Mason, 1999; Musah & Fayemi, 2000: 13–14). Furthermore the heavily armed security accompanying development efforts can also up the stakes in the eyes of the rebels, criminals, suicide bombers and kidnappers, and mean that they will use more force against a well equipped 'enemy'.

The private security company has become a player that participates in and influences both post-war recovery and state building. In the increasingly violent situation in Iraq more private security companies are being used for the protection of the private sector reconstruction and NGO activity and for the training of and support for the new Iraqi police force. In the absence of Coalition governments' desire to commit more troops, such private security companies are filling a gap. However, by their pervasive presence among local police, foreign armies and humanitarian and reconstruction organisations alike, the effect of all the international effort, in the eyes of many Iraqis, whether military or humanitarian, is deemed to be aggressive, exploitative and as such creates more grievances for those who are against the 'foreign occupation'. They are thus confirming the contention of Duffield (2001) that these same organisations which aim to help rebuild livelihoods and address issues of post-war recovery are in fact fuelling conflict, not so much through what they are doing but through the process of how they are doing it. Therefore the role of private security companies working in the process of reconstruction and humanitarian aid becomes ever more important, especially because of the confusion it creates in the minds of the local population.

Since the 1990s a number of military interventions have been based on humanitarian grounds.[11] Woodward (2001: 331) observes that humanitarian and human rights rationales justify military intervention to enable the provision of aid and relief by civilian organisations or by the forces themselves. Pirnie and Francisco (1998) counter that, already at this stage, the line between combatants and humanitarians is blurred. Military forces intervene in order to provide humanitarian assistance and commercial companies bid on contracts to provide both aid and developmental reconstruction of both infrastructure and institutions. This phenomenon is a consequence of what Duffield (2001) defines as characteristic of 'new wars' associated with the emergence of new forms of authority and areas of alternative, largely non-state, regulation of commerce and violence when global market deregulation has allowed the emergence of parallel and shadow trade. Duffield continues that these emerging political complexities are based on increasingly privatised networks of state and non-state actors working beyond the competence of territorially defined governments. The wars fought by such networked political complexes are financing and provisioning economies; this has blurred conventional distinctions between peoples, armies and governments.

These complexities become ever more ingrained when the situation becomes too volatile for the military forces to provide a secure environment for contractors and international organisations. Instead, private security companies are contracted to fill the gaps. Bhatia (2003: 85) asserts that humanitarian intervention encompasses the full range of military warfare, provision of relief, developmental assistance and state building, including public security. It is therefore in this context that the use of private security companies should be viewed—not as a single occurrence for specific projects but as part of state-building projects in an era of humanitarian intervention by states in a state.

The necessity and accompanying problems of securing law and order in Iraq were not adequately foreseen before the war had begun.[12] Private security companies are increasingly filling the gap in security needs by taking on roles that governments do not want to assign their military personnel. There are around 15 000 – 20 000 international civilians contracted to support the coalition forces inside Iraq (Brookings, 2005: 4). Even where the troops are needed for a just cause, it may be difficult for a government to commit armed forces. As Shawcross (2000: 65 – 104) observes pictures of soldiers coming home in body bags have a direct influence on domestic opinion of Western governments. Few politicians wish to cross the Mogadishu line.[13]

Duffy (2004: 29) confirms the potential dual role of private security companies, contending that they often act as a civilian security guard protecting a civilian enterprise and then participate in military combat by supporting coalition forces because their 'military colleagues' have got in to trouble close by. Human Rights Watch (2004) claims that the status of armed civilian, protecting non-combatants from harm, is immediately changed to that of soldier in civilian clothes during such circumstances.

According to Whyte (2004: 589), there are several practical advantages to using private security companies. They can deploy faster and more cost-efficiently than an *ad hoc* multinational force and the command structure is likely to be better within a private force compared with a temporary international force. Bullion (1995) implies that the level of national bias and background interest in the conflict can also be lower than with a national force provided by a supporting country.[14] In addition privatised security is seen as a simple solution to delivering immediate reconstruction programmes and aid activities in unstable environments.

The disadvantages of using private security companies are, in most cases, directly related to the advantages. Whyte (2003: 590) maintains that, if a government is less accountable when private security staff are killed in action during a just military intervention, it will probaby be held less accountable in a not-so-just intervention. The reason is that, with less public interest in government operations, scrutiny is also reduced. Muthien and Taylor (2002) say that if the company in question is contracted by both government and reconstruction company contractors, it is hard to define who carries overall responsibility. In a world where subcontracting is common practice within reconstruction, international security companies will subcontract national ones. In such cases, accountability and responsibility are threatened and often sacrificed. Who will hold a private security company accountable for its actions?

Muthien and Taylor (2002) state that, by accepting that international corporations not only conduct business in Iraq but are also building state institutions as part of commercial contracts, the authority of civil governance is surrendered. As such, as Hall and Biersteker (2002) confirm, investors are building businesses and the institutions with which they will conduct business in the future, thus creating a corporate authority. Duffield (2001) classifies this interaction of state and non-state actors building connections within and between donor governments, military establishments, ngos and the commercial sector as strategic complexes. Such complexes in this case have the consequence of reconstruction and humanitarian organisations who use private security companies for their protection incurring an association with major corporate interests. The reality is that in today's Iraq the establishment of US and other coalition countries' business is often viewed by the general Iraqi community as the commercial sell-out of the country.[15] As a direct consequence it is in the particular interest of humanitarian actors to avoid being perceived as affiliated to the commercial interests of the occupying Western world.

Many of the private security companies in Iraq are operating within an unclear regulatory framework, in environments far from Western norms, where mistakes are less rigorously investigated.[16] With governments reluctance to cross the 'Mogadishu line' their role can be compared to that of a proxy state actor, yet without state responsibility for their actions. If the trend for private security companies to take on an increased role in future reconstruction and development continues, it is in the interest of all parties involved to have their mandates and roles regulated in a manner that is commonly accepted by the international community. As identified by Slim (1997) and Coady (2002: 24) whether or not to use armed security guards supplied by private security companies is a dilemma that is increasingly faced by humanitarian and development organisations. Arms do not provide total protection and in fact can have just the opposite effect. Nor do arms negate the effective participation of the local community before humanitarian or reconstruction work as a prerequisite for a more secure environment. Nevertheless in Iraq the evolution of the armed humanitarian is increasingly common.

The armed humanitarian

Although international law allows non-combatants to be armed (Ipsen, 1999), for a humanitarian NGO to carry arms creates an ethical dilemma as well as risk. Studer (2001: 381) maintains that the NGO may be perceived as being part of a larger general group of armed organisations and this could have a devastating effect on the perception of NGO s in general. Most international NGOs have agreed or claim to work according to the humanitarian principles and the ICRC-recommended Code of Conduct. Studer (2001) argues that, although the latter does not address armaments, the ICRC implementation principles and many NGO s' general operational procedures, implementation principles and policy statements confirm that humanitarian workers should be unarmed. This theme is continued by the ICRC (1995: 139–149) which states that the principle of being unarmed is aimed at ensuring that an NGO is not perceived as a threat to any armed faction or criminals.

Many NGOs work without any armed protection in Iraq, but an increasing number are choosing to arm themselves.[17] Armed protection among NGOs may be limited to national staff hired to guard offices, living quarters and warehouses from regular criminal activity. Increasingly, however, it involves the contracting of private security companies providing 24-hour protection. Van Brabant (1998: 111) maintains that both donors and domestic organisations feel a responsibility to provide whatever protection they can for the staff. However, the reasons for not being armed are simple. Van Brabant (1998: 115) says that, by not being armed, one does not pose a direct threat to hostile forces or armed robbers, thus reducing the risk of being shot as a preventive measure. Single individuals with arms are probably more likely to have a false sense of security, resulting in those individuals venturing into unsafe situations that would probably be avoided by an unarmed person. To escalate the level of armed protection by hiring guards to secure a perimeter around worksites and provide protection during transport makes it hard to achieve any close contact with the local population. As Studer (2001: 388) says, this further complicates project implementation, since contact with target groups is essential to the provision of any form of aid, while bringing in arms can increase the likelihood of the community suffering if reconstruction/aid organisations are attacked.[18]

Thus Van Brabant (1998: 114) states that armaments may actually increase risk. In an area such as Iraq, where security is weak and resistance against military intervention is strong, reliance on armed protection may present more danger than protection. This is particularly true when, as discussed, it is hard to distinguish between private security company personnel working with: foreign military forces and reconstruction contractors and NGO workers. In addition to the many private security company personnel who resemble threatening Hollywood figures, there are numerous security personnel moving around in unmarked vehicles, civilian clothes, with firearms held discretely in order to blend in with the general community, blurring perceptions to an even greater extent.

As the ICRC (1995: 139–149) confirms, the basic principles of successful humanitarian assistance—humanitarian imperative, neutrality, impartiality and independence—apply world-wide, as does the non-arms principle. The hostile situation in Iraq puts these principles to the test and requires, as Duffield (2001) confirms, a radical reform of the institutional culture of those involved in reconstruction and aid—turning their rule-based bureaucracies into adaptive, learning and networked organisations.

Traditionally, humanitarian aid organisations work unarmed, relying on close community liaison to avoid security threats to their staff. Those organisations that are still carrying out their activities unarmed offer some advice.[19] In terms of visibility, the approach is divided between keeping a low profile in order to avoid attention and high visibility in stating the origin, purpose and activity of the organisation.[20] Liaising with the inhabitants of the project areas and with the wider community, including the local Imam and the local 'strongmen', can establish a broader power base which can 'effectively protect' the NGO. However, in all this discourse the key to local and international understanding and misunderstandings is the perception of 'the other'.

Understanding perceptions and the implications for reconstruction

Picture a section of men, often masked with the traditional Arab headscarf, armed with assault rifles escorting a smaller group of foreigners while working at a project site. In a country where secret police as well as armed Ba'ath party death squads used to act in civilian clothes, it is not hard to see how these persons are perceived as military rather than as part of a group of contractors or aid workers. The perceptions of the local population must be considered in order to better understand the risks associated with the increasing use of private security companies. For, as Hansen (2004) reminds us, legitimate and illegitimate attacks upon the coalition are often met with heavy-handed responses that have resulted in civilian casualties in the thousands, thus giving additional force to people's grievances.[21]

As Diamond (2004: 43) states, the hope that exists after war is concluded, and the consequent disappointment when the expected recovery and progress do not materialise, is common in most post-war societies. The peace dividend is often illusory (Haughton, 1998). As Collier *et al* (2003: 4) confirm, the disappointment is usually based on the lack of financial and material recovery after a conflict. For Iraqis there is the additional concern of physical safety, which compounds their grievances against the foreign invasion (Diamond, 2004; Malla, 2004: 6). Resentment among the local population towards the coalition and foreigners is increasing, to the extent that all foreign armed parties may be viewed with animosity when lethal force is used frequently in the majority of cities and towns in Iraq by foreign personnel.

The success of implementing projects, humanitarian or otherwise, in Iraq is to a large extent dependent on the co-operation and support of the local population. Association with armed personnel can be strongly disruptive to achieving the aim of the project. Ritter (2002) reminds us that the former regime nurtured a suspicious attitude towards all foreigners: as a consequence conspiracy theories of why the USA wants to control Iraq are still prevalent today. Thus, when defence contractors such as Halliburton, CSC/Dyncorp, Kellog Brown and Rooth, all protected by their hired private security companies, are contracted to conduct reconstruction it is hard for the Iraqi population to perceive this as a civilian operation.

Berger (2002) states that the motivating factor for the most extremist groups is the fight against the West's perceived actions to subordinate and enslave the Muslim world. Byman (2003: 47–55) adds that more pragmatic groups might very well see the occupation of Iraq as the primary reason for combating the West in conventional as well as unorthodox ways. NGOs meanwhile are a relatively new concept for the Iraqi population and the associated humanitarian imperatives—independence and neutrality—are not always respected. The perception of why humanitarian organisations are present in Iraq is therefore of crucial importance. If, as is the case, the private sector and humanitarian NGOs are perceived as being part of the US-led reconstruction, the risk of being attacked increases. Slim (1997) argues that organisations engaged in humanitarian and development work should always assess how others perceive them. First, organisations should define what is most visible: is it the guarded compound, expatriate staff, security guards with their rayban sunglasses, sophisticated weapons looking like Robocop, foreign flags or symbols? Slim defines such visible attributes as 'the northern face and footprint' of humanitarianism and development.

Slim asks if the actions of the organisations are being undertaken in a self-righteous or superior manner or, worse, are the actions akin to a type of colonialism? These are important issues to address when we consider, as Slim puts it, 'who is looking'. There are groups with different perceptions, including extremists, the general public, religious leaders and politicians. One way of establishing the importance of understanding perception of the non-military (that is foreign army-based) foreign intervention from a local viewpoint is to identify typologies of perception (see Box 1).

Such typologies are also influenced by the area in which the attacks are carried out. It is generally accepted that the more Kurdish areas in the north and the Shia areas in the south are deemed a safer environment for foreigners and Iraqis alike, while the central area around Baghdad is particularly dangerous, (Brookings, 2005).

Typologies of Perception amongst Iraqi Attackers

Foreigners attacked because of:

Mistaken identities

- Due to perpetrators misjudgement

Blurred boundaries*

- Confusion between civilian and military action exacerbated by private security companies accompanying reconstruction and humanitarian work. Any foreigner is a 'legitimate' target

Soft targets*

- Non military foreigners represent an easier target than the well armed coalition armies, soft targets are unable to respond as effectively and are therefore less threatening

Criminal motivations

- Foreigners are attacked so that the attackers can gain access to their spoils. The attackers have little motivation beyond wealth accumulation

* Attacks against Iraqi nationals are more likely in these instances as they are viewed as an extension of the foreign effort

Box 1

The causes of hostility and mistrust towards those involved in development and humanitarian work have four prime perceptual typologies, each of which is also reflective of the opportune basis of the attack. First, mistaken identity is of concern for humanitarian and development workers often deliberately targeted in times of conflict. Media reports highlight how many European hostages are questioned regarding their perceived links to Mossad, such is the misjudged conviction by the hostage takers that any foreigner is working for the consolidation and expansion of the Israeli state. Second, the blurring of boundaries between civilian and military distinctions means that to some attackers their motivation for attack is based on their perception that all foreigners are in some way or another working for the consolidation and expansion of the US exploitation of Iraqi society and is associated religious, cultural and economic manifestations. Reconstruction contractors and humanitarian workers are merely proxy targets. Such attacks can also be based on the desire for revenge.

Third, foreigners may be attacked because they are soft targets for any particular grievance that their attackers may have. These grievances can be based on the above or can be more personal, especially if the attack is motivated by revenge. Fourth, incorporating Shaw's (2002: 450) notion of criminality, it is recognised that for some attackers their motivation is neither ideal nor based on revenge but rather on enrichment.

The use of private security companies for protecting reconstruction, when combined with the above typologies of perceptions held by many in the general Iraqi population, has several implications for reconstruction and humanitarian effort. Within the increasingly violent context of delivering reconstruction and humanitarian aid in Iraq the use of private security companies has become inevitable and this has led to it being accepted as normal practice among foreigners and Iraqi nationals alike. This article has demonstrated that privately secured reconstruction and humanitarian activity is currently viewed as the only possible solution to ensure staff can work in a 'safe' environment. Thus, when considering the relative merits/disadvantages associated with private security companies, it must be recognised that, while levels of violence increase or remain the same, the use of private security companies will continue.

As discussed above, by their presence, the private security companies blur military and civilian boundaries and contribute to greater levels of violence against those they seek to protect, thereby justifying their employment. Nevertheless there remains a definitive link in many people's minds that transcends debate: big men with guns provide a sense of security to nervous expatriates working in a hostile environment, although it is acknowledged that even a project with private security company protection is not immune from attack. Thus there seems to be an inextricable link between the protection offered by private security companies and a feeling of relative security. This link is continually reinforced by the high budgetary allocation to security of reconstruction/aid budgets. It is also interesting to note that, despite the technological advances of modern warfare, visible men with guns invoke such a feeling of protection.[22]

In the context of private security companies becoming normal practice alternatives are not easy to define. However, there is certainly potential for different approaches towards the provision of security that are based within the normalisation of the use of private security companies and these too have implications for reconstruction and aid protection, based primarily on changing perceptions. Slim (1997) advances four ways in which organisations can minimise the consequences of damaging perceptions:

(1) Provide accurate information. Speculation about people's perceptions needs to be urgently replaced with harder surveys and insights into different people's attitudes to an organisation's work across a range of settings. Accurate information needs to be distributed so the real purpose of the activity can be disseminated to the Iraqi population. The medium through which this information is distributed must also be considered. If it through a Western agency it is unlikely to be taken as seriously.
(2) Presence and posture. Organisations have to tailor their operational style to every new situation. There is no single global way of implementing policy. Such organisational activity must include local employees as co-workers as well as security guards; they will have a better understanding of the security situation and of common perceptions among the local community.
(3) Maintaining belief in organisational values. Being disliked can make an organisation doubt itself. Many people that benefit from the organisation's services share its same values. While the majority of people may have inaccurate knowledge of an organisation, it would only ever be a minority that would be intent on seriously undermining the organisation. Therefore core organisational values should be maintained. However, the way in which these values are delivered should be changed.
(4) An ecumenical humanitarian council. A good way to maintain values is to have them challenged and refined specifically within the operating context. Establishing an ecumenical council based on the contribution of all stakeholders, potential beneficiaries, community representatives, security advisors, etc. keeps the organisation sharp and responsive to changes in their operating environment.

Walker (2004) validates Slim's (1997) strategies for overcoming damaging perceptions through an understanding that humanitarian assistance and reconstruction is not something that is delivered but something that is derived from an intimate understanding of the perception of the local population, ie the beneficiaries, and therefore requires a two-way relationship.

Van Brabant (1998: 119–120) maintains that best practice is dependent upon the organisation having an accurate understanding of the general context of the tension and possible causes of mistrust. This should lead to 'proactive positioning' so that the organisation changes the way it relates to the population on a basis of how the local population perceives it. He also advocates expatriate workers building relations with local people, as separation breeds mistrust, indifference and hostility. The main problem is trying to achieve a balance between the need for security while ensuring that the organisation is not alienated from the local population. On this basis there are several lessons-learned that could inform current and future international community reconstruction and aid activity.

In summary, the use of private security companies does not necessarily equate to better protection. Indeed, the need for such protection can become self-fulfilling mainly because of the blurring of military and civilian boundaries, which, from a local community's viewpoint, makes the military effort and reconstruction/aid activities difficult to differentiate. Therefore consideration should also be given to community liaison and information sharing regarding project purpose and rationale as prerequisites for reconstruction/aid activity as a way of reducing the potential for attacks. Foreign organisations need to understand the perceptions held by the community; on this basis they can formulate organisational responses to overcoming such perceptions, particularly by addressing the 'visibles'—high numbers of heavily armed men, a siege mentality and lack of dialogue with local communities. This will enable organisations to differentiate themselves in the minds of the local communities from the armed coalition forces' effort. These are indeed modest efforts to try and break the cycle of high reliance on private security companies, attack and then greater reliance on private security companies. However, the process of reducing reliance on heavily armed protection is as important as the end result. Organisations working in the difficult environment in Iraq can achieve more when their actions are tailored to the collective community mindset in which they interact and deliver reconstruction and aid. In so doing they can tailor initiatives that more accurately reflect the needs of those who are looking in (Slim, 1997).

Conclusions and discussion

Compared with analysis of the build-up to war in Iraq, the role and actions of the US-led coalition forces and the conflict and instability in the aftermath, relatively little attention has been paid to understanding the role of protection of the private sector-led reconstruction effort and NGO activity. This is even more surprising when the protection of the process of delivering aid and reconstruction is linked to exacerbating conflict, entrenching negative perceptions and reinforcing the perception that all foreigners engaged in aid and reconstruction activity are part of a continued political, economic and social exploitation by the victorious coalition forces.

Distinctions between military- and civilian-based action have become blurred and the protection of the private sector reconstruction and NGO effort is often reduced to being considered part of the peace consolidation strategy, which at one extreme involves suppressing uprisings in Fallujah while at another involves water projects in Basra. This is worrying as it is precisely this perception held by many that will ensure that attacks on non-military personnel continue. The use of private security companies in the protection of private sector reconstruction and aid does not allow the reconstruction and aid to be sufficiently differentiated in the eyes of the Iraqi population. In addition, where contracted companies spend large proportions of reconstruction funds on protection by subcontracted private security companies, both their independence and the humanitarian imperative must be questioned.

The lack of a sound regulatory framework within which these private security companies operate can indirectly exacerbate the aggression that those working in aid and reconstruction activities face, because of the questionable tactics used by private security personnel. National armed forces in developed countries operate under the scrutiny of internal judicial systems, elected bodies in forms of parliaments or congress and, equally important, independent human rights organisations. In the case of Iraq far too often this has proven inadequate to prevent violations of international treaties regarding conduct towards both civilians and combatants. It is therefore of the utmost importance that international legislation and control bodies are established to supervise and control the activities of these new era 21st century mercenaries.

Humanitarian and development organisations and academics have devised a range of approaches for understanding socioeconomic impact, models for popular participation and rapid appraisal, and theories for maximising the effect of local liaison (Chambers, 1998; 2002). The conditions in Iraq may be harder and more difficult than many are used to but they are not new. The main difference between Iraq and other areas of intervention or crisis does not lie in the humanitarian crisis itself or indeed in the reconstruction challenges but in the way in which these challenges evolved and are addressed. Iraq is occupied by a power that is engaged in the biggest state-building project since the Marshal Plan (Barakat, 2004: 2). The aid and reconstruction package being delivered with the occupation has brought with it a mentality that equates weapons with security because of the blurring of boundaries between the military and the civilian.

Western humanitarian and reconstruction organisations have a problem implementing projects in Iraq because of the insecure environment. Part of the problem can, however, be addressed by the humanitarian organisations adapting their way of implementing projects. The use of more national organisations and fewer armed internationals is likely to improve the security situation. By accepting alternative ways of implementing projects and thereby reducing the number of expatriates in need of armed protection, the creation of yet another $293 million private army like Aegis Defence Services might be avoided. Another substantial effect that should not be overlooked is the importance of increased public knowledge regarding civilian organisations operating in Iraq.

For the private sector reconstruction project and the humanitarian NGO activity, the protection of staff and, especially for the NGO, maintenance of its humanitarian purpose requires dissociation from military or other armed groups that give the appearance of being part of the foreign 'footprint' of war machinery. In short it requires a disarming of the humanitarian. No single conceptual lens offers a complete explanation of why foreigners are attacked and how such organisations could better protect themselves against attack. However, if organisations are to conduct humanitarian aid and avoid becoming part of the military machinery, they must step back and remember the importance of why and how they implement projects and understand the perceptions of those around them. By doing so organisations are going some way to addressing Duffield's (2001) concern to improve understanding of how human suffering can be reduced without exacerbating conflict.

Notes

1 For a similar illustration from Afghanistan, see Barakat and Chard (2002).

2 Phrases translated from interviews conducted by Bjork in Baghdad and Central Iraq, November 2003–February 2004.

3 Van Brabant (1998: 110) also confirms that the use of armed protection for reconstruction assistance has been escalating since the end of the Cold War.

4 The US military is heavily reliant upon the private sector for weapons design, procurement and supporting troops. Therefore to the USA the civil/military blurring is not as apparent as it is to Europeans, who are more reliant on in-house expertise.

5 Indeed, Barakat (2004: 23) states that reconstruction contracts can have a provision for security spending of around 40%. Therefore security companies are keen to exploit this highly profitable consequence of instability.

6 Company websites, www.sandline.co.uk; www.custerbattles.com; www.internationalriskcontrol.co.uk.

7 The BBC provides a good example. 'A British contractor has been killed in a roadside bomb attack in Zubayr, south Iraq, an Army spokesman has said. The Foreign Office confirmed a Briton had died in an incident, but gave no further details. The Army spokesman in Basra said there were two civilian casualties from the bomb on Sunday morning. "I can confirm there was a car bomb this morning. I believe they were two civilians, they were definitely not military," he said. The incident happened in Zubayr, just south of Basra. Danish television reported that the Briton was a civilian security employee, and the second casualty was a South African colleague.' BBC, 'British contractor killed in Iraq', 7 November 2004. Available at www.bbc.co.uk/1/hi/uk/3990857.

8 A few private security companies have been created specifically to support government operations and are primarily working as contractors of their respective governments. Most of the companies have a background as regular private mercenary organisations. An irregular band of redundant soldiers taking on contract killings or covert operations for governments has its roots in the Vietnam War and Africa during the evolution of independent states in the 1960s and 1970s. Since then, according to Abdel-Fatau and Kayode Fayemi (2000), regular mercenary companies have transformed into commercial companies with boards of directors, providing security services for transnational companies and governments.

9 Howe (2001) claims that this was the first time mercenary forces had been used in a way that, at least for the short term, provided stability in areas where other professional forces were lacking. Despite the title of chairman, Eden Barlow's role was analogous to that of a military commander. The difference between EO and earlier mercenary companies is its base of professional soldiers. As Isenberg (2001) quoted in Howe (2001) points out, instead of a being a ragtag band of adventurers or paramilitaries, EO offered an organised force that could not only fight but could also provide training and planning for national armies. When EO officially closed operations in 1999 this was partly the result of a changing South Africa that was starting to regulate the activities of private security operations and partly a consequence of its involvement in a failed coup in Papua New Guinea in 1997. Nevertheless Howe (2001) states that the company did not fully disappear. Part of the staff merged with the earlier sub-company, Sandline, that had been involved in the failed coup in Papua New Guinea.

10 Sandline has engaged in a number of quasi-mercenary activities over the years. In 1997 it was contracted by the Papua New Guinea government to retake control over the island of Bougainville. Landowners on the island had closed down a copper mine because of the environmental destruction caused by the mining company. Sandline was awarded a US$36 million contract to root out the local opposition to the mining in order to allow operations to continue. A member of the national armed forces in Papua New Guinea felt that the money would be better spent on its own troops and compromised the mission by making the deal public before operations commenced. The Sandline owner was arrested with $400 000 in cash but was later released. The following year Sandline was caught breaking a UN embargo on weapons to Sierra Leone. Sandline had sold 30 tons of weapons to

the former leader of Sierra Leone, Ahmad Tejan Kabbah (Chatterjee, 2004). According to Sandline's own home page (www.sandline.com) the company was closed on 16 April 2004 because of the lack of government support for private military companies willing to help in armed conflicts.

11 For example, Somalia in 1992–93, Bosnia and Herzegovina with UN forces from 1992 and NATO intervention in 1995, and Kosovo in 1999.

12 It is one thing to defeat Saddam Hussein but to ensure that every citizen obeys the law once the Saddam-era police had been disbanded was and remains much harder and must be complemented with 'constabulary support'. Graham and Freeman (2002: 4) maintain that the use of a neutral police force staffed primarily by the surrounding Islamic nations and supplemented by staff from private security companies such as DynCorps was discussed as a possible alternative before the war. However, it is now known that the neighbouring countries had little intention of providing an international police force that would secure law and order in Iraq on behalf of a US-led coalition.

13 The Mogadishu line refers to the abortive attempt that US soldiers made to stabilise the Somalian capital beginning in May 1993. The armed resistance was much stronger than had been predicted and the rationale for the intervention—protecting food and distribution outlets—became less urgent as the USA was desperate to catch one of the warlords, Aideed. Pictures of a US marine being dragged through the streets in front of the world's press caused the political will for engagement to evaporate.

14 This can help to avoid embarrassing incidences such as the 1987–90 Indian Peace Keeping Forces mission to Sri Lanka, where intervening troops were accused of having an inherited bias towards one side.

15 The commercial sell-out of the country to foreign interests was a recurring theme in interviews conducted by Bjork in the central region and in Baghdad, October 2003–February 2004.

16 Although prohibited under the Geneva Convention (Article 47), private security companies are operating in a grey area by exploiting loopholes (Whyte, 2003: 592–596).

17 ngos choosing to arm their staff, contract private security companies or train their own security force were identified by Bjork during the period October 2003–February 2004. For security reasons these organisations prefer to be unnamed in order to avoid attracting further attention.

18 Furthermore, the high cost of having a security force protecting large areas has an overall impact on the total cost of providing the aid in question. The cost of contracting security staff can exceed $1000 per member of security staff per day (Harding, 2005).

19 Names of organisations have to remain confidential for security reasons, their feedback comes from interviews conducted by Bjork, November 2003–February 2004.

20 In Baghdad a number of mine action organisations at times chose to conduct clearance operations on low or medium priority areas in order to be able to work outside the public eye, and thereby reduce the risk of becoming a target for attacks. On a few occasions where high priority tasks were in areas deemed highly hostile to a foreign presence, a different approach was chosen. The example refers to HELP-UDT working at the south end of Al Rashid district on the border of UN Area 39/40.

21 In addition insurgents and combatants apprehended may be subjected to torture and abuse, the very human rights violations for which the occupying countries heavily criticised the former regime. Many Iraqis also view the US force as an inherited enemy after the last Gulf war, with Saddam-era state propaganda demonising the West in general and the USA in particular as enemies of the Iraqi people. In addition, public security and development progress, especially in terms of socioeconomic gains and infrastructure development, have deteriorated rather than improved in many areas.

22 Technological advances do not always ensure that people feel safer. For example, the situation among expatriate staff in Iraq has parallels with the perception held by many in the UK that more policemen on the street reduces crime and makes people feel safer.

References

Abdel-Fatua, M & Fayemi, J (2000) *Mercenaries: An African Security Dilemma* (London: Pluto Press).

Barakat, S (2004) Free markets and democracy—a dangerous alliance, departmental seminar, University of York.

Barakat, SZ & Chard, MA (2002) Theories, rhetoric and practice: recovering the capacities of war-torn societies, *Third World Quarterly*, 23 (5), pp 817–835.

Berger, P (2002). *Holy War Inc: Inside the secret World of Osama Bin Laden* (New York: Simon and Schuster).

Bhatia, M (2003) *War and Intervention Issues for Contemporary Operations* (Bloomfield, CT: Kumarian Press).

Brookings Institution (2005) *Iraq Index: Tracking Variables of Reconstruction and Security in Post-Saddam Iraq* (Washington, DC: Brookings Institution).

Bullion, A (1995) *India, Sri Lanka and the Tamil crisis 1976–1994* (London: Pinter).

Bunker, R & Marin, S (1999) *Executive Outcomes: Mercenary Corporation OSINT Guide*, at http://disinfopedia.org/wiki.phtml?title = Executive_Outcomes, accessed 30 June 2004.

Byman, D (2003) Constructing a democratic Iraq: challenges and opportunities, *International Security*, 28 (1), pp 47–78.

Cannadi, J & Dollery, B (2004) An evaluation of private sector provision of public infrastructure in local government, Melbourne: Working Paper Series in Economics, University of New England: Australia.

Chambers, R (1998) *Challenging the Professions* (London: Intermediate Technology Publications).

Chambers, R (2002) *Participatory Workshops: A Sourcebook of 21 sets of Ideas and Activities* (London: Intermediate Technology Publications).

Chatterjee, P (2004) Controversial commando wins Iraq contract, special contribution to CorpWatch, at http://www.warprofiteers.com/article.php?id = 11350, accessed 16 July 2004.

Cilliers, J & Mason, P (1999) *Africa: From the Privatisation of Security to the Privatisation of War* (Cape Town: Institute for Security Studies).

Collier, P, Elliot, V, Hegre, H, Hoeffler, A, Reynal-Querol, M & Sambanis, N (2003) *Breaking the Conflict Trap: Civil War and Development Policy* (Washington, DC and Oxford: World Bank/Oxford University Press).

Coady, C (2002) *Humanitarian Action and Private Security Companies* (London: International Alert).

Diamond, L (2004) What went wrong in Iraq?, *Foreign Affairs*, September/October, 2004, pp 34–56.

Duffield, M (2001) *Global Governance and the New Wars* (London: Zed Books).

Graham, D & Freeman, C (2002) Policing is the key: rebuilding the internal security architecture of post-war Iraq, *Iraq Backgrounder: What Lies Beneath*, ICH Middle East Report No 6, 1 October 2002.

Duffy, M (2004) When private armies take to the front lines, *Time*, 6 October 2004, pp 28–29.

Hall, B & Biersteker, T (eds) (2002) *The Emergence of Private Authority in Global Governance* (Cambridge: Cambridge University Press).

Hansen, G (2004) Humanitarian action in Iraq—emerging constraints and challenges, *Humanitarianism and War Project* Tufts University, www.hwproject.tufts.edu.

Harding, T (2005) Crisis as SAS men quit for lucrative Iraq jobs: regimental chiefs plead loyalty to halt exodus to private security work, *Daily Telegraph*, 14 February 2005.

Haughton, J (1998) *The Reconstruction of War-Torn Economies*, Technical Paper (Cambridge, MA: Harvard Institute for International Development).

Hippel, K von (2004) Back-pedalling in Iraq, *Conflict, Security and Development*, 4 (1), pp 79–89.

Howe, H (2001) *Ambiguous Order: Military Forces in African States* (London: Lynne Rienner Publishers).

Human Rights Watch (2004) Legal aspects of the ongoing fighting in Iraq, at www.hrw.org.

ICRC (1995) *26th International Conference of the Red Cross and Red Crescent, 1995*, Report no 310, pp 139–151 (Geneva: ICRC).

Ipsen, K. (1999) Combatants and non-combatants, in: D Fleck (ed), *The Handbook of Humanitarian Law in Armed Conflict* (Oxford: Oxford University Press).

Klein, N (2003) 'Iraq is not America's to sell' *Guardian*, 7 November 2003.

MacGinty, R (2003) The pre war reconstruction of post war Iraq, *Third World Quarterly*, 24(4).

MacGinty, R & Darby, J (eds) (2003) *Contemporary Peace Making: Conflict, Violence and Peace Processes* (London: Macmillan Palgrave).

Malla, H (2004) Divisive force, *The World Today*, 60 (7) 2004, pp 5–6.

Muthien, B & Taylor, I (2002) The return of dogs of war, in B Hall & T Biersteker (eds), *The Emergence of Private Authority in Global Governance* (Cambridge: Cambridge University Press).

Observer (2004) Soldiers of fortune hit the jackpot, 6 October 2004.

Pirnie, B & Francisco, C (1998) *Assessing Requirements for Peacekeeping, Humanitarian Assistance and Disaster Relief* (Santa Monica, CA: Rand).

Reno, W (2004) Order and commerce in turbulent areas: 19th century lessons, 21st century practice, *Third World Quarterly*, 25 (4), pp 607–625.

Ritter, S (2002) *End Game: Solving the Iraq Crisis* (New York: Simon and Schuster).

Simons, D (2004) Occupation for hire: private military companies and their role in Iraq, *RUSI Journal*, 149 (3), pp 68–71.

Shaw, T (2002) Peace-building partnerships and human security, in: V Desai & R Potter, *The Companion to Development Studies*, pp 449–453 (London: Arnold).

Shawcross, W (2000) *Deliver Us from Evil* (London: Bloomsbury).

Slim, H (1997) *Doing the Right Thing: Relief Agencies, Moral Dilemmas and Moral Responsibility in Political Emergencies and War*, Studies on Emergencies and Disaster Relief No 6 (Uppsala: Nordiska Afrikainstitutet).

Studer, M (2001) The ICRC and civil–military relations in armed conflict, *International Review of the Red Crescent*, 83 (842), pp 367–390.
Todaro, M (2000) *Economic Development* (Harlow: Longman).
Van Brabant, K (1998) Cool ground for aid providers: towards better security management in aid agencies, *Disasters*, 22 (2), 1998, pp 109–125.
Walker, P (2004) What does it mean to be a professional humanitarian?, *Journal of Humanitarian Assistance*, 5.
Whyte, D (2003) Lethal regulation: state–corporate crime and the United Kingdom government's new mercenaries, *Journal of Law and Society*, 30 (4), 2003, pp 576–600.
Woodward, S (2001) Humanitarian war: a new consensus?, *Disasters*, 25 (4), pp 331–344.

Lessons and Controversies: planning and executing immediate relief in the aftermath of the war in Iraq

FREDERICK M BURKLE, JR, BRADLEY A WOODRUFF & ERIC K NOJI

ABSTRACT *The international community since the end of the Cold War has failed to agree on a satisfactory solution as to how it should respond to protect vulnerable populations at risk from internal state wars and human rights abuse. Western powers frustrated by this have increasingly resorted to intervention on the basis of 'right to intervene'. This paper argues that what is required is for the international community to exercise 'a right to protect' through the UN. Meanwhile the USA since 9/11 has gone down the route of unilateral intervention on the basis of 'self-defence' and in the case of Iraq has extended this concept by placing humanitarian as well as military operations under the single command of the Defense Department. The paper demonstrates how this led to the exclusion of expertise from planning, co-ordination and professional support in the field of humanitarian work. The operational lessons learned are listed and the conclusion is reached that, to avoid the problems experienced in Iraq, military and humanitarian operations should as far as possible be separated, leaving the leadership of relief to the dedicated international agencies but setting ground rules for liaison and lateral communication with the military which leave humanitarian response outside the political arena. A necessary condition for this would be the reform of the legal framework for UN response.*

Background

As the world community entered the 21st century it faced the reality that more people were being killed by their own countrymen than by outside forces. The outmoded language of the 1945 UN Charter primarily addresses cross-border wars, but is clearly ineffectual in dealing with the complicated politically driven internal conflicts and genocide that now dominate the list of human-induced disasters. At the core of debate and dispute is the UN Charter's Article 2, which does not authorise the UN to intervene in matters which are essentially within the domestic jurisdiction of any nation-state. Demands by the international community to 'do something' to protect a vulnerable population from grave harm from internal nation-state war and conflict have led to divisiveness among UN member states. Disillusionment over the lack of UN political will to address this problem threatens the future existence of this international body. When the UN Security Council has responded it has done so without a consistent, timely and effective mandate, especially in Africa.

Models of response

In 1999 the UN demonstrated success in quelling an internal conflict in East Timor through a multinational action under a UN Charter *Chapter VII* (Peace Enforcement) Security Council Resolution. This *multinational response model* approach, albeit evolving over time, is based on the 'right to intervene' and requires military intervention to stop the violence, reduce civilian mortality and morbidity, and strictly monitor human rights and international humanitarian law abuses until safe enough for the UN agencies, ngos, and other international relief organizations (iros) to enter the theatre of war. Once a peace agreement or accord is signed, a transition to a *Chapter VI* (Peacekeeping) force is prescribed (Burkle, 1999). However, the multinational model has its detractors, who claim inconsistencies from weak UN political guidance, lack of UN operational authority over troops of donor countries, deficiencies in operational command and control, and insufficient logistical support components, and political will to sustain the missions beyond the end of the initial military intervention (Western, 2004).The sovereignty-based political will to support the 'right to intervene' or not is re-debated with each Security Council Resolution. The NATO military action in Kosovo was the result of increasing frustration in the West with UN Security Council inaction. In 2002 this debate led the international community to concur that sovereign states, to remain sovereign, have the responsibility to protect their citizens. Under this model the UN would define circumstances of intervention as actual or apprehended large-scale loss of life, and genocidal intention: the UN would have the obligation to intervene by authorising force if necessary. Political will to take action in a sovereign nation-state where protection is either not exercised or refused would be based, not on the 'right to intervene', but rather on the concept of 'responsibility to protect' (Evans & Sahnoun, 2002; Roth, 2004).

Political action translates into military action. Both peacekeeping and peace enforcement are inherently political. The non-political component is assumed to represent humanitarian relief. In most situations the iros have historically retained overall leadership and control of humanitarian assistance, something that is felt to be essential for maintaining the neutrality of relief workers. However, the frustration directed at UN Security Council inaction spilled over to traditional UN sanctioned iros that were often perceived by Western observers to be bureaucratically ineffective, inefficient, and often responsible for prolonging the conflict by unwittingly providing succour to warring factions through their relief programmes.

Since the Balkan wars the military, with increased autonomy from traditional UN approaches to relief, have increased their engagement in humanitarian projects, such as community health and food programmes. The iros feel these programmes contribute to insecurity by blurring the lines between civilian and military functions, and falsely associate them with the military forces (Burkle,1999; USAID/OFTA, 1998). With increasing security problems world-wide, most will acknowledge the reality that military involvement is often essential in providing intelligence, security and logistical support to international relief organizations. However, the iros suggest the military should provide the necessary protection to ensure relief but humanitarian programmes should remain with humanitarian organisations.

Since 9/11 the USA, with its unrivalled military power, has reasserted its dominant role in international security by increasing attention to protracted crises and failed states considered bastions of terrorism (Roth, 2004). The USA developed a common strategy against Saddam Hussein's regime in Iraq that called for action based on a worst-case scenario involving threats of weapons of mass destruction (WMD), and a best-case scenario if rapid intervention would occur. The USA, along with coalition partners, disapproved of the political position and apparent lack of support from the UN Security Council and chose a *unilateral non–Chapter VII* model approach to invade Iraq (Burkle & Noji, 2004). The USA based its intervention on a country's *right to self-defence,* and not its right, or obligation, to intervene elsewhere to protect people other than their own (Evans & Sahnoun, 2002). In addition, the intervention was first considered a war to remove a hostile regime. A major humanitarian component to the war was considered unlikely. This unilateral action began a world-wide *unilateralism versus multilateralism* policy debate that exists to this day.

Planning for war

In late 2002 US government planners, influenced by a State Department-led 'Futures of Iraq' programme, considered many possible outcomes to an invasion and assumed they might face a humanitarian catastrophe (Schmitt & Brinkley, 2003). This was based on evidence that civilian health was substantially worse than in 1990, which would be especially critical if WMD were used against already vulnerable populations. Critical indicators that had suffered decline over the previous decade were as follows:

- infant mortality rates rose from 47.1 to 108/1000 live births;
- under age five mortality rates rose from 56 to 131/1000 live births;
- acute malnutrition rose from 3.6% to 11% in 1996, then declined to 4% in 2003 because of extensive UN agency- and NGO-facilitated Iraqi feeding programmes;
- there were increases in reported cases of tuberculosis, cholera, typhoid fever, amoebic dysentery, giardiasis, leishmaniasis and malaria (UNICEF;

1996; 1999; 2002; WHO, 2003a). These increases cases may reflect improvements in WHO- and UNICEF-facilitated training of Iraqi health personnel in disease reporting and outbreak investigation.

Traditionally, in such a humanitarian emergency, the State Department's US Agency for International Development (USAID) and its Office of Foreign Disaster Assistance (OFDA) deploy an operational on-site Disaster Assistance Response Team (DART) in response to natural, technological and humanitarian emergencies (Foreign Assistance Act, 1961). DART is primarily involved in assessment, co-ordination of technical assistance, development of project proposals, procurement of materiel, liaison with the military, and liaison and funding of UN and IRO programmes for immediate relief. In preparation for the war, the DART planned to provide emergency lifesaving health interventions in order to serve as a 'bridge' for up to 30 days until the iros and Iraqi national technical staff could fully re-engage. Typically, a DART includes fewer than 10 people, who are primarily involved in assessment, co-ordination of technical assistance, development of project proposals and procurement of materiel. Because of the unpredictable consequences of the anticipated conflict, the DART included 80 people, most with previous experience in complex emergencies. Specific experience included refugee care, human rights abuse and protection, epidemiology, military liaison, information management and communications, public affairs, security, environmental toxicology and biological, chemical and nuclear threat analysis. All DART members received unprecedented training ranging from chemical, biological and radiation preparedness to human rights abuse and protection procedures and anti-terrorist driving.

Simultaneously, the Department of Defense (DoD) established a Humanitarian Planning Team (HPT) instructed to conduct pre-war planning of the military Central Command (CentCom) humanitarian response (see Figure. 1), including health, and to co-ordinate those responses during the conflict. Confusion first occurred when the HPT claimed to the iros that they were the official humanitarian liaison for the US government. Many non-governmental organisations chose not to work with the military. This policy resulted in some iros questioning why USAID and other State Department offices, with whom many had established good working relationships, were not being used, and led many to believe that the planning for war might be a hoax perpetrated to drive the Saddam regime out of power. The situation was further complicated by the fact that the HPT, citing secrecy, refused to disclose crucial information needed for planning, not only to iros but also to other US military, governmental and civilian agencies working on humanitarian relief. Both USAID and the State Department's Bureau of Population, Refugees and Migration (BPRM) had representatives on the HPT, but they could not share any information with their State Department offices. In effect, the HPT became the official liaison, and unbeknown to USAID, the two planning bodies took increasingly divergent tracks.

With increased build-up of the military in Kuwait, the DoD and Coalition Forces established a Humanitarian Operations Center (HOC) in Kuwait City with the assistance of the Kuwaiti government. The HOC was to function as a clearing house for 'liaison and co-ordination' of civilian and military organisations providing humanitarian assistance. HOC activities included providing daily operational and military security briefings, making available office space for organisations providing humanitarian assistance, issuing permits and visas to work in Kuwait and cross the border into Iraq with humanitarian supplies, and serving as the point of liaison for other military organisations and donor countries. Concerns over neutrality from the military led many Iros to attend HOC operational and security briefings and request the necessary permits; however, only one IRO chose to share office space at the HOC during the war and immediate relief phase.

In January 2003, under presidential directive, the Pentagon further broke with tradition and created the Office of Reconstruction and Humanitarian Assistance (ORHA) (see Figure 1). Its job was to co-ordinate the relief and reconstruction efforts in Iraq with other US and Coalition relief organisations, and Iros. ORHA became the central US authority overseeing the efforts of the Coalition Forces (USA, UK, Australia, Poland, Denmark, Spain and Iraqi Kurdish militia) to provide humanitarian assistance during the crisis. ORHA was in charge of both operational and policy requirements in the areas of humanitarian relief, reconstruction, national and local governance, and external affairs. Concerns immediately surfaced within the State Department and USAID as to the legality, under the Congressional Foreign Assistance Act of 1961 establishing OFDA under USAID, of bringing the DART under the control of the DoD. The ongoing polemical debate was fed by discussion as to whether this presidential decision was simply a policy determination or a legal regulation.

Despite the fact that the UN did not sanction the war, iros, especially those with active programmes in Iraq, unofficially began internal planning for pre-conflict evacuation of expatriate staff and post-conflict recovery of services. There was concern that, given the already poor health situation in Iraq before the war, a major relief effort would be needed, requiring a co-ordinated effort of Iraqi nationals and iros to correct basic public health deficiencies, even without significant combat-related civilian casualties.

The iros attempted to plan for the likely humanitarian consequences of the war but they faced major obstacles. First, most organisations could not know if there would be war or not. This made it difficult to invest substantial time and resources in planning for an event which might or might not occur. Available funds for planning and propositioning supplies were limited because many major donor governments refused to commit resources to planning because of objections to the war. Appeals for funds could not be activated until organisations were sure the war would begin. Second, much of the humanitarian planning done by the major potential donor, the US government, was done by military authorities in relative secrecy. The usual source of US government humanitarian funds, OFDA and State Department's BPRM, were not fully aware of these military plans. This lack of knowledge of the principal donor government's intentions made co-ordinated planning difficult. Third, because ORHA was a part of the military force which would

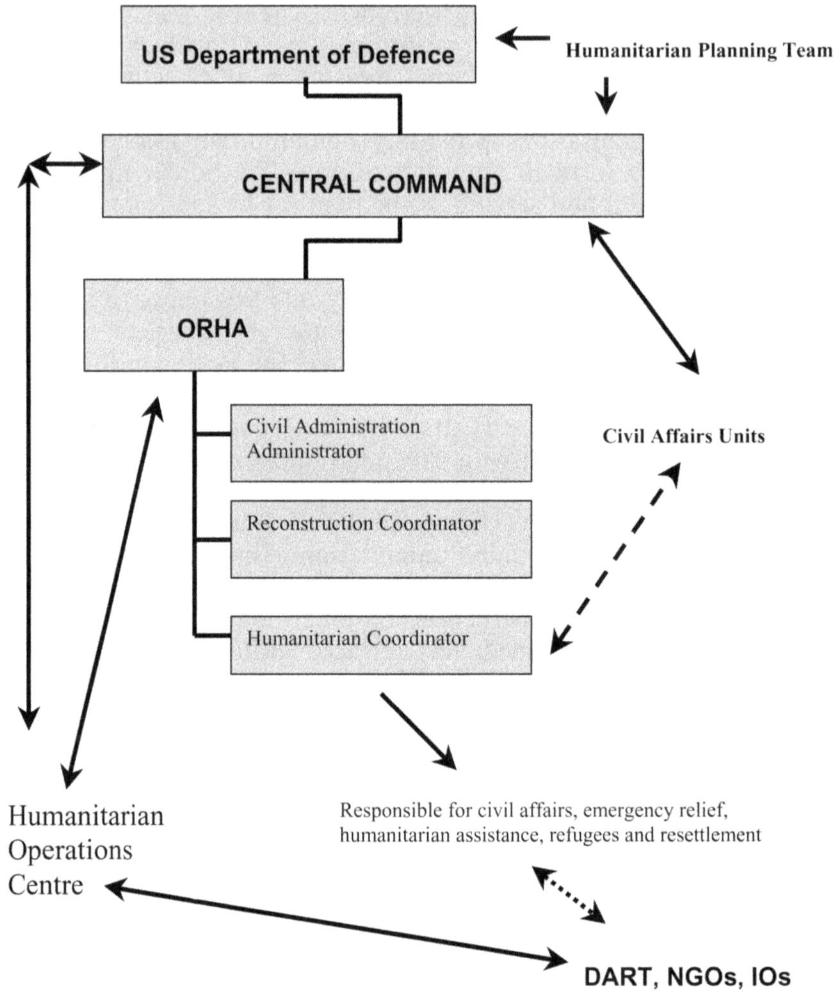

FIGURE 1.
US Department of Defense organisational chart for humanitarian assistance.

initiate the war, many organisations, including UN agencies and many ngos, feared losing independence and impartiality if they co-ordinated with or accepted US government funds.

By the start of hostilities, the following March 2003, the DoD had decided to ignore the State Department's 'Future of Iraq' task force findings in favour of assumptions that the war would be short and that it was unlikely there would be a major humanitarian crisis (Knight Rider News, 2003). DoD planners felt there would be little population displacement or public health infrastructure loss. The planners also assumed that reconstruction could be accomplished primarily by the private sector, funded by oil revenues and supported by a co-operative Iraqi population. There would be little need for the iros (McCarthy, 2003). The agencies which would provide most of the immediate humanitarian relief were Civil Affairs (CA) units of the US military and the DART. The military's CA units are comprised predominantly of reservists trained to work with US military commanders and local civil authorities to lessen the impact of military operations on the civilian population. CA specialists, including health professionals, are trained to systematically identify critical services and infrastructure needed by local citizens in war and disaster situations. However, the public health expertise of CA personnel was limited.

As it became clear that an invasion was all but certain, all expatriate UN personnel and their designated Regional Co-ordinators were evacuated to Cyprus and not allowed to return until the UN Security Co-ordinator had deemed the environment safe. The International Committee of the Red Cross (ICRC) planned to keep a small core group of expatriate (including the Head of Delegation) and national staff functioning during the conflict in Baghdad, Basra and northern Iraq. International Federation of Red Cross and Red Crescent (IFRC) Emergency Response Units (pre-packaged 150-bed mobile hospitals or clinics) were prepared for deployment. In general, the types of materials stockpiled and moved to advance positions were supplies that would be useful to treat acute combat and related injuries and illnesses, such as antibiotics, intravenous fluids and surgical supplies.

Outcome

On 19 March 2003, Coalition Forces moved from Kuwait into southern Iraq. By 14 April major combat was declared over in and around Baghdad, and on 1 May President Bush declared that the war was over.

WHO, which had provided guidance to iros by convening health co-ordination meetings in Kuwait City, later provided similar leadership in Basra in southern Iraq. During the war almost 20 health-related ngos with more than 250 international staff, with self-contained and staffed clinics and field hospitals, were either in place in surrounding countries or on standby for rapid deployment.

The conflict did not displace large numbers of people within the country nor create a flood of refugees across its borders. Fighting did not cause extensive damage to highways, bridges, power stations and other civil infrastructure. Chemical and biological weapons that US officials had said might be used now appear not to have existed. The US and Coalition military chose not to tally civilian deaths. However, by utilising a methodology developed for the war in Afghanistan using journalists' reports of war-related civilian deaths, one organisation estimated between 5966 and 7661 (1 January – 1 May 2003) civilians were killed in the war (Dardagan, 2003).

Instead, widespread looting and social disorder led to the destruction of public facilities and the disruption of essential public services. In many areas hospitals, clinics, pharmaceutical stores, public health departments, laboratories and administrative offices were ransacked, causing the collapse of the already tottering Iraqi health system (Blakemore, 2003; Physicians for

Human Rights, 2003; International Hospital Federation, 2003; WHO, 2003b; Valenciano *et al*, 2003; UN OCHA, 2003; Amnesty International, 2003a; Bacon & Rupp, 2003; Shanker, 2003; Senate Foreign Relations Committee, 2003). The greatest needs turned out not to be to be supplies to treat acute emergencies that had been stockpiled before the war but medicines for common chronic diseases of the largely urban population, such as cardiovascular drugs, and the critical diagnostic and therapeutic equipment needed to refurbish the looted laboratories and hospitals. In addition, the disruption of such essential services as electricity, water, police, judiciary, public transportation and communication systems made it impossible for patients to travel to obtain health care and for health workers to perform their jobs (WHO, 2003b; Valenciano *et al*, 2003). Lack of funds for salaries exacerbated already acute personnel shortages. The three major concerns most often cited by hospital directors and staff were the lack of security, water and electricity.

As the collapse of the hospital and public health system was occurring, the Coalition Forces initially maintained they were 'liberators' not occupying forces, forcing a debate as to responsibility for restoring essential services or providing security to the hospitals (Amnesty International, 2003b).

Relief efforts that had begun were hampered because security problems made it difficult for health assessment teams to visit sites safely. As a result assessments were rushed and incomplete. In areas newly open to humanitarian personnel security constraints prevented assessment teams from remaining overnight or establishing offices, leaving only a few hours in a day to complete the assessment. Moreover, changing security conditions sometimes made previously accessible areas inaccessible. Even when complete assessments of health facilities could be done, subsequent looting often made them rapidly obsolete.

For a short but crucial period of time, health officials had to depend on reports, often based on rumour, from military personnel within Iraq. CA units that were on the scene were unfortunately not trained in health assessment. The resulting information collected on assessment forms adapted from the UN's Office for the Co-ordination of Humanitarian Affairs (OCHA) varied considerably regarding the types of information collected, sometimes containing little or no information on primary health centres, public health capacity or civilian health status, such as mortality and morbidity indicators.

The ICRC and the IFRC continued the services they had provided before the war, including support for major hospitals. The Iraqi Red Crescent Society, perceived before the war as a potential source of volunteers who could assist in post-war relief, was not functioning during or after the war.

By the beginning of hostilities, the DART had been placed under administrative control of ORHA; however, it was to remain operationally independent. ORHA was rushed to Baghdad but soon realised that it lacked the expertise in assessment, field operations, security and communications that the DART possessed. Initially, the DART focused on the situation in southern Iraq, which was particularly poor. DART personnel, who had extensive communications systems, were deployed to the region and began to co-ordinate activities with international agencies. WHO assumed the role as lead agency for co-ordinating the restoration of curative health services in Iraq. Members of the DART, multiple UN agencies, ngos and military civil affairs units participated in WHO-led co-ordination meetings. The United Nations Children's Fund (UNICEF) officially assumed lead responsibility for education, nutrition, water and sanitation, mine clearing, child protection, and primary health prevention. WHO and DART personnel created a standardised health assessment form to assess health facilities and health status in Iraq.

Observations, recommendations and lessons learned

Planning

When multi-sectoral and multi-agency participants fail to plan and work in a co-ordinated fashion, mistakes will be made. The military remained 'vertical' in planning as USAID, DART and iros strived for a broader 'lateral' or 'parallel' decision-making and planning process. What limited preparation was done by iros occurred in an information vacuum. iros also suffered from inadequate funding. As a result, they were unable to respond swiftly.

The HPT was unprepared and ill-suited to the humanitarian task and appeared to be unaware of the functions, charter and capabilities of Iros. As a result, the HPT did not work with the iros to effectively harness their abilities and failed to appreciate the critical role they hold in humanitarian assistance, in transition to sustainable development, reconstruction, and transfer to civilian control as the military exits.

The HPT's penchant for secrecy caused confusion and denied Iros crucial information needed for planning.

The HPT's insistence that all liaison contacts go through its staff prevented non-military US humanitarian agencies, such as USIAD, which had a long history of serving as a liaison between the government and neutral iros, from salvaging the situation.

During pre-conflict planning it was USIAD that provided grants to UNICEF, WHO and an NGO consortium for health, water and sanitation that proved crucial during the war and the weeks immediately following the conflict. The squabble between DoD and the State Department over who controlled the DART and its assets should have been settled in Washington before deployment. This uncertainty placed the DART personnel in a difficult political and operational limbo that unnecessarily affected performance.

ORHA was primarily staffed by policy experts who lacked requisite relief experience and expertise, and were unfamiliar with critical issues surrounding field assessments. They did not have experience with multi-agency or multi-sectoral (humanitarian sectors of health, water and sanitation, shelter, food and fuel) decision making that was essential in understanding the diverse health roles and responsibilities across the iros and the military.

ORHA did not recognise the need to separate politics from relief and more broadly politics from public health. Pre-ORHA planning by the DART and iros strongly emphasised a decentralised public health approach to health governance. The DART Senior Medical Officer emphasised the critical need for a decentralised health outcome surveillance system approach. There existed four separate regional areas in Iraq (north, south, central and Baghdad), each with unique ethnic, tribal and religious differences, variations in health indices, security, and capacity and expectations for political governance. However, planning by ORHA emphasised a Baghdad-centric approach that dismissed the early development of a surveillance system.

Assessment

CA units acted with professionalism and good will and worked well with the iros. The iros were fully aware of the critical role these units had as an instrument of the occupying power in restoring essential services (International Hospital Federation, 2003; WHO, 2003b); Amnesty International, 2003b). However, CA units, consisting of 96% reserve forces, were under-supported, under-manned, under-prepared and under-utilised for the 'occupying power' responsibilities they faced.

In health the CA lacked needed public health expertise. For a short but crucial period of time health officials had to depend on reports often based on rumour from non-public health military personnel within Iraq. CA units on the scene were unfortunately not trained in health assessment.

The OCHA assessment form used by the CA units had a brief health section that emphasised structural loss to health facilities. Completed forms varied considerably regarding the types of information collected and the amount of detail and contained little or no information on functional capability of primary health centres, public health capacity, or civilian health indicators. Although CA units sometimes included physicians, nurses or other healthcare professionals, few had public health training or experience in rapid health assessment or outcome indicators.

A standardised health assessment and data collection form created by WHO and the DART only reached a few of the rapidly advancing CA units. As a result, most of the CA health assessments did not follow a standard format. Some CA assessments were 'classified' and therefore became unavailable to humanitarian organisations. For those assessments which were available, restrictions on the use of military communications channels made it impossible to contact the CA personnel who performed the assessments to obtain clarification or pose additional questions.

CA units should have gone through extensive training with standardised health assessment forms with assurance of a two-way communication link with public health experts in the rear. Rapid assessment, survey and surveillance requirements in humanitarian operations demand a co-ordinated effort by WHO.

Pre-conflict planning did not recognise the impact that delays in obtaining a permissive clearance from the HOC to cross into Iraq from Kuwait would have on the health assessment process. With time this situation did improve.

Immediate relief

Severe looting should have been anticipated by the DoD planners. Looting by both Iraqi civilians and military had occurred after the first Gulf war in Basra in the south and in Dohuk in the north. International relief workers had predicted that looting would occur but their warnings either never reached high echelon levels or were not heeded. This was symptomatic of a lack of military–civilian communication at levels that would have made sharing these concerns possible and credible. The resulting chaos confirmed that the unilateral US military-led relief operation had 'relatively untested capacities' (McCarthy, 2003) and lacked the expertise and resources for a complicated humanitarian effort.

US planners had been wrong to assume they would not need the assessments and assistance of the UN and IROS to restore security and public services after the war. ORHA challenged multi-agency support grants in health, questioning their political appropriateness and worth. Only as security worsened and health and water and sanitation delays occurred did ORHA seek the UN as a partner.

CA units were consistently unable to meet some of the most pressing needs discovered by their rapid health assessments. They did not usually have the orders or the necessary personnel or budget to provide large-scale health interventions. Also, because Coalition Forces moved rapidly within Iraq, their accompanying CA units may have conducted assessments only to be moved to a new location before they could take any action. As a response to these difficulties, personnel in the HOC attempted to review assessment reports to identify high-priority needs and match available humanitarian resources to those needs; however, many needs identified initially remained unmet.

When the DART was eventually placed under administrative control of ORHA the consequences to staff time and relationships were often wasteful and damaging. Nevertheless, the DART remained effective and efficient in developing and monitoring relief programmes, especially in southern and northern Iraq. The DART, UNICEF and WHO rapidly worked to re-establish core public health functions: first surveillance, then disease control measures such as vaccination, outbreak control and a reliable public health laboratory. Attention to other problems, such as access to chronic disease medications, diagnostic and therapeutic equipment such as dialysis, cardiac monitors, and defibrillators, came slowly.

The pre-conflict 10-year experience of WHO and UNICEF in Iraq proved to be invaluable in jump-starting the health and water and sanitation systems (WHO, 2003c: 1–7). Despite poor funding, WHO training of Iraqi nationals in surveillance and outbreak control, and the stockpiling of pharmaceuticals and emergency therapeutic centres by UNICEF, proved life-saving. Many others remained in a 'catch-up' mode that delayed their ability to optimise their early participation.

Security

Security and social disorder became the overriding concern in dealing with health intervention programmes and accounted for the failure of a rapid return to function of clinical and public health facilities.

Public health capacity (disease reporting and outbreak investigation) was severely compromised by lack of security.

As iros moved into Iraq, they found that the HOC was failing to provide good threat trend and security analyses, on which relief agencies depended to protect their staff. The HOC were challenged to provide credible intelligence to the iros once conventional combat activities were over and the evolving asymmetrical guerrilla type of warfare emerged. The HOC needed to be able to adjust to evolving operational and security requirements, and to be prepared to provide this non-battle intelligence and communication as an equal priority. What iros considered critical to daily security decision making, programme and living locations, and the hiring and safety of national and expatriate staff, differed from that of the military. For some in the NGO community the failure of the military to be as 'interested and sensitive' to these non-traditional security concerns of the iros underscored any lingering mistrust they had in the motives of the military. Iros, who employed their own security personnel, attempted to fill in the intelligence and security planning gaps through their own assessments. It would be useful for military intelligence and security elements to work and learn from experienced IRO security personnel who come from a different operational background.

Training

DART training was broad and first thought by some to be wasteful. Because two DART members were ambushed early on in Baghdad, the training in anti-terrorism security, security assessments and security communications in adverse environments proved life-saving.

There was a limited number of adequately trained Chemical, Biological, Radiation, Nuclear, and Explosive (CBRNE) support staff, equipment and procedural knowledge. Overall, health professionals serving the humanitarian community were not trained to deal with a CBRNE event. Evacuation from the area was the only operational strategy, one which would have ended humanitarian relief.

Unfortunately, this unconventional war in Iraq, as well as future complex humanitarian emergencies, may still require iros to train their staff in CBRNE risk assessment. Response planning must occur before deployment. Iros can only remain operational during a conflict if optimal security, protective, decontamination, isolation and management assets are available.

The media, embedded with the military, were preoccupied with the conduct of the war. Once combat was over, there was no plan for the media to engage with the relief community. The media, essential in getting the word out of a collapsing health care system, often remained preoccupied with rumours of epidemics, participating in exaggerating the gravity of reports of communicable diseases to the level of 'epidemics' and impatiently failing to understand the critical priority of disease investigation and outbreak control before any public health announcement. An accurate media portrayal of the public health situation is critical, especially when no other information system is available. It would serve the humanitarian community well to educate and embed members of the media in future humanitarian operations.

Discussion

In the run-up to the invasion in Iraq, the US administration's unilateral model gave the task of planning and the execution of humanitarian relief to the DoD. That relief effort is now widely perceived to have been mismanaged (Burkle & Noji, 2004). It would be best to keep the military out of the humanitarian business as much as possible and leave this task to US agencies that have traditionally handled humanitarian crises, and to iros. It is worrisome that DoD does not recognise and support the critical advantages of having the DART function as the US Congress intended under the Foreign Assistance Act of 1961. A military-led model runs the risk of side-stepping both OFDA and the DART and sets one standard for humanitarian assistance for war and conflict and another standard for conventional disasters. Arguably, the DART fulfils an essential role as an impartial broker to the iros that must be maintained. The military should learn to work with the DART and similar agencies and not try to replace them.

The iros have participated in various political–military–humanitarian models, all having limited success (Bacon & Rupp, 2003). Controversy centres on the appropriateness of combatants assuming traditional roles of iros such as community projects and food distribution. In future US military-led operations, the iros should not be marginalised as they were in Iraq. Much work must be done in asserting and educating for the roles that are performed best by the iros. Somehow, in the planning for Iraq, these IRO capacities were lost to either history or politics. The iros possess years of humanitarian experience, understand critical cross-cultural issues, work well in a lateral multi-agency environment, and maintain relief-related and field-tested resources such as emergency health kits. Their expertise cannot be replaced by marginalising the iros and favouring a private sector not yet functioning. That being said, a strong case can be made for reform in the IRO community. In humanitarian missions important inefficiencies remain unsettled. For example, whereas a strong WHO emergency response and surveillance team was sent to Kuwait during the prelude to the war, it was questioned whether this expertise could be sustained during the immediate relief phase by existing WHO country and regional organisation personnel. The operational tempo and tenor of emergency missions requires that WHO commit to educating and training multiple emergency response teams to supplement country teams and WHO Regional Organisations during a conflict, provide country-wide surveillance and health programme co-ordination, and maintain the functions of a ministry of health when one no longer exists.

What is lacking in the strategies and sharing of information between the DoD and iros in a military-led relief operation must be the focus in the future of transparent civil–military exercises and training that takes place before the emergency. Exercise scenarios should promote the advantages of lateral communications among agencies especially those that share sector responsibilities such as health and water and sanitation (Burkle & Hayden, 2001).

US State Department assets have extensive experience with relief operations and liaison duties between civilian and military agencies. Indeed, over the years, OFDA and similar agencies such as the UK's Department for International Development (DFID) have served as effective liaisons even between military officials of a belligerent party and the IRO community. Such liaisons are particularly crucial in the role where military officers must understand how iros operate to provide security and security communications to their organisations. Liaison must emphasise equal representation of the views of both sides, ensure that those in authority understand the mission, charter and capacity of the organisation and utilise only experienced professionals to complete the tasks (Burkle & Hayden, 2001).

ORHA lost valuable time in turning around the collapsing health system. People in leadership positions must have previous humanitarian, multi-agency and multi-sectoral policy and operational experience. In addition, the humanitarian community has for years emphasised the need to minimise bureaucracy to ensure the efficient delivery of relief. ORHA was an additional layer of bureaucracy designed to be a substitute for existing US agencies and was not successful in adding value to the relief process. It failed to serve, and generally impeded, immediate relief actions.

If the DoD insists on again taking the lead it must do it right. If the military-led humanitarian response is to be attempted in the future, then critical questions remain unanswered. Do these personnel have the appropriate multi-sectoral mix required of humanitarian operations? What transition and exit strategies will exist and who will participate? Will there be accountability for actions and who will monitor these? During the past decade minimum standards in disaster response and humanitarian assistance, called the Sphere Project, were developed for use by the iros and donor agencies (Sphere Project, 1998). Will these standards be followed by the new military-led unilateral model?

DoD needs additional active duty CA units. If not increased in number, they are at risk of losing this valuable resource through attrition. A call for a major increase in active duty CA units, first endorsed after Somalia in 1993, never materialised (Overseas Development Institute, 2003; McCaffrey, 2003; Civil Affairs Association, 2003). This is critical: given the excellent track record of CA assets in World War II, the lesson here is not so much what skills, training and levels of presence are necessary as that they need to be relearned.

Re-establishing security must take precedence over replacing looted equipment and supplies. Once security allows access, the first priority is always to rehabilitate the public health infrastructure and provide a surveillance mechanism based on outcome indicators (Roberts & Hoffman, 2004; Spiegel *et al*, 2001). Knowing this, the early health planning by the DART identified an outcome-based health surveillance system as the major public health priority. This was soon dismissed by the post-DART ORHA health authorities in favour of reporting health performance indicators that emphasised the reopening and stocking of hospitals and clinics as a measure of success. However, the question remains: can more stringent public health surveillance, critical to mitigating mortality and morbidity, be preserved during conflict? Historically, surveillance during conflict has never been fully supported and remains a gap area. The answer is found in evidence-based surveys successfully adapted to a conflict environment (Spiegel *et al*, 2001; Valenciano *et al*, 2003; Roberts *et al*, 2004). Pre-Iraq war excess mortality studies in countries in conflict proved worthwhile in the discovery of vulnerable populations and the outcome impact of violence on health indices. The recent application of these independent surveys suggests much greater civilian mortality rates than those portrayed in non-independent reports (Roberts *et al*, 2004). More qualitative surveillance studies suggest a rise in malnutrition and a near doubling of infant mortality rates (MEDACT, 2004). In a military-led model the current CA assets cannot fulfil all the evidence-based assessment and surveillance requirements required for the population they are entrusted to protect. Whatever the outcome, authority to co-ordinate surveillance should fall to WHO and its emergency response teams.

As a postscript to the background section of this article, on 16 October 2003, almost seven months since the beginning of hostilities, the UN Security Council passed Resolution 1511, setting a UN and international framework for security, political and economic progress in Iraq. This was adopted under the previously avoided *Chapter VII* of the UN Charter and called for the transfer of power from the Coalition Provisional Authority (which replaced ORHA) to the Iraqi people (UN Security Council Resolution 1500, 2003). Secretary General Annan delivered a sharply worded criticism claiming that unilateralism posed a serious challenge to UN principles. If this military model of intervention 'were to be adopted, it could set precedents that will result in a proliferation of unilateral and lawless use of force, with or without justification' (Annan, 2003).

Conclusions

The lessons from this experience will have an impact on how relief operations in complex humanitarian crises will be executed in the future. Many lessons learned will not surprise experienced professionals in the humanitarian community who forged solutions through a former multinational model. If heeded by the US government, they could have been avoided. Other lessons suffer legal, political, bureaucratic and institutional paralysis, and have done so for years. The UN is simply a Charter with an administration. The Security Council must beg and cajole its members for resources to respond to disasters, both natural and human-generated. A post-cold war opportunity to modernise has never materialised, resulting in impatient and often shameful finger pointing that repeats itself with each and every crisis. Specifically, the authors strongly recommend that, without a major UN Charter 'responsibility to protect' concept reform, one that addresses capacity to deal appropriately with genocide and internal conflict, confusion will continue to reign. Reform will not be successful without first addressing the full implementation of a UN Standing Task Force, under UN Charter Chapter VII, Article 43 (Dennehy *et al*, 1993), which enjoys the recognition, integrity, credibility and support of all UN member states. Arguably, without UN reform, *no* model of response will provide the necessary response to internal conflict and genocide. Furthermore, failure of reform will allow for future 'right to self-defence' responses to be commonplace and risk the ultimate disappearance of the UN.

Relief, whatever model emerges, should be left to those agencies and organisations with the expertise. If the military insists on unilateral control, as it would in a 'right to self-defence' model, it must develop the capabilities, from leadership to robust CA units to provide critical services, such as assessments and threat trends, and capacities to recover essential services mandated under the Fourth Geneva Convention as an occupying power. If iros decide they are going to relate to the military, they are going to have to work with them, decide on the ground rules, and then work to build relationships and the prerequisite lateral communications (Burkle & Hayden, 2001) and information-sharing capabilities in order to avoid the problems experienced in Iraq.

Public health, in whatever model of response prevails, must be seen by a broader humanitarian community, including the military, as a critical strategic and security priority that takes precedence over politics. In relief operations, public health and humanitarian actions are paramount and must never be driven by political motives and ideologies.

Note

1 An earlier version of this article appeared in the *Lancet*, 364, 9 October 2004, pp 1371–1375. The opinions and assertions herein are those of the authors only and should not be construed as official or representing the views of the US Public Health Service, US Agency for International Development, the Department of Defense or the US Government.

References

Amnesty International Iraq (2003a) Looting, lawlessness and humanitarian consequences, 11 April, at http://www.reliefweb.net/w/rwb.nsf/VOCHARUA11LatestEmergencyResponse/273C2CD2, accessed 1 August 2003.

Amnesty International Iraq (2003b) Responsibilities of the occupying powers, at http://www.amnesty.org.nz/web/Pages/home.nsf/0/d1b276cc2a0d0cc256d0a00077f80, accessed 21 August, 2003.

Annan, K (2003) Address to General Assembly on dangers of pre-emption, 23 September, at http://www.iraqcrisis.co.uk/resources.php?idtag = R3FE18083B258, accessed 20 December 2004.

Bacon, KH & Rupp, G (2003) Unready for the aftermath: Refugees International and International Committee: US unprepared for humanitarian problems in Iraq, *Washington Post*, 7 March.

Blakemore, B (2003) Robbed at the hospital: looters leave medical facilities in shambles, medicine in short supply, ABC News, Baghdad, 19 April, at http://printerfriendly.abcnews.com/printerfriendly/Print?-fetchFromGLUE = true&GlueSe, accessed 3 June 2003.

Burkle, FM (1999) Lessons learnt and future expectations of complex emergencies, *British Medical Journal*, 319, pp 422–426.

Burkle, FM & Hayden, R (2001) The concept of assisted management of large-scale disasters by horizontal organizations, *Prehospital Disaster Medicine*, 16 (3), pp 128–137.

Burkle, FM & Noji, EK (2004) Health and politics in the 2003 war with Iraq: lessons learned, *Lancet*, 364 (9442), pp 1371–1375.

Civil Affairs Association (2003) Minutes of the Board of Directors Meeting, 18 January.

Dardagan, H (2003) Iraq body count, at www.iraqbodycount.org, accessed 22 June.

Dennehy, EJ, Doll, WJ, Harper, GP *et al* (1993) A blue helmet combat force, Harvard University, National Security Program Policy Analysis Paper 1993-01.

Evans, G & Sahnoun, M (2002) The responsibility to protect, *Foreign Affairs*, 81 (6), pp 99–110.

Foreign Assistance Act (1961) US Congress (75 Stat. 424) and Executive Order 10973: Administration of Foreign Assistance and Related Functions, The White House, 3 November.

International Hospital Federation (2003) Informer: Iraq hospitals under pressure from looting and anarchy, 15 April, at http://www.hospitalmanagement.net/informer/breakthroughs/break240/, accessed 12 June 2003.

Knight Ridder News (2003) Analysis: US failed to plan for postwar Iraq, 13 July, at http://www.montanaforum.com/rednews/2003/07/13/build/safety/q-postwar.php?nnn = 6, accessed 2 June 2004.

McCaffrey, BR (2003) We need more troops, *Wall Street Journal Online*, 29 July, at http://www.washspkrs.com/prod_images/pdfs/ACF30D.pdf, accessed 20 August 2003.

McCarthy, M (2003) US military plans to lead relief efforts in Iraq, Special report, *Lancet*, 361 (9358), p 629.

MEDACT (2004) Enduring effects of war: health in Iraq 2004, at www.medact.org, accessed 11 December 2004.

Overseas Development Institute (2003) Humanitarian principles and the conflict in Iraq, HPG Briefing Note, April, at www.odi.org.uk/hpg/, accessed 21 August 2003.

Physicians for Human Rights (2003) Research & Investigations: Bulletin #1, 9 April, at http://www.phrusa.org/research/iraq/bulletin_040903.html, accessed 12 June 2003.

Roberts, L & Hoffman, CA (2004) Assessing the impact of humanitarian assistance in the health sector, *Emerging Themes in Epidemiology*, 1(3), 2004, at http://www.ete-online.com/content/1/1/3, accessed 12 November 2004.

Roberts, L, Latfa, R, Garfield, R *et al* (2004) Mortality before and after the 2003 invasion of Iraq: cluster sample survey, *Lancet*, 364 (9445), pp 1857–1864.

Roth, K (2004) Setting the standard: justifying humanitarian intervention, *Harvard International Review*, 26 (1), pp 58–62.

Schmitt, E & Brinkley, J (2003) But nobody listened: State Department study foresaw trouble now plaguing Iraq, *New York Times*, Oct 19, 2003: Late Edition–Final, section 1, columns, at http://www.nytimes.com/2003/10/19/international/worldspecial/19POST.html, accessed 12 December 2003.

Senate Foreign Relations Committee (2003) Hearing: Humanitarian Consequences related to Iraq, Statement of Record: International Rescue Committee: Testimony of Sandra Mitchell, US Senate, 11 March, p 4.

Shanker, T (2003) Safety and jobs are top issues for Iraq, Pentagon advisers say, *New York Times*, 18 July 2003, p 10.

Sphere Project (1998) *Humanitarian Charter and Minimum Standards in Disaster Response*, pp 2–56 (Geneva: First Edition).

Spiegel, P, Burkle, FM, Dey, CC & Salama, PL (2001) Developing public health indicators in complex emergency response, *Prehospital and Disaster Medicine*, 16, pp 281–285.

UN OCHA Integrated Regional Information Network (2003) Iraq: struggle to restore basic services, Relief web, 15 May 2003, at http://www.reliefweb.int/w/rwb.nsf/480fa8736b88bbc3c12564f6004c8ad5/ea52d8fdc062/, accessed 1 August 2003.

UN Security Council Resolution 1500 (2003) Adopted 16 October 2003, New York, S/RES/1511.

UNICEF (1996) *Multiple Indicator Cluster Sample (MICS-1996)* (Baghdad: UNICEF, Central Statistical Office and Ministry of Health Iraq).

UNICEF (1999) *Child and Maternal Mortality Survey 1999*, Preliminary Report (New York: UNICEF and Ministry of Health Iraq).

UNICEF (2002) *Integrated Nutritional Status Survey of Under Five Years and Breastfeeding/Complementary Feeding Practices of Under Two Years in S/C Iraq* (New York and Baghdad: UNICEF and Ministry of Health Iraq).

USAID/OFDA (1998) Northern Iraq humanitarian programs, 1991–1996, Executive summary, *USAID/OFDA After Action Report*, pp 3–6 (Washington, DC: OFDA).

Valenciano, M, Coulombier, D, Cardozo, BL *et al* (2003) Challenges for communicable disease surveillance and control in Southern Iraq, April–May 2003, *Journal of the American Medical Association*, 290 (5), pp 1–5.

Western, J (2004) Doctrinal divisions: the politics of US military interventions, *Harvard International Review*, 26 (1), pp 46–50.

WHO (2003a) *Communicable Disease Profile—Iraq* (Geneva: World Health Organisation).

WHO (2003b) *Iraq Brief for June 6,, 2003* (Geneva: World Health Organisation).

WHO (2003c) *Jump-starting the Health System in Iraq: Context and Approaches, Immediate Objectives, Activities, Milestones and Medium/Long Term Goals*, pp 1–7 (Geneva: World Health Organisation).

War and the Cultural Heritage of Iraq: a sadly mismanaged affair

JOHN WARREN

ABSTRACT *The irony of the invasion and occupation of Iraq is that nations that believe they represent the acme of human progress have, by their own ignorance and incompetence, wreaked havoc in one of the oldest lands of human civilisation in response to a perceived threat that simply did not exist. With all the current rhetoric that the imposition of a Western model of reconstruction upon Iraq implies, it is useful to remind ourselves that Iraq has a cultural heritage that spans some 7000 years of civilisation. Through art, scholarship, philosophy, medicine, engineering and religion Iraq has consolidated its position as a country where true civilising values have influenced the world as opposed to those of unilateral action, false pretexts and strategic interest. From the study of Iraq's long history the paper concludes that it is cultural and social continuity which provide the thread of progress and regeneration, suggesting that Iraq's own cultural traditions of conflict resolution can provide the key to peace with the aggressors.*

In an era when perceptions of human destiny grow increasingly coherent, when education is vastly wider and when the body of knowledge is so hugely enlarged, it is deeply disturbing that an event can occur which sets back our hopes as profoundly as the Bush/Blair attack on Iraq. It is not simply the 100 000 Iraqi dead (the large majority innocent of offence);[1] it is not even the motivation where power commands oil, although both are significant in terms of setting back human aspirations. It is the sheer nature of the conflict. Nations which imagine themselves at the acme of progress have adopted the bully-boy tactics of the children's playground to smash into submission one of the oldest lands of human civilisation. What is profound and fundamental in this conflict is that it was totally unnecessary. There was no threat. The pretended cause simply did not exist.

How many times since cities first arose in the land between the rivers has this land been devastated, and with no more reason than greed for land or resources? The history of Iraq has been a story of cultural evolution in slow steps interrupted by the wars of the power hungry, even sadly into this century.

The prime ancestor of all human kind, Mitochondrial Eve,[2] almost certainly lived in Africa rather than in that legendary Garden of Eden between the Tigris and the Euphrates, but when humans had come out of Africa, it was in this great river basin primarily that the tribes first welded human lifestyle into the complex organisation of cities. Where history reaches so very far back, memory is supplanted by legend, in which the distant haze is pinpricked by the clarity of an occasional archaeological searchlight. At the furthest reaches a first flush of cities, indefinite but undeniable, appears in southern Iraq some 7000 years ago. Specialist trades such as metal working, coupled with writing and formal religious culture, identify consolidated urban development which by 3000 BCE had produced the rich heritage of intensively organised cities whose remains have come down to us at archaeological levels and survive in standing monuments, such as the earliest ziggurats, and in traces of canal systems. Importantly we understand them better perhaps than any ancient civilisation because so much has survived of their daily life in the form of the written records—the huge libraries of cuneiform (inscribed tablets, many still awaiting translation)—and graphic pictorial records on bas-relief panels.

The mismanagement of this affair sadly includes failure to anticipate cultural chaos. The mute incompetence which presumed that Iraq would emerge from its doorways clutching American flags was matched by the dream that Saddam's capture would blossom into national compliance. Dissolution of the Iraqi army and police compounded the blunder and lack of evident arrangements for the protection of cultural property provided a huge window for looting both at archaeological sites and in the collections, particularly the great national collection of the Baghdad Museum, by any standards one of the world's foremost repositories of material relating to ancient civilisations.

A crucial difference between the past and present is the widespread modern market in antiquities, much of it in the USA itself. The cupidity of collectors fuels the drive to loot museums and pillage sites as never before. Failure to anticipate this fallout of war and disorder must represent a signal failure to honour the terms of the Hague Convention on Cultural Property.

Shortly after the invasion of Iraq, by 10 April, the fabric of Iraqi society was in tatters and evidence was emerging of serious danger to the artefacts in the collections and on the archaeological sites.[3] In the absence of a protective military response under the terms of the Hague Convention on the Protection of Cultural Property, staff at the Iraq Museum took what action they could, with the result that losses from display items have been estimated as limited to about 5% of the items of greatest interest on public display and 9800 items in storage. This loss amounts to some 2% of the half a million items in the museum's collections[4]—a number which might have been far greater but for the tenacity and determination of museum staff who had, in some cases, to resort to arms to protect national property. The museum compound became momentarily defended by government forces and then a battle-damaged trophy. Only later in June 2003 did it take on the aspect of a protected fortress with a battle tank stationed in the entrance. In many cases isolated archaeological sites were offered no such protection, and have fallen prey to looters with as yet no measurable results of loss.[5]

It is the most visible and attractive objects of antiquity that are on display and most at risk. The greed of collectors, the connivance of middlemen and the determination of looters is a fearsome combination, aided sometimes by corruption among staff. The losses, therefore, may include many of the prime items, among them treasures recovered by Sir Leonard Woolley from Ur, and apparently a substantial number of ivory cylinder seals. The worst of the looting was evidently carried out by astute and well informed robbers who took the most valuable and attractive items, leaving replicas and copies untouched. Some 8500 objects on display are estimated to have disappeared.[6] Some were returned during an amnesty.

The National Museum in Baghdad was the prime repository of archaeological material and as such was afforded the greatest protection. None was given to the Museum of Manuscripts,[7] to other collections and museums elsewhere nor to sites where archaeological material was accessible. For the failure to anticipate the problems and to provide protection the US military bears heavy responsibility.

It is ironic that a cultural heritage continuous over 7000 years and persistently overrun by invaders with more than half an eye on the riches of its lands should, even in this 21st century, be made the target of armies invading on false pretexts: but this is more than an irony. Given the overwhelming force used and the wide cultural background knowledge available to the aggressors, it is a matter of profound incompetence that these prime reservoirs of historical knowledge should have been put again at risk and loss. The history of Iraq has been a sequence of disastrous losses to which this century has unwisely added another sad chapter.

Major floods, perhaps the Flood of legend and the Bible, added to the burden of man-made disasters but, with the aid of decipherable records emerging some 5000 years ago, the evidence can be reconstructed. Fine cultural objects are paralleled by written evidence of dynasties, rulers and lifestyle. Across central and southern Iraq in the so-called Jemdet Nasr period extending from Babylon to Qut in the south we know the culture collectively as Sumerian, but the lifestyle was that of local city states sharing a mutual background but not yet anywhere near nationhood.[8] They, even then, looked back to a distant past and recorded the dynasties and rulers preceding the Flood in what inevitably has become known as *The Book of Kings*.

This enormous cultural span gives Iraq (together perhaps with parts of riverine China, Egypt and possibly the Indus Basin) a valid claim to have been the longest cultural entity on the planet. Iraq has had a history of urban continuity second to none. Although this territory has never been ethnically simple, its mixture of population has, through most of history, had a fissured coherence which gave justification to the ultimate formation of a single state lying across most of Mesopotamia. From the time of the Greek invasion under Alexander until the 20th century, however, Mesopotamia formed part of one or another wider empire. For one remarkable and crucial period under the Abbasid Caliphs it was the capital of the largest empire in the mediaeval, world stretching from Morocco to the frontiers of China. Ultimately and almost by default the modern independent nation of Iraq emerged after World War I out of a fragment of the collapsed empire of the Ottoman Turks. At that point the bemused governments of Britain and British India found themselves in charge of an emergent nation sufficiently coherent to acquire a monarch and an independent status in the world.[9] Out of a mixture of Arab nationalism, Kurdish hopes and imperialist idealism a nation was forged. The same process of establishing a contemporary independent society is now repeated in the tragic aftermath of another invasion with uncomfortable parallels.

Surprisingly, at the outset of its cultural history, Iraq was home to an extraordinary mathematical florescence. With the emergence of the cuneiform script as pictograms and subsequently as phonograms it became possible to express not only the spoken word but the abstract complexities of mathematics.

The evolving cuneiform scripts of the Sumerian era embraced a mathematical system that has resonated through the ages, leaving a permanent mark on present society. 60 minutes of arc, 360 degrees of angle, 60 seconds in the minute of time, 60 minutes in the hour and 24 hours in the day all derive ultimately from the comprehensive arithmetic of ancient Iraq. Four thousand years ago cuneiform script shows the mathematicians of old Babylon using a complex system of notation where place values ran in units of 60. This allowed their two symbols, repeated in varying orders, to construct all the integers. Fractions, multiplication and division became straightforward and the sexigesimal system allowed the use of a wide range of factors, 60 being divisible by a remarkably large series of base numbers.[10] Even logarithms became accessible, although their usefulness in a contemporary sense was not understood. The later clumsy and inhibiting Greek and Roman systems of mathematics stand in discomforting contrast to this earlier and (geometry apart) more skilful system of calculation.[11]

With these sophisticated mathematical tools astronomical calculation became possible, the value of pi was identified and exploited while square roots were used to solve both practical and theoretical problems. Sumerian mathematicians even achieved and used solutions to the quadratic equation, a feat achieved by the Greeks only by the imprecise and difficult routes of geometry.

Sophisticated three-dimensional thinking and plan making is also evident at this stage in the third century BCE.[12] The earliest known physical planning derives from a clay tablet inscribed with plots, canals, roads, temples and settlements in Nippur, all identified by drawn boundaries and described in cuneiform

Intellectual resources of the calibre and the flexibility offered by the cuneiform script made it possible to organise, manage and control large communities with complex interactions and so the building of cities and the establishment of trading empires became feasible. Surviving tablets have been found to record even such mundane items of commerce as a computation of contents or 'delivery note' for a cartload of vegetables. Weightier matters were recorded *in extenso* to come down to us in the permanence of baked clay tablets.[13] Many tens of thousands of tablets have yet to be deciphered and translated. Out of this demanding and painstaking scholarship deeper understandings will emerge. The evident robbery of a number of collections is, therefore, the more to be regretted.

Calculation and speech were thus made timeless in Uruk (now Warka in southern Iraq) about 4000 BCE. Although some of the earliest languages remain indecipherable, there is, from the succeeding Sumerian and Akkadian periods, a wealth of comprehensible literature from an epoch embracing the city states of Uruk, Kish, Nippur and others across central and southern Iraq. The direct cultural influence of this vibrant heartland left evidence as far west as Mari (towards Aleppo on the Euphrates in Syria) and east as far as Kerman in the uplands of Iran. It was inevitable that power would coalesce around dynasties where populations pioneered the arts and culture of living in closely organised urban societies. An urban explosion between 4000 and 3000 BCE produced a plethora of city states by about 2000 BCE which we identify as Sumerian from their linguistic commonality—sharing a language apparently unrelated to any other and which died out after the Akkadian conquests of 2300 BCE under Sargon I.[14] Sumer had dominated southern Iraq and Akkad the central area round present day Baghdad and the north around Mosul. The Akkadian grouping was also linguistically based but in this case the language was Semitic. It evolved through Babylonian and Assyrian to father Aramaic, Hebrew and most importantly Arabic, now the common language of Iraq and surrounding regions. With language had come literature in the form of factual record, myth, recitation and the literary epic. The story of Gilgamesh is pre-eminent among the many Sumerian myths and is itself a coalescence of preceding tales. It tells of the hero of the Flood—perhaps the Flood of Noah—which 'swept through the lands for seven days and seven nights...until the sun returned and brought daylight to Heaven and Earth...and the rays of the sun came into the great ship'. The version of the epic from the library of Nineveh runs across 12 closely inscribed tablets. The legend recurs in several sources.[15] Another myth recounts the rebuilding of the devastated temples by Gudea,[16] and others describe in detail such pacific enterprises as trading voyages and market practices regulating internal trade, as well as commerce by sea to the further reaches of the Gulf and even to the Indus.

With urban expansion and the organisation of populations came building on a monumental scale. Rulers now demonstrated the aggregation of their powers in the building of ziggurats, as monumental as the pyramids but unlike them at once citadel and home of the gods rather than tombs. The great stepped ziggurats, which included those at Ur, Agadai, Eridu, Uruk, Lassa, Ashur, Borshippar, Nippur and above all at Babylon, were huge structures of solid masonry rising by multiple terraces to a temple complex on the upper platform. Babylon, with its ziggurat shrine to the god Marduk, came to dominate the region but by 1595 BCE its dynasty had peaked and was at an end. The Akkadian empire had faded. Through the confusions of the subsequent 'dark age' the Assyrians emerged to dominate the region in the last millennium BCE from a heartland in northern Iraq. At this point begins the age of eight Mesopotamian empires, where the dominant powers embraced not only Babylonia and Akkadia but extended into Palestine and Anatolia and the Iranian uplands. Administrative skills had grown and empire building had moved up in scale. The Assyrian capital moved north to Kalhu (now Nimrud near Mosul) where a 15-kilometre wall enclosed the city and palace. There huge bas-relief panels have survived to provide graphic proof of its history and artistic capabilities. A new cultural vigour was apparent.

Iraq, as Akkadia, Sumeria and Assyria, had established (in parallel with Egypt) a rich artistic legacy in the arts of sculpture, ceramics, fabrics, goldsmithing, jewellery and works in the baser metals. Mathematics, literature and expressive forms of music and poetry were at the forefront of cultural achievement in the middle of the first millennium BCE when the first evidence of Greek intellectual power became apparent in the region. Long before this the earliest detailed written codes of law had been promulgated. A tradition of laws established over a millennium reached an apotheosis in the Code of Hammurabi, written in 'clear vigorous Akkadian' and covering the whole conspectus of life in Southern Mesopotamia.[17]

Iron, a material so rare that it was sometimes more valued than gold, now insidiously dominated warfare, farming and the cultural arts. It gave armies enhanced power, agriculture became more productive and building techniques advanced. On this wave Assyria created its greatest capital at Nineveh opposite modern Mosul on the Tigris. Like Nimrud the site had been used in prehistory. Almost as large as Nimrud it was encompassed by even greater walls, the outer of which in towered crenellated stone has been reconstructed. The huge inner wall was of mud brick. Despite these fortifications Nineveh fell in 312 BCE to the Medes and Babylonians, an event which marks a major cultural turning point in the history of Iraq.

This sudden reversal returned Babylon to dominance under Nebuchadnezzar, second of the new dynasty, and saw the reconstruction of this long-established city on the scale of Nimrud and Nineveh. In the process Babylon gained its famous ceramic-faced walls and gates. These have survived sufficiently to have been faithfully reconstructed. The more ephemeral arts flourished in parallel. The Oud, a traditional musical instrument of the Babylonians, is traceable from this period onward and, at a more mundane level, elements as basic as recipes remain traditional today. A neglected facet (vernacular architecture is often neglected) was the distinctive courtyard house—a type already apparent in the upper levels of cities such as Ur and well developed in the Akkadian and Sumerian periods. This remained the standard and distinctive urban form of Iraqi cities until the 20th century. There were sophisticated adaptations but little fundamental change. The essential characteristic of these houses was that they were agglomerative, clustered like cells in a honeycomb, although normally rectangular in plan. The houses gained their light and air only from a central courtyard with minimal windowing on to the streets. The result was a tightly knit urban fabric intersected by narrow chasms. The interdependence of the inhabitants of the city has rarely been more powerfully expressed. The advantages of this structure lay in high density with maximum privacy. Heat penetrated only through minimal openings into the courtyards and into the narrow streets. The defensible urban perimeter was minimised and the carriage of clean water and other supplies was shortened.

Although frequently reconstructed, these courtyard houses have remained the essential component of Iraqi cities through the ages and domestic lifestyle within them has likewise been remarkably constant. They have provided for a lifestyle in which extended families could flourish, caring for every generation and every family circumstance. As the climate varied throughout the year the daily routine fluctuated, the family moving around the house like nomads according to season. This traditional family structure has survived in modern Iraq as a cultural force that has been the source of vitality and cohesion. In this final *floruit* of Babylon in the sixth century BCE occur the great schemes of building that signal its prosperity down the ages—Nebuchadnezzar reigned for 43 creative and constructive years. The hanging gardens and the glazed bricks of the processional way were glories that barely survived Belshazzur whose reign ended in 539 BCE with the return of his father Nabonidus, who tamely surrendered the city 10 years later.[18]

In economic terms this was an event of expansion under yet other invaders. The first of these invading powers was barely foreign. Cyrus the Great (d 529 BCE) arose as leader of the Persians from the southern province of present day Iran (Fars). He welded the great river basin of Mesopotamia into a political entity which was extended by his son into Palestine and Egypt. Babylon figured centrally in its government and in the reign of Darius I the capital was moved to Susa in eastern Mesopotamia (now in Iran), while its territories extended to Libya, the Nile, Anatolia, Bactria and Sogdia in Central Asia, continuing eastwards to the Indus and south into the Arabian peninsula. Thus by 500 BCE Iraq was at the centre of a vast empire and found itself at the beginning of a pendulum swing of hostilities that was to bring the young Greek prince Alexander into Iraq as a conqueror and finally to his debauched death at Babylon. This lightning strike might have been a mere flash on the stage of history had it not been for the staying power of Alexander's generals, particularly Seleucus, whose control over the Mesopotamian part of Alexander's conquests brought in Greek culture and Greek colonists on an important scale. Seleucia-on-the-Tigris (a little south of Baghdad) became a regional capital. Meanwhile the Medes and Persians of the Bible, subsumed into the Parthian dynasty, came to rule the region south of the Caspian sea from about 230 BCE. As their territories grew, dependence on the fertile farmlands of Mesopotamia grew equally. Iraq was again central to the functioning of an empire stretching from Babylonia to Bactria, continually disputed with the Greeks. In time this led to the conflict of the Parthians with the emerging power of Rome as it penetrated the East in the first century BCE, while Babylon and the south were intermittently in revolt from or independent of Parthia. Seleucia remained Greek in language and culture, while Hatra, on the Euphrates further north, was culturally

Hellenistic and resolutely Parthian in politics, resisting Roman sieges under Trajan and Septimus Severus. It is possible in Hatra to see a monumental temple complex in Oriental classical style engulfed in an urban layout of courtyard houses built in a fundamentally Mesopotamian manner. Mixed with Persian features are items of purely Roman and Greek jewellery, coinage and artefactual design. The west had come to Iraq and, over the centuries following Alexander, was firmly entrenched with clear cultural consequences.

Linguistically Akkadian, transmuted into Arabic, has remained the speech of the people and there seems little doubt that, with successive admixtures, it is genetically the Sumerian and Akkadian root stock that has populated the fertile soils of the twin river basin for some 5000 years, surviving into recent times the invasions of other powers on the wider world stage.

After 2500 years the fragile mud mounds that are the remains of this once wondrous and immense city have been the billet of 2000 invading US troops, succeeded by a multinational contingent under Polish command. Deep trenches (one over 185 yards long) have been cut through archaeological layers, large areas of hardstanding have been put down, fuel depots established with consequent leakages and damage done in defiance of archaeological advice.[19]

The decline of Babylon was complete 2000 years earlier, although even in its final years it remained an outpost of the earlier culture, producing cuneiform tablets still in the first century CE and remaining a minor trading centre while the great power struggles moved north.

The next long chapter is of the Persian/Parthian and Sasanian conflict with Rome—Rome in the east that is, Byzantium, whose aspirations intermittently turned to territories beyond the uplands of Anatolia and Syria towards the great Mesopotamian plain. Iraq remained central to this struggle which, like many sustained conflicts, was the crucible of a cultural revival that was the basis for all subsequent Persian Art.

In its surviving fragments the art of the Parthian dynasty (247 BCE–224 CE) demonstrates powerfully the continuity between Assyria and Persia. Its successor, the Sassanian empire, extends the cultural genre. The Sassanian winter capital was established on the banks of the Tigris opposite Seleucia, the ageing Greek colony. Their new capital, Ctesiphon, boasted one of the most magnificent of all palaces, the Tak-i-Chisra, of which a dramatic part of the great facade and the central *iwan* survives. This vault, the largest unreinforced brick vault ever built, was 35 metres high, 25 metres wide, 50 metres long and stood on a wall seven metres thick at its base. It opened its giant semi-parabolic arch between wings faced with rising tiers of blind arcading. This was an architectural form entirely eastern in its evolution and inspiration, without a hint of the classical west. In essence the *iwan* is a huge cave deriving fundamentally from the open fronted tent where a chief would receive his guests and tributaries. Its form was destined to recur extensively thereafter in Muslim art.[20]

So rich was this palace that in the Muslim conquest of 641 CE its conquerors were overwhelmed at the task of distributing the spoils. Carpets, tapestries, silks, curtains on an enormous scale were the background to the Sassanian royal presence.

This was a period when diverse religions flourished across Iraq: the numerically largest were Christianity and Zoroastrianism but neither was predominant and their cultural effects are now barely visible. This circumstance was dramatically reversed after 643. Islam, which had begun its expansion by moving rapidly both east and west out of Arabia, had taken Mesopotamia almost immediately, driving the Sassanian dynasty to extinction. A mere century later Iraq was to become the heartland of Islam, largely through an internal dynastic dispute. The Prophet Mohammed came of an Arabian tribe of which an earlier Ummayad branch soon took up the succession (the Caliphate) until a century after the Prophet's death. However, his direct descendants had their adherents and became identified as the Shi'a—literally 'The Party'—whose leadership in the Imans Hassan and Hussein was effectively eliminated in the battle of Kerbala. So the soil of Iraq became the focus of lament for the lost family of the Prophet, an event that carried with it major cultural implications. The direct blood of the line of the Prophet had been spilled in Iraq, which thenceforward was to be a soil particularly precious to Islam and emphatically so to the Shi'a. Pilgrimage to Iraq, to Kerbala and al Najaf became extended to Samarra and Kadhimain (Baghdad) by virtue of the shrines to Imans of the bloodline of the Prophet; with the pilgrims came the oriental influences of Persia, Afghanistan, Central Asia and India.

The defeat and annihilation of the Ummayad dynasty and Caliphate by 750 produced a radical reorientation in Muslim culture. The Ummayads, whose capital was Damascus, had absorbed Byzantine and Hellenistic influences to the extent that much of their art is a sub-sect of Oriental Hellenism. Now the capital of the Caliphs, momentarily transferred to Harran in northern Syria by the last of the Ummayads, was brought by their Abbasid conquerors, with only a brief halt on the upper Euphrates, to a new city, Baghdad, founded at a new site on the Tigris in 762. The Abbasids were neither Shi'a by blood nor by persuasion, being from another preceding generation of the Prophet's tribe. They were nevertheless acceptable to virtually the whole of Islam and until the Mongol invasions they provided a Caliphate generally recognised from India and Central Asia to the middle reaches of the Mediterranean. Only in the western Mediterranean—the Maghrib—did the surviving branch of the Ummayads hold political sway through their fluctuating rival Caliphate. For the rest of the vast Muslim world Iraq was the centre. Initially the Caliphate was contained in a huge new fortification, The Round City of Baghdad,[21] of which there is now no visible trace.

There had been round or near round cities before, but the timing and precision of this venture was on a scale unprecedented. As reconstructed from written accounts the city appeared in 762 as a geometrically exact circular fortress about 8000 metre in circumference. It was double-walled with diametrically opposed gates and, within the walls, built hard against them, were ranges of compounds for barracks and official housing. The great wall of the city stood 18 metres high and was some 15 metres wide at the top. In the centre, isolated in a great open *maidan* stood the caliphal palace and the Friday mosque. The Round City was both a military base and the working government entity.[22] Outside its four gates spilled irregular agglomerations of which the principal surviving feature is the necropolis, which became the cemeteries, with the shrines of two Imams. By accretion this became the separate town of Kadhimiye, only recently absorbed into the metropolis.

Culturally Caliph al Mansur's Round City was as important and extraordinary as its walls were dominant. It drew from all quarters of its vast empire the ambitious, the highly skilled, the capable and creative. It took on a vibrant life of its own and significant cultural developments originated here. The earliest lustre pottery seems to date from this time and the carving of gypsum dados inherited from the Sassanians took on seminal new forms. Much can be inferred from the visible differences between the final stages of Sassanid art before 650 and the emergence of a full blown style of Islamic architecture as we see it surviving in Samarra in the ninth century. Under the Abbasids a new and visibly different aesthetic approach was forged in Iraq and it is to this that we can first attach confidently the description 'Muslim Art'.

But the Round City stood in a bend of the Tigris over which spread the flood waters of the spring thaw from the mountains of Kurdistan and Anatolia. Frequently the river rose to damaging heights and the mud-brick walls sagged and collapsed. The city became a burden on the Caliphal Treasury. Early in the ninth century a new site was selected further upstream at Samarra, where a low rocky shelf stood above the turbulent Tigris even at spring high water. Although trading and commercial life continued in Baghdad, the Caliphal court moved upstream. Mosques, palaces, *maidans*, barracks and residential quarters stretched out on a spine of some eight miles running parallel to the river. But the economic life of Iraq continued to focus on Baghdad and by the end of the ninth century commerce had won. Samarra was abandoned in favour of Resafa, a site on the left bank, a little downstream from the old Round City. Here medieval Baghdad flourished.

Since it has been abandoned we can see at Samarra the telling sequence of extant great monuments of that first age of Islamic architecture, which was not derivative and not based on an alien culture. Here was built the first mausoleum in Islam, the Sulaibbiye,[23] a Caliphal burial place which became the archetype of the greater and more famous domed tombs of Asia, India and North Africa. While it clearly has an antecedent in the Dome of the Rock in Jerusalem, which is a celebratory structure not a tomb, it transposes the central dome surrounded by an arcade into a peculiarly eastern form. In its next transmutation four external *iwans* were placed on the cardinal axes. This was then the model for the rich heritage of Muslim mausolea.

Stone and gesso dados had long been used as a protection from damp rising from the moist soils of Mesopotamia. Samarra leaves us with the clear evolution of decorative carving on these dados in sweeping curvilinear patterns that produced the universal arabesque running like a theme tune through the manifold styles that were to follow. A feature of even wider implication is the evolution of the pointed arch which is clearly evident. At Samarra the earliest buildings, such as the Waziriya, employed simple intersecting curves consistently. By the time the Caliphal court moved back to Baghdad the four-centred arch had been developed and purposefully employed in the fortress-like Kasr Ashiq, the last great building of the Caliphal period in Samarra. The two greatest mosques in Caliphal Samarra were built with a distinctive form of minaret, perhaps based on earlier precedents in Iraq. These minarets were placed on axis and, rather than containing a staircase, they featured a spiral ramp rising round a solid core and diminishing with height as in some ziggurats.[24] This distinctive helical form was carried to Cairo, where it occurs in the Ibn Tulun mosque as perhaps the most salient example of the outward spread of Caliphal influence in the ninth, 10th and 11th centuries when Iraq was the focus of the Muslim world. On its return to Baghdad the Caliphate was at the heart of the creatively burgeoning city, which it enriched with gates, bridges, mosques, colleges and palaces in a mature brick style. The city became a byword for civilisation and luxury. But even this more permanently built city has left relatively few tangible works of creative art, for it was to suffer the ferocity of the Mongol invasion and the overthrow of the Caliph in 1258. Even before this savage event political overlordship had been wrested from the Caliphs by dynasties such as the Seljuks and the Atabegs; but nevertheless the overall picture of Iraq in the Abbasid period is one of evolution in the arts and sciences unparalleled elsewhere at the time.

Of the Abbasid monuments surviving outside Samarra the most notable is the isolated desert palace at Ukhaidir near Kerbala,[25] where much of the architectural vocabulary of later Islam can be seen in an emergent stage—evocative, gaunt in its wilderness and enigmatic in its origins. From a later period in Baghdad there survive the Bab al Wasitani, the Mustansiriye, and the 'Abbasid' palace of the later Abbasid period. Despite the colossal destruction of the city under the Mongols, its cultural vitality persisted through the reigns of Ilkhamids and succeeding Turkoman rulers until the next eruption from Central Asia, when Tamburlane again sacked and ruined Baghdad (in 1392). Four successive forays by Tamburlane proved a profound setback both to the city itself and to Mesopotamia, which recovered only to the status of a province.

During these years preceding the devastations of Tamburlane there were two prime centres of Islamic thought, Cairo and Baghdad. Some might defer also to the capital of the rival Ummayad Caliphalate in Cordova.

Because Islam is a total way of life,[26] an integral religion, it has a unifying quality which puts all branches of knowledge within one overriding concept. Consequently scholars have moved with ease from religion to philosophy, mathematics, the physical and chemical sciences, medicine and zoology, astronomy and their integration with the arts. In Islam the pursuit of knowledge has always been gnostic in nature, pursuing parallel levels of enquiry as part of the integral spiritual whole. Iraq in the Abbasid Caliphate was part of the heartland of Islam and with Egypt it was the point of entry of western knowledge into Islam. Both had ready access to Greek sources but Baghdad was tempered in addition by wisdoms of the east. Scholarship has always been important in Islam and every mosque was traditionally a centre of education and frequently the focus of a college. This was certainly true in Baghdad, where the Mustansiriye was among the foundations leading debate and theoretical evolution of Muslim thought. Names among the famous of the Baghdadi scholars were Abu Hanifa (d 767), who originated one of the more orthodox schools of Sunni philosophy; and Ibn Hanbal (d 855) who founded another which was among the most strict of the orthodox sects, particularly influential under the Ottomans. By contrast Al Junayd (d 911) and his pupil Al Halaj (c 922), the earliest Sufis, integrated mysticism with God. Among others was Al Ghazali and the 10th century theologian al Gaylani, whose philosophical school thrives in Baghdad to the present day.[27]

While Greek treatises were known and translated in mediaeval Baghdad they may not have been the sole source of ancient wisdom. The routes across Central Asia to China were an active channel of exotica—in commerce and knowledge. The sciences advanced in parallel with philosophy and mathematics. Use of the sexegesimal system persisted but with the seminal introduction and adaptation of Indian numeration the essential structures of modern mathematics emerged. Al Kwarizini (d 846) gave clear expression to decimal notation and he invented the techniques of algebra. The basic trigonometry of Hipparchus was extended by scholars in Baghdad into spherical trigonometry under the stimulus of astronomical calculation. Al Farghani (d 861) first calculated longitudes and wrote down the elements of analytical astronomy. Al Battani (d c 930) has been described as the creator of modern trigonometry. He calculated the precession of the equinoxes and the obliquity of the ecliptic using the observations of Hipparchus. At about the same time Al Farabi (d c 950) advanced the work of Ptolemy, while Al Kindi (d 876) worked on optics and gravity and wrote some 200 books. All these scholars worked in Baghdad where, by the end of the 10th century, a group known as As Safa (The Pure) created an encyclopaedia embracing the sciences, the principles of government and philosophy set against a cosmological background.[28] This work was paralleled by the writing of Al Tabari (d 923), who settled in Baghdad to write a universal history embracing all knowledge. Another encyclopaedic creation was the work of Al Masudi (d 956) who travelled widely and described all known wisdoms in a comprehensive book of which the *Golden Meadows* is the shortened version. Al Ya'qubi (d c 900) wrote the earliest Arabic general history with extensive descriptions of both Baghdad and Samarra.

This was an age of universal enquiry, of conflicting thoughts and emerging coherence stimulated by a flow of translated Greek scientific and philosophical treatises no longer thought important in Greece itself, where the ancient schools of philosophy had been closed in favour of the monastic life.

The precepts of Greek medicine were analysed, questioned and amended by the work of Al Razi (d 932),[29] who created the great hospital in Baghdad. He amended long-held precepts and was the author of works on subjects as diverse as disease, music and chemistry. Jabir bin Hayyan, who lived in Kufa in the 8th century, was an alchemist whose rational mind led him to analytical understandings which have given him the title of the Father of Chemistry.

A succession of distinguished poets of this period in Iraq might begin with Abu Nuwas (d 810), a favourite of Harun al Rashid, to continue with Ibn Qutaiba (d 890), a prolific writer in all forms of literature, and include Ibn Mutazz (d 908), who also rose momentarily to be Caliph, before his assassination. He wrote the standard Arabic work on rhetoric. Most famously Hariri (d 1122) wrote a series of tales of great popular appeal which were illustrated with miniatures and repeatedly copied. Of painters the best known miniaturist was Al Wasiti, who illustrated Hariri's *Maqamat.*

A particular factor in the spread of the arts and culture of Islam was the convergence of people from diverse parts of the empire in the annual pilgrimage enjoined on every Muslim. Those who had travelled to Mecca and had so become a Haji fulfilled the duty and objective of the pious. Between the Hejaz (Mecca and Medina) and Iraq ran a pilgrim route protected by forts and caravanserais. This route took a direct line across the northern plains of Saudi Arabia to what is now Kuwait and the Euphrates–Tigris confluence. It was known as the Darb Zubeida. Many a traveller combined the Haj with business in the Caliphal capital, a concurrence producing interaction between all parts of the Muslim world, including even those of the rival Caliphate in Spain

The land routes into Arabia, Turkey, Palestine, Persia and Central Asia intersected water-borne traffic through the Gulf and up both the Tigris and Euphrates to the region of Baghdad. From the Gulf trade went out to India, Indonesia and East Africa. Even after the Mongol conquest in 1258 and the savage destructions of Tamburlane a century and a half later a powerful cultural continuity and its focal point on the trade routes kept Iraq at the heart of cultural development. The trade of the Turks, the Mongols and the growing Muslim territories in India all flowed into, through and between the rivers. Across what is now Iraq the arts developed in parallel with the wider pattern of Timurid and later Ottoman and Mughal evolution. Baghdad, however, had lost the great revenues which came from being the capital city. It fell back to being, with the other cities of Iraq—Samarra, Kufa, an Najaf and Kerbala—the focus of secondary pilgrimage to its great shrines at Kadhimiye and Bab-al-Sheikh.

A diminishing Mongol presence in Mesopotamia gave way almost inevitably to the rule of the emergent Persian dynasty under Ismail as Safawi. This Persian province in turn tempted the rival Ottoman dynasty, dominant in Constantinople from 1453. Selim I had conquered Tabriz and northern Iraq by 1516 and his son, Sultan Suleyman the Magnificent, took lower Iraq south of Baghdad in 1534. Although the Ottomans lost control momentarily when Shah Abbas retook the city, Iraq finally and permanently became part of the Ottoman empire under Murad IV in 1639. Until 1917 and the Ottoman defeat in the first World War, Iraq became a backwater under Turkish governorships and Baghdad a neglected provincial capital, although there was, in the late 18th century, a period of virtual independence when the governorate passed to the Mameluke (Egyptian) protégés of the Ottomans. Under Daud Pasha political independence ended peremptorily in 1831. At this time the Ottoman capital itself was coming under strong European cultural influence and its arts and architecture began to reflect the prevailing Franco-Italian tastes being adopted in Istanbul. In the major civic buildings, decoration, planning and stylistic attributes betray the growing impact of European technology, trade and aesthetics.

In the provincial backwater that Mesopotamia had become a profound and deep-seated cultural continuity was provided by the traditional house and the urban neighbourhood.[10] As a cultural entity with its local mosque, school, market and compact cluster of houses, each close-knit neighbourhood within the city perpetuated a lifestyle which had barely changed over thousands of years. The extended family was the determinant, its continuing lifestyle the raison d'être. The cohesive mass of courtyard housing intersected and interlinked by a filigree of narrow lanes overhung by balconied windows—*shanashiels*—was the permanent cultural legacy from antiquity. Superimposed on this pattern were stylistic overlays fashionable in Ottoman Istanbul, interspersed with the occasional stylistic influences from the Arabian Gulf and India. In the grander houses there are direct reflections of European impact which created the Ottoman baroque. A railway crept out to link Constantinople with Baghdad and so connect ultimately with Basra, the Gulf and the east. With such communications came the trappings of western technology. Other Europeanisation occurred by commercial infiltration then by imposition, as the British army painfully pursued the Ottoman troops northwards to find itself ruling briefly and then hastily setting up a puppet government out of which emerged the conservation and academic study of Iraqi culture, the creation of the National Museum and the care of monuments.

This new facet initiated by Gertrude Bell includes the great Iraqi Museum in Baghdad and the huge buttress which saved the collapsing south wall of the Taq-i-Khisra at Ctesiphon. The newly independent state began to generate its own cultural identity in literature, the arts, education and ethnic traditions. The smooth evolution was punctured by the overthrow of its monarchy after a couple of generations. In cultural terms the imposition of western technology was the prelude to an explosive expansion funded by oil revenues.

Rapid absorption of industrial technology in the second half of the 20th century was the product of educational exchange in which Iraqi scholars went abroad for education while foreign teachers and consultants came into the country. Universities were founded and flourished. Commercial expansion produced a vibrant modern nation, which even during the Iran–Iraq war of 1980–88 was strongly supported by Western Governments. Not until Saddam Hussein invaded Kuwait did this support diminish. In parallel its cultural background was derived from Western nations. Iraqi painters reflected capably almost every artistic movement in Europe and distinguished themselves internationally. Among them were painters such as Hammoudi al

Jadir, ad Dabbagh and al Azawi. Groupings such as the New Vision and the Innovationists succeeded earlier obviously derivative schools such as the Baghdad Group for Modern Art and the Impressionist Group.[30] A political revolution and invasion have intervened: now a new generation will arise from a diaspora which took, among many others, the two most distinguished Iraqi architects of the later 20th century, Mahummed Makiya and Rifat Chadirji, out of their homeland at the height of their creative careers.

It is an almost universal facet of oligarchy that it seeks to perpetuate itself in monumental structures—often with militaristic or palatial overtones—and the Ba'athist regime was no exception. The warring period—the Iran–Iraq war and the two Gulf wars—produced sycophantic grandiose monuments, palaces and mosques, some now toppled and none likely to achieve the status of great art or architecture. They represent nevertheless an emphatic cultural event of which history deserves some record.

This was also a period of cultural vandalism aimed at minority groups, of which the attempted elimination of the Marsh Arab culture is the outstanding disaster, fortunately not beyond retrieval. Of the huge areas of delta wetlands which were the base of an ancient culture only 10% survived the deliberate drainage policies of the Ba'athist government. Its recovery, planned and painfully started, will be slow and difficult. The damage to the indigenous culture will be even harder to repair and without a massive injection of aid may not be achievable in real terms and in a time scale sufficient for a full cultural recovery.[31]

An essential element of cultural survival is continuity; continuity in creative matters, in human behavioural patterns and in the traditions which underlie social behaviour and tribal lifestyles and provide that continuing thread of progress which renders every society distinctive. Such traditions can be profoundly important and are neglected at pain of loss.

One such value has an important bearing on recovery. There is in Arab behavioural culture a very important and deeply understood tradition known as Sulha, reconciliation. With it feuds can be settled; in its absence the feud goes damagingly on. And the process demands the commitment of both parties. A wrong has been committed; reconciliation can be achieved only when the wrong doer's tribe or family seeks, through an intermediary, to make amends, payment—usually blood money. There is then a duty on the family of the wronged to negotiate and, the matter settled, the whole community rejoices. It is a process as deep-seated and culturally significant as a wedding. By it the cycle of revenge and counter-revenge is broken.

On the admission of guilt by the wrong doer society rebuilds. But can Israel confess its theft of Arab lands and seek reconciliation? Can the USA confess its pursuit of control of oil in Iraq and seek reconciliation? Unless cultural understanding can reach so far that the USA communicates at this socio-cultural level the invasion will be seen by Iraqis for what it is. In the words of Bishop Riah Abu El Assal of Jerusalem: 'If there had been no oil in Iraq there would have been no war in Iraq'.[32]

We have, on this evidence, failed to advance culturally from the conflicts that tore apart the kingdoms of Mesopotamia 3000, 4000 and 5000 years ago.

Old Europe—wise old Europe—knew better, but the advice was not heeded. Now it remains for the aggressors to make amends.

Notes

1. *The Lancet*, Vol 364, Issue 9448, Nov 20, 2004, pp 1857–1864.
2. For example, S Oppenheimer, *Out of Eden*, London: Constable & Robinson, 2003.
3. While the US government bears a grave responsibility for the 'storm of ignorance, greed, revenge, zeal and mayhem that swept through the Iraq National Museum after the invasion' (http://cctr.vinkc.edu/user/fdeblauwe/iraq.html), it did subsequently (3 December 2004) pass into law an enactment empowering the president to impose 'import restrictions' on materials illegally removed from Iraq. By then the horse had bolted.
4. See http://cctr.vinkc.edu/user/fdeblauwe/iraq.html.
5. Among the very important sites reported to have lacked protection stand Nimrud (Barsippa), Hatra (el Hadr), Nineveh (Kuyunjik), Ctesiphon (el Madain), Nippur (Nuffur), Ur, Larsa and Uruk (Warka). See web pages The 2003 Iraq War; and Archaeology, 2005, available at http://cctp.umkc.edu/user/fldeblauwe/iraq.htm. Many other sites (at least 30) of less prominence but great importance have been reportedly left vulnerable if not pillaged.
6. This information derives from Internet contributions by Dr Francis Deblauwe.
7. *Guardian*, 21 December 2004. The national collection of ancient manuscripts and subsequent archives was burned early in the occupation.
8. Succinct accounts of the many early kingdoms are to be found in F Masmachi, *Treasures of the Iraq Museum*, Baghdad, 1975.
9. There are divergent views on this period 1918–24 when a new kingdom was hastily forged. King Faisal was crowned in Baghdad on 23 August 1921. For a detailed account of events leading to this, see E Burgoyne, *Gertrude Bell, From her Personal Papers*, Vol 2, London: Ernest Benn, 1961.
10. J Warren & I Ferhi, *Traditional Houses in Baghdad*, Horsham: Coach Publishing, 1983.
11. J Warren, *Greek Mathematics and the Architects to Justinian I*, London: Art and Archeology Research Papers, 1975.
12. The clay tablet exhibiting the plan is illustrated in anon, *Mesopotamia Yesterday, Iraq Today*, Sartec Sa, Lausanne and Baghdad: 1977.
13. N Postgate, *The First Empires*, Oxford: Oxford University Press, 1977, pp 26 *et seq*, 76 *et seq*.
14. *Ibid*, p 80.
15. J Black & A Green, *Gods Demons and Symbols of Ancient Mesopotamia*, London: British Museum Press, 1992.
16. M Roaf, *Cultural Atlas of Mesopotamia*, Oxford: Oxford University Press, 1990.
17. Postgate, *The First Empires*, p 99.
18. *Ibid*, p 136.
19. BBC interviews, 27 February 2005.
20. See R Hillenbrand, *Islamic Architecture*, Edinburgh: Edinburgh University Press, 1994, where the crucial relationship between this pre-Islamic palace, the Taq-i-Khisra at Ctesiphon and subsequent Caliphal building is explored. See also KAC Creswell, *Early Muslim Architecture*, Vol 11, Oxford: Oxford University Press, 1969; and G Hermann, *The Iranian Revival*, Oxford: Oxford University Press, 1977. In Stierlin, *Islam*, Vol 1, Cologne: Taschen, 1996, the palace is shown in its current state of reconstruction.
21. Creswell, *Early Muslim Architecture*.
22. Of the many accounts of the Round City, the supportive analysis of Herzfeld is set out in Creswell, *Early Muslim Architecture*.
23. Creswell, *Early Muslim Architecture*; and Hillenbrand, *Islamic Architecture*.
24. See Stierlin, *Islam, in extenso* on Abbasid Samarra and Baghdad.
25. G Bell, *Ukhaidir*, Oxford: Oxford University Press, 1914.
26. A Guillaume, *Islam*, London: Penguin, 1954.
27. A comprehensive overview of early Muslim scholarship is to be found in A Papadopoulu, *Islam and Muslim Art*, London: Thames & Hudson, 1980.
28. SH Nasr, *Science and Civilization in Islam*, World of Islam Festival Publishing Company.
29. *Ibid*.
30. N Salim in *Iraq Contemporary Art*, Sartec SA, Lausanne and Baghdad 1977.
31. *New Scientist*, 26 April 2003.
32. At the University of York, 20 October 2004.

Attributing Value: evaluating success and failure in post-war reconstruction

SULTAN BARAKAT, MARGARET CHARD & RICHARD JONES

ABSTRACT *External analysts are already trying to evaluate the impact of the reconstruction strategies of the occupying powers in Iraq. However, those with long experience in this field caution against a rush to judgement and emphasise that it will be the Iraqis themselves who will eventually make a value judgement on how the occupation has affected their nation. The paper seeks to define a possible approach to facilitating such an evaluation at the appropriate time. Study of current evaluation theory and practice leads to the conclusion that aid evaluation, particularly in post-war contexts, tends to be almost exclusively geared to the purposes of project accountability and performance. Thus it largely fails to question the culturally and ideologically determined assumptions of value which underpin post-war reconstruction interventions. As a result a satisfactory methodology for the evaluation of the long-term impact has not been developed. Concluding that a participatory approach is the key to developing such a methodology, the methodological challenges to participatory evaluation are defined, paying particular attention to approaches, attitudes and indicators. These challenges are then practically demonstrated through case studies of project evaluation in Burundi, sector evaluation in Mozambique and an interim country evaluation in Iraq. This evidence suggests that participatory methods enable understanding of both the visible effects of war and reconstruction and the invisible, emotional and attitudinal changes which are the determining factors in developing a harmonious nation.*

On receiving the Dag Hammarskjold Medal (8 July 2004) Lakhdar Brahimi (2004) reflected on his 'peace-related activities'. Exhibiting a high degree of humility in the face of the complexities of human conflict and reconciliation, he first recalled that no two situations are alike but nevertheless offered the following four general lessons: 1) 'The only prudent starting point...is to try and understand as best you can why there was a conflict in the first place' and to ask 'what is the context in which you find yourself?' That requires time 'to talk to a lot of people, over and over again'; 2) unfortunately ' the most important decisions end up having to be taken...before we are knowledgeable enough to anticipate what their implications might be'; 3) when it comes to declaring the mission successful 'it is better to resist the temptation to declare victory prematurely'; and 4) 'our expectations and agendas are not becoming any more realistic. Instead, they have become more ambitious and multi-faceted' and we want everything to happen 'now, immediately, even in the midst of conflict'. A timely reminder to us all that 'fools rush in where angels fear to tread'.

What we learn from Brahimi's narrative of his experiences is that attributing value to a nation-building exercise like the reconstruction process itself, is no easy matter and cannot be undertaken in haste. Applying the logic of his discourse, evaluation of the long-term impact of interventions needs to be undertaken many years after the period of reconstruction. It is those stakeholders who made the necessary 'hard compromises' to ensure a durable peace, the citizens of nations that emerge from war, who will be best able to say what value they attach to the results and to what extent they think that international efforts assisted or hindered them.

However, although assessments of 'success' and 'failure' have been attributed retrospectively to a number of post-war reconstruction processes, these evaluations have been based on the criteria of external actors, not those of national stakeholders. This point can be illustrated by referring to two 'successful' nation-building exercises, which are being critically re-examined at this time: those of Germany and Japan. These should perhaps now be capable of being evaluated with some degree of confidence, since enough time has elapsed for the citizens of these now sovereign nations to assess the outcomes and voice their considered judgements without fear of reprisals or rejection.[1] However, it is US analysts who are revisiting these experiences as previous US nation-building exercises, because of their perceived relevance to the reconstruction of Iraq.[2]

Thus criteria of value seem to be based on assumptions that are determined by the dominant international culture, such as the existence of structures for liberal democracy and a market economy. Commonly, rather than 'talking to a lot of people' and engaging in 'painstaking dialogue', as Brahimi suggests, measurable indicators, such as the absence of violent conflict, the holding of multiparty elections and the growth in GDP are taken as the sole indicators of success.

Dobbins *et al* (2003) have refined these criteria and applied them to evaluating past nation-building efforts using the classic approach of aid and social programme evaluations: the input/output assessment using measurable indicators. However, although on this basis they detect a clear correlation between external inputs of time and resources to reconstruction ('effort') and outcomes in terms of 'democratic institutions and economic growth', they perceive that other factors are at work. The way the assisted population responds and the way the conflict was brought to an end are significant: total defeat, as in the case of Japan, or a negotiated settlement with some of the protagonists, as in Afghanistan. These were countries that received comparable amounts of per-capita inputs but where the post-war compliance with the post-war authority is markedly different. However, this tool is also unsatisfactory; we are still looking in from the outside and attributing external measures of value, that is, assessing what value the intervention has been to the intervening actors not to the recipients.

We clearly do not have any consistent method of evaluating nation building as a whole, but we are in the habit of regularly evaluating its parts. All major donors, international agencies and banks constantly evaluate their programmes of post-war reconstruction. At the micro level too, projects are increasingly subject to formal evaluation exercises. For this reason we start by looking for lessons that can be learned from the general theory and practice of evaluation that could assist us in defining an approach to evaluating the long-term impact of post-war reconstruction. We suggest that aid evaluation, particularly in post-war contexts, by being almost exclusively geared to the purposes of project accountability and performance, has largely failed to question the culturally and ideologically determined assumptions of value which underpin post-war reconstruction interventions. However, experiences in participatory evaluation, although not widely practised, are seen to provide the basis for an approach to long-term impact evaluation and this is examined through three case studies of evaluations in the war-torn contexts of Burundi, Mozambique and Iraq. First, however, evaluation as a concept must be examined.

Understanding evaluation

Rebien (1996: 1) states that '"Evaluation" in its usual sense is basically a reflexive process which every human is engaged in every day'. In common usage it is usually calculated in terms of 'material or monetary worth' but it has a broader meaning of 'that which is worthy of esteem' or 'has intrinsic worth' (OED, 1965: 2332). In other words, value can be seen as either objectively quantifiable or subjectively 'in the eye of the beholder'.

The same contradiction is apparent in the development of the academic discipline of evaluation. When seeking to define it, Rebien (1996: 13–18) quotes Rossi and Freedman: 'Evaluation research is the systematic application of social research procedures in assessing the conceptualization, design, implementation and utility of social intervention programs'. Rebien (1996: 13–18) adds his own caveat: 'that evaluation is not merely the application of research methods in order to uncover facts about social interventions but it is an applied science with a managerial and political purpose' where 'moral and ethical considerations are inherent to all. . .decisions. . .In short, evaluations are not value-free.' [3]

Nevertheless, the academic discipline of evaluation was from the start grounded on the belief that it could be objective in the attribution of value to social interventions by standing apart from the everyday personal judgements of individuals. It was therefore for a long time only concerned with the attribution of the first kind of quantifiable value. As the aims of social interventions came to be increasingly defined in qualitative terms, so evaluation now began to seek to enter the difficult terrain of trying to determine what was 'worthy of esteem' or had 'intrinsic worth', while nevertheless believing that this could and must be objectively determined in order to provide normative guidance for future work. It is therefore concerned to demonstrate a causal relationship between programme and outcome.

This 'experimental' approach has been called into question from two perspectives: the 'pragmatic' and the 'naturalist'. Pawson and Tilley (1997: 11–17) state that the pragmatic approach sees the role of evaluation as based on the acknowledgement that 'the very act of engaging in evaluation constitutes a political statement'. Rebien (1996: 171) confirms that this 'led from a knowledge-driven to a use-led model of research', in which evaluation research provides 'ammunition for debate and intra-organizational arguments' or for the purposes of legitimation. For Pawson and Tilley, the 'naturalist' perspective is the alternative approach to evaluation that Guba and Lincoln proposed in 1989 for their 'fourth generation'. It was part of the general constructivist trend in social science which rejected the notion of single verifiable realities in favour of 'value pluralism'. The belief that the diverse stakeholders in a social programme each have their own construction of reality which they bring to bear in the negotiation of outcomes also led to a focus on the use of evaluation information as empowerment.

Both Rebien (1996) and Pawson and Tilley (1997) see the next stage in evaluation as the 'pluralist' approach and they take Cronbach as the main proponent of matching research evaluation approaches to the circumstances and purposes of each specific intervention. The pluralist approach seeks to combine the objective 'experimental' approach with the subjective 'multiple perspectives' rather than allowing them simply to continue alongside one another.

This is because evaluation, by its nature, needs to attribute value and influence practice, and is therefore necessarily concerned with causation. As we have seen, Pawson and Tilley (1997) suggest that the constructivist generation went down a blind alley in rejecting this role, while justifiably seeing the need to examine the process of how stakeholders interact with social interventions. On the other hand, the 'experimentalist' generation pursued the issue of causation by such a narrow input/output route as to exclude most of what is relevant to the way change occurs in society. From this perspective change is seen to take place both internally as well as externally. It is the result of a combination of potential or opportunity with conditions within the social context and the volition of subjects. Logically this requires not restriction of the information base but greater breadth and depth of understanding (similar to Brahimi's approach to understanding conflict). The issue of causation is thus not irrelevant but infinitely more difficult to determine than the input/output model suggests.

Evaluating aid

Cracknell (2000: 39) suggests that 'From the start...aid evaluation had a strong pragmatic character, with the emphasis on the practical usefulness of the results in improving aid operations'. It did not concern itself with the theoretical considerations discussed above, but in the first instance only with the effectiveness of a particular project or programme in achieving its goals or producing benefits. In essence each project or programme was thus a kind of case study. However, as with other case studies, it then became 'concerned not just with whether the policy or programme has worked in the case investigated, but also whether it would work elsewhere' (Gomm, *et al*, 2000: 99). Thus, the main purposes of aid evaluation were defined in 1991 and re-endorsed in 1998 as 'to improve future aid policy, programmes and projects through feedback of lessons learned' and 'to provide a basis for accountability, including the provision of information to the public' (DAC, 1998).

However, as the aims and objectives of aid programmes evolved to encompass broad social issues such as poverty alleviation, good governance, institution building, community empowerment and, more recently, peace building, so logically the aid world was led to consider other styles of evaluation. For example, participatory evaluation, using Participatory Rural Appraisal (PRA) methods or action research have become more prominent. Oakley *et al* (1998: 48–49) state that 'Conventional and largely quantitative evaluations are more concerned with inputs and outputs... Social development evaluation, on the other hand, is not so amenable to such limited methods and demands an approach which is...capable of picking up and explaining the qualitative change which may have taken place'.

The new goals for social development, and indeed the declared aims of most post-war reconstruction, are therefore qualitative, long-term, holistic and political. At the same time they are not specific and so not easily measurable by conventional input/output methods conducted during and immediately after the completion of projects or programmes. This has induced recognition of the need to assess wider social and political impact, not just measurable and immediate socioeconomic outcomes. Thus Oakley *et al* (1998: 26–35, 59–136) believe that aid evaluation has also moved in the direction of a mixed method or 'pluralist approach which entails using different methods to ensure a representation of the views of different stakeholders' and a recognition of different purposes, including the need for long-term social impact assessment. However, they confirm that the assessment of impact is rarely reached. Yet it is precisely this purpose of evaluating impact (the wider and ultimate effects of interventions) which concerns us when attempting to evaluate reconstruction and nation building.

There has been noticeably little mention so far of the involvement of the citizens of countries where interventions take place, except in the role of recipients. Participatory evaluation is a common concept in the present day literature on aid. But as Chambers comments (1998: xiii) 'as usual with concepts which gain currency, rhetoric has run far, far ahead of understanding, let alone practice'. Samset (1998: 122–123) also raises the question of which criteria may be used to measure the success of projects and demonstrates that different criteria deliver different verdicts on success and failure. For example, his study of the Refugee Enterprise Project finds that it was highly efficient and effective and so, 'successful' in donor terms. However, from the recipients' point of view, it was found to be 'not relevant' and so a failure.

Here, we could usefully look at an analysis by Arnstein (1971) of the real nature of eight types of activity commonly labelled 'participation' in the context of public programmes in the USA. Only three, those that involve 'various degrees of citizen power' are deemed to involve 'real' participation and of these only the third, 'partnership', is legally possible in the context of international co-operation. The givers of aid are accountable to citizen control, but in their own country. No control can be exercised directly by the citizens of recipient countries. Similarly, no power can be delegated by donors, accountable to their own citizenry, to those of another state. Aid is therefore given and received on the basis of partnership but, even in the best cases, still an unequal partnership. In the case of a country devastated by war, the 'various degrees of. . .power' exercised by its citizens can be very limited.

Having moved on from the apparent certainties of input/output calculations and accountability auditing through the uncharted territory of multiple constructed realities and the contradictions of participation, evaluation researchers are faced with a number of choices. What is it appropriate to evaluate in a particular case? Who evaluates and for whom? If evaluation is in essence a judgement of value, whose criteria of value should be applied? They clearly recognise that the answers they give to questions of purpose and value in respect of a particular evaluation will directly influence the choice of methodology adopted.[4]

This recognition is still far from being translated into a consistent approach to the design of evaluations of aid programmes. In the particular case of post-war reconstruction evaluation is still largely carried out to examine the delivery of aid for purposes of accountability and implementation. The more difficult exercise of assessing the long-term effects of intervention on national development is not normally attempted, mainly because the recognition of this need has not yet given rise to the development of a body of practice involving evaluators from recipient countries. Cracknell (2000: 357) at the end of his book on aid evaluation calls the next big challenge facing the profession.

Methodological challenges to participatory evaluation: approaches, attitudes and indicators

If it is the case that social impact evaluation of reconstruction efforts must be participatory, then there is a number of methodological challenges to consider. These are based on approaches and associations of participatory evaluation, and practitioner perceptions in regard to evaluating the effectiveness of aid and the establishment of indicators. The purpose of this section is to elaborate these methodological challenges.

Approaches to participatory evaluation

Participatory evaluation is underpinned by several core themes: 1) The importance of harnessing collective knowledge of many stakeholders, especially at the community level, to reflect on the development intervention;

2) the need to adapt the evaluation to particular circumstances and contexts, thus requiring flexibility and reliance on qualitative rather than quantitative data; 3) the need for participation between evaluators and constituents; 4) the need to ensure that participants become beneficiaries, meaning that the evaluation becomes associated with joint benefits that evaluation participants obtain from taking part, particularly in terms of empowerment. Patton (1990) contends that one of the negative connotations often associated with evaluation is that it is something done to people. One is evaluated, usually by rigid adherence to objectively verifiable indicators. However, participatory evaluation ultimately helps to contribute to constituents' own socioeconomic development and informs policy implementers of their real priorities and needs as the basis for formulating development strategies. The core themes are reflected by the following approaches in Table 1.

The Institute of Development Studies (1998) has shown (see Table 2) that participatory evaluation differs from conventional evaluation in several important ways:

Many of the core elements of a participatory evaluation have their roots in different aspects of participatory enquiry, a process, which has also evolved from the conventional approach. For example, Chambers (1998) cites three common elements found in a PRA approach: *responsibility* (individual responsibility and judgement exercised by facilitators, with self-critical awareness, embracing error); *equity and empowerment* (a commitment to equity, empowering those who are marginalised, excluded and deprived, especially women); and *diversity* (recognition and celebration of diversity).

These core elements fit in well with the participatory evaluation, for an equitable process is essential, as the essence is to engage with as broad a

TABLE 1. Approaches to participatory evaluation

Approaches	*Advantages and disadvantages*
Participatory evaluation aims to create a learning process for the programme recipients that will help them in their effort to reach desired goals (Greenwood & Levin, 1998)	Emphasises continued learning, whereby participants' capacities are built up through the evaluation process. However, this does not always satisfy the donor agencies' need for prompt accountability
Participatory evaluation is a process of self-assessment, collective knowledge production and co-operative action in which the stakeholders in a development intervention participate substantively in the identification of the evaluation issues, the design of the evaluation, the collection and analysis of the data and the action taken as a result of the evaluation findings (Jackson & Kassam, 1998)	Particularly useful to assess evaluatees' own strengths and weaknesses as part of the overall evaluation processes, it emphasises how people directly connected with the intervention can improve the initiative. However, such a process can be hijacked by powerful subgroups.
Participatory evaluation is a process controlled by the people in the programme or community. It is 'something they undertake as a formal, reflective process for their own development and empowerment' (Patton, 1990)	This approach again emphasises how the individual can benefit but this can at times be to the detriment of the measurement of overall programme effectiveness.

TABLE 2. Differences between conventional and participatory evaluation

	Conventional evaluation	*Participatory evaluation*
Who plans and manages the process?	Senior managers, or outside experts	Local people, project staff, managers and other stakeholders, often helped by a facilitator
Role of 'primary stakeholders' (the intended beneficiaries)	Provide information only	Design and adapt the methodology, collect and analyse data, share findings and link them to action
How success is measured	Externally defined, mainly through quantitative indicators	Internally defined indicators, including more qualitative judgements
Approach	Predetermined	Adaptive

Source: Institute of Development Studies (1998).

representation of interests as possible. Often, by its very nature, an evaluation is taking place among a diverse range of stakeholders, and although it is not always easy, their opinions must be articulated.

However, Chambers (1998) states that a major challenge for the PRA is 'how to further develop and spread evaluation in which poorer people and communities do their own evaluations and how to enable women and the poor to become more involved in the policies and initiatives that affect their communities'. These priorities confirm the need for participatory evaluation as a methodological process that links from programme to sector and country evaluation.

Practitioner perceptions

Further methodological problems include the perception among practitioners of participatory evaluation. In their experience there maybe a causal link between inputs and subsequent development. However, the time frame and the number of other variables that must also be deemed to combine and influence that outcome make it impossible to test this relationship by conventional quantitative methods alone. As Cracknell points out (2000: 357), it is the current emphasis on long-term social and political aims (such as good governance, institution building and policy development), and the need to move away from project aid to sector and programme support, that are creating unease about how to evaluate the effectiveness of aid. As already mentioned, this kind of enquiry needs to be informed, and preferably led, by researchers from the recipient society. It is this understanding that has particular relevance when establishing indicators.

The use of indicators in participatory evaluation

So far consideration has been given to our understanding of participatory evaluation and its links to more general approaches of participation.

Consideration must now be given to the establishment of primarily qualitative indicators as a method for summarising the opinions and feelings of constituents and conceptualising the programme from a local viewpoint.

Development indicators are used extensively to get some form of measurement of aspects of macro or micro developmental progress. Many organisations (such as the UN and World Bank) have lists of indicators to measure such progress.[5] The received wisdom is that such indicators give as accurate a description as possible of the overall situation in a country. Therefore it can be seen from the beginning that there is a bias towards economic indicators and other indicators that lend themselves to relatively easy quantification. The majority of these indicators are concerned with the more macro achievements and broader development gains and have little relevance to the type of indicators necessary for participatory programme evaluation.

Goodhand (2001) confirms that in the post-conflict setting a participatory evaluation's attempt to explain or understand social, political and economic processes as interactive functions of social production will be concerned with two key areas. First, the impact of the development intervention (programme) and, second, how the causes, evolution and effects of armed conflict among different belligerent population groups (ethnic, religious, class, etc) have changed as a result of the programme.

The findings of such an evaluation will have immediate relevance to the recovery of that society and for the prevention of a recurrence of violent conflict. Thus indicators of peace are essential to the understanding of the conflict and how the very people who are affected by the conflict define the nature of the peace desired, which in turn provides important lessons for the post-conflict reconstruction task of building a positive peace (Barash & Webel, 2002: 8).

Where signs of ethnic or religious tension, or indeed any form of tension, are not obvious, it is easy to assume that, as people are living in what appears to be peaceful circumstances, where different ethnic groups appear to mix, coexistence does not seem to be an issue, or that the violence is only taking place on a small scale.

Commentators such as Young (in Darby & MacGinty, 2003: 15) would argue that in countries characterised by high levels of conflict occurring in frequent yet relatively constrained time frames the dynamic in play often means that obvious physical signs are difficult to detect. Although violence often occurs, it is not always happening when foreigners are trying to evaluate a programme. The evaluator does not usually arrive on the scene and see shoot-outs in the marketplace or people running for their lives in the fields. Thus, some way of establishing indicators for non-obvious phenomena needs to be developed through the participation of the local stakeholders as part of the participatory evaluation process.

Such a process, while relevant to programme evaluation, has several limitations for participatory evaluation, at a sector or country level. Such evaluations, as Cracknell (2000: 263) states, require information regarding long-term impact in an attempt to establish the 'ultimate effects' of a number of interventions, which by their nature contribute to changes which are cumulative. These changes are evident five, 10 or more years after the events of the intervention and are diffuse. They are not directly linked to one specific aid project or programme objective (although these may contribute to changes) but to more general social goals (such as good governance). They are the result of programme outcomes (planned and unplanned) interacting with factors in the wider society, many of which may even first occur after the intervention.

In the case of such impact evaluation in war-affected countries (evaluation of nation building for example) we have additional challenges. First, differential survival and rapid and unpredictable changes result in data gaps and inconsistencies so that, even if baseline data sets exist, they are less likely than in societies with political stability and social continuity to relate to many of the most significant factors for evaluating impact. Second, the sensitivity of issues and the drama and trauma of events make it difficult for those involved to examine certain subjects critically or to put events into perspective, especially in the immediate aftermath of violent conflict. Thus taboos on open discussion can constitute a limitation on retrospective evaluation by recipient stakeholders to a greater or lesser degree, depending on the social issues concerned and how central they were to the conflict.

We have to conclude, then, that the impact of social development aid, whether in a war-torn context or not, is proving both difficult to identify and virtually impossible to measure through the use of traditional indicators.[6] Hallam (1998: 79) identifies 'three principal challenges for those wishing to measure through indicators the impact of an humanitarian intervention' which, as will be shown, are equally applicable to social development: 1) a lack of consensus on what constitutes a desirable outcome; 2) the problems of data collection and data availability; and 3) attributing impact to an intervention.

Considering these in reverse order, it is possible to make the following observations. An important consideration in attributing impact to particular social development interventions is that significant extraneous variables often only emerge or become apparent after the intervention ends, so that the extent and nature of the impact goes beyond limited project objectives, spilling over (negatively or positively) into other contexts (point 3). As a consequence of this, there is then no ready-made baseline information on these aspects for purposes of comparison (point 2). Contemporary records (including pre-programme appraisals, etc) can be used to establish the context in which the intervention was made but will not necessarily cover aspects which subsequently prove significant. Even if we 'rediscover the baseline' as Oakley *et al* suggest (1998: 140 – 143) with a view to accumulating relevant information for subsequent impact evaluation, it is inevitable that the definition of significant indicators will have to be revised in response to changing events. In such cases the baseline data are likely to be inadequate or missing. In the end we have to rely on a combination of inadequate baseline information and retrospective reflection (and attribution of value, point 2) by diverse, but mainly recipient stakeholders, through a combination of participation and the setting of proxy indicators, as the following case studies illustrate.

Reflecting on the need for participatory evaluation: project, sector and country-level case studies

The differing approaches to participatory impact evaluation, the perceptions of practitioners influencing the evaluation process and the establishment of relevant indicators have resonance in the following case studies of project evaluation in Burundi, sector evaluation in Mozambique and interim country evaluation in Iraq.

Participatory evaluation of a project: Burundi

During a participatory evaluation of a peace programme in Bujumbura that addressed both social and economic aspects of livelihoods,[7] signs of tension were not immediately visible among the people. While the buildings evidently bear scars of conflict, people are at work in the fields, children are running around and the market is busy.[8]

Initially desk research was undertaken to gain an accurate knowledge of the conflict before the evaluation and to become familiar with key issues. Once in Burundi key informants were identified to establish indicators that would be an essential component of the participatory evaluation. In this particular instance one group of key informants was especially relevant: the community judges (*Bashingantahe*), who have a unique knowledge of the social and economic dynamics of the local communities. Throughout the initial phase of the evaluation it was essential to establish the participants' expectations of the evaluation and the process for articulating views. This had two benefits: 1) everyone, evaluators and constituents, knew what was expected of them and 2) confusion was avoided. In this atmosphere of mutual co-operation, specific and general indicators were established (Box 1) to evaluate the peace programme. After initial pilot testing, some of the indicators were altered; this set the scene for the participatory evaluation to take place.

As participation is the key, consideration was given to the relevant ways that information could be collected. Local consultants and translators were used who could speak the local language. Participants best express themselves in their local language, in this case Kirundi. Evaluators should not assume that everybody will be fluent in the colonial language, for this is simply not the case at the impoverished subsistence level.

Once the data had been collected and processed, the results were presented back to the stakeholders. This enabled them to clarify points, identify possible gaps, validate the results and, importantly, to feel a continued sense of active involvement in the process. In contrast to many evaluations, in which the results are never presented to the actual people who were the subject of the evaluation, in this participatory process feedback to constituents was a priority.

Examples of indicators used for the participatory evaluation of a peace programme in Burundi.

Specific

- Visits take place among former neighbours (now living in different areas because of the ethnic segregation of quarters);
- Relations between different groups are more stable;
- Relations have remained multi-ethnic and balanced in terms of gender and participants;
- More people approach the *Bashingantahe* (community judges) for help because they are in a fixed location;
- The population goes to the *Bashingantahe* as a first resort for resolution of their conflicts;
- There is a reduction in delinquency among the young because young people are occupied in employment;
- People who have been trained are now working.

General

- The participants have taken up their own economic and civic activities after training;
- There has been a reduction in tensions because of greater community cohesion;
- There is a greater solidarity a) between community associations from different quarters; b) between different ethnic groups in the same association and the community associations support vulnerable groups;
- The community associations are functional

BOX 1.
Examples of indicators used for the participatory evaluation of a peace programme in Burundi.

The main results of the evaluation, based on the participatory definition of proxy indicators, were that the programme had contributed to peace, because former neighbours were beginning to visit each other, even though they now lived in ethnically defined areas. The dialogue and trust that formed as a result would prove to have a lasting benefit despite the continued violence.

Examples of this approach to project evaluation are less common than the literature might suggest and the lessons learned at this level have generally not been scaled up to country-level evaluations.

Participatory evaluation of a sector: Mozambique

An example of the participatory approach being applied to a sector in a war-torn country is a study carried out in Mozambique with the Ministry of Education.[9]

The purpose was to examine the impact of capacity-building strategies (by both government and international partners) on the development of the education sector and the role that this played in post-war recovery. Although this was a historical study, looking back over the education and careers of the post-independence generation of Mozambicans, the initial approach was similar to that adopted for the Bujumbura project evaluation. The researcher discussed an initial concept for the research ideas and strategy with senior staff in the ministry and other key informants in the education sector and developed the research instruments with them. These included designing a quota sample and an interview strategy based on four topics.[10] The first of these was a semi-structured questionnaire designed to record the participants' individual education and career history along with their reflections on it. Three other topics (their perception of the role of government and perception of the role of international co-operation in developing the education sector, as well as the causes and effects of the civil war) were introduced by means of 'cue' questions which invited the participants to reflect without suggesting how they should order their ideas.[11]

The results of these reflections were analysed by post-coding, which revealed some consensual views on the positive and negative aspects of the roles of government and its partners, including those that were seen to have contributed to war and those which were facilitating recovery. These were taken as 'folk theories' and the basis for formulating indicators of good governance (Box 2) with which to 'interrogate' the documentary record (literature, media and documentation from government and donors), while the individual histories were used to understand the realities behind the statistical record of education, growth, set-back and recovery.[12]

The final outcome of this 'composite' research strategy (as in Barakat *et al*, 2002) was thus not simply to make an external evaluation of the impact of multiple international interventions in the education sector over the 25 years of Mozambican independence, but to reach an understanding of the interaction between those interventions, the context in which they were made and the volition of their subjects.

Key indicators of good governance

- promoting inclusion and equity;
- policy/strategy development;
- leadership/vision;
- participation of public and international partners;
- respect for diversity;
- space for dialogue;
- capacity (effectiveness and resources) to deliver.

BOX 2.
Key indicators of good governance.

A crucial factor was found to be that the Mozambican government and public shared a vision of education as the motor for personal and national development. This in turn conditioned proactive strategies to seek and use international assistance in support of a national agenda. Responsibility for governance was largely attributed to government, but the public was also seen to contribute positively or negatively to the quality of governance. In this scenario, international co-operation was seen to have an essential supporting role, especially in the early years, when technical assistance was crucial in developing the capacity of the ministry to make its aspirations a reality. However, it was deemed to have been only truly effective when integrated in a comprehensive government strategy. This three-cornered relationship was seen to have broken down under the pressures of war and economic collapse, when government and people were concerned with survival and donors resorted to a proliferation of uncontrolled projects. Regaining the policy initiative and enlisting donor support for an integrated sector plan, evolved in consultation with parents and teachers, has been a key recovery strategy in the post-war years.

Interim country impact evaluation: measuring Iraq's reconstruction—the big picture

Recent research by the Centre for Strategic and International Studies (CSIS, 2004) provides us with a good example of an evaluation of the reconstruction progress in Iraq, in which many aspects of the approach discussed have been scaled up to the national level. However, the first point to make is that what can be evaluated at this stage is process, not ultimate effect. The purpose is thus to identify immediate effects and trends in order to adjust intervention strategies, although data collected and understanding gained at this stage might be a useful input to future evaluation of the impact of coalition interventions on nation building. The key research method was to cross-reference the results from the different data sources, both qualitative and quantitative, against responses to a series of simple statements that served as a barometer of progress in five areas of Iraq's reconstruction. The statements were: *Security* (I feel secure in my home and in my daily activities); *Governance and participation* (I have a say in how Iraq is run); *Economic opportunity* (I have a means of income); *Services* (I have access to basic services, such as power, water and sanitation); and *Social well-being* (my family and I have access to health care and education). The findings are displayed graphically in figure 3.

The paradigm shows that none of the five key reconstruction areas is in the 'viable zone'. Security is firmly in the danger zone while the other areas are all in the grey zone—moving in the desired direction, but still with negative public perceptions. The report concludes that Iraq has not yet reached the realistic goals outlined as the tipping points in any of the five sectors of reconstruction.

Thus the report represents a very thorough example of process evaluation for the purpose of correcting an ongoing intervention. Its authors also see it as establishing a baseline not only to 'describe the status of Iraq's reconstruction...to assess whether Iraq is progressing, regressing or

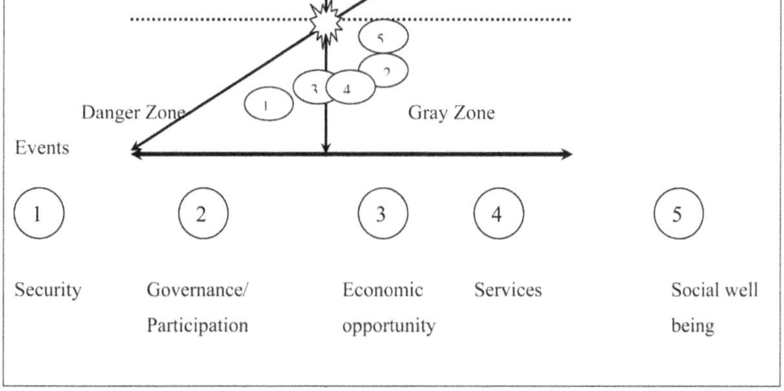

FIGURE 3.
Cumulative view of reconstruction in Iraq (June 2003 – July 2004). *Source*: CSIS (2004: iv).

remaining static' right now, but to 'provide an index for future measurement of progress' (CSIS, 2004: ii–xi).

The conclusions of the report are probably the best assessment to date of the largely negative status of reconstruction in Iraq and reflect Iraqi opinion on the five key areas on which the evaluation is based, which are certainly pertinent to their situation. However, despite the extensive interview survey by Iraqi researchers using a 'structured conversation' methodology based on response to cue statements, it fails to focus clearly on what Iraqis see as the root causes of their situation and key conditions for long-term solutions. It can be argued that this is a methodological issue rather than one of purpose.

The research design shares many of the methodological approaches outlined above and in Barakat *et al* (2002), such as the use of multiple data sources to identify 'popular theories' and the emphasis on qualitative measures of progress and a quota sampling approach. However, it differs in one important respect from the project evaluation in Burundi and the sector evaluation in Mozambique. The original research design did not contemplate using Iraqi researchers; these were recruited when security concerns would have made access by CSIS researchers problematic. As a result, Iraqis had no involvement in the research concept or, more importantly, in the choice of statements to represent the 'successful end-state for Iraq' and levels of progress towards it, including the tipping point on each of the five indicators. The Iraqi researchers were brought into the project at the preparation stage for the field research they were to carry out, thus making an important contribution to the validity of the data collection and its interpretation, but within parameters already set by the external research team. (CSIS, 2004: 6–10). The research design is therefore composite and mainly qualitative but it is not participatory.

The questions to ask are, first of all, in the very difficult conditions in Iraq today could this research have been participatory? The quality of the field research carried out by the Iraqi researchers, which depended not only on their competence and motivation but also on the motivation to participate on the part of their subjects, suggests that it would have been possible. The second question is: what advantages would a participatory approach have contributed beyond what was achieved by this already very thorough research exercise. The answer lies in the research team's own conclusions after completing the research: 'Progress should be measured in terms of Iraqi priorities' and 'Iraqis at all levels must be more directly involved in reconstruction efforts'. As discussed above, these are the very benefits that can flow from a participatory enquiry. Such an enquiry provides a better understanding of the reconstruction process, particularly the priorities and volition of the war-affected people and it begins to transfer control and the capacity to plan solutions to them so that they become directly involved in their own reconstruction.

For example, the five statements that were developed through 'brainstorming' within the research team could be seen as simple indicators, (CSIS, 2004: 4). People would not misinterpret such indicators and they would fit in well with the other data sources, such as media and public records, used in a triangulation exercise to give extra validity to the findings (Burns, 2000: 419). The fact that the interviewees responded to these statements is a clear indication that they touched on issues of immediate concern to them. In addition, the mapping of a downward trend in all these key indicators over the first 12 months of the occupation is a valid and important conclusion. This enabled the researchers to argue for redoubled efforts in each of these key areas, starting with security as the immediate priority and precondition for progress in all other aspects of recovery.

Iraqi priorities within the parameters set by the researchers were clearly demonstrated. However, there are indications in the field research results of the CSIS (2004) that, with Iraqi participation in setting the research agenda (defining the 'end-state' in the researchers' terminology) and formulating the key statements, different issues might have been addressed or the same issues addressed differently. The researchers wanted to tackle the issue of security based on interviewees' personal experiences. However, 'Across the country, respondents demonstrated a reluctance to base their assessments of the security situation on their personal circumstances' and apparently wanted to look at the bigger picture (CSIS, 2004: iv). Yet even the indicators of levels of personal security, based on the extent to which people leave their homes and circulate beyond their immediate neighbourhood, were probably misleading, measuring the need to go out rather than how safe it was to do so.[13]

On the issue of governance it is clear from the researchers' recommendations, as well as the research instruments, that this too was considered by the researchers at the level of personal participation in local governance. However, it can be argued that the research did not tackle what may be the key issue for Iraqis at this time: the recovery of sovereignty.[14] The results of the evaluation show that negative perceptions predominate. There are two prime reasons for this: first, there are undeniably fundamental problems in Iraq; second, attitudes are formed on the basis of factors which the environment is perpetuating. For example, if, as seems to be the case, foreign occupation is now perceived by most Iraqis as an inherently negative situation, people's mindsets are likely to be that things will never improve while the coalition forces remain.

It needs to be said that this critique of the CSIS research can be made precisely because the team made a virtue of necessity and supported an excellent team of Iraqi researchers in the field to collect rich data. This would repay further analysis and could provide the proxy starting point for a next stage participatory enquiry.

Lessons learned and the potential for scaling up

Two main lessons learned can be drawn from the experiences in participatory evaluation at a local and sector level. First, the use of participatory enquiry as part of a composite evaluation research strategy leads to a more accurate assessment of the long-term impact of interventions to assist the recovery of people and institutions in war-torn societies.

The second lesson learned is that, in addition to contributing to the general level of understanding of the reconstruction process, this approach to evaluation brings with it concrete benefits for those individuals and institutions that are its subjects, in the form of capacity building and empowerment. Empowerment occurs when the participants involved in the evaluation process can set the record straight. In addition their capacity is increased because the process itself leads to new insights and understanding which can be used to improve the planning and implementation of further development programmes.

From the third case study in Iraq, which was conducted nation-wide but was partial in the sense that it was an evaluation of trends and immediate impact of a process still in its early stages and did not use participatory methods, we can draw some conceptual and practical lessons. The definition of end states for key issues and a hierarchical progress towards these goals is a useful structure for charting broad social changes through proxy indicators at the national level. The field research demonstrated that, even in the midst of conflict and after the virtual collapse of public order, it was possible to collect qualitative data from a broadly representative sample of willing participants by involving national researchers. As in the other two cases, this was the core component in a composite research strategy drawing on other quantitative and secondary sources.

Having demonstrated that participatory evaluation can be used at micro and sector levels and that nation-wide research is possible in conflict situations, the potential for scaling up the methodology for the evaluation of 'nation building' can now be considered. Four key issues would seem critical to evaluating the impact of reconstruction in Iraq.

Timing

The period that has elapsed since the war ended is a key consideration and there is no such thing as a 'standard length of time', nor in many cases a definitive moment in time when hostilities can be said to have ceased. One of the main determinants will be the depth of the national trauma experienced, as in the total defeat of Japan and Germany in World War II. Another necessary condition is the absence of fear of reprisals or social sanctions. In short, the moment has to be right for people to feel able to participate. It is certainly too early in present day Iraq, Afghanistan and Kosovo for a participatory evaluation aimed at assessing the long-term impact of post-war reconstruction, although there may be scope for assessment of progress towards reconstruction.

Data

Data and documentation are important to a composite approach to evaluation. However, when reviewing these studies it is important to remember the partial nature of documentary evidence: it is both fragmentary and created for particular administrative and personal purposes, mostly by the privileged and powerful. This applies equally to the collection of social statistics. All these sources represent 'the *social perception* of facts; and are. . .subject to social pressures from the contexts in which they are obtained' (Thompson, 2000: 124, original author emphasis). In the case of Iraq we are dealing with a defeated nation which is under foreign military occupation. The results are therefore weighted in favour of the victor's point of view, despite any honourable attempts to seek out contemporary accounts from the vanquished.

Resources

Careful consideration will need to be given to human resources. The key issue is that the research team should be essentially national, although it might include foreigners.[15] Finding key informants to participate in the research design is essential, especially for sampling. This should draw on the national research team's knowledge and understanding of the society, and it is considerably more complex at national level than in the sector and programme cases discussed above. A cautionary lesson can be drawn from the ill-fated caucus model adopted by the Coalition Provisional Authority in Iraq to select a representative authority, which was universally decried by Iraqis—external actors alone trying to set up a quota sample will almost certainly get it wrong and provoke rejection of the evaluation process.

Undertaking such an evaluation would not require significantly greater financial resources than the CSIS study cited above. The time (six months) and human resources deployed (under 20 field researchers and academic contributors) were comparatively modest in comparison with other forms of national surveys.

Resolving these issues would not be easy but, as the CSIS programme evaluation has shown, it is by no means impossible. So since it therefore appears that such an evaluation is technically feasible, the crucial factor for it to take place in a country such as Iraq is the motivation of its citizens to participate. This would most probably be derived from a belief that an understanding of their experience can contribute to the development of their own country and provide lessons to the international community for its future conduct of nation building after war.

The crucial difference between this method of participatory evaluation and the social survey approach is that it allows us to understand not only the visible effects of war and reconstruction but also the invisible, emotional and attitudinal changes, which are the real determining factors in developing a harmonious nation. In contexts of violent change and instability, it pays to combine different data sources and research methods in a composite methodology, but the core concept for understanding what these data reveal of post-war development is the participatory enquiry.

Evaluation, as we have seen, does need to establish causal relationships if it is to be a useful tool for future planning. However, it is not a purely objective process because it involves attributing value, and different stakeholders assess value in different ways. Thus relating the value of outputs to the level of inputs in terms of resources and effort, in the manner of aid evaluations, is an attempt to establish a causal relationship. Such a relationship can lead to conclusions as to why some interventions for nation building appear to be successful and others do not. However, the critical issue for sustainability is what value is attached to the outcomes of intervention by those who receive them. Criteria of value attributed by donors and recipients are likely to overlap but they are unlikely to be identical, especially in the ordering of priorities for reconstruction. It is particularly necessary to know if interventions deliver value for effort in the eyes of the recipients. In some cases, as we saw above, they may feel that what they have gained in material terms is outweighed by what they have lost in terms of sovereignty or choice. Their final judgement will in any case not be clear until many years later, by which time the international community has usually moved on to the next crisis.

Thus, how recipients evaluate the post-war reconstruction assistance they receive, what inputs they perceive as making a crucial contribution to recovery, and which effort and resources brought no tangible benefits or were actually counter-productive, is of crucial relevance not just to them but to how those future crises may be handled. A more compelling reason for participatory evaluation in post-war reconstruction is that it enables those recovering from war to negotiate an 'end-state' or shared vision for themselves that will meet their needs and aspirations in a way that is politically and culturally acceptable to them and therefore more likely to be sustainable. As others in this volume have argued, this is the fundamental condition for the future development of Iraq.

Notes

1 Such as MacArthur's censorship of criticisms of the emperor in post-war Japan. See Salvatore Jennings (2003).

2 Pei and Caspar (2003). See also the work of Salvatore Jennings (2003); and Dobbins *et al* (2003).

3 Rebien (1996: 13–18) identifies three distinct purposes of evaluation: *accountability*, which is the requirement to show those funding social interventions that the funds have been spent as intended and achieved the desired results; *implementation*, which is concerned with performance evaluation in order to improve the management of the implementation process more effectively; and *strategy/policy*, in which evaluation is used 'to accumulate knowledge in order to make informed decisions regarding future policies and strategies'.

4 See Bickman and Rog (1998) on the need to understand the rationale for an evaluation and the context in which it is to be carried out, since this will inform the research questions and in turn the potential answers.

5 Some of the most high-profile compilations of indicators are from the World Bank the UNDP. The World Bank uses some 800 indicators in 87 tables, organised in six sections: World View, People, Environment, Economy, States and Markets, and Global Links. The UNDP has similar indicators for measuring health, education, access to resources needed for a decent standard of living, environmental sustainability, protecting personal safety, equality, and technology. Much reliance is placed on such indicators by bilateral institutions and ngos, which incorporate them into their strategies and programmes. See World Bank (2004); and UNDP (2003).

6 Indeed, aid interventions in general have provoked cries of frustration such as: 'the problem with discussing the impact of international assistance on the people of Afghanistan is that none of us can really claim to know what the impact has been' (Donini, in Hallam, 1998: 79); 'a clear concept and definition of "impact" is missing' and 'there is no linear or tangible relationship between project output and impact' (Oakley *et al*, 1998: 37). Furthermore, social development interventions are also

undertaken 'with goals that are inherently non-material, and hence not amenable to understanding through the use of surrogate economic indicators' (Brown, 1991).

7 The Post-war Reconstruction and Development Unit, University of York carried out this evaluation of the 'Community Based Bujumbura Peace Programme' for CARE, The Netherlands, in December 2003.

8 Since independence from Belgium in 1962 there has been almost continuous political unrest, including *coup d'états*, politically motivated assassinations and episodes of ethnic violence. However, the latest socio-political crisis started in October 1993 when Tutsi army officers assassinated the democratically elected Hutu president and several leaders of his political party. The event triggered reprisal killing of over 150 000 Hutus and Tutsis, the segregation of Bujumbura into Tutsi- and Hutu-dominated living quarters and the proliferation of mutual fear and distrust among Burundians.

9 Chard (2003) carried out this participatory enquiry in 2003 in the course of her doctoral studies at the University of York.

10 For discussion of sampling in war-affected contexts, see Barakat *et al* (2002). Thompson (2000: 145–146) also discusses the issue in relation to oral history.

11 Participants spoke as much or as little as they chose on each topic, ranged over several topics without interruption if they wished, and their silences were respected. All the discussions and interviews were carried out in the working language of the ministry and schools, Portuguese. The scope of the research did not include rural populations who were not habitual speakers of Portuguese; otherwise a similar strategy to the Bujumbura case would have been necessary. In multilingual Mozambique the 'colonial' language is in general use in urban and semi-urban contexts.

12 An approach similar to that used by Pawson and Tilley (1997: 87–88) in their study of adult education in prisons

13 One respondent pointed out that 'Iraqi men will always leave their homes even in the middle of live battle', (CSIS, 2004: 16).

14 The response of one man to this set of statements was 'I am now free to vote [statement considered a 'tipping point' for governance]. But the new government was appointed by the Americans, not elected by the people of Iraq. I look forward to having a government elected by the people' (CSIS, 2004: 16). Is this last statement an expression of the 'optimism' detected by the researchers or the retreat of the powerless into irony?

15 Piccioto (1999: 12) suggests that where 'transacting parties have widely divergent interests and perspectives, independent evaluation may help to mediate'.

References

Arnstein, S (1971) A ladder of citizen participation in the USA, *Journal of Town Planning*, 57 (4), pp 176–181.

Barakat, S, Chard, M, Jacoby, T & Lume, W (2002) The composite approach: research design in the context of war and armed conflict, *Third World Quarterly*, 23 (5), pp 991–1003.

Barash, D & Webel, P (2002) *Peace and Conflict Studies* (London: Sage).

Bickman, L & Rog, D (1998) *Handbook of Applied Social Research Methods* (London: Sage).

Brahimi, L (2004) Statement by Mr Lakdhar Brahimi, Special Adviser to the UN Secretary-General, on the Occasion of the Awarding of the Dag Hammarskjold Medal by the German UN Association, Munich, at www.un.org/apps/news, accessed 15 July 2004.

Brown, D (1991) Methodological considerations in the evaluation of social development programmes—an alternative approach, *Community Development Journal*, 26 (4), pp 259–265.

Burns, R (2000) *Introduction to Research Methodology* (Harlow: Longman).

Chambers, R. (1998) Foreword, in J Blackburn & J Holland (eds), *Who Changes? Institutionalizing Participation in Development* (London: Intermediate Technology Publications).

Chard, M (2004) Capacity building in the Ministry of Education in Mozambique, case study for doctoral research, University of York.

Cracknel, BE (2000) *Evaluating Development Aid: Issues, Problems and Solutions* (London: Sage).

Centre for Strategic and International Studies (CSIS) (2004) *Progress of Peril: Measuring Iraq's Reconstruction. The Post-conflict Reconstruction Project* (Washington, DC: CSIS).

DAC (1998) *Review of the DAC Principles for Evaluation of Development Assistance* (Paris: OECD).

Darby, J & MacGinty, R (eds) (2003) *Contemporary Peace Making: Conflict, Violence and Peace Processes* (London: Macmillan Palgrave).

Dobbins, J, McGinn, J, Crane, K, Jones, SG, Rollie, L, Rathmell, A, Swanger, R & Timilsina, A (2003) *America's Role in Nation-Building: From Germany to Iraq* (Washington, DC: Rand Publications).

Gomm, R, Hammersley, M & Foster, P (2000) *Case Study Method* (London: Sage).

Goodhand, J (2001) Violent conflict, poverty, and chronic poverty, *Chronic Poverty Research Centre Working Paper 6* (Manchester: CPRC and Intrac).
Greenwood, D & Levin, M (1998) *Introduction to Action Research*, (Thousand Oakes, CA: Sage Publication Inc). p 239
Hallam, A. (1998) Evaluating humanitarian assistance programmes in complex emergencies, *Good Practice Review*, 7, Relief and Rehabilitation Network, Overseas Development Institute, London.
Institute of Development Studies (1998) *Participatory Monitoring and Evaluation: Learning from Change*, Issue 12, University of Sussex, Brighton.
Jackson, E & Kassim, Y (1998) *Knowledge Shared* (ET Jackson and Associates: Ontario), pp 199–216.
Oakley, P, Pratt, B & Clayton, A (1998) *Outcomes and Impact* (Oxford: INTRAC).
Oxford English Dictionary (OED) (1965) p 2332.
Patton, M (1990) *Qualitative Evaluation Methods*, (Newbury Park, CA: Sage), p 129
Pawson, R & Tilley, C (1997) *Realistic Evaluation* (London: Sage).
Pei, M & Caspar, S (2003) Lessons from the past: the American record on nation building, *Policy Brief*, 24 May (Washington, DC: Carnegie Institute).
Piccioto, R (1999) Towards an economics of evaluation, *Evaluation*, 5 (1), pp 7–22.
Rebien, CC (1996) *Evaluating Development Assistance in Theory and Practice* (Aldershot: Avebury).
Salvatore Jennings, R (2003) The road ahead. Lessons in nation building from Japan, Germany, and Afghanistan for postwar Iraq, *Peaceworks*, 49 (Washington, DC: US: Institute for Peace).
Samset, K (1998) Project management in a high-uncertainty situation. Uncertainty, risk and project management in international development projects, PhD thesis, Norwegian University of Science and Technology, Trondheim.
Thompson, EP (2000) *Voices of the Past: Oral History* (Oxford: Oxford University Press).
UNDP (2003) *Human Development Indicators 2003* (Geneva: UNDP).
World Bank (2004) *World Bank Development Indicators 2004* (Washington, DC: World Bank)

Index

For Product Safety Concerns and Information please contact our EU
representative GPSR@taylorandfrancis.com
Taylor & Francis Verlag GmbH, Kaufingerstraße 24, 80331 München, Germany

www.ingramcontent.com/pod-product-compliance
Lightning Source LLC
LaVergne TN
LVHW080645011026
849160LV00014B/1331

* 9 7 8 0 4 1 5 4 6 4 2 4 6 *